THE RISE AND FALL OF MODERN BLACK LEADERSHIP

Chronicle of a Twentieth Century Tragedy

H. Viscount "Berky" Nelson

University Press of America,® Inc.
Lanham · New York · Oxford

Copyright © 2003 by
University Press of America,® Inc.
4501 Forbes Boulevard
Suite 200
Lanham, Maryland 20706
UPA Acquisitions Department (301) 459-3366

PO Box 317
Oxford
OX2 9RU, UK

Library of Congress Cataloging-in-Publication Data

Nelson, H. Viscount.
The rise and fall of modern Black leadership : chronicle of a
twentieth century tragedy / H. Viscount "Berky" Nelson.
p.   cm.
Includes bibliographical references and index.
1. African American leadership—History—20th century.
2. African Americans—Civil rights—History—20th century.
3. United States—Race relations. I. Title.

E185.6.N445 2003
303.3'4'08996073—dc21   2003050402 CIP

ISBN 0-7618-2562-2 (paperback : alk. ppr.)

This book is dedicated to three special people:

My mother and original role model,
Mrs. Leanna Nelson Johnson;

My late and dear friend who provided inspiration,
Professor Stanley Coben;

My dear wife Joan K. Nelson,
who lived many days and nights in solitude.

ABOUT THE AUTHOR

Dr. H. Viscount "Berky" Nelson was born and bred in the small town of Oxford, Pennsylvania. He received his baccalaureate at West Chester University and earned an M.A. and Ph. D. in History from the University of Pennsylvania. For more than thirty years he has been a college educator—a history professor and administrator—at Dartmouth College and UCLA. Currently he is the Director of the Student Activities office at UCLA. His publications include: Nelson, et. al. *America: Changing Times: A Brief History*, (John Wiley and Sons, 1980); Philadelphia's Thirtieth Ward, 1940-1960," *Pennsylvania Heritage*, Spring, 1979; and "Before the Revolution: Crisis Within the Philadelphia and Chicago NAACP, 1940-1960, *Negro History Bulletin*, January-March, 1998. His wife Joan K. Nelson is an Associate Dean of Students at UCLA.

In Aristotelian terms, the good leader must have ethos, pathos, and logos. The ethos is his moral character, the source of his ability to persuade. The pathos is his ability to touch feelings, to move people emotionally. The logos is his ability to give solid reasons for an action, to move people intellectually.

— Mortimer J. Adler, American Philosopher

CONTENTS

PART III
CONSCIOUSNESS OF SELF

PREFACE

For the past two decades I have been deeply troubled by the limited progress a significant segment of the black population has made in attaining the education, housing, and employment opportunities necessary to maintain a middle class lifestyle as citizens of the United States. This became particularly troubling because high-profile people like Ward Connerly, Clarence Thomas, J.C. Watts and others of African ancestry projected a sense of well-being and contentment and eschewed any degree of favoritism that might be directed toward black Americans. Given the high incidences of poverty, incarceration, the deteriorating family structure, and other societal aberrations inherent in black communities, I wondered how blacks speaking confidently about true egalitarianism in American society could ignore the black underclass with impunity. Traditional black leaders and organizations offered no sustained rebuttal to those who, in my estimation, would betray their race. *The Rise and Fall of Modern Black Leadership: Chronicle of a Twentieth Century Tragedy* attempts to answer that question.

Several books have been published about black leadership, two of the most recent being *African-American Leadership* by Ronald W. Walters and Robert C. Smith, and Earl Ofari Hutchinson's *We Have No Leaders*. Walters and Smith present an esoteric, well-researched scholarly tome that defines black leadership and provides insight about the methodology and nuances about blacks and leaders from the 1960s to the end of the century. Hutchinson, conversely, offers a reflective, personal critique that questions the dearth of race consciousness displayed by men and women of the 1990s who would lead African Americans into the new millennium. *The Rise and Fall of Black Leadership*, however, examines those who guided and represented the race during the previous century. No one book can address every important detail or adequately discuss all the personalities who played a role in the evolution of contemporary black leadership in the United States. This writer makes an honest effort to offer a comprehensive disquisition about the most influential people who shaped the course of modern African American history. Nevertheless, I apologize in advance to those individuals of significance, past and present who played a leadership role but were omitted from the ensuing discussion.

Many people directly or indirectly are responsible for the completion of this manuscript. My graduate school mentors, Professors Thomas Cochran, Morton Keller, Wallace Davies, and Alex Riasanovsky offered encouragement and advice. Others who deserve thanks include members of the UCLA family—Drs. Lawrence Gower, Rick Tuttle, Terry Saunders, Joan Brown, Messrs. Mike Cohn, Kenn Heller, Tim Ngubeni, Jimmie White, Ms. Flare Johnson and librarian Miki Goral of the Young Research Library. Professor Elliott Barkan of California State University, San Bernardino also deserves my profound appreciation for making constructive comments on the manuscript. Howard Dodson Jr. of the Schomburg Library and Venis Marsh of York College in New York City provided advice and support. Finally, I would like to express my deepest gratitude to Ms. Susan Peabody who applied the final touches to the manuscript. Despite the assistance rendered from those mentioned above, I must take full responsibility for the content, interpretation, and errors presented in this book.

H. Viscount "Berky" Nelson
May, 2002

INTRODUCTION

During the "Golden Age" of television—the 1950s—Art Linkletter served as the popular host to "Truth and Consequences." He also enjoyed children and would ask them questions to adult-like situations on a live T.V. show entitled "Kids Say the Darndest Things." One day a most interesting dialogue occurred between Linkletter and a little Negro boy.

Linkletter: What do you want to be when you grow up?

Boy: A white man. [Audience laughs]

Linkletter: Why do you want to be a white man?

Boy: Because Niggers ain't shit. [T.V. goes immediately to black]

The dialogue above may be subjected to many different interpretations—none favorable to African Americans. The child's parents and relatives taught him not to like black people. He revealed self hatred inculcated at an early age that reflected the feelings many African Americans maintain toward their race. No positive black role models existed for the impressionistic boy. Instead, he displayed a longing to be white rather than black, reflecting a long-held opinion of racial inferiority based more on fictitious musings than fact. No self-respecting African American would ascribe to the utterance of the young boy cited above. But given the abject condition of low income blacks, self-serving motives of the black bourgeoisie, and most importantly, the questionable role played by contemporary black leaders—or leaders who happen to be of African ancestry— a critical review of African American society seems warranted. We should reexamine the past, evaluate contemporary society, and anticipate—as best as possible—the direction toward which African Americans are headed in the twenty-first century.

One of the more traditional methods used for evaluating a people occurs through the discussion about its best representatives—its leadership—and how they responded to challenges of the era in which they lived. *The Rise and Fall of Modern Black Leadership* is a book designed to evaluate the role played by African American leadership during the twentieth century. While most books on leadership dwell on the personalities of those individuals who strategize and direct others to do their bidding, this endeavor is designed to reveal how whites and the larger society determined the direction and behavior of blacks who would lead their race. Like most leaders, prominent blacks who represented their race never acted in a vacuum. Instead, they responded to the pressures that white society hurled at the African American community. The negative aspects of racism—white violence toward blacks, segregation, and the various forms of discrimination attributed to "the color line"—caused African American leaders to think of ways to ameliorate their race's abject condition.

Black leaders of national renown evolved from a myriad of sources. Some gained initial fame through the church. During the early nineteenth century Richard Allen of Philadelphia laid the foundation for subsequent leaders by gaining the loyal support of his congregation to promulgate the direction for racial amelioration. This tradition continued through the late nineteenth, and early twentieth and mid twentieth centuries under the direction of Bishop Henry Turner, Adam Clayton Powell Sr. and Jr., and Dr. Martin Luther King Jr. respectively. Others, like W.E.B. Du Bois acquired leadership by displaying extraordinary intellectual prowess. And still others like Marcus Garvey and Jesse Jackson evoked a philosophy, or presented a program that catered to the interests of a significant number of people. Of course a dynamic personality or some kind of recognition from influential whites propelled certain African Americans into the limelight. Unlike white leaders of prominence, blacks never derived leadership from personal wealth or from affirmation gained from a national political election. Instead, a nationally known black would be more inclined to acquire recognition by being selected for prominence by a white benefactor or influential members of a white oligarchy.

It is also important that the reader understand the context in which black leaders acted as leaders. From the "Jim Crow" era of the 1890s through the 1920s and 1930s, African American representatives laid the foundation for what became the Civil Rights Movement of the 1960s. The acquisition of human rights became the clearly articulated goal of virtually every prominent black leader. Even when certain leaders appeared to have other motives in mind, which could be observed in Booker T. Washington's industrial education philosophy or Marcus Garvey's Back to Africa Movement, the objective always remained the same—acquiring freedom from the degradation of white racism. From World War II to present, however, the objectives of black leaders became clouded and somewhat confused. In part, this confusion may be attributed to the increasing enlightenment of white society toward blacks. Without changes in white attitudes toward African Americans, the successes of black leaders would have been severely limited. Therefore it is important to ascertain why racial norms in America affected and altered the role black leaders played in mitigating white racism and creating greater opportunities for African Americans.

Of course with every leadership cadre, there are favorable and unfavorable elements and factors that produce both heroes and villains. However for African Americans who existed as the largest and most consistently persecuted minority in the United States, decisions made by black leaders had life or death consequences. These decisions could not only result in success or failure for immediate followers, but also have a lasting impact on the black community many generations into the future. While white leaders could make decisions without believing those decisions could impinge upon an entire race; black leaders had no such luxury. Instead, every black spokesperson with a conscience had to feel that their very bearing, style, thoughts, and success or failure would impinge on the very fortunes of the larger African American society.

Before any further discussion can properly ensue on black leadership, it is necessary to define the meaning of leadership as it applies to African Americans. In *The Rise and Fall of Modern Black Leadership* some of those who lead are measured by their commitment to ameliorating the condition of the African American majority. These leaders headed and belonged to civil rights organizations ranging from the Niagara Movement, the NAACP, National Urban League, the Universal Negro Improvement Association, and the National Negro Congress to the March on Washington Movement, to the Student Non-Violent Coordinating Committee, the Southern Christian Leadership Conference, the Black Panthers, and the Nation of Islam. Fraternal and church leaders, individuals holding legislative offices and other positions of prominence also deserve mention.

Until the 1980s and 1990s there were few doubts that the black leader represented his/her race. Even the most self-centered black politician was largely elected by and responsible to the black electorate. On the other hand, African American leaders comprise individuals who either use or allow race to be used on behalf of those who would slow black amelioration and curtail prospects for equal rights desired by all black Americans. Like those of liberal orientation who headed organizations and belonged to institutions that espoused equal opportunity for blacks, conservative elements within the African American community also gained positions of prominence in civil rights agencies and played influential roles in the public and private sectors of the nation.

For most of the twentieth century African American leaders maintained a deep commitment to serving their race despite colossal disagreement on how to achieve defined goals. From the Washington-Du Bois controversy to the differing philosophies of Malcolm X and Dr. Martin Luther King Jr., there was little doubt about the commitment of black leadership. These people dedicated their lives to their race's improvement. Even professional athletes who became the first to break color barriers were perceived first and foremost as representatives of African American society. Track star Jesse Owens, boxer Joe Louis, and the famous Jackie Robinson who integrated major league baseball instilled pride in the hearts of every African American man, woman, and child. Whites might have been hostile or indifferent to the exploits of the black athlete in the boxing ring, on the gridiron, or on the baseball diamond. The black community, however, seemed joyously united in supporting the exploits of their trail-blazing athletes. African Americans felt rapture for every boxing blow delivered, celebrated every touchdown scored, and reveled in every outstanding play made by the black athlete. The African American athletes, without any doubt, served as models, representatives, and leaders of their race.

Measuring the commitment of those working to achieve racial equality may be deemed judgmental. Nevertheless certain specific qualities may be applied to identify individuals who served as leaders and representatives of African American society. Initially, these men and women were selected or supported by some segment of the black community. Although an influential white could anoint a black to some position of responsibility, the individual chosen usually held prestige and influence within the African American community. It would be inconceivable that a black selected to any position of prominence could be considered for any post without first attaining respect from African Americans. Anyone selected to do the bidding of a white benefactor alone would be excoriated in the black press and labeled as an "Uncle Tom." This individual would also be instilled with such self-loathing that he/she would cower privately in fear rather than face the wrath of an enraged black community. The integrity of the black leaders seldom remained in doubt. The sincerity these men and women had for black America remained inviolate. Philosophical arguments and political inclinations aside, the mission of African American leaders had been clear—protect the dignity of their race, speak on behalf of the speechless black majority, and work relentlessly to enhance the fortunes of black Americans.

Some African American leaders focused attention on white America, appealing to democratic principles to mitigate the hostility of white racism. Some carried themselves as dignified human beings that served as positive examples of successful African Americans. Some engaged in efforts to demonstrate that blacks were human, capable of having emotional feeling, possessing the capacity to learn, and possessing the necessary qualities to succeed in any chosen profession. And still others directed their time and energy to black uplift—exhorting their race to strive for social equality, economic development, and political prominence in the larger society.

More recently, blacks in leadership positions have adjusted to the variances within American society. The Second World War, the Cold War, Civil Rights Movement, demise of the Soviet Union and other factors dramatically affected all Americans and forever altered race relations in the United States. Recognizing the currents of change, new black leaders evolved with a different sense of purpose. Integration and an easier rapport with white people led to an establishment of new paradigms in race relations between blacks and whites as well as a different perception of leadership roles played by blacks in prominent positions. Indeed, the evolution of black leadership—from being race specific in one extreme to being color-blind on the other—reflects change in the larger American society. The only constant about race relations in the United States is the inconsistency of inter-racial relationships. Given the increased responsibilities, expanded job opportunities, and diminution of overt racism in contemporary society, the role of blacks in leadership positions understandably changed dramatically. As mayors, judges, members of congress, speakers in state assemblies, chief executive officers, and individuals holding positions of responsibility in the public and private sector, black leaders no longer represent African American society alone. They are beholden to white benefactors, often represent a white constituency, and become idolized by white Americans who appreciate and respect talent, intelligence, and charm. The alternate acceptance and rejection of African Americans by white Americans has depended upon mitigating circumstances that represent the changing landscape of race relations in the United States. Correspondingly, black leadership alternated between being change agents and responders to the vagaries of white racism. *The Rise and Fall of Modern Black Leadership* might imply that the role African American leaders have had in society diminished. While the title is suggestive, one should not draw conclusions about the book's intent. When perusing this book, the reader may assess whether black leaders could have acted more effectively in meeting the challenges they faced as spokespersons for their race and as the conscience of America, and decide whether current leaders maintain the legacy of pride and altruism established by noble predecessors.

PART I

CONSCIOUSNESS OF RACE

1

LATE NINETEENTH CENTURY LEADERS AND THE PRELUDE TO MODERN LEADERSHIP

The 1890s represented a nadir in the status of African Americans. On February 20, 1895 Frederick Douglass, the anti-slavery orator and most prominent black leader of the nineteenth century died. On September 18, nearly six months after Douglass' death, Booker T. Washington renounced equality in his Atlanta Address. And on May 18, 1896, the United States Supreme Court handed down a decision in Plessy v. Ferguson that legalized state mandated segregation. The demise of Douglass brought to a close the aggressive, uncompromising brand of leadership that encouraged blacks to demand all the freedom and equality guaranteed American citizens in the United States Constitution. Washington's highly acclaimed address signified and represented an abrupt end to a century of aggressive black agitation for human rights. His brand of leadership stood for survival through accommodation and surrender. And to make certain that blacks would not enjoy the privileges of citizenship in American society in the forthcoming century, African Americans were reduced to second class status through the infamous "separate but equal" doctrine outlined in *Plessy v. Ferguson*. All of these events impacted the condition of African Americans and altered the future course of race relations in the United States.

African American leaders of the early nineteenth century recognized that institutional slavery provided the platform for establishing racial unity.

As long as the "Peculiar Institution" existed, black leaders could demand a forum, become heard nationally and internationally, and prick the conscience of all Americans who professed to embrace the utopian concepts of life, liberty, and the pursuit of happiness. Thus, the tasks of early leaders seemed contradictory—easy and hard simultaneously—convincing prejudiced whites that blacks were human. Logically, the very nature of human rights—the right to be free—could not be defined or confined by race. Perceptive African American spokespersons knew that no asterisk appeared in the Declaration of Independence or Constitution that proclaimed unequivocally that blacks were inhuman and therefore could never be free and treated with dignity. And since every renowned nineteenth century black leader was free—Richard Allen, James Forten, David Walker, Robert Purvis, and Charles Remond—the inconsistency of slavery in America referenced by free Negro spokesmen demanded attention. On the other hand, the overwhelming majority of white citizens of the United States, including Presidents of the United States, sincerely believed blacks were inferior to whites.[1] Outspoken whites cast doubts on the humanity of the African race. Therefore black leaders, and most accomplished African Americans of the nineteenth and early twentieth centuries, would spend considerable time and effort trying to convince whites that blacks deserved to be treated like free human beings rather than former slaves.[2]

Frederick Douglass represented the last and most prominent nineteenth century African American leader to devote his life to the eradication of slavery and racial discrimination. No other contemporary leader rivaled Douglass' oratory, uncompromising stance against slavery, and fame as a civil rights advocate. Born to an anonymous white man and a black woman in Talbot County on the Eastern Shore in Maryland in 1817 with the given name Frederick Augustus Washington Bailey, Douglass deeply resented the inhumanity of slavery. Douglass' thirst for freedom evolved during his employment at the Baltimore shipyard—a thirst that became satiated in 1838 when he disguised himself as a sailor and ran away to New York City and eventually New Bedford, Massachusetts. While in New Bedford, he adopted the name Douglass, became a family man, joined the local anti-slavery society, and came under the influence of William Lloyd Garrison.

Under Garrison's tutelage Douglass honed his speaking skills, acquired instruction in criticism, and broadened his repertoire in attacking the evils of slavery. Between 1844 and 1847 Douglass arguably became the most prominent abolitionist on the lecture circuit. He published his widely acclaimed memoirs—*Narrative of the Life of Frederick Douglass*—toured the British Isles as a proponent for the abolitionist cause, and became heralded as "one of the greatest phenomena of the age."[3] After returning from England, Douglass settled in Rochester, New York where he published *The North Star*, an abolitionist newspaper that again attested to his mastery of the English language and devotion to freeing his race from bondage.

The North Star enabled Douglass to pursue a course independent from white Abolitionists. As the publisher and editor of the most prominent black newspaper in the United States, Douglass transcended the limited white emancipationist views of the Garrisonians and delved into "quality of life issues" deemed pertinent to black people. All concerns pertaining to the "color line"—ranging from the multiple aspects of segregation to inequalities based upon racial discrimination—received attention. Through his paper Douglass also implored blacks to be self-respecting and take pride in literary attainments, demonstrated the virtues of being financially independent, and gave voice to race conscious African Americans.[4] After the Civil War Douglass became an ardent Republican and in 1872, removed from Rochester to Washington, D.C, the seat of Republican power. As a resident in the nation's capital, Douglass gained distinction as president of the Freedman's Bank, delivered the oration at the unveiling of the Emancipation Monument, and received the appointment from President Hayes as Marshal of the District of Columbia. Douglass finalized his career as the most renowned representative of his race through his appointment as Minister to Haiti, a position that garnered acclaim from Haitians as well as black and white Americans.

In 1891 Douglass resigned his commission in Haiti and returned to his Washington residence at Cedar Hill. He spent his remaining years enjoying his family, and writing and hosting Americans of either race who coveted his friendship and wisdom. The majesty that Douglass conveyed refuted any possibility that black men were inferior, subhuman, and should be relegated forever to the status of chattel. Throughout his long career, Douglass called upon fellow "race members" to agitate incessantly for quality schools, black suffrage, and legal rights, and demand that privileges be bestowed by character rather than color should be enacted. These views seemed prescient and enabled Douglass to be perceived as a precursor to the Civil Rights Movement of the twentieth century.

The opprobrium of slavery, the subsequent demand for recognition as humans, and the debate over citizenship dominated the thoughts of nineteenth century black leaders. Although the Civil War technically ended slavery and Reconstruction legislation had been designed, in part, to integrate the freedmen into the larger American society, white Abolitionists, with the exception of Senator Charles Sumner of Massachusetts and Representative Thad Stevens of Pennsylvania, ignored the plight of black Americans. Only propitious timing related to northern revenge, political expediency, the forcefulness of strong white men of conscience, an exhausted South, and the agitation of black leaders like Douglass allowed for the opportunities and hope afforded blacks during the Reconstruction era.

Throughout Reconstruction Douglass and other black leaders like Congressmen Joseph H. Rainey and Robert B. Elliott of South Carolina, and Senators Hiram Revels of Mississippi and P.B.S. Pinchback of Louisiana continued their quest for black human rights. Others used a collective voice to acquire justice. On December 19, 1873, prominent blacks convened a National Civil Rights Convention in Washington, D.C. to address Congress and demand the rights of United States citizens. Under the leadership of chairman George T. Downing, a successful caterer and the wealthiest black man in America, the membership called for equal access to hotels, non-discrimination in public conveyances, and fair treatment of African Americans in the judicial system and resolved: "That the protection of civil rights in the persons of every inhabitant is the first and most imperative duty of the Government.... [and] That no people can aid in sustaining and upholding either themselves or the nation unless they are fully protected in their pursuit of happiness."[5] Downing concluded the gathering's plea by imploring Congress to pass a comprehensive bill to protect the rights of African Americans.

Black leaders toiled for their race cognizant that white people could eventually tire of bestowing largess upon the freedmen. Indeed, after the demise of egalitarian Negrophiles like Charles Sumner and Thaddeus Stevens, subsequent Congressional leaders believed zeal for the freedmen kept the nation divided. Opportunities to terminate Reconstruction and curtail burgeoning rights for freedmen occurred through the controversial Hayes-Tilden presidential election of 1876. Northern and southern businessmen recognized a need for inducing peace in the old Confederacy. Former Confederates abhorred Reconstruction governments that not only offered political and social rights to freedmen, but more importantly, suggested that Negroes, regardless of talent or status, would hold power comparable to whites. To regain hegemony in the South, redeemers seized upon opportunities derived from political discord that occurred in

Louisiana and South Carolina during the 1876 presidential election. Democrats and Republicans reached a compromise. In return for Hayes' confirmation as President, the G.O.P. agreed to remove federal troops from the South (actually only Louisiana and South Carolina) and leave freedmen to the "tender mercies" of southern whites.

The symbolic Compromise of 1876 enabled the South to become part of the "Gilded Age" of the 1880s. The power vacuum created during Reconstruction allowed the former planter class—the Bourbons—to seek restoration and dominance in the South's political affairs. But these changes had national overtures as well. Executive and Legislative branches of the Federal Government catered to the interests of the "Captains of Industry." The nation's chief executives—Presidents Garfield, Arthur, Harrison, and Cleveland—would remain true to the task of regional reconciliation at the expense of the Negro. No president placed the rights of freedmen before that of the party, business interests, or white social contentment. Likewise, Congress placed issues of national interests—the tariff, currency, civil service reform, and federal regulation of interstate commerce and burgeoning corporations and foreign affairs—before the South's "Negro question." While each major party addressed the necessity for promoting freedom, equality, and the constitutional right to suffrage, they offered platitudes rather than make sincere efforts to enforce the Constitutional rights of Negroes.

Contemporary black leaders held limited influence with United States presidents, Congress, or the white electorate. Nevertheless, someone had to speak up on behalf of black people. One individual who articulated the cause of the Negro race hailed from the West Indies, a black man named Edward Wilmot Blyden. Born in St. Thomas in the Danish West Indies on August 3, 1832, Blyden entered the world of a relatively privileged family. His father (a tailor) and mother (a teacher) were both free and literate, and resided in a predominantly Jewish and English speaking community in the capital city of Charlotte-Amalie. When young Edward became ten, the family moved to Venezuela where he displayed high intellect and a facility for foreign languages. After returning to St. Thomas, Blyden met a white American, Reverend John P. Knox, a man who sponsored the precocious boy's study in the United States. By 1850 Blyden reached American soil and prepared to enter the Rutgers Theological College. Although admission was denied him because of race, Blyden had the opportunity to meet Presbyterians who belonged to the colonization movement. Through discourse with those who counseled blacks to return to Africa and engage in black altruism, Blyden would spend most of his life as a pan-Negro nationalist, a proponent of colonization, and an outspoken advocate for the black race.[6]

Between 1850 and 1862 Blyden resided in Liberia and engaged in several occupations—the ministry, an educational tutor, and principal at a high school. At this time Blyden also came to the realization that he must refute charges of Negro inferiority. Therefore, he engaged in historical, linguistic, and liturgical research and commenced writing designed to elevate the Negro race to equal status with whites. By the 1870s Blyden's writing reached maturity and enabled him to become the foremost black intellectual of his day. He spoke of past achievements of the Negro race and praised the "African Personality." Blyden's writings were original, ingeniously argued, and gained additional credence since he displayed intimate knowledge of English, French, German, and Arabic literature, and had his writings published in the United States and England.[7] In 1887 Blyden presented his "magnum opus" before the world, a book entitled *Christianity, Islam, and the Negro Race*. Scholars on both sides of the Atlantic Ocean praised his work and marveled that the tome had been written by a "Negro."

Blyden's reputation as an original thinker and writer, coupled with his charm, brilliance in conversation and eloquence in speech, made him the darling of the lecture circuit in England and the United States, and gained him acclaim in the Muslim world. He gained additional recognition through membership in Athenaeum—one of the most exclusive gentlemen's clubs in London—as a Fellow of the American Philological Association, and as an honorary member of the American Academy of Comparative Religion. A recipient of several honorary degrees, Blyden forced white intellectuals to recognize his talent, and by default, dispelled the myth of Negro inferiority. But for blacks, his accomplishments as a litterateur, a man of culture, and prideful Negrophile, established a foundation that would be replicated by other black leaders of the late nineteenth and early twentieth centuries.

Despite the lofty example of racial accomplishments established by Blyden and his efforts of moral suasion on behalf of blacks, presidents of the United States and members of Congress had little use for the Negro. The Executive and Legislative branches of government focused almost exclusively on developing the nation economically. Therefore, the judicial arm of government remained the sole institution capable of enabling blacks to retain social and economic rights achieved through Civil War and instituted during Reconstruction. Unfortunately, the judiciary's behavior comported with other branches of the federal government. The Supreme Court displayed its indifference toward African Americans in a series of decisions handed down in the 1870s and 1880s. The Court's initial callousness toward blacks appeared when the justices overturned the Civil Rights Act of 1875. The Civil Rights Act had prohibited discrimination attributed to race in inns, public transportation facilities, and theaters. It also forbade the exclusion of blacks from serving on juries. Reflective of the unfathomable "wisdom of that day," the Court declared the Act unconstitutional, arguing that the "Due Process Clause" of the Fourteenth Amendment prohibited discrimination by race solely in regard to states, a clause allowing bigoted individuals to persecute blacks at will. In response to this unfortunate development, in a lucid, calm, calculating voice, Douglass raised embarrassing questions about the Court's reasoning by declaring:

> Only base men and oppressors can rejoice in a triumph of injustice over the weak and defenseless.... In humiliating the Colored people of this country, this decision has humbled the nation. It gives to a South Carolina, or a Mississippi Railroad conductor more power than it gives to the National Government.[8]

Douglass' eloquence could not mitigate the severity of the Court's finding. Moreover, its interpretation on racial discrimination became even more disappointing to African Americans because alleged "friends," northerners and Republicans, dominated the Court. Since decisions rendered by the Court impacted the legal treatment accorded blacks in the entire nation, black leaders recognized their race faced a dire future.

Douglass' retort to the Supreme Court hardly appeared as the first or only response to the rising tide of racial discrimination directed toward blacks. A Douglass contemporary and fellow Marylander, Reverend Henry Highland Garnet, also served as a champion of his race. Born a slave in New Market, Kent County, Maryland, Garnet, like Douglass escaped slavery and moved to New York City where he completed his education and launched his career as a Presbyterian minister. As a fiercely militant foe of slavery, Garnet participated actively as a member of the Liberty Party, called for a general rebellion at the Convention of Free Men held in 1843, and founded the African Civilization Society. Collectively, these deeds caused Garnet to be a rival of Douglass and earned him the opposition and enmity of Douglass himself. In Garnet's later years he served as the United States Minister to Liberia and died in 1882, one year before the repeal of the Civil Rights Act. Despite their differences, Douglass respected Garnet as a sincere and dedicated African American leader who served as a positive role model for the race. While he toyed at one time with the idea of emigration, Garnet spoke for generations of future black leaders and African Americans when he said:

> America is my home, my country, and I have no other. I love whatever good there may be in her institutions.... I love the green hills which my eyes first beheld in my infancy. I love every inch of soil which my feet pressed in my youth.... I love my country's flag, and I hope that soon it will be cleansed of its stains.... [9]

But like many African American nationalists, Garnet spoke critically of the inequities rendered blacks. In an address before Congress, Garnet asked a rhetorical question about the time when reformers (critics) will no longer castigate America and declared: "When there shall be no more class-legislation, and no more trouble concerning the black man and his rights.... When, in every respect, he shall be equal before the law, and shall be left to make his own way in the social walks of life."[10] These words reflected the dogged determinism that the nineteenth century vanguard passed on to future black leaders.

The humbling effect of white hatred and indifference directed toward blacks impinged most severely upon self-respecting African Americans. In both South and North, African American leaders became objects of violence. Alamance County, North Carolina, became the site of the hanging of black Republican leader Wyatt Outlaw in 1870. The following year, the prominent African American Philadelphian, Octavius V. Catto, was assassinated for exercising his right to vote. Douglass and other aggressive black leaders nevertheless persisted in working tirelessly to achieve equality for African Americans. Meanwhile, other blacks used a more subtle and safe means for addressing racism. Throughout the nation these African Americans of substance created a black aristocracy to shield themselves from the heightening tide of racism. Acquiring wealth through business, banking, farming, catering, and the medical profession, the Churches of Memphis, Bruces of New York, Cheathams of Washington, D.C., Adgers of Charleston, and Mintons of Philadelphia maintained extremely close family ties, intermarried, and established a long-standing leadership cadre.[11] By example, this black aristocracy aided outspoken militants who argued that African Americans were as accomplished and human as whites.[1]

Even during Douglass' heyday as an outspoken leader who advocated that blacks assimilate into the larger American society, several blacks displayed little confidence in white America. Black leaders embarked upon different strategies in response to the heightening racism. Some like Edward Wilmot Blyden, Bishop Henry McNeal Turner, and Martin R. Delaney recommended expatriation to Africa. Although Blyden represented the bridge between earlier colonizationists like Paul Cuffee and John Russworm, most of his time was spent in Liberia; thus his extreme fervor for expatriation to Africa had a limited impact upon African Americans.

Bishop Turner proved to have a greater impact than Blyden as a proponent of the colonization movement. Born near Abbeville, South Carolina in 1834, Turner enjoyed several careers. At some time in his life he found employment as a cotton field worker, blacksmith, author, editor, minister, chaplain in the Union Army, and eventually Bishop in the African Methodist Episcopal Church. Turner gained favor among the Republican Party, serving as one of the G.O.P.'s founders in Georgia and received a presidential appointment as the Macon, Georgia postmaster. Despite the successes he enjoyed in his varied career, Turner became an advocate for emigration to Africa and, in 1876, accepted the Vice Presidency of the American Colonization Society. Annoyed by the second class status all African Americans experienced regardless of accomplishments or station, an angry Turner vilified the United States. The increasingly harsh treatment accorded blacks during the late nineteenth century caused him to declare: "[I] wish it (the United States) nothing but ill and endless misfortune, wish I would only live to see it go down to ruin and its memory blotted from the pages of history." Turner encapsulated the reason for his bitterness by proclaiming: "A man who loves a country that hates him is a human dog and not a man."[13] Undoubtedly, Turner spoke for many accomplished African Americans who felt betrayed by white society and the federal government, and who were incensed by the reluctance of whites to provide freedom and equality to people of darker hue.

Martin Robinson Delany, the final member of the expatriate triumvirate, was one of the most accomplished Americans of any era. Born free in Charles Town, Virginia [now West Virginia] on May 6, 1812, Delany spent his formative years in Washington County, a region inhabited and controlled by George Washington's family. Deeply infused with the spirit of freedom and equality that the family represented that naturally became disseminated throughout the community, Delany had a profound sense of the contradictions evident in a slave society. By 1823 Delany's mother Pati moved the family to Chambersburg, Pennsylvania because she had broken Virginia law by teaching her children to read. At age 19 Delany left home and traveled to Pittsburgh to continue his education. There, he came under the tutelage of John B. Vashon who instilled him with a sense of racial pride, encouraged him to pursue a career in medicine, and inspired in Delany a profound desire to help the Negro race.[14]

Delany initially displayed his race consciousness as a newspaper editor. *The Mystery*, the first black newspaper published west of the Alleghenies, was devoted to the anti-slavery movement and published under his editorial direction. As editor, Delany's untiring efforts to place blacks in the most positive light as unwarranted victims of slavery caused him to be tried for his vicious attacks against "the peculiar institution."[15] In 1850 Delany entered the Harvard Medical School to complete a two-term requirement and receive a medical degree. Protesting Harvard students caused the dean, Dr. Oliver Wendell Holmes, to dismiss Delany and two additional black students four months prior to graduation.[16] This unfair decision embittered Delany and stimulated his interest in expatriation.

Later in his career Delany became an author, the first black to explore Africa, and the first commissioned field officer serving as a major in the Union Army. Toward the end of the Civil War Delany was stationed in Charleston, South Carolina and remained there throughout Reconstruction. He acquired the office of trial judge and became deeply involved in that state's Reconstruction politics. Yet despite his willingness to work within the system, Delany became extremely disillusioned because hopes for his people steadily declined. This reality caused him to adopt a black-nationalist position replete with a strong sense of African American pride that caused him to perceive the great Frederick Douglass as an appeaser to whites.[17]

Blyden, Turner, and Delany represented the views of sensitive and angry blacks who tired of the inconsistencies between American pronouncements of freedom and corresponding denial of rights to African Americans during the late nineteenth century. These men were accomplished in their own right and could not accept humbling themselves before whites in order to gain the safety of their person or attainment of a goal. The primary motive for expatriation existed in the deep sense of racial pride held by each man. Yet they realized that the America in which they lived would not tolerate expressions of racial pride and demands for racial equality. Flight to Canada, the West Indies, or Africa therefore seemed logical and worthy of pursuit. The individual who forged a relationship between expatriation and black racial pride, and who garnered respect from whites and blacks alike, was the Episcopal priest Reverend Alexander Crummell.

Crummell served as the bridge between colonization, black-nationalism, and domestic economic self-help among blacks of the post Civil War era. Born in New York in 1819, Crummell—along with classmate Garnet—attended Oneida Institute, received an A.B. from Queens College, Cambridge in 1853, and served as a pastor and missionary in Liberia and Sierra Leone for twenty years.[18] He founded the American Negro Academy and served as rector of Saint Luke's Episcopal Church in Washington, D.C. Race restrictions proved particularly embittering to him. He resented being excluded from Episcopal seminaries in the United States, causing him to study in England to earn his college degree. Understandably, racial discrimination that prohibited Crummell from acquiring an education in the United States contributed to his receptivity toward those blacks that espoused expatriation.

With a highly acclaimed degree from one of Europe's finest universities, Crumell's experience convinced him that a black man, regardless of talent, could never be considered the equal to a white man in America. A means for addressing this dilemma required blacks to become interdependent, developing reliance upon what he deemed "social cohesion," a mutual-support system which required the sable race to look after its own. He held other strong beliefs as well. His Victorian principles encouraged him to demand that blacks develop high moral character. He eschewed black involvement in politics and instead, urged the race to tend to weaknesses perceived as being related to The Status of the Family, The Condition of Labor, and the Element of Morals. He also embraced the concept of freedom, and maintained a strong sense of American nationalism. While racial turmoil during the 1890s made it difficult for many black leaders to embrace the United States of America, Crummell remained optimistic. As a man of the cloth and a devoted Anglophile with missionary zeal, Crummell blamed African Americans for their debased condition. However when Crummell founded the American Negro Academy in 1897, he declared that the black elite must maintain a sense of responsibility for the masses. This organization and Crummell's belief in altruism served as the model for a subsequent concept ascribed to a group known as the

"Talented Tenth."[19] Although a combination of factors ranging from self protection to sincere altruism propelled prominent black citizens like Crummell into action, a spirit of black-nationalism nevertheless pertained in this proud, ebony black man which became handed down to impressionistic young men like W.E.B. Du Bois.

Despite the acclaim achieved by other leaders, it was the steadfast Douglass who spoke for the African American majority. Douglass pitted his anger, intellect, and energy against the rising tide of racial discrimination. By gaining fame as a proud African American, Douglass established a precedent for subsequent black leaders to follow. Complex issues arising during the late nineteenth century in regard to race indicated that an array of black leaders would evolve and extend the quest for human rights into the next century. However before Douglass could inject all African American leaders with his unwavering passion for justice and equality for blacks, the first evidence of acquiescence appeared in the guise of Booker T. Washington.

In many respects, like Douglass, Booker Taliaferro Washington established precedents for the behavior of many black leaders of the twentieth century. Born in 1856 to Jane, a slave on the James Burroughs farm near Hale's Ford, Virginia, Booker never knew his paternal father. As a boy he experienced the harshness of slavery and acquired survival instincts that proved beneficial throughout his life. When he was ten the Civil War ended and an era of optimism pervaded recently freed blacks. The industrious youngster absorbed the feeling of optimism and retained a positive view about America throughout his life. Like many former slaves reared in harsh circumstances, as an adult Washington would wax nostalgic about his enslavement and reflect publicly on the positives rather than negatives regarding his slave heritage.[20] Having been befriended by supportive whites in his rural community, Washington perceived white people as being essentially good. Quiet, pensive, ambitious, and highly intelligent, Washington believed that the key to any personal success he might enjoy depended almost entirely upon white beneficence.

By stealth and natural instinct Washington ingratiated himself with white people. General and Mrs. Lewis Ruffner (for whom Washington served as a house boy) and General Samuel Chapman Armstrong, the principal of Hampton Normal and Agricultural Institute, acted as his initial role models. General Armstrong left an indelible imprint on Washington. During Washington's years of study at Hampton between 1871 and 1874, Armstrong personified the father Washington never knew. The General also provided Washington with a powerful god-like image and imperial presence that the young man emulated. Moreover, Armstrong personified important attributes—discipline and hard work—essential for success in late nineteenth century America. Under the guidance of Armstrong and training received at Hampton, Washington ventured forward to found Tuskegee Institute in Alabama. There, virtually everything Washington learned at Hampton became instituted at Tuskegee. Industrious, meticulous, practical, demanding, conservative, and with a military bearing, Armstrong proved not only an embodiment of the age, but also a perfect model for the founder and principal of Tuskegee.

In order to survive in the "Unreconstructed South" of that day, Washington relied upon his common understanding of nineteenth century America. The dominating aspect of Washington's seminal years appeared in contrasts between slavery and freedom, blacks and whites, rich and poor, and North and South. The dichotomies inherent in his experiences caused him to believe that success could be determined only by adopting a dogged, single-mindedness in action and deed. These contrasts and the demands for compromise produced within Washington a multiple personality far more complex than the "twoness" Du Bois would discuss later in *The Souls of Black Folk* when he described the condition of the Negro American.[21] The bifurcation in Washington's background enabled him to function confidently and self righteously as one of the most complex but heralded leaders in African American society.

Issues of the 1890s became issues of power—its acquisition and retention. Washington and the post-bellum United States, with its fledgling industrialism and quest for power, evolved simultaneously. The "New South," the new America, the newly created wealth, and the recently freed Negro embraced unique qualities that extended far beyond the comprehension of the "Founding Fathers." It was a new beginning for Americans generally, and for freedman like Washington in particular. Indeed, for black people in the "New South" the issue of leadership and power became extremely important because the overwhelming majority of African Americans resided south of the Mason-Dixon Line. This would suggest that a black leader of national import should be southern born and aware of the folkways and mores of southern life in order to have a constructive impact on the African American masses. Southern whites recognized the need for preserving order in their "New South" and selected a man suitable to their tastes and interests. Equally important, northern whites concurred with their southern counterparts and supported Washington, anointing him to become the leader of the African American majority. Since power became the key to late nineteenth century leadership, Washington decided that acquiescence to whites would enable him to acquire power and eventually lead his people into the next century.

Both Washington's southern upbringing and his comprehensive understanding of the nuances of the age—typified by the aggressive behavior of the Robber Barons—placed him in good stead as a leader. But his leadership also evoked the Social Darwinism of the era. He knew how to sidle up to whites of prominence, allowing himself to be "used" to achieve his own personal ends. His understanding and application of the cliches "the survival of the fittest," "ends justifying the means," and "might makes right," made Washington the most appropriate black leadership symbol of the age. But perhaps best of all, Washington learned the concept of organization from the "Captains of Industry." In many respects, he anticipated the thoughts and deeds of black leaders during the 1890s. He identified with the white power structure and recognized the need to develop a broad power base acceptable to influential whites. Washington also appeared to be ruthless, willing to undercut anyone who threatened his power base, economic and political interests, or role in the larger society. Although his behavior often reflected a man with flawed character, Washington never wavered in his unfaltering mission to protect and heighten prospects for African American amelioration.

Given the conditions in the "New South" of the 1890s, blacks placed survival as their first priority. Washington, more than anyone else, epitomized the survival instincts necessary at that time. Ruthlessness abounded. Intimidation and killing became more commonplace. Life in the South proved more lawless than popular folklore attributed to cowboys of the "Wild West." Recognizing this, Washington made certain that the students, faculty, and alumni of Tuskegee refrain from exercising basic freedoms of speech and press so that the institution could operate unfettered. Black resentment of white bigotry, he recognized, could only be addressed in a non-threatening manner with guile and cunning. Thus, Washington applied a clandestine methodology when attacking rivals and achieving goals. He eschewed compromise with fellow African American leaders and appeared acquiescent before influential whites. Consequently, winning at all costs dominated his thought, even if dignity and honor became sacrificed in the process.

In response to the Social Darwinism of that era, Washington endeavored—like Douglass before him—to show that blacks were human.

He sincerely believed that the more successful blacks became, the more they would become accepted by whites. In response to the demise of the Civil Rights Act of 1875 Washington said: "Brains, property, and character for the Negro will settle the question of civil rights."[22] By seeking respect for black humanity a primary goal of Douglass and Washington became enjoined.

One logical question that must be raised, of course, had to do with where the line of demarcation should be drawn between appeasement and integrity. Louis Harlan noted that Washington "traded political independence for educational and economic gain."[23] At best, Washington exhibited far more overt race consciousness than William Hooper Council, a contemporary nemesis who served as President of Alabama Agricultural and Mechanical College located in Huntsville. In competition for limited resources available to black students, Washington believed Council went too far in surrendering black dignity to acquire white largess. Perceiving Council as the prototype of an "Uncle Tom," Washington spent considerable time pre-empting Council's extreme eagerness to appease southern whites.[24] But at worst, Washington never developed alliances or created trusting relationships with fellow African Americans from the South or North. Invariably, the solitary, self-contained style Washington adopted often transcended his purpose to the disadvantage of his beloved race.

Washington's problems as a leader may be attributed to several additional factors that hampered his role as the preeminent representative of his race at the dawn of the new century. First, his enormous ego from which he gained strength also instilled within him an innate weakness. Only an individual with enormous self-confidence, industriousness, and intelligence could overcome the enormous obstacles Washington faced to achieve national notoriety and success. Self-assuredness naturally ensued, suggesting that no young black man or woman encountered during his formative years could be deemed a peer in leadership ability. And second, the development of a trusting relationship with fellow African Americans also appeared conspicuously absent. Whether this problem proved specific to Washington's personality, or rather, may be attributed directly to his slave heritage remains speculative. However, the concept of trust can prove difficult to comprehend when the heritage of slavery was marked by pejoratives—betrayal, inferiority, and the absence of positive black role models. For these reasons alone, Washington never acquired a southern black confidant—save his personal secretary Emmett Jay Scott—with whom he could share confidences about his strategic plans and practical thoughts.

As the last black leader of national repute born into slavery, Washington would have more reasons for demonstrating personal deficiencies as a leader than subsequent spokespersons of the race. Thus, Washington's worst faults must be evaluated in juxtaposition to his heritage within the context of slavery and manumission in the South, the region in which he resided his entire life. By contrast, Douglass, his predecessor, lived most of his adult life outside the "deep South" and enjoyed far more latitude as an advocate for freedom and equality on behalf of the Negro. Unlike Washington, Douglass exhibited pride, dignity, and self assuredness that enabled him to engage in social intercourse comfortably with dignified whites within the United States and Europe as well as refined blacks residing in the North.

Washington's most glaring deficiency existed in his inability to work cooperatively with members of his own race, a problem that appeared initially when Washington first came to national prominence in the mid 1890s. His white-controlled industrial education at Hampton never prepared him for interacting with proud, college trained black professionals schooled in the classics familiar with breathing the relatively free air of the North. Those he could influence and control became friends and pawns.[25] However, other than inviting this African American intelligentsia to address the student body of Tuskegee, Washington eschewed the classical education experienced by his sable guests. Instead he mandated that faculty at Tuskegee must provide instruction from the perspective of an industrial rather than academic curriculum. Washington told students: "We are not a college, and if there are any of you here who expect to get a college training you will be disappointed."[26] At most, Washington allowed for "dovetailing," a co-mingling of the industrial and academic in instruction. Clearly, the principal at Tuskegee made certain that industrial education took precedence over academic instruction in Greek, Latin, and mathematics. Even here, the dogmatic Washington refused to have questions raised about his policies, a phenomenon more likely to occur if students acquired broader thinking made possible through the breadth of a liberal arts education. This feeling became even more pronounced as he gained greater influence during the early twentieth century.

When Washington addressed the populace attending the Atlanta Exposition in 1895, he presented a position against which twentieth century black leadership would rebel. Of particular interest to those who observed and studied the address was the "separate as the fingers" clause.[27] Observant whites and blacks recognized that this reference to racial separation revealed that Washington approved of segregation. The address garnered thunderous approval from whites who subsequently anointed Washington the leader of his race. Reflective blacks, however, thought differently. While Washington counseled blacks to adopt patience in regard to social equality—the kind of patience preached by southern ministers and adopted by both religious and secular blacks in the "deep South"—the speech served as a galvanizing force for black proponents of racial equality. The pragmatic Washington accepted racial segregation. However, other black leaders, specifically accomplished blacks in the North, would devote considerable time and energy to eradicate the stigma of "Jim Crow." It would become increasingly evident that blacks differed on the "Race Question," a factor that certainly divided whites and blacks (and even blacks among themselves) far into the next century.

When Washington accepted the concept of segregation in his Atlanta Address, he inadvertently allowed himself to become identified with Senator John T. Morgan of Alabama. Supported by his interpretation of science and religion, Morgan spoke of the Negro's biological and mental deficiencies which justified segregation of the races. In 1890, Morgan declared: "The negro [sic] race in their native land ... have not contributed a thought, or a labor ... to aid the progress of civilization. The inferiority of the negro (sic) race, as compared with the white race, is ... essentially true and ... obvious.[28] "Rednecks," like "Pitchfork" Ben Tillman of South Carolina, Charles B. Aycock of North Carolina, and Hoke Smith of Georgia, rabid racial supremacists who cast an everlasting stain on the virtues of American democracy, also undermined Washington's rationale for separation.[29] Washington would find it difficult to maintain the confidence and support of African Americans while simultaneously endorsing the demeaning views of avowed white segregationists. When the Supreme Court handed down its opinion on the Plessy case Washington, through his Atlanta Address, had already identified with and acquiesced to the "separate but equal" doctrine. While the Court's decision regarding Plessy gave whites license to become more aggressive in segregating blacks, it contributed to enormous black resentment, caused progressive race conscious leaders to challenge white bigotry, and by circumstance, placed Washington in an awkward situation.[30] The disgruntled black opposition failed to realize that while Washington would bristle at criticism and maintain a jaundiced view toward the northern black elite; this feeling never deterred him from his fundamental goal—enhancing the life of the larger black society.

Plessy v. Ferguson impinged on the well being of every African American generally, and the black elite in particular, on a nationwide scale. While the case originated in New Orleans, a rising "color line" had evolved throughout post Civil War America. Historian C. Vann Woodward's discussion about "Jim Crow" suggests that the black elite, African Americans who set outstanding examples for the black masses to emulate, had to be stifled in some way. The emergence of Washington, coupled with the Plessy case, presented an immediate challenge to northern black leadership that functioned largely outside the grasp of virulent southern white racists. Douglass' death and the leadership void filled by Washington would force these new leaders to take up the mantle of freedom. The person who evolved to challenge Washington's leadership was William Edward Burghardt [W.E.B.] Du Bois.

Du Bois, an early proponent of Washington, would become one of the Tuskegee Wizard's staunchest adversaries. Young Willie Du Bois entered the world on February 23, 1868 in a modest home on Church Street in Great Barrington, Massachusetts.[31] Like Washington, Du Bois experienced dualities during his childhood—black and white, poverty and wealth, weakness and strength—as part of the dichotomy of being an African American. Also, like Douglass, Washington, and other prominent black American leaders, Du Bois sprang from a decidedly multi-racial lineage. Sensitive to his mixed ancestry, Du Bois clarified his origins, claiming that he had "a flood of Negro blood, a strain of French, a bit of Dutch, but thank God! No 'Anglo-Saxon,'" an observation revealing a profound sense of alienation he would have with the predominant white society in the United States.[32]

Most members of his mother's family, the Burghardts, made their living in service as cooks, waiters, and domestics. Within black circles the family seemed positioned to make a respectable living. Northern black service workers closely observed whites, aped white folkway and mores, and thereby assumed refined airs of the white upper class. Unlike whites whose class designation depended largely on wealth, Du Bois, like other self-respecting African Americans, relied on "haute culture" as the determinant for class standing. Although sired by a father he never knew and reared by a mother who sank deeper into poverty during his formative years, Du Bois nevertheless viewed his hardscrabble past in idyllic tones that became manifested in a positive image of self. This feeling became underscored when, as a pre-adolescent, he "annexed the rich and well-to-do boys as his companions.[33]

Outside of his immediate family, white men of prominence had the greatest impact on Du Bois' life. This very fact presented Du Bois with an interesting dilemma, a unique aspect of "twoness" missing from the autobiographical accounts he left for posterity. While racist whites denigrated African Americans, white people were also responsible for providing him with direction, encouragement, intellectual stimulation, financial support, and the ammunition with which to fight the foes of African American society. Therefore it became difficult, if not dishonest, for him to condemn the entire white race and attain credibility with blacks when a white patron of some sort launched the careers of many successful blacks. Du Bois certainly recognized the awkwardness of being a beneficiary of both white largess and white animosity.

Frank Allen Hosmer, a white Congregationalist, Amherst graduate, and principal of the newly established Great Barrington High School, became Du Bois' first adult male role model. From Hosmer, Du Bois learned about the value of education, an appreciation for literature and writing, and indirectly, the need for white moral and financial support. Hosmer guided the talented black youth through his adolescence in Great Barrington until he met his second role model, Erastus Milo Cravath, the president of Fisk University.

A descendant of New York abolitionists and former chaplain of the 101st Regiment of Ohio Volunteers in the Civil War, Cravath instituted the classical ideal of education within the Fisk curriculum. As an Oberlin graduate with a degree in divinity, Cravath remained mindful of Oberlin's origins as the first college in the United States founded with the mission to educate blacks. The school's fascination with blacks and greater propensity to admit and train talented African Americans and whites collectively remained with Cravath after his Oberlin experience.[34] Seeing blacks as equals rather than curiosities, Cravath knew from personal experience that African Americans could perform academically as capably as whites, and should be introduced to a rigorous academic curriculum. Fortunately for Du Bois, matriculating to Fisk and falling under the tutelage of Cravath and his faculty, proved ideal for Du Bois' social proclivities and intellectual growth.

During his three years in the South (1885-88) attending Fisk and learning the ways of black folk at the University and in the Tennessee hinterlands, Du Bois augmented his feelings of racial pride. College classmates provided Du Bois with the absented sense for racial belonging missing from his rustic origins in Great Barrington. Summers spent in the country teaching the black masses—the earthy men, women, and children of humble origins who comprised the majority of black people—gave him a positive sense of his African American roots. Yet one as sensitive as Du Bois could not speak objectively about his positive experiences with blacks without extolling the virtues of Cravath whose direction as the Fisk President, made Du Bois' college experiences fulfilling and enormously positive. Fisk Dean Adam K. Spence, former professor of classical Greek at the University of Michigan who possessed a profound commitment to educating black college students, also deserved praise. Spence fiercely defended Fisk's classic curriculum and made the institution a flagship for training African Americans in the "deep South." These and other like-minded, dedicated men enabled Du Bois to acquire a life-long interest in scientific research, gain a penchant for studying people, and develop techniques for recording notes that enabled him to become the first modern sociologist. Unlike Washington who never lived in the North, Du Bois' southern sojourn enabled him to gain a deeper emotional understanding of Americans generally and African Americans in particular.

Perhaps the most fortuitous aspect of Du Bois' matriculation to Fisk appeared in his ability to mingle with and respect elite [or potentially elite] peers who would comprise the black aristocracy of twentieth century America. The privileged educational background and training acquired by Fisk students prepared them for responsible positions that led to acclaim and high status in African American society. The denial of human rights in late nineteenth century America would instill many Fisk alumni with an uncompromising demand for equality on behalf of all African Americans. With the bravado of a budding genius, Du Bois saw a role for himself and other students at Fisk. He envisioned all of his peers working toward the betterment of black Americans when he wrote: "Through the leadership of men like myself and my fellows, we are going to have these enslaved Israelites [freedmen] out of the still enduring bondage in short order."[35]

Like Washington, Du Bois also became influenced by powerful forces inherent in the late nineteenth century, but unlike his future adversary, Du Bois displayed propensity for broadening the context of the black struggle to include not only the United States, but the entire world. At Fisk's Thirteenth Commencement in 1888, Du Bois demonstrated that he had become influenced by power in a global sense as evidenced by his selection of Otto Von Bismark "my hero," as the object of his commencement address. In his oration on Bismark, Du Bois said: "The life of this powerful Chancellor illustrates the power and purpose, the force of an idea."[36] Many interpretations may be gleaned from the object lesson Bismark posed for Du Bois. Nevertheless the abject condition of black Americans caused Du Bois to see a need for developing cohesion among African Americans just as the "Iron Chancellor" effectively used the powerful elite of Germany to create a strong national bond through discipline and hard work. Already, Du Bois demonstrated an expansive reality and placed his beloved race in the larger context of world society. With respect for his ability and at complete peace with his African American heritage, Du Bois prepared to move from Fisk to Harvard.

William James, the last significant and probably most influential instructor among Du Bois' white mentors, taught philosophy at Harvard. James, along with George Santayana, instilled in Du Bois an appreciation for ideas and a profound love for learning. Few black leaders, then or now, had been sufficiently advantaged to be served by faculty operating on the "cutting edge" of modern thought in history, philosophy, logic, and psychology, an academic background that enabled Du Bois to exude the confidence to lead blacks into the twentieth century.

Du Bois graduated cum laude from Harvard on June 25, 1890, enrolled the following year as a Ph.D. candidate in history and political economy, traveled through Europe, studied in Germany, and became the darling of Boston's elite black set. During his tenure at Harvard Du Bois met Archibald Grimké, Harvard Law School graduate and litterateur, and Joseph Charles Price, President of Livingstone College in North Carolina. Price also served as president of the Afro-American League and the National Equal Rights Convention, and espoused black unity, college training, participation in politics, and African American pride. This race conscious black southerner certainly impressed Du Bois. He was an individual Du Bois identified as a man who died before his time.[37]

During his years of graduate study Du Bois adopted the imprimatur of a benevolent despot stating what he would do "if he were king." More a moderate in economic and political theory, he, as biographer David L. Lewis asserts, "... feared both vulgar wealth and vulgar democracy."[38] Again, Du Bois' duality became extant. His humble class and racial origins caused him to identify with the black masses. However, the significant privileges he acquired as a student and eminent scholar—an extremely rare happenstance at that time—compelled him to accept and endorse the elitism of white teachers and benefactors.

The 1890s ushered in profound thinking on public education that transcended the limited concept of industrial instruction espoused by Booker T. Washington. Powerful interests from North and South focused on the pragmatic needs of the larger society, and the kind of education needed to train the masses to meet the employment expectations of a burgeoning capitalistic society. Each geographical region saw a need to educate laborers to serve their area of the United States. The South depended upon black laborers, and in the North, European immigrants with limited knowledge of English and American culture, supplied the work force for industrial America. In the two Lake Mohonk Conferences of 1890 and 1891, the most influential men and women of the day—exclusively white northerners and southerners who molded public opinion—discussed the educational needs of society generally, and blacks in particular. Eventually the gathering reached a general consensus that placed emphasis on training the masses to perform basic skills needed for industry and agriculture. "Mohonkers" became the antecedents to progressives who regulated the access to education, instituted the means for social control of the lower classes, and determined the kind of functional training required of America's inchoate laboring force during the next century.[39]

The larger interests of the United States took precedent over providing classical education for African Americans. The few who supported this concept, like southern folklorist Albion Tourgee, Torrey Harris, the United States Commissioner of Education, and New York Baptist Bishop Malcolm Mac Vicar, held limited, and eventually waning influence on national policy makers. Thus, to Booker T. Washington's credit, industrial education seemed far more in tune with the pragmatic norms of late nineteenth century America than liberal arts training endorsed by Du Bois. But it should also be understood that proponents of classical education largely intended such education for the so-called "better classes" of either race. African Americans who insisted upon making classical education available to blacks—who in later decades would propose school integration—were thinking primarily about the availability of education for their class, the middle class, rather than the masses. Few leaders of either race envisioned education as a means for the economically and culturally disadvantaged to enhance their socioeconomic station.[40]

The debate over public education generated contradictory behavior from Du Bois, conflicts pertaining to his endorsement of elitism and simultaneous identification with the masses. As a Harvard trained Ph.D., Du Bois had reason to display a supercilious attitude toward the general public. However the socialistic training he received at the University of Berlin instilled him with a desire to serve as a champion for the unrepresented proletariat. In this respect, he resembled idealistic members of the white hierarchy who spoke for the masses without caring whether they jeopardized their status as members of the cultured elite. Du Bois never felt sufficiently comfortable with whites to shun his African heritage and never wavered in maintaining pride in his people. Upon his return to the United States after years of study in Germany, Du Bois wrote: "I dropped suddenly back into 'nigger'-hating America."[41] Though Du Bois would speak glowingly and repeatedly about "his people," no one would mistake the haughty sage from Great Barrington for being an "average Negro." Indeed, his moral outrage against wrongs committed against African Americans never abated.

As a prognosticator of future inter-racial problems, Du Bois recognized the need for studying African Americans and explaining how poverty and racism impinged on black society within the United States. When asked to conduct a study of black Philadelphians commissioned by the University of Pennsylvania, Du Bois responded favorably. Little did the University or Du Bois realize that his research, a classic study entitled *The Philadelphia Negro*, would speak to multiple issues that would challenge future African American leaders. Racism, intra-racial class conflict, leadership voids, helplessness endemic to the urban underclass, and American indifference to scientific discovery regarding the plight of the Negro characterized black life in the United States. In short, *The Philadelphia Negro* became the first comprehensive treatise that challenged white Americans to redress problems attributed to racism. Equally important, the study outlined the responsibility of black leadership, a "Talented Tenth," to lead a despised race from purgatory to equality and success.

Although influenced by numerous white men, Episcopal priest Alexander Crummell provided Du Bois with the "noblesse oblige" concept of a "Talented Tenth," a select group expected to serve their race.[42] Aside from his grandfather, Crummell became Du Bois' first black mentor. Du Bois first met the seventy-six year old Crummell at Wilberforce University in the spring of 1895 and became immediately impressed by the cleric's dignity and noble bearing. Subsequent conversations eventually evolved into mutual respect and the discovery of similar sensibilities. Just as Crummell initially praised then criticized Washington's work, Du Bois would also support then decry the leadership role played by the Wizard of Tuskegee. Disillusioned by Washington's sycophantic behavior toward whites, remarks attributed to Washington exasperated Crummell. The dignified cleric disapproved of Washingtonian homilies that praised the institution of slavery, and reached a final breaking point with Washington after the Tuskegean said: "If in the providence of God the Negro got any good out of slavery, he got the habit of work."[43] Given the need to demonstrate the race's humanity, Crummell initiated the attack on "The Tuskegee Machine" in Washington D.C. on October, 1896 at a meeting of the American Negro Academy. Crummell voiced the opinion of race conscious African Americans when he said that a race was deemed civilized when it produced "letters, literature, science, philosophy, poetry, sculpture, architecture [and] all the arts."[44] The pronouncements of this august man, which combined race consciousness, erudition, and criticism, could hardly be lost on Du Bois.

For Washington, Du Bois, and other black leaders, the 1890s represented a decade of contrasts. Although reference to the "Gay Nineties" has proven a misnomer, certain developments gave rise to altruism and hope. In contrast to Social Darwinism initiated by Englishman Herbert Spencer and popularized in the United States through William Graham Sumner's endorsement of "the gospel of wealth," humanistic forces evolved that black leaders embraced and used in their quest for racial equality. Hope for the disillusioned and dispossessed appeared through the settlement house movement.[45] Originated in England's Toynbee Hall in London in 1884, Stanton Coit, an American social reformer, transported the concept of the settlement house to New York City in 1866. By 1889 Jane Addams, arguably the most progressive, socially minded white woman in America, opened Hull House in Chicago, the most famous settlement house in the United States. Addams' humanism eventually extended to the plight of African Americans when she befriended Du Bois and became a founder of the NAACP. Another example of humanism directed toward the urban poor originated in the Social Gospel Movement. Christians and Jews decided to follow tenets contained in the Judeo-Christian ethos by providing assistance to the indigent.[46] Quakers in Philadelphia demonstrated their concern about the urban poor by commissioning Du Bois to investigate black life Philadelphians. By accident or design, a representation of "Social Gospel" interests appeared in Du Bois' scholarship when he advocated the concept of service—the duty and responsibility of the upper classes to assist those of lower station.[47] As a unique black reformer reflective of the era, Du Bois participated in the late nineteenth century intellectual response to industrialism, imperialism, and racism.

Perhaps the most confusing reformist movement exemplifying contradictions of the late nineteenth century appeared in the Populist movement. Populists, members of a nascent urban labor and agrarian movement from the South and West vied to unseat the eastern political establishment. Conflicts between opposing political forces threatened the political stability of the nation. Western Populists called for higher farm prices, lower freight rates and extended credit;[48] but the greatest threat to the status quo in American politics occurred in the South. Southern Democrats and Republicans feared that the Populists' efforts in soliciting black support for their cause—preaching the commonality of poverty and offering egalitarianism to these potential allies—would undermine the hegemony of the white ruling class. The political pronouncements of Georgia Populist, Tom Watson, created deep concern for traditional white politicos when he said:

> You [blacks and whites] are kept apart that you may be separately fleeced of your earnings. You are made to hate each other because upon that hatred is rested the keystone of the arch of financial despotism which enslaves you both. You are deceived and blinded that you may not see how this race antagonism perpetuates a monetary system which beggars both.[49]

Watson's declaration suggested that for the first time since Reconstruction, African Americans of the South existed as an integral part of southern society, playing a legitimate role in the region's economy. The intensity of regular party fears about the Populists, coupled with long standing white concerns about blacks as a political force, threatened the prevailing culture of late nineteenth century America.[50] However, by the 1896 presidential election the Populist movement was rendered moribund. Democrats and Republicans successfully used race as a dividing factor and regained political dominance among the electorate. Reassured whites looked forward to stability at home and expansion abroad. For blacks, however, a prominent role in national politics became dashed by the Populist defeat and rendered African Americans politically impotent for an entire generation.

Despite the hope and despair blacks encountered in the social and political capriciousness of the era, a spirit of tenacity, industry, and racial consciousness prevailed among African American females culminating in the formation of the National Association of Colored Women [NACW].

Founded within two months of Plessy v. Ferguson, the NACW proposed to be a social, economic, and moral force that would guide and protect African American society generally and specifically target black women as their primary focus for assistance. The NACW endeavored to improve conditions for the race by easing the burdens faced by working women. Among the panaceas envisioned by the NACW were kindergartens, day nurseries, and mothers' clubs, institutions and social organizations that provided training, relief, and mutual support for desperate, overburdened, disadvantaged black women. The founder, first president, and force behind the NACW was an aristocratic woman of noble bearing and impeccable manners named Mary Church Terrell.

Born on September 23, 1863 in Memphis, Tennessee to former slaves, Robert Reed and Louisa Ayers Church, Mary enjoyed a sheltered, upper middle class existence. Educated at an "integrated model" school connected with Antioch College in Ohio and graduated from Oberlin College in 1884, Mary Church taught at the renowned M Street Colored High School [renamed Paul Lawrence Dunbar] in Washington, D.C., and traveled throughout Europe before marrying Robert Heberton Terrell.[51] Since married women were prohibited from teaching and her husband, a Harvard graduate, was an educator and budding attorney, Mary Terrell could have enjoyed a quiet life as a homemaker. Instead, as a representative of the "new woman," she devoted her life to acquiring civil rights for her gender and race.

As president of the NACW, Mary Church Terrell created policies that would be emulated by subsequent female organizations. She established communication through a monthly newsletter that disseminated information about the organization, made provisions for biennial conventions to be held in cities with large black populations, and devoted the organization to elevating black women to the highest level of attainment.[52] As the first national organization created and run by black females, the NACW catered to the needs of women who were married with children and to single professionals. The NACW also afforded women an opportunity to acquire leadership skills. Members of the NACW would develop the female version of the "Talented Tenth" and serve as a guide for service emulated in the twentieth century by African American sororities.

Anna Julia Haywood Cooper, another black female influenced by the mores of Victorian America, also became instrumental in establishing a role for women in the long struggle for civil rights. Born from a union between a slave woman, Hannah Stanley and her master, George Washington Haywood in Raleigh, North Carolina in 1858, Anna proved extremely precocious and possessed a burning desire for education. After completing her secondary education at the St. Augustine's Normal School and Collegiate Institute in Raleigh, Anna Haywood married, matriculated to Oberlin and graduated with an A.B. and M.A. in 1884 and 1887. Like her classmate Mary Church, Cooper moved to the District of Columbia, rented quarters with the Alexander Crummell family, taught at the M Street School, and prepared for a life of social activism. Cooper spoke before the white Women's Congress at the Chicago World's Columbian Exposition in 1893 on the "Intellectual Progress of Colored Women Since Emancipation." She also became the only woman elected to the American Negro Academy, and promoted opportunities for black youth and women through clubs, organizations, and an uncompromising defense of African American rights.[53]

Booker T. Washington, W.E.B. Du Bois, Mary Church Terrell, Anna Julia Cooper, and other black leaders would have to marshal all their strength and energy to contend with forces evolving during the 1890s that would have a deleterious effect on African Americans. The decade represented an age of industrialization, greed, and human despair, fostering a sense of insecurity among white Americans. These frustrated Americans looked for scapegoats to rationalize their problems and used blacks as the primary focus for attack. Blacks bore the brunt of demeaning jokes and became the objects of functional racism in America. The editors and writers of the northern press and magazines made a comfortable living lampooning the Negro. Historian Rayford Logan found that late nineteenth century stories, poems, cartoons, and anecdotes referred to African Americans as "'nigger,' 'niggah,' 'darkey,' 'coon,' 'pickaninny,' 'Mammy.' 'aunt,' 'uncle,' 'buck,''light-complected-yaller man,' and 'yaller hussy.'"[54] Negro physical features discussed derisively—thick lips, kinky hair, black skin—added to implications of limited intelligence emphasized through the use of "Negro dialect," reinforced in white minds, the reality of African American inferiority. Caricatures of the "lazy, improvident, dishonest Negro" offered justification for treating African Americans as second class citizens.

Indignities blacks faced during the 1890s gave rise to the "color line" of the twentieth century. Segregation, lynching, and disregard for civil rights, impinged negatively upon every black man, woman, and child in the United States. Historian C. Vann Woodward reported in *The Strange Career of Jim Crow* that racial segregation, initially a northern creation, existed long before Plessy.[55] During the Reconstruction and Redemption period segregation became increasingly popular as a practice in the South. So by the unsettling decade of the 1890s, genteel and radical southerners as well as northern liberals acquiesced to the pervasive hostility directed toward African Americans that continued unabated since the end of the Civil War.[56]

In many respects the 1890s gave rise to the dawn of modern black leadership. The issue of how best to lead became prescribed from Douglass to Washington and Du Bois. Douglass established the role of responsible leadership by acting with dignity and pride, serving as a role model for the race, and invoking fiery oratory to champion the cause of black people. This great man believed that threats to African Americans required a suitable response. Douglass even tested his right to enjoy all privileges available to American citizens by marrying Helen Pitts, a white woman from Rochester, New York. Washington, on the other hand, represented cautious, pragmatic leadership. He protected his beloved Tuskegee and would endeavor to prepare blacks for what he believed were challenges of the twentieth century. For Washington, a man who directed the race from his base in Alabama, marriage to a white woman would be inconceivable. Correspondingly, Du Bois, epitome of the black intelligentsia, used literary talents rather than oratory to gain respect for African Americans. Aloof and correct, he would apply his considerable skills to organize, stimulate, and unify black people to fight against the advancing tide of racism.

Black leaders of the twentieth century relied upon patterns of leadership established by nineteenth century precursors. Douglass offered prideful, uncompromising demands for equality, Washington represented compromise, and Du Bois prepared to stand for excellence that demonstrated unequivocally that African Americans were equal to whites as a cultured, competitive, industrious race. It is also important to keep in mind that many influential black leaders were influenced and assisted by prominent whites. Douglass had white abolitionist friends, though he refused to be compromised in order to court favor with prominent whites. Washington seemed entirely intent on using his survival instincts to acquire necessary assistance to aid and abet dependent southern blacks. Du Bois, who placed dignity before pragmatism, had difficulty acting subservient to anyone. Yet, like Washington, he too possessed survival instincts. He studied and lived in the North and South and proved capable of functioning in a society where inequality existed and economic dependency limited options for ambitious black people.

One consistent theme regarding nineteenth century African American leaders held true; all were deeply race conscious. They had a profound sense of responsibility to their race, a race demeaned, hated, and reviled by white society. Few, if any, African Americans found a sanctuary safe from racist hostility. Both white northerners and southerners maintained a deep animosity toward blacks, an animus steeped in America's history as a slave holding nation. Every nineteenth century black leader had intimate knowledge of the racism that permeated American society. The only issues of contention among black leaders pertained to the response to racism—emigrating abroad, compromising to achieve domestic tranquility, or fighting incessantly for rights as American citizens. Although a small retinue of African Americans harbored black nationalistic ideas and continued to believe in emigration, the overwhelming majority of blacks thought of the United States as home and prepared to fight for recognition as humans and American citizens.

When northerners accepted and eventually promoted the southern concept of white supremacy and black inferiority and endorsed the universality of segregation, reconciliation between the North and South became complete.[57] For most whites the "Negro Problem," as a divisive force, no longer existed, but for blacks further ignominy awaited. The inferior status of African Americans that evolved through the three branches of government, the media, and national politics became finalized in 1898 through America's victory in the Spanish-American War. With thousands of new, "inferior colored" people from the Caribbean and the Philippines incorporated into the American sphere of influence, "The White Man's Burden," domination of inferior and dependent races at home and abroad became undisputed. For people of color racism had no boundaries. The most learned and accomplished African American enjoyed no greater rights than the most debased and ignorant southern freedman or black guttersnipe residing in the North. The rising "color line" forced black leaders to stay the course and maintain a relentless push for equality. Generations of leaders would be involved in the quest for human rights, a march toward freedom that consumed African American leaders for most of the twentieth century.

2

THE RISING COLOR LINE

"The Problem of the Twentieth Century is the Problem of the Color Line."
With these prophetic words delivered at the first Pan African Conference
in 1900, W.E.B. Du Bois introduced a cadre of prominent leaders to their
primary challenge. Familiar with the burgeoning industrialism of the United
States and troubled by the increasingly harsh treatment accorded his sable
countrymen; the clairvoyant Du Bois anticipated clashes between blacks
and whites. The omnipresent "color line" permitted whites to enjoy a sense
of superiority. However, the negative manifestations attributed to racism
forced black leaders to take a more aggressive stance against racial
discrimination. The daunting task at that time required black leaders to
initiate the quest for human rights and equal opportunity for African
Americans during a period of continuous, and invariably, heightened white
repression toward blacks. Black leaders had the unenviable responsibility
of reminding a proud nation of the inconsistency between the avowed
principles of democracy and freedom evident in the Constitution, and the
woeful discrimination practiced by white Americans toward people of
color.

Du Bois' portent of a century consumed with racial problems hardly
represented the perspective of the American majority. At the dawn of the
new century Americans seemed optimistic and looked toward the future
with confidence. Victory in the Spanish-American War enabled the United
States to savor the taste of empire and become recognized by the English,

French, and Germans as an incipient world power. Astute politicians like Mark Hanna who represented the heart and soul of the Republican Party made certain that President William McKinley would prepare for re-election in 1900 without serious challenges from remnants of a defunct Populist Party or from the Democrats. Unbridled wealth made possible by the continuous growth of trusts and the financial empire of J. Pierpont Morgan enabled an increasingly powerful economic oligarchy to control the nation's wealth. Europeans continued migrating to the United States in search of fortune, adding to the mystique that America was the land of opportunity for ambitious people in the new, vibrant century.

Applying the euphoria of this era to African Americans, Booker T. Washington published *A New Negro for a New Century* in 1900. This discourse, rendered in the positive Washingtonian style, spoke optimistically of the future. The following year Washington's classic autobiography *Up From Slavery* appeared, offering black and white Americans alike a sense of the nation's destiny. According to Washington, poor, humble, but industrious people, regardless of race, could attain success in the United States. By avoiding the controversial "race" question, Washington afforded white people a clear conscience in regard to the Negro. Respecting the sensibilities of white America and speaking to the needs of the majority of blacks who remained rooted in the South, Washington solidified his position as the preeminent black leader of the era. For better or worse until his death, Booker T. Washington would function as the spokesman for his race.

Du Bois' admonitions and Washington's optimism revealed decidedly different perspectives on the future for African Americans. Evidence suggested that the pessimistic theory posed by Du Bois held greater validity. In 1900 nearly ninety percent of all African Americans resided in an unrepentant South, and life expectancy for African Americans nationally comprised only 34 years as opposed to 48 years for whites.[1] With Plessy v. Ferguson guaranteeing white hegemony and the black majority confined to penury as the primary labor force, Washington's optimism seemed illusionary and misguided. Moreover, by 1901 eradication of black voting rights became finalized when North Carolinian George H. White, the last black Congressman, served his final term in the House of Representatives. With White's retirement Congress would remain lily-white for a generation. Rabble rousing southern white demagogues had license to spread their infectious venom throughout Congress with impunity. Unbridled racism placed the entire African American population in jeopardy as white animus toward blacks became normative and served as the cornerstone for race relations far into the twentieth century.

The lack of respect accorded African Americans gained further support from genteel white academicians steeped in the late nineteenth concept of scientific inquiry. Rather than accept the original premise that classified all races as being one species of the animal kingdom,[2] scholars searched for different answers. The Scotsman, Lord Kames, who in 1774 published *Sketches of the Human History of Man*, presented the initial theory on racial differences that denigrated people of African ancestry. First, Kames presented the premise that the races evolved from different stocks. Then, he spoke pejoratively of the Negroid race, citing the black color, "thick lips, flat nose, crisped wooly hair, and rank smell" of Negroes that suggested the African race was different, and by description, inferior.[3] Lord Kames' philosophy gained additional credence from Dr. Charles White, an English surgeon, and an American physician, Dr. John Augustine Smith, president of William and Mary College and of the College of Physicians and Surgeons of New York. Both men believed that Africans were not only physically different from Europeans but also mentally inferior to Europeans, the race ranked first in "the immense chain of beings."[4] But Dr. Samuel George Morton, more than any other scholar, established the foundation for scientific racism through an academic medium known as phrenology—the measurement of brain size in relation to race and intelligence. Possessed with a profound interest in research, Morton collected specimens of fauna throughout the nation and became particularly fascinated by human skulls. His crania collection, the largest in the world, enabled Morton to speak as an authority in several academic realms. With the 1839 publication of *Crania Americana*, Morton recorded several scientific firsts. He initiated a new approach in anthropology; he provided credence to phrenology; and he developed a scientific rationale for the enslavement of African Americans.[5]

American ethnologists played an unwitting role in maintaining African American unity in the struggle for dignity. Unlike Latin-American nations that recognized people of mixed ancestry and accorded greater status to individuals with some Caucasian blood, whites in the United States and scholars specifically held different opinions. To white Americans, anyone with African blood received the sobriquet "Negro," and suffered the consequences for being black. Dr. Joseph Clark Nott of Mobile, Alabama and graduate of the University of Pennsylvania's School of Medicine presented a more explicit view of mulattos. In an article entitled "The

Mulatto a Hybrid—Probable Extermination of the Two Races If the Whites and Blacks Are Allowed To Intermarry" published in the *American Journal of the Medical Sciences* (circa 1842), Nott perceived miscegenation as being detrimental to both races. Although it was generally assumed that the admixture of white blood provided the mulatto with higher intelligence than the pure Negro, Nott believed this mixed race to be less hardy than the parent races and therefore inferior.[6] By identifying mulattos in the same or worse manner as pure Africans, Nott and other white scholars kept African Americans of mixed ancestry like Booker T. Washington, W.E.B. Du Bois, and others within the Negro race. Nott's characterizations, which seemed to hold credence with the white majority, determined that those with an infinitesimal admixture of African blood—including the descendants of the most esteemed white people—could play a leadership role only in black America.

While politics surrounding the Civil War and Reconstruction brought the issue of black humanity forward, the notion of African American inferiority never subsided. Rather, intellectual justification for racism evolved through a fledgling academic field that became known as sociology. In 1883 Lester Frank Ward published a seminal book, *Dynamic Sociology* that applied the theory of artificial control to Social Darwinism. Ward suggested that humans exercise some control over environment and influence the direction of human development. In 1890 Ward founded the *American Journal of Sociology*, providing scholars with a forum to rebel against the conservative thought of the Victorian era and instill a sense of liberalism within the American intelligentsia. Unfortunately, the continuous strain of racism in the United States eliminated objectivity and liberalism in regard to African Americans. At best, "objective" white sociologists attributed the rise of a nascent black middle class primarily to beneficent whites.[7] But most sociologists writing at the turn of the century, like Sarah E. Simons, W.H. Thomas, Paul S. Reinsch, and Charles A. Ellwood held African Americans in disdain and referred to a Negro as one of "inferior capacity," displaying "no tendency toward development," and remaining "a savage child of nature."[8] More often than not, white intellectuals mirrored the racist beliefs of the larger white society rather than honor the credo of objectivity that would support egalitarianism in regard to the African American.

While sociologists provided an intellectual framework for the inferior status of African Americans, another more pernicious threat to the humanity of African descendants, and challenge to black leadership, existed in lynching. In many respects, lynching, America's most infamous domestic pastime, became the phenomenon that caused blacks to question Booker T. Washington's influence as a black leader. The accommodationist policy Washington adopted failed to protect blacks—residing in the North and South—from the vicious attacks of white racists. Between 1895, the year of his Atlanta Address, and 1900, nearly 500 blacks died at the hands of lynch mobs. Since Washington's deference to whites made him ineffectual in attacking lynching, someone had to step forward to launch a frontal attack against this nefarious, inhuman practice. On January 20, 1900, Representative George White introduced the first anti-lynching bill to the United States Congress. Unfortunately, the bill died in committee despite 105 African Americans dying in the centennial year alone.

After White left Congress, a feminist firebrand known as Ida B. Wells-Barnett worked incessantly to place lynching on the forefront of the national consciousness. Born to enslaved parents on July 16, 1862 in Holly-Springs, Mississippi, young Ida had only a vague recollection of slavery. Her parents, Lizzie Warrenton Wells, who suffered severely under the yoke of slavery, and her father Jim Wells, a carpenter, who vividly remembered his mother being severely beaten by his father's jealous wife, instilled her with a profound sense of independence and an abhorrence of repression.[9] In her sixteenth year, Ida's parents died in a yellow fever epidemic, leaving her to care for five younger siblings. Although forced to leave her college studies at Shaw University prematurely because of an argument with the College president, Ida Wells passed the teachers examination and began instructing students near Holly Springs. Eventually, new teaching opportunities beckoned in Woodstock, Shelby County, Tennessee. While teaching in Tennessee, Wells displayed her combative nature when segregation practiced by the Chesapeake, Ohio, and Southwestern Railroad encouraged her to initiate and win a law suit against the company.

Eventually tiring of teaching in the primary grades, Ida Wells ventured into the newspaper business. With the guidance of *New York Age* editor, T. Thomas Fortune, Wells made her living as an essayist and "Afro-American agitator" for the *Free Speech and Headlight* newspaper of Memphis. Her acerbic editorials spared no one, white or black, who fell short of her expectations. Therefore, "with the ability to articulate grievances and the passion to persist in a cause," Wells seemed equipped to tackle the odious practice of lynching.[10] After a brutal lynching in Memphis cost three innocent self-sufficient middle class black men their lives, Wells became an untiring crusader against the heinous practice. She spoke out about the mythology of rape as the primary cause for lynching, a position that caused her to flee Memphis in 1892 and find work at the *New York Age* headquarters. As an outspoken critic of lynching, she faced a formidable opposition and enlisted the assistance of her husband, Ferdinand Barnett, a Chicago attorney she married in 1895, as her ally.

The Barnetts and their supporters faced a formidable challenge because most white people believed in the innate inferiority of the Negro. In addition, the Barnett family had to contend with the likes of Quincy Ewing, a white contributor to the prestigious magazine *Atlantic Monthly*, who echoed the thoughts of scientific racist scholars and whites. Ewing provided justification for those who would lynch blacks by saying:

> The Negroes, as a rule, are very ignorant, are very lazy, are very brutal, are very criminal. But a little way removed from savagery, they are incapable of adopting the white man's moral ideals. They are creatures of brutal untamed instincts, and uncontrollable feral passions, which give, frequent expression of themselves in crimes of horrible ferocity. They are, in brief, an uncivilized semi-savage people, living in a civilization to which they are unequal.[11]

The attitudes voiced by Ewing and others pressed Ida Wells-Barnett into action. She wrote articles that vigorously protested lynching, used public forums to defend black men, and attacked anyone inclined to accept the southern myth about black rapists.[12]

Interestingly, Ida Wells-Barnett, an African American woman, could be identified as the most renowned black militant of the late nineteenth and early twentieth centuries. She carried a pistol and encouraged blacks to arm themselves for self-defense. Nevertheless, she was a rational militant and provided her listeners with practical advice. She encouraged blacks to use economic boycotts and emigrate from the South. The intellectually astute Wells-Barnett also recognized that successful blacks who refuted the concept of racial inferiority attracted the wrath of white racists. When an infamous lynching in Memphis occurred in 1892, she realized that resentful whites viewed successful blacks with disdain. Lowly, petulant whites had more reason to attack an "uppity," successful black than the uncouth, impoverished Negro who knew his place. At the very least, Wells-Barnett could take comfort knowing that lynching ensured racial solidarity between upper and lower class African Americans.

In addition to leading the anti-lynching crusade, Wells-Barnett criticized the legal system for disregarding the rights of Africa Americans. Indeed, most whites assumed that African Americans victimized by "Judge Lynch" were guilty and therefore received proper punishment for their "despicable acts." By exposing southern injustice in the press and on the lecture circuit, she revealed that white professionals joined with lower elements of white society as perpetrators of mob violence. Wells-Barnett did not limit her exposé to the South. In her mind racism permeated every stratum of white society. She extended her fury to the press, the federal government, the Republican Party, and the white clergy.[13] Naturally white America preferred the homilies of Booker Washington to the fiery rhetoric of Ida Wells-Barnett.

Booker T. Washington's cavalier treatment of lynching contributed to Wells-Barnett's split with the "Wizard." She deplored the Tuskegee principal's response to lynching as characterizations that placed blame entirely upon the victim and became one of the first prominent African Americans to criticize Washington publicly. Mockingly, Wells-Barnett presented the Washingtonian view to be: "Give me some money to educate the Negro, and when he is taught how to work, he will not commit the crime for which lynching is done."[14] After publishing an article in *World Today* in April 1904, Wells-Barnett placed herself clearly in the anti-Bookerite camp and joined W.E. B. Du Bois as one of Washington's most staunch adversaries.

The rising "color line" gave impetus to the dispute between Booker T. Washington and W.E.B. Du Bois. According to journalist Ray Stannard Baker, the South, unlike the North, was consumed by what he deemed the "Negro Problem." White southerners had concerns that race relations in the "New South"–namely, alterations in labor-management relationships in the new economy, the role of blacks in state politics, and the potential threat to customary folkways and mores—might prevent white people from keeping the African American population subservient. Therefore, as people accepting Negro inferiority as a universal truth, southern whites felt justified maintaining the "status quo" by marginalizing—by any means necessary—the millions of blacks residing in "Dixie." Through lynching, economic intimidation, segregation, a "lily white" legal system, limited access to education, and the systematic elimination of blacks from politics, African Americans residing in the South found themselves in a tragic situation. Since whites visited blacks daily with some kind of atrocity, the black condition seemed increasingly desperate.

Baker observed that the North had its racial problems too. Most African Americans residing above the Mason-Dixon Line lived in cities. As the numbers of blacks moving into cities increased, housing became cramped, sanitary conditions worsened, and low-income migrants became objects for derision. The situation became exacerbated when black migrants competed against whites for jobs. In every major city—Indianapolis, Cincinnati, Philadelphia, New York, Boston, and Chicago—Baker found that racial discrimination and racial tension heightened. African Americans of long standing, the elite of the black community, also felt the sting of discrimination. Public establishments that had welcomed black trade refused service to all African Americans including the established black bourgeoisie. Even Boston, center of the Abolitionist Movement, contained residents who perceived blacks as threats. Speaking for his congregation, a white church leader stated: "What shall we do with these Negroes! I for one would like to have them stay ... but the proportion is growing so large that white people are drifting away from us.[15] Conscious of the ever-increasing racial slights and chagrined by the lack of respect accorded them from the white public, anger festered among African Americans residing in the North. These blacks would be among the first to challenge the endearing platitudes of Booker T. Washington.

Evidence of black leadership's concerns about the Washingtonian strategy emerged almost immediately after his Atlanta Address of 1895. African American newspapers like the *Cleveland Gazette* and *Washington Bee* voiced their opposition. Prominent black Philadelphian, Dr. Nathan F. Mossell, also expressed disillusionment with the "Wizard of Tuskegee," pronouncing Washington's surrender of the ballot "the most damnable heresy."[16] Still, as a spokesman for the African American majority who resided in the South and as a man recognized and respected by southern politicians and northern industrialists, Washington remained a powerful force that many black leaders initially chose not to oppose.

Blacks critical of Washington soon received a justifiable reason for holding their tongues. On October 16, 1901 Washington reached his apogee as an African American leader. That momentous day Booker T. Washington culminated a series of firsts for African Americans. Aside from being the founder of Tuskegee Institute, the first black to receive an honorary degree from Harvard [M.A. in 1896]; the first president of the National Negro Business League [1900]; he became the first African American officially invited to dine in the White House with the President of the United States. Since Roosevelt assumed the presidency the previous month, the timing of his social appointment with Washington had momentous significance. While blacks expressed heartfelt delight, the white South, conversely, immediately voiced outrage with Washington's breach of social convention. Washington came to realize the dinner invitation placed him in a political dilemma. He feared alienating white southerners by dining with a white man—particularly the President of the United States. Nevertheless, he dined with President Roosevelt and eagerly took the risk because of the portent for power the social encounter conveyed to black and white Americans.

The October dinner demonstrated before blacks and whites in the entire nation that Washington had became the undisputed leader, representative, and power broker for all African Americans. The politically astute Washington appreciated the augmented leverage he enjoyed. Access to Roosevelt enabled Washington to become the sole presidential advisor on Negro affairs. As August Meier observed, Washington—through Roosevelt—had a number of positions at his disposal, including collectorships of ports and internal revenue, receiverships of public monies in the land office, diplomatic posts, register of the Treasury, and recorder of the deeds. Equally astonishing, Roosevelt asked Washington to advise him on the selection of whites to fill positions of influence in the South.[17]

Washington obviously savored the personal notoriety and enormous prestige he gained by dining with the President of the United States. But in fairness to Washington, his motives remained consistent; he acted to benefit his race within an overwhelmingly hostile environment. Social intercourse with the President comported with "The Wizard's" political objectives. In addition to support from the Chief Executive, Washington sincerely believed that the salvation of African Americans depended upon a coalition with conservatism—southern patricians and wealthy northerners. Washington firmly believed in black self-help and racial solidarity, and clandestinely acted as an African American power broker who supported black voting rights and opposed segregation. Yet he also knew that his race would never become free of oppression without political and economic assistance from white people. Although he publicly denounced political activism among African Americans, Washington contributed his personal wealth to support political causes advantageous to blacks. Washington even encouraged white benefactors to provide financial support to political test cases that would aid and abet the role of blacks in American politics.[18]

Knowing the age and understanding the vagaries of racism better than any other American of that day, Washington, also known as the Tuskegean and the Wizard, played the role of a chameleon. By wearing different masks to achieve specific goals, Washington acted as a tyrannical overseer at Tuskegee, exhibited deferential dignity before white northern benefactors, acted as a paternal father toward southern blacks, used cunning and guile to control the black North, and kept "his place" within the white South.[19] Directly and indirectly, the Washingtonian strategy seemed correct. Despite southern repression, in nearly twenty years after the 1895 Atlanta Compromise Address, the number of black owned businesses doubled from approximately 20,000 to 40,000, and more than 200,000 black southern farmers owned land.[20]

Unfortunately, Washington's style, colossal ego, and obsession with power detracted from his objectives. These factors, added to the rising "color line," caused the number of anti-Bookerite detractors to grow. Indeed, Washington's excessive efforts to act as an accommodator and toady to whites exacerbated the differences between himself and openly race conscious blacks of the North. His public deference to white people became particularly demeaning for a race of people endeavoring to attain human respect from whites. As David Levering Lewis reveals, a perusal of Washington's speeches encapsulated in 1898 in *Black-Belt Diamonds* contained elements offensive to proud African Americans of the North. Few, if any, could countenance the notion that lynching "really indicates progress [because] there can be no progress without friction." Few would agree that slavery provided African Americans with "the habit of work." In addition, Washington's "darkey stories" proved extremely odious to northern blacks. When addressing the Harvard audience upon receiving his honorary Masters degree Washington stated that he "felt like a huckleberry in a bowl of milk."[21] This flaw in Washington's strategy of appeasement can hardly be overemphasized. Given the strident attacks against the race by white politicians and eugenicists, and the universal disrespect given blacks regardless of status or accomplishment, the leading "nigger" telling "nigger stories" transcended the satire Washington tried to evoke. It stood to reason that if a man like Washington could elicit disrespect from southern whites—as seen in vitriolic attacks against him after dining with President Roosevelt—no other self-respecting black could expect civil treatment from white Americans.[22]

While Washington could be deferential to white people, he sought to dominate northern born blacks in possession of degrees from prestigious white universities. By emphasizing success derived from pragmatism and hard work while belittling African Americans with a classical education,

Washington exhibited deep insecurities. Accolades accorded him by the white press, politicians, and financiers, and even the President of the United States could not overcome his acceptance of inferiority in regard to whites, and resentment toward elite blacks, who by northern birth and subsequent opportunity, exhibited the attributes of white gentility. When given the opportunity to hire teachers for his academic program, Washington usually hired graduates of Fisk rather than black alumni from white universities in the North.[23] Even Washington's endeavor to lure Du Bois from Atlanta University to Tuskegee seemed less designed to elevate the status of Tuskegee's faculty than to control Du Bois, and correspondingly by stealth and guile, dominate the African American intelligentsia.[24]

Like many insecure people, Washington exhibited an obsession with power. Initially, this quirk in Washington's personality became evident through his creation of the "Tuskegee Machine." Even before the Atlanta Address, Washington plotted to direct the African American race. Washington seemed willing to use any means at his disposal to maintain his dominant role as the leader of his people. The initial test of his resolve occurred in 1899 when Sam Hose, a black farmer in Palmetta, Georgia became the victim of a lynch mob. After Washington's equivocation following the vicious lynching and his public pronouncements on positive race relations in the South, a concentrated onslaught against the Tuskegean commenced. The Afro-American Council, headed by Reverend Reverdy Cassius Ransom of Chicago, B.T. Thornton of Indianapolis, and Ida Wells-Barnett led the attack.[25] Using Tuskegee as his base of operation, Washington devised a plan to seize control of the Council. By 1902 his plan succeeded. Washington deftly changed the Council's composition by placing cronies like T. Thomas Fortune in positions of power.[26] The so called "Bookerites" changed the Council from being a militant organ of black discontent to a mouthpiece of Booker T. Washington.

The National Business League [NBL] aided Washington in his quest for power. As the director of the Atlanta University Studies, Du Bois envisioned the creation of Negro Businessmen's Leagues in every area where a community of African Americans lived. Washington recognized the importance of Du Bois' design, usurped the idea and, in 1900, convened the first NBL meeting in Boston. Washington used the League primarily as a force to undermine opposition from African American opponents of the North and dominated the proceedings with more than 300 Bookerite delegates. He selected his personal secretary, Emmett J. Scott to head the organization, and quelled any discussion about the atrocities whites inflicted upon blacks.[27] By solidifying his power through the NBL and engaging in political intrigue more capably than any black politician in the nation, Washington resembled national Republican boss Mark Hanna—the dominant political power broker in America. While these developments more than likely incensed those already in opposition to Washington, Du Bois seemed unperturbed. At this time the Atlanta University professor perceived himself as a scholar rather than as a "leader of men."[28]

Although Du Bois held some misgivings about Washington, the relationship between the two men had been cordial, if not mutually respectful. In March 1899 Washington recommended that Du Bois join him on the platform during a Tuskegee fund raising campaign in Boston. Three months later Du Bois gained Washington's favor at the Afro-American Council convention when he openly defended the Wizard against detractors. Washington seemed pleased by Du Bois' support, and at the urging of Albert Bushnell Hart, Du Bois' mentor at Harvard, proposed that Du Bois leave Atlanta University and join him at Tuskegee. Flattered by the offer and enticed by a raise in pay, Du Bois gave some consideration to Washington's overture. Some time would elapse before Du Bois became alienated by Washington's egotism and control tactics.[29]

Meanwhile, anger toward Booker T. Washington accelerated. An increasing faction of black leaders abhorred Washington's toadying, denigration of academic training, and public declarations exhorting blacks to refrain from participation in suffrage. During a northern fund raising trip, Dartmouth and Harvard Law graduate and black Bostonian William H. Lewis told Washington to return to the South, continue his work on vocational education, and "leave to us the matters political affecting the race."[30] Although the Wizard's dominating style grated on Du Bois, he remained dispassionate and evaluated Washington and his work objectively. In addition to Ida Wells-Barnett and former Harvard classmate Monroe Trotter, a strong, trusted personality would be required to lure Du Bois into the anti-Bookerite camp.

John Hope, a professor at nearby Atlanta Baptist College (later renamed Morehouse) and friend and confidant to Du Bois decisively moved Atlanta University's most prominent scholar toward an eventual break with Washington. Blue-eyed with wavy brown hair, white in complexion and a native of Augusta, Georgia, Hope maintained a strong identification with the African American race. As an eight-year old, Hope witnessed a vicious attack against blacks by white racists in Hamburg, South Carolina. This incident caused him to identify exclusively with his black heritage and promoted a sense of equality and justice that demanded satiation. Washington, his antics, and his accommodationist policies, therefore, became anathema to Hope—a resentment he privately conveyed to Du Bois.[31] In a review of *Up From Slavery* that appeared in the July 16, 1901 issue of *Dial Magazine*, Du Bois, possibly because of Hope's influence, presented a prelude to the epistle against Washington that eventually appeared under the heading "Of Mr. Booker T. Washington And Others" in *The Souls of Black Folk*.

At the turn of the century the Atlanta University community, including Hope and Du Bois, evaluated the race's progress in the South. Since the slaves received freedom, the scholars found that African American leaders—ministers and teachers—and sympathetic whites encouraged blacks to engage in uplift and self-help endeavors. For at least a generation, blacks accepted the folkways of America that proclaimed industry, loyalty, diligence, and respect for authority would result in economic success. They knew that Washington profoundly believed in these concepts and ardently articulated the opinion that black material success would elevate the Negro in the eyes of whites. Moreover, they also knew that Washington offered several clichés to prove his point. "No race can prosper till it learns that there is as much dignity in tilling a field as in writing a poem." "The trouble with the Negro is that he is all the time trying to get recognition, whereas what he should do is to get something to recognize." "In the future let us emphasize our opportunities more and our difficulties less. Let us talk more about our white friends and about our white enemies less."[32] However, research demonstrated to Hope, and eventually Du Bois, the problem with Washingtonian homilies; blacks worked hard but without achieving desired results. African Americans remained poor and experienced unrelenting discrimination at the hands of racist whites.

Even without Hope's influence, Du Bois' views toward the Tuskegean could only harden. Du Bois grated over the fact that racial discrimination harbored no difference according to class. Well respected, urbane, intelligent black men and women received the same disrespect from white Negrophobes and segregationists as the most disheveled, uncouth, undeserving black field hand. Therefore, Washington's public remarks that emphasized economic development and industrial education at the expense of social amenities for deserving African Americans seemed far more than the proud, meticulous Du Bois could tacitly accept.[33] Given Du Bois' temperament, criticisms of Washington that appeared in *Dial Magazine* and *The Souls of Black Folk* were hardly unanticipated.

In the initial passages about Washington in *The Souls of Black Folk*, Du Bois praised the Wizard and respected Washington's value as an African American leader. He considered the Atlanta Compromise Address that gained sympathy and understanding from the white South, by surrendering the desire for equality and working toward inter-racial understanding, "the most notable thing in Mr. Washington's career." He also touted Washington for accurately assessing the driving spirit, and successfully courting the favor, of the dynamic, industrial North. Unfortunately, Washington failed to recognize that sophisticated, urbane blacks could not accept social degradation at the hands of whites with impunity. Therefore, in *Souls*, Du Bois spoke for himself and other highly educated African Americans who could not countenance Washington's acceptance of social inequality.[34]

In what served as a critical rebuke to Washington's policies, Du Bois spoke of the "two classes of colored Americans" who disagreed with the Wizard's approach to achieve black salvation. First, Du Bois spoke of the militants who abhorred the white race and would become expatriates from the United States. He dismissed the radical contingent by inferring that it was impossible to find a sanctuary on earth beyond the grasp of white people. But then Du Bois spoke for the reticent black people—the "thinking class." Here, Du Bois spoke at length and reasoned that this faction of Negroes respected Washington for his earnest endeavors to help blacks and use diligence under the yoke of southern oppression. Du Bois found fault with the Washingtonian plan for resolving racial problems by counseling against the need for political power, eschewing the importance of civil rights, and denigrating the significance of classical education for African American youth.[35]

Yet there were things that Du Bois implied but failed to cite in his critique of Washington. The cultured elite he identified that comprised the Grimké family, Yale graduate Kelly Miller, and others who devoted years of study to acquire an education and master the folkways and mores of an educated aristocracy, could not be bartered away for economic pragmatism beneficial to the black masses. It was impossible for the well-bred intelligentsia to engage in the freedom of ideas worthy of their station and education and simultaneously accept a lower social position dictated solely by race. In speaking for the "Talented Tenth," Du Bois embraced a class consciousness indicative of learning and achievement, and spoke for those who embraced self-determination and the classical education available for blacks at Fisk and Atlanta Universities in the South and prestigious white colleges and universities in the North.[36]

Although Du Bois consistently praised Washington for his achievements and leadership, Washington felt stung by the criticism. The Wizard overlooked a central theme in the book that spoke of the ambiguity that characterized African American life. Du Bois said: "One ever feels his twoness—an American, a Negro; two souls, two thoughts, two unreconciled strivings; two warring ideals in one dark body, whose dogged strength alone keeps it from being torn asunder."[37] Washington, unfortunately, failed to interpret "twoness" broadly or comprehend the larger construct of Du Bois' ideas. Without the formal training presented in liberal arts colleges, Washington seemed incapable of appreciating the objective criticism of Du Bois or sensing that the color problem required more than one solution and leader. Instead, the Wizard perceived Du Bois' essay solely as a personal affront. Although the piece appeared temperate in tone, it angered the Tuskegean and fostered an irreparable schism between the principal and the professor.

The criticism contained in *The Souls of Black Folk* proved difficult for the tender ego of Booker T. Washington to accept from an African American. Though he had steeled himself from the numerous affronts directed toward him by whites, Washington would not countenance attacks emanating from a fellow race member. For his part, Du Bois must have recognized that *The Souls of Black Folk* marked a break with Washington, but with the mind of an academician Du Bois might not have appreciated the degree to which Washington took offense. Looking back to that earlier era, Du Bois recalled: "… he couldn't quite think of me as a man with purely scholastic ambitions…. He was a terribly suspicious man."[38]

With publication of *The Souls of Black Folk,* Washington reached a final impasse with his detractors and saw Du Bois as his primary nemesis. Louis Harlan, Washington's biographer, succinctly outlined the dilemma between the two men as a result of Du Bois' critique in *Black Folk* when he observed:

> The burden of Du Bois' rejection of Washington was that his materialism and his compromises with white tyranny denied blacks their right to dream, to aspire, to master the world around them. The very restraint with which Du Bois presented his case, conceding Washington's genuine fostering of black self-help and acknowledging that he often opposed racial injustice in his own way, rendered Du Bois' arguments … persuasive … and made Du Bois clearly the intellectual of the anti-Washington faction.[39]

The final split between Washington and Du Bois occurred on July 30, 1903 when Washington agreed to address the National Negro Business League at the Columbia A.M.E. Zion Church in Boston. A coterie of black Bostonians decided to embarrass Washington, and the protagonist leading the attack was a man of free Negro lineage, William Monroe Trotter. Trotter hailed from proud success-oriented stock. His father attained the rank of lieutenant in the famous 55th Massachusetts and led his fellow soldiers in refusing pay lower than white recruits, causing the regiment to serve without recompense until the government acceded to their wishes. The senior Trotter returned to Boston after the war and made a comfortable living in real estate, politics, and the post office. He acquired sufficient funds to raise his family in the suburbs, enable young Monroe to attend the best primary and secondary schools, and eventually gain entrance to Harvard College. Monroe Trotter excelled in academics, earning Phi Beta Kappa recognition as a junior and graduating from Harvard with honors. Proud, arrogant, vain, and combative, Trotter devoted himself to proving that blacks were equal, if not superior to, whites. He relished demonstrating his academic prowess before white peers, and decided upon a career in journalism as editor of a black newspaper, *The Guardian*, a decision, in part attributed to a need to prove that the C grades he received in English must be transcended.[40]

Given Trotter's combative, competitive nature, Washington's accommodationist policies became intolerable. Trotter seethed with loathing for Washington and virtually everything he represented as a promoter of vocational education, apologist for segregation, and as an opponent of black participation in politics. Equally disconcerting to Trotter and others with similar sentiments, Washington represented a public insult to the race. By accepting social segregation and the loss of suffrage, Washington decreed that blacks were inferior beings that should accept second class citizenship.

On his part, Washington misunderstood the opposition of African Americans to his policies and became convinced that personal jealousy, attributed to his close relationship with President Roosevelt and the power he derived from being a presidential confidant, served as the underlying causes for the attacks. Indeed, Washington became obsessed with maintaining his power, causing him to value loyalty over talent. However even more disconcerting was Washington's display of racial self-hatred and insecurity which caused him to prefer white counsel and black sycophants to African Americans who presented him with legitimate criticisms.

Trotter gleefully awaited Washington's appearance at the church. He enlisted a number of friends—including his sister—to undermine the Wizard and disrupted the proceedings by using tactics ranging from personal invective and physical force to the application of cayenne pepper on the dais which caused coughing, sneezing, and mayhem. Washington remained above the din, and after those creating the disturbance were removed from church, addressed the congregation. In white newspapers Trotter's antics were denounced unanimously; for white members of the press Washington remained the undisputed leader of the African American people. Furthermore, Washington's defenders smugly reported that Trotter and his associates, Granville Martin and Bernard Charles, were arrested for disturbing the peace by instigating the so-called Boston Riot.

At first glance Washington's hegemony as the primary leader of his race remained intact. Washington firmly believed that only a boisterous minority opposed him and his ideas. Unfortunately, he underestimated his adversaries, feeling his life experiences offered greater preparation for the tasks at hand than those trained at "Ivy League" institutions. But while the "Boston Riot" received national coverage and bolstered empathy for Washington, it simultaneously gained positive notoriety for Trotter. The incident enabled Trotter to show whites that an extremely vocal minority rejected Washington's leadership and his strategy for African American success. The white majority could no longer believe that all blacks acquiesced to the harshness inflected upon the race by callous whites and accepted Washington as their black messiah.

Washington's rancor toward Trotter resulted in vindictiveness that caused him to overestimate his abilities and misjudge the support generated for Trotter. Boston Bookerites, led by Reverend James H. McMullan, pastor of the church and admirer of the Tuskegean since his dinner at the White House, pressed charges against Trotter. These men hired the services of G. R. Swasey, a white attorney who failed to convict Charles. However Swasey defeated the defendants' black attorneys, and forced the unrepentant participants to serve thirty days in jail. Trotter capitalized on his martyrdom in *The Guardian* by accusing Washington of paying for the expensive white lawyer to the detriment of race champions like himself. Regrettably for Washington, his confidence in knowing people by experiencing the trials and tribulations of life caused him to underestimate Trotter. Washington forgot that the shrill but shrewd, erratic but brilliant Monroe Trotter possessed a Phi Beta Kappa Key earned at Harvard University.

Washington won a Pyrrhic victory in the aftermath of the "Boston Riot." This fact became glaringly evident when the thirty-day jail sentences gained sympathy for Trotter and his imprisoned friends. Among supporters of the newly martyred Trotter were two Atlanta University professors, the lesser known George A. Towns and W.E.B. Du Bois. Alliances among wearers of the Crimson of John Harvard ran deep and strong; both Towns and Du Bois held degrees from America's most venerable and esteemed university. Both men voiced support for Trotter, and in response, Washington prepared himself for combat with Du Bois, the man he considered the architect of the embarrassing Columbia Street Church disturbance.

Now that the issue had been enjoined, pretenses of civility between Washington and the Tuskegee Machine, and members of the "Talented Tenth" disappeared. Washington, the more pro-active party in the imbroglio, embarked on a mission to destroy his opposition with guile, patronage, influence peddling, and innuendo. Atlanta University became the initial object for attack when the Bookerite faction blamed the entire school for instigating the Boston Riot. However the Wizard devoted his primary attention to Trotter and Du Bois. Washington used espionage to embarrass the *Guardian's* editor and mitigate the effectiveness of Trotter's newspaper. To achieve this goal, Washington created and funded rival newspapers, and clandestinely had libel suits directed toward Trotter. But ultimately, Washington recognized that the key to maintaining his dominance as the pre-eminent black leader depended upon harnessing Du Bois. The Wizard recognized that the strident Trotter could never supplant him. But Du Bois' status as a brilliant scholar stood to rally the black intelligentsia in opposition to the Tuskegee Machine. Washington recognized that Du Bois must be neutralized and ultimately defeated.

Washington made one final attempt to dominate the intellectual radicals by organizing a clandestine conference held in New York City's Carnegie Hall in January, 1904. For the Wizard, as David L. Lewis suggests, much was at stake; his power to make or destroy careers, maintain a monopoly over philanthropic money directed toward blacks, and ability to apply effective strategies designed to enhance the race's future.[41] Again, Washington displayed his penchant for duplicity by offering an olive branch to the dissidents, but in reality, devoted himself to outmaneuvering and controlling the opposition. The wary Du Bois attended the conclave, but recognized almost immediately that Washington had stacked the conference with Bookerite delegates and opted for dominance rather than cooperation. The New York Conference failed to reach the objectives outlined by the Wizard. Du Bois would become firmly ensconced in the anti-Bookerite camp and Washington failed to silence critics and reassert his dominance as the ultimate African American leader.

If African American leaders appeared inconsistent and self-defeating, it seemed understandable given the pressures the race faced at that time. Washington's staunch friend and supporter, Theodore Roosevelt, long harbored racist views toward blacks not too dissimilar from the James Vardamans and Ben Tillmans of the South. Just prior to inviting the Wizard to dinner at the White House Roosevelt had said: "A perfectly stupid race can never rise to a very high plane; the negro (sic), for instance, has been kept down as much by lack of intellectual development as by anything else."[42] And to remove any certainty that the dinner invitation mitigated his views toward the black race, Roosevelt retreated somewhat from his association with Washington (referring to the dinner as a luncheon) and displayed a consistently racist attitude toward African Americans.[43]

An event in Brownsville, Texas that occurred on August 13, 1906 afforded Roosevelt the opportunity to correct any misconceptions of favoritism his enemies believed he harbored toward African Americans. On the date in question, unknown assailants in Brownsville killed a white man and wounded a police official. Black soldiers in nearby Fort Brown were accused of the crime. Although the soldiers unanimously professed their innocence, President Roosevelt refused entreaties on the soldiers' behalf and dismissed three companies—167 men including 5 Congressional Medal of Honor recipients—of the Brownsville regiment without trial. Although black leaders voiced outrage about the injustice, Roosevelt remained steadfast in his decision to cashier every soldier despite the regiment's history of meritorious service. African Americans had nowhere to turn outside their race to find redress from grievances directed toward blacks.[44] Equally disturbing for Washington, the incident in Brownsville placed the Wizard in a quandary. By attacking Roosevelt for his intemperate behavior toward the Brownsville soldiers, Washington could lose influence with the President. Conversely, if Washington remained silent on the matter, he risked losing support within the African American community. Washington decided to remain mute, a decision that cost the Tuskegean the support of an invaluable ally, the black Boston Brahman, Archibald Henry Grimké.

Given the commonalities Grimké had with Washington and Du Bois, it seemed highly improbable that the Brownsville incident would cause him to deviate from his neutral stance regarding the warring camps. In many respects, Grimké acted as the bridge between Washington and Du Bois, owing to his slave heritage and high intellectual attainments. Born a slave in South Carolina in 1849 to slave owner Henry Grimké and Nancy, his mulatto nurse, "Archie" Grimké personally experienced the brutality of slavery. Despite his wretched origins, he gained access to an education—attending Lincoln University in Pennsylvania and Harvard Law School—acquired fame through the assistance of his famous aunts (Angelina and Sarah Grimké), and became an avid foe of racial discrimination. After working as an attorney and acquiring notoriety as a journalist, he eventually served as the American consul to the Dominican Republic. Throughout his career Grimké maintained a strong independent streak and, depending upon the issues, divided his loyalties between the Republican and Democratic parties. As an eminent writer, lecturer, and intellectual, Grimké played a complex and ambiguous role among the bevy of black leaders of the 1890s and early 1900s. Urbane and erudite, he resided both in Boston and Washington, D.C and thoroughly understood the political machinations of the era. By 1905 both Niagarites and Bookerites solicited his support, recognizing his influence could tip the balance of power between the opposing factions.

For practical purposes Grimké maintained a relationship with Booker Washington. As the most influential, cultured African American figure of the day, Grimké realized that working with the Tuskegean could prove beneficial for African Americans. And yet Grimké's independence and more outspoken militant positions about racial discrimination made him attractive to "radicals" like Monroe Trotter and eventually Du Bois. Grimké had consistently criticized United States presidents when they failed to uphold the rights of African Americans. Therefore, Roosevelt became particularly odious to Grimké when the President terminated the careers of the Brownsville soldiers. Grimké perceived the President's egregious behavior to be beneath contempt. He expected Washington to express outrage about Roosevelt's callous decision like other black leaders. When the Wizard refused to speak, the relationship between Grimké and Washington essentially ended.[45] Washington's position on "Brownsville" placed Grimké firmly in the radical camp, provided impetus for greater militancy among black leaders, and marked the decline of Booker T. Washington as the single, most powerful race leader of the early twentieth century.

September 24, 1906, one month following the Brownsville incident, marked an even more horrendous episode in the declining fortunes of African Americans. On this date the first major race riot of the twentieth century originated in another Brownsville—a suburb of Atlanta, Georgia. In the months prior to the riot, Atlanta's leading citizens focused more on economic development than mounting social tensions developing in the city. White anger toward blacks intensified when the press alluded to higher incidence of urban crime, cast aspersions toward African Americans, and incited white mobs to attack blacks. After the *Atlanta Journal* irresponsibly published sensationalized accounts of five incidents where black men allegedly attacked white women, according to journalist Ray Stannard Baker who investigated the riot, "a trivial incident fired the tinder." Several factors in addition to "Yellow Journalism" contributed to the tension. With the rising "color line," problems in race relations pervaded the entire South. Whites aggressively instituted limitations upon black in politics, systematically eliminated blacks from participation on juries, and imposed segregation indiscriminately to keep African Americans in "their place." Coincidentally, "The Clansman," a popular rabble-rousing play, raised feelings among the white population to a fever pitch. White residents of Atlanta also became agitated by the presence of idle blacks despite high labor demands and wages.

Most disconcerting to African American leaders who followed the riot were reports that blacks victimized by the mob proved to be African Americans of substance rather than low income vagrants. Law-abiding, upright black citizens who supported themselves, their families, and dependent relatives suffered grievously from the attacks.[46] These collective events caused Washington and his policy of accommodation to fall into even greater disrepute among those identified as the black elite. As David Levering Lewis wryly observed: "There was bitter justice in the fact that the Atlanta Compromise of 1895 would end in the Atlanta riot of 1906.[47]

Because of the expanding "color line," responsible African Americans redoubled efforts to retain confidence in their race and display black accomplishments. Racism practiced by professional organizations particularly galled the African American elite. Mindful that the most accomplished black doctor, lawyer, or dentist was excluded from membership in national professional associations, African Americans founded their own organizations. In addition to the first black medical and business associations formed at the turn of the century (the National Medical Association founded in 1895 and Negro Business League in 1900), African Americans organized the National Association of Negro Musicians and the National Association of Teachers of Colored Schools in 1902 and 1904 respectively.

As though anticipating the racial conflicts of 1906 and recognizing a need for developing mutual support in the face of rising racial tension, the African American elite founded other organizations to bolster the morale of a fledgling black establishment. The first elite association appeared in Philadelphia, Pennsylvania under the name of Sigma Pi Phi, more popularly known as the Boulé. On May 15, 1904 the wealthy pharmacist and physician Dr. Henry McKee Minton spoke to Dr. E. C. Howard and encouraged him to invite Dr. Algernon B. Jackson and Dr. William Warrick to his home at 508 S. 10th Street. Minton convened the meeting to discuss the possibility of organizing a fraternity in Philadelphia comprised of the best men of color in the city. Its primary purpose "was to serve as a medium for the expression of the social instincts and the intellectual convictions of a small group of men with similar accomplishments and ideals."[48] Qualifications for membership included graduation from an accredited college, dedication to high ideals, capacity for fellowship, and promise of creative and effective work.[49] Since convention prevented African Americans of the highest stature from developing inter-personal relation-ships with white peers, Sigma Pi Phi provided a formal social outlet for the black elite. When the group met the following fortnight at Dr. Minton's home, the men had finalized the name of the organization, with the Greek letters representing congeniality, tolerance, and constructive effort. Dr. Minton, selected as the first Sire Archon (chairman), wrote the constitution and took responsibility for establishing a nationwide organization comprising the best men of the race.

Of southern mulatto stock and member of one of the oldest black families in Philadelphia, Minton possessed the pedigree to promote the organization among members of the "Talented Tenth." As a graduate of Phillips Exeter Academy, the Philadelphia College of Pharmacy, Jefferson Medical College, and a founder of Douglass and Mercy Hospitals, Minton possessed the demeanor of leadership, a commitment to selecting the finest men of his race, and a genius for organization. After establishing Alpha, the initial Boulé, Sigma Pi Phi expanded to Chicago (Beta) in 1907, Baltimore (Gamma) in 1908, and Memphis (Delta) in 1910. The Grand Boulé, created in 1908, existed as a confab where individual members (Archons) of all Boulés gathered with wives (Archousas) to enjoy intellectual stimulation and establish bonds of friendship across the nation. Not surprisingly, W.E.B. Du Bois belonged to the organization, as did surgeon Daniel Hale Williams of Chicago (the first physician to perform successful open heart surgery), Judge Robert H. Terrell of Washington, John Hope of Atlanta, and other African American intellectuals and professional men of good character and standing who hailed from the best families in black society.[50]

From this initial foray to develop a spirit of congeniality among African Americans, a second fraternity, Alpha Phi Alpha [Alphas] was founded at Cornell University in December 1906. Unlike the Boulé that comprised men of accomplishment, the Alphas and subsequent black fraternities focused attention primarily on the undergraduate college population. The Alphas evolved from a Social Study Club, prided themselves on selecting the best and brightest black students on campus, and selected the platitudes "manly deeds, scholarship, and love for all mankind" as the principles of their fraternal organization. To fill a void in their education at Cornell, the fraternity men insisted that the membership become grounded in Negro life and history to highlight its significance as an African American fraternal organization.[51] Soon after the founding of Alpha Phi Alpha, the notion of fraternal organizations evolved among women. In 1908 women at Howard University, under the direction of Ethel Hedgeman Lyle, founded Alpha Kappa Alpha [AKA], the first African American sorority in the United States. Like the Alphas, AKA evolved with the understanding that blacks must select the best students available, those with an appreciation of culture and merit who would provide service to the race.[52]

While the first decade of the twentieth century offered little for which blacks could feel elated or proud, some positive aspects of the Progressive Era appeared that mitigated the harshness of racism and provided hope for African Americans. Blacks took the initiative to establish a number of self-help organizations. In addition to the aforementioned Negro Business League (1900), blacks founded the National Afro-American Council. In 1904 Booker T. Washington created a short-lived organization known as the Committee of Twelve that evolved from the January meetings held in Carnegie Hall. By 1905 prescient blacks provided the foundation for the National Urban League. However none of these organizations, save the future Urban League, had the lasting impact of another short-lived organization organized by W.E.B. Du Bois. A gathering comprised of the leading black intellectuals of the day met in Niagara Falls, Canada and became known through posterity as the Niagara Movement.

Du Bois' ideas for the Niagara Movement, and subsequently the NAACP, evolved from his joint work with Washington as a member of the Committee of Twelve. He, along with Washington and Hugh Browne, principal of the black preparatory school Cheyney Teachers College in Pennsylvania, had been charged with developing an agenda for a meeting to be held in February or March 1904. In response, Du Bois drafted a proposal designed to develop a communication network linking prominent blacks nationwide to address and rectify the racism which impinged on African American society. Not viewing the plan as being feasible, Washington made his intentions known to Du Bois with anticipation that the idea would die aborning.[53] Meanwhile, Du Bois began planning for the secret retreat. On the advice of two anti-Bookerite friends from Chicago, attorney Frederick McGhee, and Dr. Charles E. Bentley, the founder of Provident Hospital—the first black hospital in the nation—Du Bois moved forward.

In June 1905 Du Bois wrote to more than fifty-nine African American men from different regions of the country, asking them to convene in Buffalo, New York with two purposes in mind. First, Du Bois asked prospective participants to organize and adopt a means for aggressive action against the repression experienced by African Americans. And second, he proposed that the men join him in devising a plan to oppose Washington, a man who stifled "honest criticism." Of the fifty-nine men who answered the call, comprising the "Talented Tenth" of black society—educators, lawyers, physicians, businessmen, ministers, and publishers—twenty-nine men and a teenage boy attended. Although lodging had been booked in Buffalo, racial hostility directed toward the attendees by hotel management caused the Niagarites—as they came to be known—to remove the gathering to the Erie Beach Hotel at Fort Erie on the Canadian side of the Niagara Falls.

The conference lasted three days (July 10 to 13) and functioned without the Wizard's spy, Boston attorney Clifford Plummer who never learned of the switch to Fort Erie.[54] Among those in attendance were the Bostonian Monroe Trotter, Frederick McGhee and Dr. Charles E. Bentley from Chicago, Harvard classmate Clement Morgan, and J. Max Barber, a Virginia Union University graduate who would distinguish himself as a dentist and an honored NAACP member in Philadelphia. Several formidable men, though willing, found it impossible to attend. These men included Du Bois' close friends John Hope and George Towns of Atlanta, sociologists Monroe Work, noted later for producing the *Negro Year Book*, and Richard R. Wright, Jr., A.M.E. bishop and future president of Wilberforce University. Despite these notable absentees, the conference continued unabated. The delegates drafted a "Declaration of Principles" that succinctly expressed the "Talented Tenth's" point of view, declaring: "We refuse to allow the impression to remain that the Negro American assents to inferiority."[55] The conferees also agreed to endorse ideas Du Bois presented to ameliorate the condition of African Americans. These Niagarites called for legal redress, public action, social reform, economic cooperation, and an organizational structure designed to carry forward ideas to promote African American rights. Although Washington endeavored to squelch the organization by using every means at his disposal to discredit the Niagara Movement, the Niagarites prepared for the next annual conference.

Planners for the second Niagara Convention decided upon Harpers Ferry, West Virginia to commemorate the 100th anniversary of John Brown's birth. The sleepy town nestled in the Blue Ridge Mountains also proved appealing because Brown's attack on the federal arsenal in the town's center represented the initial blow struck to free the slaves. To the planners it seemed fitting to strike a renewed blow for freedom nearly half a century after Brown's raid. The Harpers Ferry convention, held August 15-18, 1906 at Storer College, functioned rather uneventfully. The only crisis of significance occurred when women endeavored to attend the meetings, an issue representative of the nascent black feminism that continued throughout the century. Over the sole objection of Monroe Trotter, women became equal partners within the gathering. Throughout the conference attendees reaffirmed their determination to strike against "Jim Crow" with unabated vigor and provide relentless attacks against those who endorsed the accommodationist principles of Booker T. Washington.

Although the Niagara Movement would continue until 1909 when it merged with the NAACP, its structure, organization, and membership paled significantly when compared with Washington's Tuskegee Machine. Abolitionist in origin, shrill in tone, and elitist in membership, the Niagarites never gained the mass appeal comparable to the Bookerites. Idealistic rather than pragmatic, the men and women engaged in the Niagara Movement never resorted to using the debased tactics of Washington and his followers to dictate polices designed for black amelioration. The Niagarites were also wary of whites, a feeling hardly uncommon among the black elite who had excelled despite the roadblocks to success established by their white counterparts. Unlike Washington and his cronies, the proud Niagarites seemed less beholden to members of the white power elite. However, the organization would be short-lived. Devoid of a white base of support, lacking the ability to court favor among middle class blacks, and without an organizational and ruthless genius like Booker T. Washington to keep the membership in line, the Niagara Movement was destined to become moribund. Still, the seed for unremitting protest had been planted. Its gestation proved essential for the creation of the NAACP, a progressive organization that operated as the most preeminent civil rights organization of the twentieth century.

As an organization demanding reform, the Niagarites represented an African American contingent of the Progressive Movement, an era when an early twentieth century bourgeoisie sought to address problems inherent in early twentieth century America. The Progressive Era contributed to the complexity and the duality Du Bois spoke of in *Souls of Black Folk*. Middle class activists known as progressives responded to the excesses of an industrial, urban society by seeking economic, political, and social reforms to enhance the quality of life in American society. Progressive reformers endeavored to disseminate the wealth concentrated in the hands of the wealthy few, broaden political opportunities for the politically dispossessed, and extend social justice to the less advantaged members of the American public. The Progressive Movement, however, hardly represented uniformity. Individual progressives and progressive organizations represented variegated interests that could appear contradictory. Those who aggressively promoted changes to enhance economic opportunities could simultaneously oppose extended political involvement and expanded social justice toward specific disadvantaged groups. While most white progressives ignored blacks in their reform efforts, progressive ideals were manifested among blacks. Washington and Du Bois represented the sable contingent that applied progressive ideals to enhance life for fellow African Americans. Although linked with prominent conservative industrialists, Washington operated as an economic progressive, envisioning industrial education as the means for attaining salvation for his people during an era of harsh racial repression. Du Bois conversely, believed that political activism and social amenities guaranteed to every American citizen should never be sacrificed for enhanced economic opportunities. Thus, the Washington-Du Bois controversy represented clashes between progressives deeply committed to improving the condition of their race.

By the end of the century's first decade, a coterie of white and black progressives sought to redress the racism that impinged upon African Americans. Resentful of the ever expanding "color line," white progressives like John Edgar Milholland and Mary White Ovington of New York and Francis Garrison of Boston combined their idealism with the objectives of the Niagara Movement. Collectively, they would combine forces to mount a challenge to America's racist heritage. To succeed in their quest for an egalitarian society, these neo-abolitionists would contend with both white racists and black proponents of the Tuskegee Machine. A formidable task awaited these agents for change.

3

PROGRESSIVES AND THE SEARCH FOR OPPORTUNITY

A brutal incident that occurred on August 14, 1908 initiated a transformation in African American leadership that forever altered race relations in the United States. On that date a race riot occurred in Springfield, Illinois. A fallacious rumor that a black man had attacked a white woman incited white men into frenzied excitement. While race riots in the early twentieth century hardly proved exceptional—Atlanta, Georgia had already witnessed two racial conflicts—circumstances in Springfield aroused different passions. Unlike the Atlanta riots that took place in the South, the Springfield riot occurred in the North and more importantly, in the hometown of the Great Emancipator, Abraham Lincoln. After two days of rioting, two blacks were lynched (one a successful businessman), fifty people wounded, and 2,000 African American residents fled the city.[1] Oswald Garrison Villard, grandson of the fiery abolitionist William Lloyd Garrison, registered his shock over the atrocities in Springfield in the *New York Evening Post*. William English Walling, a southern born white aristocrat voiced similar outrage in an article, "The Race War in the North." Walling's writings inspired Mary White Ovington, a Unitarian, socialist, and descendant of an abolitionist, into action. She encouraged Walling to form an organization to fight against the demonic outrages inflicted upon blacks. As a result, Walling, Ovington, and Dr. Henry Moskowitz, a social worker among the New York City immigrants, formed the first triumvirate of what would later be known as the NAACP.[2]

Feeling that Lincoln's memory had been desecrated, the triumvirate decided to stimulate the complacent black bourgeoisie of the North and inspire black leaders to take action. Their task would prove arduous. When prominent black leaders spoke out against racism, the anger became outer-directed; the South rather than the North served as the object of black wrath. Though the South's overt racism demanded a strong counter response, astute African Americans recognized that attacking the white South from a distance contained less risk than critiquing northern white neighbors. Evidence of black reluctance to engage fellow northerners in civil rights efforts appeared when Oswald Garrison Villard issued a "Call" for a conference on the Springfield riots. Garrison's quest for a response to the Springfield atrocity received scant attention from the African American community. The black press essentially ignored the "Call." The *New York Age*, in typical Bookerite form, skirted the race issue entirely. Equally important, only New Yorkers Bishop Alexander Walters of the AME Zion Church, Reverend William Henry Brooks of St. Mark's Methodist Episcopal Church, and Dr. William L. Buckley, the only African American public school principal in the city, attended the initial meetings.[3]

Only after a group of attendees gathered at Charity Organization Hall in New York in late May, 1909, at a meeting that became known as the National Negro Conference, did blacks of significance play a role of some import in working toward African American amelioration. Although most in attendance were white, many of the most prominent African Americans in the nation attended. Du Bois journeyed north from Atlanta. He was joined by Monroe Trotter and Archibald Grimké of Boston; Ida B. Wells-Barnett of Chicago; Mary Church Terrell, Reverend J. Milton Waldron, President of the National Negro Political League of Washington, D.C.; Bishop Walters of New York; and William Scarborough of Wilberforce University, Ohio.[4] Booker T. Washington had been invited. But distrustful of Villard and other blacks and whites of liberal persuasion, Washington decided not to attend. Nevertheless, Washington offered opinions on the convention, and through his literary mouthpiece, the *New York Age*, rendered contrasting views about the people in attendance. With typical Washingtonian panache, the Wizard enabled white conferees—though he never liked or trusted white people—to receive praise while black delegates, upon his advice, were denigrated.[5] In a bizarre sense, Washington's insecurity as a marginally educated leader generated in him the counter-snobbery of a self-made man. According to a Cornell alumnae friend of Mary Church Terrell, Washington made the terms "college" and "degree" anathema at Tuskegee.[6] Because Washington distrusted independent minded, "degree-rich" blacks and held little confidence in their ability to form a successful African American organization, he characteristically attacked members of his own racial group.

The acrimony between the Washington and Du Bois camps represented far more than a clash of egos. Instead, the persistence of black self-hatred remained in evidence. Washington made a revealing statement which exonerated Villard, the individual responsible for leading the effort to fight black racial injustice when he said: "Mr. Villard, in my opinion, is a well-meaning, unselfish man, but he does not understand people. He has gathered about him a class of colored people, who have not succeeded, (and) who are bitter and resentful...."[7] Obviously Washington found it easier and safer to lash out at fellow blacks than challenge whites. The negative opinions Washington held toward liberal black leaders represented a curious theme that plagued African Americans of the era and continued into the distant future.

Washington's sable allies seemed equally adroit in casting aspersions at fellow blacks, playing the race card to the Wizard's advantage. A well known but anonymous African American leader (presumably Emmett Scott) claimed that comparisons between Washington and Du Bois proved unfair to the latter, noting: "Dr. Washington is at the head of a large institution.... Dr. Du Bois, on the other hand, is a mere hired man ... in an institution (Atlanta University) completely controlled by white people."[8] The fact that Washington had supporters who would stoop to any level of intrigue to further Washington's cause appears particularly curious. Although the Bookerites firmly believed in Washington's plan for black amelioration, the issue seems far more complicated than the adulation of henchmen for their chief. Actually, the deep sense of mission and the need to identify with a powerful black personality propelled Washington's supporters into action.

Without questioning means or motives, members of the Tuskegee Machine plotted, lied, and used every devious means at their disposal to discredit the opposition. Knowing that white women attended the conference with black men, Washington and his cohorts even circulated false rumors suggesting that Du Bois and his supporters advocated inter-racial marriage.[9] Moralists and fair play advocates would decry the methods of the Tuskegee Machine. Unfortunately the desperate nature of the African

American condition and the need to support a messiah who would lead their race to the "promised-land" contributed to the harsh Bookerite attack. Desperate African Americans, including scores of black professionals, offered unwavering loyalty to the charismatic Washington.[10]

The anti-Bookerite faction also engaged in recrimination. Du Bois declared that only those who agreed with Washington's policy of "giving up agitation and acquiescence in semi-serfdom" support the Tuskegeon.[11] An exasperated Moorfield Story, the white Boston attorney who presided over the NAACP, described the difficulties between the Washington and Du Bois factions as being "almost racial."[12] However Story understated reality—the disagreements were deeply intra-racial in tone and substance. The demoralizing force of racial self-hatred fostered internecine warfare that proved all consuming among African American leadership.

Conflicts between the warring African American factions nevertheless failed to deter Oswald Garrison Villard from his mission. Villard kept the Conference on task until the conferees eventually decided upon a common theme; human equality for African Americans—a theme that would be central to the purpose of black leadership throughout the century. To realize his goal, Villard directed the Conference toward the issue of black suffrage "and the collective action designed to bring that about" as the primary focus of conferee efforts.[13] As a white man, Villard became the object of acid tongued black dissenters. These critics, however, could not prevent Villard from moving the conference forward.[14]

In addition to gathering purposeful blacks and whites together, the Convention represented an opportunity to heal rifts between black leaders, progressive white males, and feminists. While the first decade of the twentieth century revealed deep passions among Americans firmly committed to "Progressivism," those committed to temperance, consumers' leagues, universal peace, social settlements, and prison reform ignored the rights of women and African Americans. Ante-bellum reformers linked the abolition of slavery with the feminist movement. However, the mutual support derived from combined efforts of blacks and women to fight discrimination ended after the Civil War. Relations between black civil rights activists and white women deteriorated during the late nineteenth century as each group sought primacy for its cause. Villard's 1909 Conference rekindled the alliance between blacks, fair-minded white men, and female activists.

On Thursday, May 10, 1910, the second National Negro Convention opened at the Charity Organization Hall in New York City. This time the

Convention established its identity as the National Association for the Advancement of Colored People. A Committee of Forty [or National Negro Committee] served as a planning board for the organization. It entertained contrasting opinions about the most efficacious means for attaining human rights. The Negro committee was particularly mindful of racial sensitivity, making certain that the views of African American leaders received recognition.[15] Moorfield Story, former president of the American Bar Association became the organization's first President. William English Walling served as Chair of the Executive Committee; John E. Milholland, Treasurer; Oswald Garrison Villard, Disbursing Treasurer; and Frances Blascoer, Executive Secretary. Du Bois became so enthralled in work undertaken at the Conference that he would prepare to leave the confines of Atlanta University to become the NAACP's Director of Publicity and the only African American executive officer.

Within two weeks of the Second National Conference a subcommittee formed to find worthy African Americans who could serve as members of an incipient National Committee of One Hundred. This subcommittee would be responsible for offering advice to the parent body. It would also find funding for the Association, publicize the organization's activities, and perform investigations into discriminatory practices against African Americans. The inter-racial composition of the committee appeared as a radical departure from previous civil rights organizations. It was designed to show that blacks and whites could work collectively, promote sensitivity of whites toward blacks, and chart a positive direction for all Americans. Among the notable men and women who became active in the Association during its fledgling months were whites like writers Lincoln Steffens, Ray Stannard Baker, and William Dean Howells; reformers Lillian Wald, Jane Addams, Mary White Ovington, and Rabbi Stephen S. Wise; and educator John Dewey. Included among the prominent blacks were educators Mary Church Terrell; crusader Ida Wells-Barnett; journalist Archibald Grimké; and Reverend Alexander Waters.[16]

Circumstances dictated that Du Bois would become an integral part of the NAACP. In fact, the National Association was conceived during a critical time in his career. Du Bois' scientific research stood far in advance of traditional "respectable" scholarship; he addressed unpopular issues dealing with race and class discrimination. Yet, Du Bois bristled at the realization that his ground breaking research failed to diminish white brutality directed toward blacks.[17] In part, Du Bois blamed Washington's accommodationist policies for white disrespect of African Americans. His criticism of Washington angered white philanthropists who endorsed the "Tuskegee Idea" and funded Atlanta University. As long as Du Bois remained on the faculty, the institution remained in a precarious financial situation. In addition, Du Bois' criticism of southern black leadership generally, and the Wizard in particular, alienated the Atlanta professor from virtually every member of the southern business and professional class. For example, when Du Bois criticized the black business community in Norfolk, Virginia for its weak leadership and meager support for racial progress, Washington's renown ascended. The Washingtonian philosophy of self-help and solidarity cemented a bond between the Tuskegean and the black elite of Norfolk. Pragmatic conservatism espoused by Booker T. Washington pervaded every fabric of southern society including members of the precarious black professional and business class.[18] Therefore, Du Bois had little choice in making an important career decision; he left the increasingly restrictive confines of Atlanta and moved to New York City.

As a fledgling organization, the NAACP needed Du Bois' erudition, polemical inclinations, and facility for encouraging people to fight the rising "color line." The NAACP would use his removal to New York to hasten the change in African American thinking from accommodation to protest. When Du Bois became the Director of Publicity and Research for the NAACP, he changed his career responsibilities from social scientist to propagandist. Rather than publishing research treatises, Du Bois would concentrate on mobilizing blacks and instilling African Americans with racial pride with selected feature stories and editorials. As editor of the Association's official organ, a magazine known as *The Crisis,* Du Bois would gain notoriety far in excess of any previous or contemporary black professor in the nation.

During the first decade of its publication under Du Bois' stewardship, the circulation of *The Crisis* increased from 10,000 to 104,000 annually.[19] Changes in America, coupled with Du Bois' genius for raising issues paramount for African American advancement, revealed that whites generally and blacks in particular, began to reflect more deeply about the nation's Negro problem and "color line." Equally important, through *The Crisis*, Du Bois allied the nascent "Negro movement" with political and social progressivism.[20] This publication served as the most acclaimed militant voice of the black bourgeoisie during the twentieth century.

From 1910 forward the NAACP's role as a viable civil rights organization increased appreciably. Peonage, police brutality, legal cases, and other problems involving the "Negro Question" received the organization's undivided attention. Within a year of its genesis, the Association supported or successfully resolved a myriad of cases and established the NAACP as an organization fighting incessantly for African American rights. Du Bois' intellectual reputation lent credence to the NAACP and attracted the black bourgeoisie to the Association. These developments, coupled with Villard's genius for organization, established the foundation for the most successful black civil rights organization in history. Association founders created the means for legal redress by founding local branches through which aggrieved blacks could solicit legal council. By soliciting dues paying members who provided funds for branch and national office operations, Du Bois, Story, Villard, and others within the NAACP hierarchy developed the financial stability that would ensure the organization's longevity throughout the twentieth century.[21]

Ironically, the righteousness of the NAACP's cause evolved from an assault upon Booker T. Washington. On March 19, 1911, Washington received a severe beating at the hands of an unsavory white New Yorker named Henry Albert Ulrich. While the reasons for Washington's presence in a seedy white neighborhood, the locale of the attack, remain unclear, all evidence suggests that Ulrich beat Washington without cause except for race. Ulrich was arrested and tried for assault. When the jury found Ulrich innocent, Washington finally recognized that racism thrived in America regardless of his efforts, optimism, and positive notoriety. As Washington's biographer, Louis Harlan observed, the Wizard became touched by: "his self-recognition as he ran bleeding through the New York streets, that in the atmosphere of American racism even Booker T. Washington was lynchable."[22] Thereafter, Washington became more inclined to denounce racial discrimination publicly. The assault on Washington also contributed to the eventual coalescence among African American leadership. Du Bois, the militants, and the NAACP demonstrated they understood America far better than the Wizard of Tuskegee and his Tuskegee Machine.

Further reason for blacks of stature to embrace the NAACP occurred with the election of William Howard Taft and Woodrow Wilson as Presidents of the United States. When Theodore Roosevelt served as the Chief Executive, African Americans received recognition—through presidential appointments arranged by Booker T. Washington—from the highest office in the nation. Soon after Taft became president, however, he removed African Americans from several patronage positions granted during the Roosevelt Administration. Unlike Roosevelt, Taft refused to appoint blacks to federal posts that would offend southern sensibilities and disrupt the work at hand.[23] By implementing his "southern policy," Taft not only ignored Washington's advice and removed additional African Americans from office, but he also made blacks realize the importance of an organization like the NAACP. African Americans could no longer depend on support from the Executive Branch of government. The only victory African Americans claimed early in the Taft administration occurred when the Administration retained a handful of patronage positions traditionally earmarked for blacks. However, by the end of Taft's term in office, southern blacks seeking federal patronage were disillusioned and thoroughly discouraged. Taft only appointed blacks that filled offices in the North.

The Election of 1912 presented the nation with three presidential candidates—Taft, the incumbent, former president Roosevelt of the Progressive Party, and Woodrow Wilson, the Democratic Party nominee. Although the national electorate may have been confused, blacks faced an even greater dilemma trying to ascertain which candidate deserved African American support. Roosevelt's racist inclinations, his infamous Brownsville decision, and the subsequent exclusion of blacks from the Progressive Party Convention disappointed African Americans. Taft's indifference to the race and the "cold shoulder" offered blacks by Taft Republicans also proved disheartening. Therefore the unknown Wilson deserved serious consideration from the African American electorate. But Wilson's record concerning racial equality hardly proved stellar. As the president of Princeton University, the Virginia born Wilson headed the only "lily white" Ivy League institution. Equally chilling, by placing a Democrat in the White House, southern democrats—party stalwarts who endorsed white supremacy—could use the Executive Branch to reduce blacks to an even more servile position.

Prior to the 1912 election Wilson intimated he would be fair to black people. As the Democratic Party candidate, Wilson promised to make appointments solely on merit and declared he would be "President of all the People." He promised to veto legislation inimical to black interests and inferred that he would not discriminate against blacks seeking bureaucratic appointments because of color.[24] Despite his southern heritage, some blacks perceived Wilson to be honorable and worthy of their votes. Others were apprehensive about Wilson because of the unsavory reputation of the Democratic Party in regard to the "Negro Question," and because the "Democracy" functioned for years as the party of black disenfranchisement and segregation.[25] Pundits critical of Wilson seemed prescient. A sense of foreboding occurred almost immediately after Wilson won the election. Members of the Tuskegee Machine's Black Cabinet, District of Columbia residents who served as Booker T. Washington's regional link to the White House, sensed Wilson's hostility. They voluntarily disbanded rather than be ignored and disgraced by the President-elect.[26]

Among the early twentieth century presidents, Wilson's administrations proved most inimical to African Americans. Wilson reneged on his commitments to blacks, removed black civil service workers from long-held jobs, and became solely responsible for imposing segregationist policies in federal agencies. During Wilson's first term the Executive Branch extended the "color line," offering no refuge or hint of equality to self-respecting African Americans. Using disingenuous terminology under the guise of the National Democratic Fair Play Association (anticipating California's Civil Rights Initiative by eighty years), the Wilson Administration segregated federal offices in an attempt to prevent white female secretaries from reporting to black men. Elsewhere, separate toilets were established in the Bureau of Printing and Engraving—a decidedly insulting gesture on the part of Wilson Democrats. These displays of insensitivity were followed by the selection of a white man to serve as the minister to Haiti, a traditionally black appointment. Obviously, black militants like Du Bois and Trotter, who endorsed Wilson believing that his Ivy League pedigree would invoke fairness to the race, became outraged by Wilson's betrayal.

Although Wilson proved extremely unsympathetic to African Americans, the racial insensitivity his administration displayed proved a godsend to black leadership and the NAACP. Wilson's callous disregard for African Americans caused Booker T. Washington—the appeaser and NAACP foe—to lose face and support. If anything, the course of events since the renowned 1901 White House dinner proved Washington and his machine's vision for the future in race relations to be naïve, short-sighted, and wrong. Events would prove that Wilson's second term further discredited Washington's policies and gained support for aggressive human rights activists.

Recurring health problems forced Washington to rewrite his will and purchase a life insurance policy. Unfortunately, he neglected to train a successor. The only instructions Washington offered during his final days pertained to mundane administrative duties and housekeeping tasks. He directed Emmett Scott to attend the Fisk inauguration in his stead and asked A.J. Stewart, his personal business agent, to "keep his yard clean."[27] Washington's actions demonstrated unequivocally that he preferred to be the existing boss rather than a mindful visionary.[28] Given the daily crises blacks faced to survive, even someone with Washington's dedication to racial elevation had difficulty preparing African Americans for the future.

On the eve of Washington's death, differences between warring black factions somewhat abated. The infamous African Exclusion Bill that required separate accommodations in railroad cars, persistent residential segregation, and other indignities to blacks served to unite African Americans. An article by Washington published posthumously entitled "My View of Segregation Laws" appeared in *The New Republic*. It revealed that the Wizard's thinking finally approximated the thoughts of former adversaries. For the first time Washington openly attacked segregation, suggesting the Wizard masqueraded before white people to acquire economic power and political influence to help his people. Probably feeling vindicated, Du Bois published portions of Washington's anti-segregationist views in *The Crisis*, highlighted by Washington's panned review of "The Birth of a Nation," the highly innovative but racist movie produced by D.W. Griffith. After death, Washington enabled his legions to find common cause with his nemesis, W.E.B. Du Bois and the NAACP.

The timeliness of Washington's death late in 1915 prior to the United States entry into World War I appeared fortuitous. This proud, race conscious-man would never personally witness his miscalculations and errors in judgement that conceivably retarded prospects for intra-racial accord in America. He could not anticipate that circumstances created by the war—the decline of southern agrarianism, black migration from South to North, and the resurgence of Negro pride—placed his philosophy at odds with the new direction taken by an increasing number of African Americans from the lower echelons of black society.[29] The Wizard would also be prevented from learning that his attacks on Du Bois and other northern black militants enabled white southerners to feel justified in maintaining discrimination and blaming "outsiders" for protesting against the racial status quo. Despite the excellent service Washington provided Tuskegee Institute and other black southern educational institutions, his death prevented him from learning that in the long-run, his leadership might have done African Americans more harm than good by retarding the march toward equality.

Despite possibilities for rapprochement between the Washington and Du Bois camps after Washington's death, black leadership remained disorganized. Personality conflicts, jealousies, and distrust created an animus between Bookerites and the NAACP that prevented the development of a concerted national African American effort to fight racial prejudice. Progressive white men and women within the NAACP discovered that the divisiveness within the black bourgeoisie stymied the organization's growth. Internal bickering caused the initial attempt to found a branch in Harlem to fail. The irascible Ida Wells-Barnett, to the detriment of the Chicago branch, promoted disharmony and animus. Dissension among black leaders in Philadelphia stalled the establishment of a branch in the "City of Brotherly Love." Similar problems plagued African American leaders in Columbus, Ohio, Indianapolis, Indiana, Louisville, Kentucky, and St. Louis.[30] Rather than deal with the issues at hand—the pejorative aspects of the "color line"—prominent blacks in virtually every major city engaged in constant internecine warfare.

An additional problem undermining unity among responsible blacks appeared in the observations of a white NAACP field worker named Kathryn M. Johnson. Johnson contended that the so called intelligent African Americans "everywhere were backward and timid and lacking in pride."[31] Her opinion comported with other progressive white thinkers. Francis J. Garrison, a descendant of abolitionist William Lloyd Garrison, believed that five to ten years would elapse before prosperous African Americans would provide the financial resources necessary to help their race. Prominent African Americans like John Hope of Atlanta agreed with white critics. Hope contended that black intellectuals took an isolated view toward their problems and eschewed collective efforts to resolve racial issues. He acknowledged that two white men, Joel Elias Spingarn and Charles Edward Russell helped him realize the role of African Americans in the larger world context. Black novelist Jesse Fauset concurred with Hope and revealed her debt and appreciation to Spingarn when she said: "prod us, prick us, goad us on by unpleasant truths to ease off this terrible outer self of sloth and acceptance.... Some of us need to be told that we should be men...."[32] The race needed to be elevated; realities of the era suggested that the temperamental spirit and individualism of black leaders would not suffice.

The first signs of a new, concentrated effort to strengthen black leadership appeared at the Amenia Conference of 1916. Held at Troutbeck Estate, home of Joel Spingarn, the Conference intended to reconcile differences between supporters of Washington and Du Bois. Recognizing the need to mitigate tensions, Spingarn proved an ideal host. A wealthy Jew with experience as chair of the Department of Comparative Literature at Columbia University, Spingarn enjoyed sufficient respect from all parties to heed his call for reconciliation. Du Bois, who organized the conference, also sought to avoid dissension. Wisely, he kept himself off the program and eliminated anyone likely to resurrect past grievances from either opposing camp. With Washington's recent death and Du Bois' reluctance to antagonize the Wizard's supporters, the Conference proceeded to address substantive issues of the day. Topics for discussion included education, industry, politics, civil rights, legal and social discrimination, and plans for the future.[33] The stage had been set for collective leadership to evolve and battle proponents of racial discrimination.

Du Bois' willing subservience, coupled with Joel Spingarn's visionary purposefulness, allowed for the selection of James Weldon Johnson to head the Association and subsequently amalgamate the warring factions. Empowered by his appointment as the National Field Secretary, Johnson appeared the ideal mediator. Born on June 17, 1871 to a headwaiter father and musically talented mother in Jacksonville, Florida, and as an overt supporter of Washington, Bookerites trusted him. Fortuitously, Johnson also satisfied the radical black contingent. Johnson was college educated, fluent in Spanish, served as the United States Consul in Venezuela, and held enormous respect for scholarship. Radicals also appreciated Johnson's early entry into the NAACP (1912) and his effective role as Vice President of the New York City branch.

Unfortunately, Johnson's appointment as the NAACP National Field Secretary failed to establish a complete rapprochement between Bookerite and Niagara factions. Members of the Tuskegee Machine eschewed activism, and the radicals led by Du Bois still voiced strong opinions against industrial education, the cornerstone of Washington's ameliorative strategy. On the other hand, the Amenia Conference and Johnson's appointment as Field Secretary established the NAACP as the foremost black civil rights organization in the nation. These developments also determined that African Americans would be guided by an urbane, northern based intellectual class and would be headed by a visible, congenial leadership cadre who would endeavor to gain equality for African Americans.

Given the rising "color line" evident during the Taft and Wilson Administrations, African Americans needed the intrepid leadership of the NAACP. As early as December 10, 1910 Baltimore, Maryland enacted the first residential segregation law in the United States. The ordinance confined blacks living within the city to separate residential areas. Other cities adopted similar policies.[34] Racial discrimination also extended to schools, another development that revealed white resolve to control African Americans. Sensing that education would further emancipate blacks and make them more difficult to intimidate, white southerners withheld or reduced state and local appropriations to black schools. Correspondingly, in more northern regions—from Washington, D.C., Ypsilanti, Michigan and Hartford, Connecticut to the hallowed halls of Cornell University and Smith College—African Americans seeking educational advancement suffered from various forms of racial discrimination. The NAACP received ample opportunity to test its skills as the nation's primary civil rights organization.[35]

With the rise of racial consciousness in response to heightened racism, the NAACP had access to a number of intelligent young men and women who could be tapped for membership. The training ground for these potential leaders existed in newly created fraternities and sororities forged on black and integrated college campuses throughout the nation. These organizations provided undergraduates with the opportunity to enhance their organizational skills and develop a sense of responsibility to prepare for the eventualities of leadership. Concepts of personal pride, ethical standards, mutual respect, scholarship, and service to their race became instilled in the hearts and minds of all African Americans initiated into the "Black Greek system." After the founding of Alpha Phi Alpha Fraternity [Alpha] in 1906 and Alpha Kappa Alpha Sorority [AKA] in 1908, several additional Greek letter organizations emerged during the second decade of the twentieth century—Kappa Alpha Psi Fraternity [Kappa] (1911), Omega Psi Phi Fraternity [Omega] (1911), Delta Sigma Theta Sorority [Delta] (1913), and Phi Beta Sigma Fraternity [Sigma] (1914). Joining two of the charter members of the NAACP—W.E.B. Du Bois [Alpha] and the white reformer Jane Addams [AKA]—were other leaders and founders of other early twentieth century organizations like Eugene Kinkle Jones [Alpha] of the National Urban League, A. Philip Randolph [Sigma] of the Brotherhood of Sleeping Car Porters, Carter G. Woodson [Sigma] of the Association for the Study of Negro Life and History, and Sadie T. M. Alexander [Delta].[36]

The evolution of the NAACP and its strategy for applying the law to redress racial grievances provided the impetus for black college trained men and women to act more aggressively as race leaders. Black attorneys particularly required prodding as evidenced by the NAACP's attack against the American Bar Association [ABA]. When the ABA refused to extend membership to African American attorneys—Moorfield Story, a white man who headed the NAACP, led the opposition against the Bar Association. Story encouraged three African Americans, William H. Lewis, William R. Morris, and Butler R. Wilson to apply for ABA membership. The applications were processed and the applicants gained acceptance into the ABA. When the ABA discovered the new inductees' race, however, national officers rescinded admission to the Bar Association. Story prepared for a protracted fight. But to Story's chagrin, Wilson and Lewis, a Boston Bookerite, accepted the ban; Morris resigned from the Bar Association.[37] Racism kept African American lawyers out of the ABA. Equally significant, the timidity displayed by black lawyers demonstrated that if attorneys trained to protect rights contained in constitutional law acquiesced to racial slights and had no recourse for defense, the black bourgeoisie remained powerless, fearful, docile, and inclined to accept the intractable racism inherent in American society. Obviously, the formation of the NAACP occurred at a propitious time.

Despite facing enormous opposition from virtually every segment of American society, the determined, predominantly white NAACP leadership engaged in a relentless attack against racism. The Association established local NAACP chapters, hired lawyers to fight prejudicial laws, and fought relentlessly against an intransigent white society that displayed omnipresent racism. Throughout the decade it waged onslaughts against segregation practiced by hotels and restaurants, "Jim Crow" imposed on railroad cars, and disenfranchisement that relegated blacks to constant subordination. After establishing its first branch outside New York City in Chicago in 1911, the Association added nine new branches the following year and doubled the number of branches between 1913 and 1914.[38] Through the NAACP magazine, *The Crisis*, Du Bois provided readers with information about National Association activities, published stories on lynching and mob violence, and garnered support for the Association. With the NAACP providing the organizational framework to defend black rights and attack those who sullied the principles of justice and equality outlined in the Constitution, an increasing retinue of blacks envisioned the Association as an organization worthy of support.

Knowing lynching cast aspersions on the entire nation, the NAACP applied pressure to state and national officials to end lynching and mob violence. Their efforts produced limited results. When President Taft learned about a particularly brutal lynching in Livermore, Kentucky, the portly President hid behind States Rights and declared the Executive Branch powerless to intervene in the lynching debate. Equally disconcerting, poor whites in the rural South initiated a systematic effort to scare black competitors off the land. These intimidating tactics declined only when middle class whites, dependant on cheap black labor and feeling the adverse effects on their personal finances if blacks fled the South, began to quell the disturbances.[39] However when lynching did occur, none of the cowardly participants faced justice. White juries simply refused to indict the perpetrators and Congress never felt obligated to pass a federal anti-lynching bill. Despite NAACP prodding, the public expressed little concern about protecting African Americans against lynching.[40]

The fortunes of African Americans would be altered significantly by changes created by the First World War. Hardly anyone anticipated the impact of the Great War on American society. During the early stages of war in Europe, the United States existed as a non-belligerent and manufacturers stood to make enormous profits as a supplier of war materials. Unfortunately for the American industrialists, the conflict raging in Europe curtailed European immigrant labor to the United States. Because of the dearth of immigrant laborers, war production industries hired agents to lure southern black laborers to urban industrial centers in the North. Initially, white southerners seemed unperturbed by the African American flight. Poor whites felt relieved when economic competitors and their racial "inferiors" vacated their beloved South. Those of higher classes dependent on black labor initially took comfort believing blacks remained cowed into submission by long standing intimidating practices that guaranteed servility to whites. However when the white power structure eventually felt threatened by the loss of their cheap black labor force, efforts were made to keep blacks in "Dixie." Despite exerting considerable force and intimidation to keep blacks home, black southerners left in droves. Attracted by higher paying jobs and enhanced opportunities to escape from harsh southern oppression, thousands of blacks streamed into northern and mid-western cities. With the black influx to the North, race relations within the United States would never be the same.

The "Negro Question" and the "color line," problems confined primarily to the South, would become national in scope and profoundly challenge the spirit of American democracy. As southern migrants broadened the economic base of northern black communities, they emboldened the black bourgeoisie and propelled black spokespersons into a more active role as race leaders. When the United States entered the war in 1917, an opportunity to extend civil rights for blacks fortuitously appeared. Astute African Americans recognized the nation required fighting men, a reality that offered blacks the chance to demonstrate patriotism and gain respect by measuring arms with the enemy. They also knew that racist civilians and military leaders intended to prevent blacks from gaining honor as warriors. Ensuing events caused the NAACP to seize the moment. The Association presented a series of allegations about the military's reluctance to enlist African Americans for the war effort. National officers revealed that the commissioning of black officers had been delayed and units of the field artillery, navy and, and air corps refused to accept African Americans into their ranks. When the military insulted the ranking black officer Colonel Charles Young by retiring him on unfounded grounds of physical disability, the NAACP adroitly used Young's plight as a devise to increase membership in the National Association. Although Young demonstrated his physical prowess by riding horseback from his home in Chillicothe, Ohio to Washington, D.C., a feat that demonstrated his physical prowess, the army returned the Colonel to active duty but prevented him from serving in Europe.

The treatment accorded Young hardly caused black leaders to become petulant. Instead, they played a strong leadership role by exhibiting an earnest public display of patriotism in the belief that black loyalty during the war would advance prospects for racial advancement when hostilities ceased. Editors of thirty-one African American newspapers, for example, agreed unanimously to set aside grievances to support the war effort. Du Bois summarized the editors' views by encouraging blacks to remain loyal to the United States in a "Close Ranks" editorial published in *The Crisis*. As with previous wars, Du Bois and other African American leaders believed the sacrifice of black lives in defense of the United States would enable their race to acquire and enjoy the respect guaranteed to all American citizens.[41]

For "Closing Ranks" and supporting their country, black leadership and the larger African American society saw an opportunity to reap benefits derived from participating in a successful war effort. Black solders experienced a sense of pride when the French received them as heroes and liberators. Even efforts on the part of Charles C. Ballou, the American general who encouraged the French to adopt segregationist practices, could not dampen black troops' morale or deter African Americans at home from celebrating the exploits of their boys "over there." Equally important, blacks on the battlefield and at home expected better treatment from white America as a reward for services rendered to win the war. John Russell Hawkins, a Baltimore high school teacher and Executive Secretary of the National Race Congress, even devised Fourteen Articles—akin to those of President Wilson—that outlined expectations for the Negro in post war America.[42]

The National Urban League appeared as another organization that made its presence felt during the First World War. Like the NAACP, the Urban League was conceived and developed during the Progressive Era largely by white liberals. And like the NAACP, the need for an active Urban League became hastened by a steady migration of southern blacks to the industrial North. Precursors for the Urban League occurred as early as 1905 when a black school teacher named Dr. William L. Buckley and William Schieffelin founded the Committee for Improving Industrial Conditions of Negroes in New York City. Three years later John Emlen, a white Quaker, founded the Armstrong Association in Philadelphia to address the housing needs and job prospects for southern migrants. And six years later Mary White Ovington, a charter member of the NAACP published an insightful sociological study, *Half A Man*, a monograph that underscored the inequities southern black migrants faced after moving to New York City. That same year the Urban League represented a coalition of organizations involving individuals concerned about a myriad of issues ranging from the adjustment of black women to an urban industrial milieu, to making decent housing available for the thousands of African American migrants from the South. White reformers Frances A. Kellor, Mrs. William Baldwin Jr. and Abraham Lefkowitz, along with philanthropist Julius Rosenwald contributed to the League's formation. The collective efforts of these white liberals represented the best of a truly principled white elite class in the United States.

The dedicated men and women dedicated to ameliorating black urban life also elicited the support of progressive African Americans, the most prominent being a graduate student at Columbia University named George Edmund Haynes. Born in Pine Bluff, Arkansas in 1880, Haynes attended Fisk, graduated in 1903, and matriculated to Yale University where he studied under Social Darwinian theorist, William Graham Sumner. A sensitive, caring young man, besides his graduate studies, Haynes supported his widowed mother who labored as a domestic servant and younger sister before returning to his graduate studies. While a student at the New York School of Philanthropy, Haynes became absorbed with the topic of Negro migration and migrant adjustment to urban life. He discovered that black migrants suffered grievously from historical subservience, limited skills, and racial prejudice. In short, Haynes discovered a pattern that plagued scores of African Americans. Disadvantages attributed to race and penury contributed to a dysfunctional family life, limited black opportunities for success, and kept a disproportionate number of blacks mired in poverty. To rectify the problems, Haynes proposed that welfare associations incorporate blacks into their organizations, that educational institutions train social workers, and that interracial committees be established to accomplish social and economic justice for black migrants.[43] Although a visionary and mere graduate student, Haynes provided the foundation for an organizational structure designed to improve the socioeconomic condition of the black masses.

The National Urban League [NUL] represented an amalgam of black conservative and liberal thought. Booker T. Washington and Robert Russa Moton, along with Kelly Miller and Dr. W. H. Brooks became early supporters of the League. By operating without the burden of political ideology that fostered dissension and limited the effectiveness of other organizations, the League established branches throughout the North—St. Louis, Chicago, Detroit, Philadelphia, and New York—without the rancor and in-fighting that would characterize the NAACP.[44] Except for a minor rift between Dr. Haynes and Eugene Kinckle Jones who eventually became the National Urban League Executive Secretary, circumstances dictated a marriage between conservative and liberal African Americans. Rivalries between Bookerite and Niagara factions never materialized to jeopardize the NUL. An African American truce may be observed in a statement which appeared in the *Washington Bee* which declared: "What are rights without bread to eat, houses to live in, clothes to wear and some simple luxuries? Let us have our political rights, but also the rational means to enjoy them."[45]

Leaders within the Urban League used the war to advance the cause of African Americans. As early as January 1918, the League arranged for conferences with the Department of Labor, serving as a precursor to A. Philip Randolph's efforts to place African American workers in defense industries.[46] That same year the League, in concert with the NAACP, endeavored to link the black urban worker with the American Federation of Labor. War-time labor shortages enabled the League and the NAACP to wrest some concessions from organized labor, the Department of Labor, the Executive Branch, and even some southern white employers. Although members of the NUL successfully enlisted the aid of industrialists, civic leaders, and municipal governments to ease the social and economic plight of southern migrants, a significant segment of the black population demanded emotional leadership replete with appeals to racial pride. Neither the NAACP nor NUL could fill this void. The time seemed propitious for a new kind of leader.

The trials African Americans faced during the Progressive Era created the viability of nascent black-nationalism and black-nationalist leaders in the United States. By the second decade of the century Washington's accommodationist policies had clearly failed. Moreover, the NAACP's endeavors to attain full citizenship and equal rights for the nation's sable population boasted minimal success. Consequently, some prideful African Americans who held little hope for black equality in the United States remained open to black-nationalist views prevalent during the 1890s. They required direction and a spokesperson who could galvanize support and lead the race out of "Canaan and into the Promised Land." That leader who provided an alternative to the Tuskegee Machine and the NAACP was an unpretentious appearing but dynamic man from the Caribbean, Marcus Garvey.

Born in 1887 in St. Ann's Bay, Jamaica, Marcus M. Garvey contained few attributes likely to propel him to leadership in the United States. As a West Indian alien, Garvey would have limited understanding of racial nuances peculiar to America. After all, native born African Americans had made little headway in uniting their race. Also, Garvey's dusky, dowdy appearance placed him at odds with most African American leaders of prominence who were usually mulatto, physically attractive (by European and black bourgeois American standards), and college trained profession-als. Moreover, spheres of influence had already been established within the black leadership cadre between the radical and conservative factions. Nevertheless, Garvey defied all odds, and for a brief period, provided hope and offered salvation for scores of African Americans.

Like many foreign blacks, Garvey read Washington's autobiography, *Up From Slavery* and viewed Washington as the most prominent black man in the world. However, far more than a book linked Garvey with the Wizard of Tuskegee. The inter-racial climate of Jamaica mirrored that in the United States. Tensions between blacks and whites existed, but positive accords were also reached between some black and white Jamaicans. Garvey's organization, the Universal Negro Improvement Association [UNIA] received its initial endorsement from liberal whites rather than members of the island's black bourgeoisie. Consequently Garvey, like Washington, identified more with philanthropic whites than with blacks. In preparation for his visit to Tuskegee, Garvey told Washington: "Up to now my one true friend as far as you can rely on his friendship, is the whiteman (sic)."[47] The persistent Garvey made overtures to visit Washington in Tuskegee, but financial difficulties and Washington's death prevented him from consummating the meeting. Accustomed to rebuff and hardship, Garvey remained committed to his race and decided to migrate to the United States to test his leadership skills and present his ideas to African Americans. When Garvey established the UNIA in the United States in 1917-1918, he founded an organization that appealed to the alienated, impoverished, disaffected angry members of the race mistreated or overlooked by the black and white elite.[48]

Given the impoverished state of black Jamaicans, Garvey became enamored by the potential African Americans had for acquiring wealth. Sensing where black earning potential was greatest, Garvey decided to settle in New York City. While there, he observed how World War I improved black economic prospects. Garvey sensed that as trade between America and Africa increased (from $47 million in 1914 to $325 million by 1920), African Americans rather than West Indians became the group most likely to take advantage of the burgeoning economic opportunities. Garvey's instincts proved correct. With money raised through stock options sold to African Americans with investment capital, Garvey founded the Black Star Line, a shipping company designed to transport goods between the United States, the West Indies, and Africa. African Americans from every socioeconomic class initially supported the venture, including the upwardly mobile working class and prominent blacks like Yale graduate, Dean William Pickens of Morgan College and W.E. B. Du Bois.[49] William Ferris, literary editor of the AME Church's *Christian Recorder* and Yale alumnus also joined the Garveyites. Ferris eventually served as chancellor and Assistant President of the UNIA. The interest of black leadership, heretofore political and social, now expanded to encompass economics and international business.

Garveyism, the UNIA, and black-nationalism would prove timely and appropriate responses to the dynamics affecting national and international affairs. Almost immediately after the United States entered the World War, African Americans recognized the need to focus primarily on race relations at home. Racist whites insisted on keeping African Americans, particularly soldiers in uniform, subservient. Workers from the south who trekked north to improve their condition also became targets for oppression. Initial indications of inter-racial trouble surfaced as the tide of migrants swept north and broke in a huge wave beginning at Chester, Pennsylvania in the east, St. Louis in the mid-west, and Los Angeles in the far west. The crest of the wave broke in Detroit, Chicago, Philadelphia, and most significantly, East St. Louis, Illinois.

Events in East St. Louis, Illinois strengthened Garveyism and gave credence to black-nationalist sentiments, as the city became the scene of the most violent race riot in the nation's history.[50] Despite prosperity in the city—owing to its role as a war materials supply center—fear of labor competitors, black slums, and the corrupt infrastructure of machine politics made African Americans the beneficiaries of uncommon white vitriol. After rumors and innuendoes about a race war surfaced in the spring, a racial clash occurred in early July, 1917, resulting in 39 blacks killed (as opposed to 9 whites), hundreds wounded, and nearly 6,000 African Americans displaced from their homes.[51]

The response of the black intelligentsia to the rising tide of racial hatred seemed timely, justifiably angry, and properly articulate. The editor of the *California Eagle* immediately spoke of revenge, declaring: "It's up to the Negro to strike the first blow ... be not afraid to die."[52] In response to the harm inflicted upon blacks, and as a means for redressing grievances, the NAACP received support from black secret and fraternal organizations—entities which heretofore disdained involvement in civil rights activities.[53] In *The Crisis*, Du Bois declared that to prevent future riots, whites must stop lynching, mob violence, disfranchisement, and "Jim Crow." The NAACP, in turn, used the riot to attack American racism while simultaneously garnering support for the Association. It published the horror of East St. Louis by conducting a silent march in New York City, disseminating literature on segregation and "Jim Crow," and contributing to the formation of the congressional investigating committee to gain an understanding of the violent unrest.[54]

The Red Summer of 1919 highlighted by the Chicago race riot brought renewed attention to the nation's racial problems and the importance of black leaders in addressing racial discrimination. The incident began after a black youth swimming in Lake Michigan crossed into the imaginary white bathing area. Convinced that the boy violated their space, whites threw stones at the youngster who subsequently drowned. After hearing of the boy's death, blacks and whites spoiling for a fight engaged in a melee which resulted in 38 deaths (23 black and 15 white) and scores of arrests. An investigation was launched to determine the cause of the racial confrontation. Like East St. Louis, an incendiary press, political corruption, poverty related problems, economic rivalry, and racial prejudice caused the riot. Once again, the NAACP obtained favorable publicity by establishing a legal defense fund for those involved with or victimized by the riot.[55]

Throughout the second decade of the century a certain realization became abundantly clear. A "New Negro" had emerged as a result of the World War. Heightened militancy appeared as southern migrants in northern cities experienced greater freedom, acquired wealth, and for the first time, had the opportunity to join other African Americans to confront their oppressors. White rioters entered the black community at their own risk, a factor explaining the high number of white fatalities in East St. Louis and Chicago. The African American propensity to fight back (voiced exceedingly well in Claude McKay's poem "If We Must Die") pervaded black communities throughout the nation. Whites recognized that quiet, contented "Uncle Toms" had been replaced by proud and assertive African Americans. Evidence of the aggressive spirit appeared from Longview, Texas to Washington, D.C. In each city African Americans—civilians as well as those in army uniform—fought gallantly and heroically against whites who attacked their race.[56]

With increased militancy exhibited by black citizens, African American leadership had little recourse but to take a more aggressive stance in support of human rights and freedom from oppression. Du Bois even engaged in fiery rhetoric, urging blacks to defend themselves with "bricks, clubs, and guns."[57] In the annual NAACP conference held in Cleveland in July 1919, for the first time blacks dominated the proceedings. The conference represented the largest annual gathering in NAACP history with delegates from 34 states in attendance. Taking his cue from the increased militancy from the black man on the street, Bishop John Hurst addressed the conference of delegates imploring them to die, if need be, to obtain their rights.[58] Every black socioeconomic class in the North demonstrated that whites could no longer attack African Americans with impunity.

Heightened race consciousness among African Americans energized leaders within the NAACP. In defense of blacks charged with murder in Phillips County, Arkansas, the Association raised more than $50,000 which helped gain freedom for the African American defendants.[59] Under the guidance of the NAACP, black leaders also worked aggressively to have an anti-lynching bill passed by state legislatures, governors, and the United States Congress. In 1919 the bi-racial Anti-Lynching Conference spear-headed by NAACP directors provided a platform that enabled blacks to express their views on the most despicable aspect of racism. And the following year, an amalgam of black leadership appeared at the NAACP's national convention in Atlanta. The conference not only conveyed the Association's growing confidence and comfort in the righteousness of its work, but also revealed that the schism between northern and southern black leaders had significantly diminished.[60]

Black leadership had a great deal to be proud of on the eve of the century's third decade. The rift between the Tuskegee Machine and the old Niagarites ended, and a coalition among black leaders had become firmly established. No one on either side could deny that leaders from Washington to Trotter had the very best interests of the race in mind. Du Bois himself declared that "no difference of aim and desire" existed between northern and southern Negroes.[61] Equally important the masses, comprised of non-descript, hard-working African Americans, openly displayed confidence in the work and direction offered by black leadership. The NAACP no longer carried the opprobrium as a white directed organization. *The Crisis*, controlled and dominated by Du Bois, boasted more than 10,000 subscribers, the largest number to that date in history.[62] Thanks to black leadership, the "color line" had become a nationally recognized problem with viable solutions emanating from the federal government. Yet more importantly, blacks had a collective sense of purpose. In May, 1919 Du Bois spoke for scores of African Americans and their spokespersons when he said: "We are cowards and jackasses if we do not marshal every ounce of our brain and brawn to fight ... the forces of hell in our own land."[63] For the first time since the demise of slavery African American leadership approached unity in design and purpose.

The NAACP provided the opportunity for a rising black bourgeoisie to become involved in civil rights activities. Blacks with leadership ability gained heightened prominence within their community by speaking in unison for African Americans—ranging from farm workers and urban laborers to professional men and women. The few apologists for racism like Bookerites Emmett Scott and Robert Russa Moton (Washington's successor at Tuskegee) were critiqued and denounced without creating a split within African American ranks. And if the NAACP appeared insufficiently race conscious among Pan-African segments of the black middle and working classes, Garvey's UNIA provided an alternative for these race conscious people. In the North and South, black spokespersons evolved and prepared doggedly to acquire full citizenship for their race.

Further evidence of a nascent black militancy among African American leaders evolved when the National Equal Rights League [NERL] convened in 1918 and sent a black delegation to the Paris Peace Conference to present African American grievances. Marcus Garvey, fledgling labor leader A. Philip Randolph, and Adam Clayton Powell, Sr., head of the prominent Abyssinian Baptist Church in New York City, headed the contingent of delegates.[64] NERL sought to use the black elite of America, the West Indies, and Africa to rid Africa of European colonialism. Even people of color in Japan and China were perceived as guides capable of training Africans until colonized Africans could care for themselves. NERL, joined by the newly created African Blood Brotherhood [ABB], a militant organization conceived by the young West Indian intellectual Cyril Briggs, also advocated unionization and armed revolution. Garvey, Briggs, and particularly Randolph would push mainstream black leaders toward the left; and sable leadership seemed inclined to drift toward a stronger, collective militancy.

During the Progressive Era Americans began to address the "color line," enabling certain realizations to become abundantly clear. Black leadership could boast of significant accomplishments despite overwhelming odds. The East St. Louis and Chicago riots strengthened the hand of African American leaders and generated a sense of black unity unprecedented during the twentieth century. These horrific events also gave race leadership the determination to fight incessantly for human rights and the ability to elicit financial and numerical support from the masses to promote human rights for African Americans. Nevertheless, questions remained about the ability of black spokespersons to "go it alone." Without prodding or support from liberal whites, the most prominent organizations dedicated to ameliorating the social, political, and economic status of African Americans—the NAACP and National Urban League—might not have existed. On the eve of the "Roaring Twenties" a transition of power occurred. Highly principled white men and women who created and supported civil rights organizations relinquished leadership to African Americans. Whether newly empowered blacks could sustain the organizations and promote new directions to meet unanticipated problems remained an open question.

4

THE 1920S: A RESTRUCTURING
OF BLACK LEADERSHIP

Despite intra-racial rivalries and power struggles evidenced among the fledgling leadership cadre, black leaders attained their apogee as a collective force during the 1920s.* No decade before or since rivaled the dynamism, creativity, and cultural pride evident among African American representatives as those who gave rise to "Negritude," the "New Negro Movement," and the Harlem Renaissance of the "Roaring Twenties." The dissipation of the Washington-Du Bois controversy, inception of the NAACP and National Urban League, the great migration of southern blacks to northern cities, and the rise of a burgeoning black bourgeoisie—events of the previous decades—had prepared blacks for the mantle of leadership. Leaders brought together black and tan, wealthy and poor, rural and urban African Americans from North and South to participate in a cultural metamorphosis and unity of purpose previously unseen in the annals of

---

* African Americans achieved significant gains during the decade of the 1960s. However, intra-racial dissension attributed to class interests and generational differences, combined with the absence of an evolutionary generic sense of African American culture, minimized the collective purpose of the black leadership cadre. See Chapter VIII below.

United States history. Simply put, the time proved propitious for a visible black leadership prepared to encounter the machinations of the "Roaring Twenties."

Ironically, the impetus for African American leadership's rise to prominence evolved, in part, from the black lower class through an idiom known as jazz. An expressive, rhythmic, original style of music that originated in New Orleans' Storyville district during the turn of the century, within twenty years this black cultural norm came to represent the symbol of an era known as the "Jazz Age." During the 1920s the black and liberal white cognoscenti of New York broadened the concept of jazz to encompass all artistic aspects of African American culture. This original black culture became publicized and enhanced through the writings of Langston Hughes, the musical stylings of Duke Ellington, and the hospitable Harlem ambiance created by the black heiress and hostess, A'Lelia Walker. Throughout the 1920s African Americans established the cultural norms for the entire nation, and for the first time in history, became recognized as significant people who added a unique vibrancy to American society. However another more serious mien than a cultural race consciousness also became captured during the age. Repression and strife visited upon African Americans contributed to the presence of leadership unparalleled since the emancipation of the slaves.

Events that caused blacks to "close ranks" behind leaders and take pride in their race evolved during the post-war era. First, the steady migration of southern blacks to northern cities enabled black culture—music, art, and literature—to be injected into mainstream America. This kind of respect from whites must have pervaded the black community and elevated African American confidence. Migrants also allowed for an augmentation of the black professional class. As black communities expanded in northern cities, the black bourgeoisie grew in stature, influence and wealth, pressuring their leadership to demand equal rights for the race. Second, African Americans took pride in the contributions made by gallant black soldiers who risked their lives and died, in President's Wilson's words, "to make the world safe for democracy." With heightened self-esteem and expectations, black soldiers and civilians alike gleefully anticipated the fortunes of democracy being visited upon African Americans. Finally, the militant rhetoric and pride evidenced in *The Crisis* and other black newspapers circulated among scores of African Americans, served as a call to arms that united the black community. The black press revealed a nascent self-importance never before witnessed in African

American society.[1] These combined factors meant that African Americans, the traditional objects of white oppression, would no longer accept racial attacks with impunity.

White people recognized the currents of change evident after the Great War and acted to stem the tide of liberalism that threatened the "old order." Overt manifestations of a frightened America appeared in the rise of white vigilantism represented most noticeably in the rise in the new Ku Klux Klan. But unlike the Klan of old, the new Klan expanded beyond the "deep South" to contain white men from the North Central, Southwest, Midwest, West Coast, and North Atlantic regions of the United States.[2] At the height of its influence during the mid-1920s, the Klan boasted 5,000,000 members and held political influence in several states. While the new Klan devoted especial attention to ridiculing Catholics and Jews, the popularity of the KKK placed black leaders on notice; they realized that the entire race could still be victimized by white racists. Evidence of the brutality of racist attacks, attempts to intimidate intrepid leaders, and white complicity in the degradation of African Americans may be gleaned from events that occurred in Tulsa, Oklahoma between May 31-June 1, 1921. Racial conflict in Tulsa represented black militancy and the universality of racism that characterized the decade. Atrocities committed against African Americans proved most disturbing because of the phenomenal success the city on the Arkansas River enjoyed during its brief history. Since the discovery of oil in 1910, Tulsa had become a boomtown. Blacks and whites migrated from the "deep South" and border-states to Tulsa in search of fame and fortune. By 1921 the "Magic City" contained two distinct communities—one black and the other white. Racial separation contributed to black prosperity in the segregated "Greenwood" section. A prideful African American community boasted two black schools and newspapers, thirteen churches, three fraternal lodges, two theaters, a hospital, and a public library.[3] The heart of the African American community's business district, "Deep Greenwood," became known as the "Negro's Wall Street." It contained a myriad of commercial establishments, including confectionery and grocery stores, numerous restaurants, eleven rooming houses, and four hotels. The offices of black physicians, lawyers, and other professionals could also be found there. The most well-to-do African Americans boasted assets in excess of $100,000.[4]

The infamous Tulsa incident began when a nineteen-year old boot-black, Dick Rowland, accidentally stepped on a seventeen-year-old white female elevator operator's foot. When the surprised girl screamed and

Rowland ran away, rumors immediately circulated that a black man had assaulted a white woman. When the Tulsa police arrested and immediately imprisoned Rowland, blacks became fearful of Rowland's fate because the previous year, a white man had been taken from the jail and lynched. Consequently, leaders in the black community armed themselves and marched to the jailhouse to protect Rowland and prevent a possible lynching. When a white man attempted to seize the weapon of a black veteran, shots rang out resulting in the death of ten whites and three blacks. A melee ensued. No black socioeconomic class stood exempt from white repression. During the next twenty-four hours 40 city blocks within the black community were looted and razed, more than 1,000 homes and businesses ruined, and 23 churches destroyed. The black community lost property valued at $1,500,000. More importantly, hundreds of innocent blacks were killed and wounded by bloodthirsty white mobs.[5]

Perhaps the most egregious aspect of the Tulsa Riot may be gleaned from the realization that nothing short of racial hatred and resentment toward successful blacks caused the conflict. Unlike other cities whose populace erupted out of frustration attributed to labor conflicts, significant demographic changes, or a depressed economy, Tulsa, only slightly touched by the 1921 recession, enjoyed bountiful economic success. Equally significant, African Americans profited directly or indirectly from the discovery of oil, the "Black Gold" of the southwest by developing a black community "showcase." Attainment corresponded with pride, and black pride proved far more than even the most prominent whites of Tulsa could accept.

Almost immediately after the riot, Walter White, Assistant Secretary of the NAACP, investigated causes for the racial confrontation and chronicled the events for the entire country in *The Nation*. White described the sweeping, all inclusive aspects of white bigotry as being the primary reason for the riot when he said: "... [I]n the sudden prosperity that has come to many ... white brothers ... there are some colored men there who are wealthy. This fact has caused a bitter resentment on the part...of whites who feel that these colored men ... are exceedingly presumptuous in achieving greater economic prosperity than they ... of a divinely ordered superior race."[6] Walter White's perspective on white hatred of successful blacks received credence when he noted that Dr. A.C. Jackson, a wealthy, successful physician—deemed "the most able physician in America," was murdered in cold blood by white vigilantes. Speaking for the tenor of the times, and on behalf of African Americans nationally, White concluded his observations by saying:

> Dick Rowland was only an ordinary bootblack with no standing in the community. But when his life was threatened by a mob of whites, every one of the 15,000 Negroes of Tulsa, rich and poor, educated and illiterate, was willing to die to protect Dick Rowland.[7]

Thus, middle and upper class blacks maintained affinity with their low-income brethren because racist whites displayed animus toward all African Americans regardless of status.

The NAACP immediately raised money for riot victims, collecting nearly $2,000 for its "Tulsa Relief and Defense Fund." Given the national race consciousness among blacks, far more money could have been donated to aid Tulsa's African American community. However Tulsa's white leadership engaged in deceit and duplicity; they declared that Tulsa residents were solely responsible for the riot and that local citizens would rebuild the African American community. Intent on reducing the black populace, their ruse enabled whites to prevent "Greenwood" from being rebuilt and forced most blacks to vacate the city.

The Tulsa riot forced African Americans to realize the need to be constantly vigilant and to recognize that survival depended upon mutual self-defense. No longer could indigent, disadvantaged blacks be held solely accountable for white recrimination. The Tulsa incident proved that elite and middle class African Americans were the objects of as much, if not more, white opprobrium as downtrodden members of the race who represented the popular demeaning stereotype of the lackadaisical "darkey." The lessons of Tulsa were hardly lost upon black leaders of the era. Mary E. Jones Parrish, a reflective eye-witness wrote:

> The Tulsa disaster has taught great lessons to all of us ... some of our group who have been blest [sic] with educational or financial advantages are oftimes [sic] inclined to forget ourselves to the extent that they feel their superiority over those less fortunate, but when a supreme test, like the Tulsa disaster comes, it serves to remind us that we are all of one race.... Every Negro was accorded the same treatment, regardless of his education or other advantages.[8]

Under these conditions African Americans of high profile would find themselves thrust into a new and challenging role as leaders.

Although black leadership with national recognition responded nobly to the horrors of Tulsa, they remained unaware of every manifestation of racial hatred. Atrocities committed against blacks in Rosewood, Florida, for example, remained unknown to Du Bois, Walter White, and other contemporary race leaders.[9] On January 1, 1923, black residents of Rosewood, Florida experienced the wrath of lawless whites. Problems began after a black convict escaped from a road gang and allegedly raped a white woman. A white mob formed in the nearby town of Sumner and marched to the prosperous black Rosewood community to seize and kill the perpetrator. Brandishing rifles and shotguns and using hounds to follow the scent of the purported black felon, the mob was out for blood. When the dogs came to the house of Aaron Carter, a World War veteran who was not at home, the mob became frenzied. Although the incensed mob eventually found and killed Carter, it remained disgruntled and thirsted for more "nigger blood."

Few people recognized or learned of the stand made by Sylvester Carrier, a man whose heroism should have been disseminated throughout the entire black populace. In Carrier the mob encountered a proud, angry man—a "New Negro." Reflecting the hauteur of a proud black man Carrier prepared for action. He collected his relatives from the town, brought them together under his parents' roof, and prepared to defend his family. When the mob heard of a black buildup at the Carrier home and attempted to seize Sylvester, he killed the white ringleaders and enabled his family to escape into the woods. Sylvester Carrier died in the firefight and scores of innocent black men and women were killed in cold blood. After black people fled, white men razed the town of Rosewood.[10] Although the bloody incident failed to attain the recognition of other racial clashes, the indomitable spirit of newly found self-esteem and leadership manifested in Rosewood appeared elsewhere, particularly in the North.

In early September 1925 a more celebrated case involving a white mob and blacks in defense of home and hearth occurred in Detroit, Michigan. Detroit had experienced a continuous influx of blacks who trekked north to work in the auto industry. In just over a decade the African American population increased from 10,000 to 75,000. Finding suitable housing for this burgeoning population became a problem. Because established black residents in the African American community initially felt inconvenienced by overcrowded conditions, those with means became the first to leave the confines of the black neighborhood to seek more spacious homes in white residential areas. Several African American families moved into white communities, but verbal intimidation and violence caused them to vacate their newly purchased homes and retreat to safety in black enclaves.

Events came to a head when Dr. Ossian H. Sweet, a black physician recently returned from Paris after studying the effects of radium with Madame Curie, purchased a home in a white neighborhood. After waiting nine months to allow his would-be neighbors to prepare for life in an integrated neighborhood, the Sweet family moved into their home. Since Sweet and his wife had been subjected to death threats, they brought guns, ammunition, relatives, and friends with them on moving day for self-defense. On the first night a white crowd gathered outside the Sweet residence. The following evening the crowd grew ominous. When friends and relatives came to provide additional support to Dr. Sweet, the mob charged the newcomers. Dr. Sweet recalled the event and provided insight about his emotions by declaring:

> When I opened the door and saw the mob, I realized that I was facing the same mob that had hounded my people through its entire history. In my mind I was pretty confident of what I was up against. I had my back against the wall. I was filled with a peculiar fear, the fear of one who knows the history of my race. I knew what mobs had done to my race before.[11]

Those within the Sweet residence represented a new attitude reflected by African Americans during the post-war era, and like courageous middle class residents in Tulsa and Rosewood, prepared to make the ultimate sacrifice to protect their dignity. When someone within the enraged mob fired shots at the house, the Sweets returned fire and a white man fell dead. The police then bolted into action, arrested all within the residence, and charged the entire group (including Mrs. Sweet) with murder. The NAACP immediately entered the fray, acquired the legal services of Arthur Garfield Haynes and Clarence Darrow, and raised $75,000 in Sweet's defense. At the conclusion of an emotional trial, the entire Sweet retinue was acquitted. Although race relations in Detroit suffered and Dr. Sweet would be deemed a "trouble-maker," the incident demonstrated unequivocally a collective militancy within African Americans unseen since the days of the black Abolitionists.[12]

Dr. Sweet reflected the black elite of the post World War I era. This incipient bourgeoisie equated wealth with status and thereby demanded the same privileges accorded white peers. Less concerned about the accoutrements of assimilation and strongly identified with the masses, the new leadership pushed relentlessly for gains beneficial to the entire race.[13] As Willard Gatewood has observed: "Their role as cultured brokers between the black and white worlds underwent transition, shifting from an emphasis on assimilation to an emphasis on black culture and a closer identity with the black masses."[14]

The individual most responsible for recognizing a shift in leadership and espousing the demise of pretentiousness which characterized the African American aristocracy was a man of elite bearing named Langston Hughes. James Mercer Langston Hughes, Poet Laureate of the Harlem Renaissance and son of James Nathaniel and Carrie Mercer Langston Hughes, entered the world on February 1, 1902 in Joplin, Missouri. Hughes possessed the pedigree of an African American aristocrat. The family was politically prominent and well educated. Lewis Sheridan Leary, a grandfather through marriage, participated in the Harpers Ferry Raid with John Brown. His great uncle, John Mercer Langston, for whom Hughes was named, had been a lawyer, appointee to the Freedmen's Bureau, a college administrator, diplomat, and the first African American to serve Virginia as a congressman.[15] Grandmother Mary Langston attended Oberlin College, his mother studied at the University of Kansas, and his father prepared for the bar and eventually practiced law. Despite his noble bearing, young Hughes had been born into a dysfunctional family. Alternately, he resided with his mother, father, and stepfather, and lived an insecure, nomadic existence.

Hughes' hardscrabble upbringing provided him with a profound understanding of African American travail. Through his literary genius, Hughes spoke passionately and accurately about black culture. Prior to his matriculation to Columbia University, Hughes published "The Negro Speaks of Rivers" in *The Crisis'* June 1921 edition. Between January and June, 1922, Hughes published an additional thirteen poems in *The Crisis* which spoke of African American culture, history, and pride. The following year Alain Locke, a Harvard Phi Beta Kappa and Rhodes Scholar contacted Hughes and asked him to contribute to *The New Negro*, Locke's seminal work which initiated a cultural movement known as the "Harlem Renaissance."

One of Hughes' most significant contributions to African American society, however, existed in his use of the literary mien to bridge class differences in the black community. As the era's most renowned African American of letters, Hughes garnered respect that enabled him to condemn the black elite's haughtiness and speak glowingly of the African American masses.[16] Hughes' derisive expose of elitist African Americans angered the black establishment.[17] While it would be ludicrous to assume that Hughes' critique of the black elite would imbue them with an urgent need to serve the disadvantaged masses, his critical revelations addressed the inappropriateness of black snobbery. Because of Hughes, the old, self-serving, self-contained elite atrophied somewhat as the cornerstone of African American leadership.

Hughes' acclaim, as with many other high profile blacks, evolved from a close relationship with prominent whites. Like Booker T. Washington who had William Baldwin, Collis P. Huntington and Andrew Carnegie, and Du Bois who gained support from the Spingarns, John Mulholland, and Mary White Ovington, Hughes also received patronage from white people. Playwright Carl Van Vechten submitted Hughes' poems to Alfred A. Knopf, introduced him to the editors of *Vanity Fair*, and enabled the young author to acquire a national reputation. Vachel Lindsay, the most prominent poet of the decade, also promoted Hughes and contributed to the aspiring writer's success. And during his formative years as a writer, Mrs. Charlotte Mason, a wealthy New York socialite, became Hughes' most influential supporter. She financed Hughes' college education at Lincoln University, Pennsylvania and even assisted him after graduation. These people, coupled with African Americans like Walter White, Jesse Fauset of *The Crisis*, and Professor Alain Locke of Howard University provided Hughes with immediate recognition and respect.

Aside from his literary talent, one of the Hughes' most significant contributions to the African American community existed in his ability to demonstrate that a "New Negro" had arrived. His views appeared to be on the cusp of African American introspection. While Hughes appeared as the first strong voice that openly critiqued the contented black bourgeoisie, he simply anticipated the feelings others had about the African American establishment. A combination of factors—the continuous black migration from the South, the rise of an African American nouveaux riche, and the constant reminder of omnipresent racism—allowed Hughes to become the conscience and voice of the "New Negro."

The "New Negro" became epitomized in leadership circles by a fledgling professional organization known as the National Bar Association [NBA]. A group of African American attorneys from mid-western cities in Chicago, St. Louis, Kansas City, and Des Moines recognized the need to elevate the stature of black lawyers in the United States. Founded by Des

Moines attorney George H. Woodson in 1925, the NBA endeavored initially to eliminate competition among black attorneys and develop a spirit of professional support and cooperation. African American lawyers recognized a need to enhance the reputation of sable barristers to acquire black clients and gain respect in the overwhelmingly white judicial system. Almost immediately after its inception, however, the NBA evolved into an organization with far greater interests than the professional enhancement of its membership. Racial repression of the era dictated that the quest for African American amelioration would serve as the primary focus of the NBA. Therefore every local bar that joined the Association was expected, as one NBA member recorded: "to cooperate with all Negro progressive and constructive movement for [the race's] advancement."[18]

Boasting the best legal minds in African American society, the NBA raised money through membership fees to share information about economic, political, and social issues that had legal ramifications for African Americans. Believing that barriers to racial progress evolved from legal restraints and quasi-legal legislation inherent in American racism, Harvard trained officers in the NBA like Philadelphia barrister Raymond Pace Alexander envisioned the work of black attorneys as being all encompassing for African Americans. Skilled and unskilled black laborers needed advocates to remove race-based restrictions that undermined employment opportunities. The NBA would also endeavor to make certain that municipal, state, and national governments represented African Americans as well as the larger white society. Recognizing that in American jurisprudence everyone should be treated equally, the NBA would dedicate its membership to gain equanimity for black Americans.[19]

As watchdogs and protectors of African American interests, the NBA began establishing chapters throughout the nation. Within four years, the NBA membership increased from approximately 200 to nearly 500 black male and female attorneys nationwide. By the end of the decade the NBA founded chapters in Chicago, Philadelphia, New York, Boston, Baltimore, Washington, Detroit, Cleveland, and had regional offices in North Carolina, Texas, and California. Since many black lawyers also belonged to the NAACP, the NBA played the multiple functions of providing soldiers to fight against the omnipresent "color line," defending African American rights, and keeping black barristers employed. The networking established by the Association proved to be comprehensive and efficient. Given situations that arose during the 1920s, lawyers within the "Talented Tenth" received ample opportunity to demonstrate their leadership ability.

Field Secretary James Weldon Johnson of the NAACP served as an excellent bridge between Hughes, the National Bar Association, the "New Negro Movement," and the trials and tribulations that plagued African Americans during the 1920s. Johnson, like Du Bois, proved both a literary genius and an activist. Introduced to literary classics by his mother during his pre-school years, Johnson became a voracious reader. His love for the printed word continued through college into adulthood.[20] As a lawyer, former editor of the *New York Age*, poet, diplomat, and lyricist who wrote the Negro National Anthem ("Lift Every Voice and Sing"), Johnson proved not only a leader, but a "Renaissance Man" as well. By October 1920 Johnson's performance as the Field Secretary impressed the Board sufficiently to enable the NAACP hierarchy to select him as the Association's Executive Secretary, the first African American to hold the most powerful position in the entire organization.

Under Johnson's direction, the NAACP increased its surveillance on racial discrimination and heightened African American determination to combat racism. Almost anticipating the concern of African Americans in Tulsa who feared mob rule, the NAACP prepared to move an anti-lynching bill through Congress in the spring of 1921. As Executive Secretary of the Association, Johnson approached Senators Arthur Capper and Charles Curtis of Kansas and, Representative L. C. Dyer of Missouri and asked them to spearhead the anti-lynching fight in Congress. Dyer, who previously voiced his sentiments against lynching and believed in making the odious practice a federal crime, introduced the Dyer Anti-Lynching Bill [H.R. 13] on April 11, 1921. The bill was referred to the Judiciary Committee and Johnson made certain that the NAACP would use every procedure available to the Association to champion the anti-lynching cause. Johnson personally contacted key members of the House and Senate, and had the New York Office rally support for the bill's passage. Black people jammed the congressional galleries to view the debate, and vociferously expressed support for the anti-lynching advocates. Although it took nine months, the Dyer Bill finally reached the House floor and passed 230 to 119. As Johnson recalled: "The Dyer Bill brought out the greatest concerted action I have yet seen the colored people take." He then observed: "A wave of thanksgiving and jubilation swept the colored people of the country."[21]

As a skilled lobbyist who understood congressional caprice and the inclination for individual members to maintain party loyalty, Johnson recognized that the most difficult fight lay ahead. Senators tended to be mutually supportive, held enormous prestige, and curried greater power than members of the House. Johnson lobbied Henry Cabot Lodge, the ranking Republican Senator, and enlisted his support. Other NAACP committee members gathered petitions of support for the Dyer Anti-Lynching Bill from 24 state governors, 26 mayors, 88 bishops and numerous members of the clergy.[22] The NAACP also placed advertisements in support of the Anti-Lynching Bill in the *New York Times*, *Washington Star*, *Atlanta Constitution* and other newspapers, reaching nearly 2 million people. Knowing that the public had become fully aware of the stain of lynching upon American democracy, Senators Lodge and Curtis assured Johnson personally that the bill would not be abandoned. But when the legislation came before the Senate in December 1922, the Republican senators reneged on their promises, abandoned the bill, and in a private caucus, decided to allow the Dyer Bill to die.

Although Johnson learned that the Republican senators supported the Dyer bill "just for the record," he took comfort in knowing that his efforts and those of the NAACP could be deemed responsible for bringing lynching before the halls of Congress and the American people. Walter White, Johnson's able lieutenant, also used his considerable talent to combat lynching. In addition to writing *Thirty Years of Lynching in the United States, 1889-1918*, the book used to bolster the anti-lynching argument in Congress, White authored *Rope and Faggot* in 1928, a study designed to undermine the fallacy of white superiority. Therefore, defeat of the Dyer Bill never deterred the NAACP from continuing the onslaught against lynching. More importantly, NAACP actions—directly or indirectly—drastically reduced lynching for the remainder of the decade. Johnson proudly proclaimed that the Association's efforts awakened decent southerners and caused them to begin initiating steps to curtail lynching. Johnson appeared correct in declaring: "This, I think, was its [the NAACP anti-lynching effort] most far-reaching result."[23]

Throughout the 1920s the NAACP not only provided legal support for African American defendants (as in the Sweet Case), but also addressed the pernicious and demeaning aspects of racial discrimination. White animus toward blacks remained nationally omnipresent; the NAACP had to husband its resources and exercise prudence when defending African American rights. Knowing that segregation was firmly entrenched in the South, the NAACP selected northern cities as targeted sites where lawsuits had the greatest possibility for success. Public institutions that demeaned and insulted blacks seemed omnipresent. Upscale hotels and restaurants refused to accept black trade. Motion picture theaters relegated blacks to the "crow's nest," the least desirable section for viewing films. As one NAACP attorney recalled, "The old civil rights act of May 1887, without teeth or brains, was for all practical purposes ineffectual."[24] However by the end of the decade, black leaders within the NAACP began, and often succeeded, in breaking down the barriers of segregation. Johnson, White, and the NAACP reached a common accord with African Americans. Clearly, blacks of every socioeconomic class identified with and supported the work undertaken by the NAACP and its leadership.[25]

The NAACP and NBA hardly existed alone as the sole black oriented organizations that came to prominence or reached an apogee during the 1920s; the National Urban League also enhanced its status as an industrious, committed, advocacy organization. As early as January 1918 the National League on Urban Conditions Among Negroes (NLUCAN) held a three day conference in New York City. Eugene Kinkle Jones, the National Urban League secretary, enlisted Dr. Robert Russa Moton to preside over the meeting organized to discuss "Negro Labor in America." Since the American Federation of Labor [AF of L] nominally extended union membership to blacks, the League felt obligated to address the AF of L's demonstration of beneficence toward African Americans. The League reacted favorably to the AF of L overture and pledged itself to promote the incorporation of African Americans into organized labor.[26] By November 1918, however, the invitations offered by AF of L leadership proved irrelevant. Local unions almost unanimously barred blacks from membership. Therefore, the National Urban League found itself forced to devise means for ameliorating the "Negro Labor" situation.

The Urban League task at hand required two distinctly different stratagems. The first borrowed a chapter from the NAACP that encouraged cooperation between blacks and whites of prominence and with like minds who agreed to work jointly toward uplifting the Negro race. By 1919 the League proved adroit in developing inter-racial alliances in 32 cities. The second goal—that of elevating low income blacks to bourgeois status—occupied the thoughts of NUL leaders throughout the 1920s and extended far into the twentieth century. Converting a rural peasant class into sophisticated urbanites proved an arduous undertaking. Like virtually every member of the black bourgeoisie—comprising members of the Urban League, the NAACP, or other established organizations engaged cooperatively with whites—attaining middle class status for the masses became the primary objective.

The Urban League's Eugene Kinkle Jones emerged as a promising young leader who headed a prominent organization endeavoring to improve the economic condition of African Americans. As the son of Joseph Endom and Rosa Daniel Kinkle Jones, young Eugene Jones was born in 1885 and resided in a decidedly middle class household in Richmond, Virginia. Jones' father graduated from Colgate University and became one of the first educated blacks in the Old Dominion. The elder Jones taught at the Richmond Theological Seminary (currently Virginia Union) and his mother, who graduated from Howard University and the New England Conservatory of Music, instructed students at the Hartshorn Memorial College. After graduating from Virginia Union, Jones matriculated to Cornell University where he earned a Masters degree. While at Cornell, Jones became the first initiate of Alpha Phi Alpha fraternity, became instrumental in marketing the Alpha concept to other colleges and universities, and gained experience that proved invaluable for a future executive of a national social service organization. After taking leave from his teaching position in Louisville, Kentucky, Jones moved to New York in 1911 to serve as a field secretary of the Committee on Urban Conditions Among Negroes [CUCAN].[27] Named the NUL Executive Secretary in 1917, Jones decided that the League would gather information, continue developing new branches, and advise local chapters on day to day operations.

One of Jones' most valuable contributions to the African American masses may be attributed directly to a personnel appointment. In 1920 Jones named and funded sociologist Charles S. Johnson to head the League's Research and Investigations Department. For the first time ever, a national service organization acquired statistics and other information to learn about the living and economic conditions experienced by African American urbanites. Rather than merely obtaining facts and figures, Charles Johnson sought to acquire scientific evidence which would destroy negative stereotypes used to justify white discrimination toward blacks. Another important aspect of Johnson's work existed in his study of African Americans in relation to labor unions. Here, Johnson focused on the primary concern of the African American majority—prospects for gainful employment. No issue spoke more directly to the black masses than work. Since the rising "color line" related directly to African Americans, Johnson spoke to the fundamental issue that plagued race relations throughout the twentieth century and explained the desultory condition of the black majority in contemporary society. White people refused to allow blacks equal opportunity for gainful employment. In *Negro Membership in American Labor Unions*, Johnson and his associates concluded: "The Negro is yet on the fringe of America's industrial life. He continues to be a marginal worker."[28]

In addition to primary scientific research, Johnson also produced *The Urban League Bulletin* in 1921 to disseminate information about the status of African Americans throughout the nation. However, his most significant contribution toward destroying myths about African American inferiority while simultaneously addressing the race's practical concerns appeared in *Opportunity: Journal of Negro Life*. First published in January 19, 1923, *Opportunity*, in Johnson's words, was: "... to present objectively, facts of Negro life."[29] Mindful of the need to demonstrate the human qualities of African Americans, Johnson made certain that both black subscribers and the white public recognized talent within the race. This served to glorify African Americans, generate respect for black culture, and develop among readers an appreciation for the sable race's potential for making an even larger contribution to the United States. Contributors to *Opportunity* included every noteworthy figure in African American political, social improvement, and literary circles. In the first year of publication alone, Robert Russa Moton of Tuskegee, Alain Locke of Howard, Kelly Miller of Morgan State, as well as poet Countee Cullen, insurance magnate C.C. Spaulding, and Monroe N. Work of *Negro Year Book* fame were published in *Opportunity*. Through these efforts the concept of "the Negro Renaissance" became disseminated throughout the country. Equally important, the magazine publicized the social needs of and altruistic services provided for African Americans.[30] With this publication the link between cultural pride, social activism, scientific research, and prospects for economic ameliora-tion became complete. Evidence of the "New Negro Movement," African American militancy, explanations for the black condition, and the "Negro" quest for self-sufficiency became encapsulated in Charles S. Johnson's "Journal of Negro Life." No better magazine addressed the condition of Negro life as understood by leading blacks of the era than *Opportunity*.

More than any previous organization, the National Urban League worked on behalf of the "average Negro," developing strategies to place African Americans in the United States labor market. Evidence of this concerted effort appeared through the NUL's creation of the Department of Industrial Relations [DIR]. Between 1924 and 1925 E. K. Jones and others within the Association acquired money to sustain the DIR. T. Arnold Hill, the thirty-nine year old field secretary and executive of the Chicago

Urban League (and like Jones a Virginia Union graduate) was selected to head the new office. Hill saw his responsibility as advancing economic opportunities for African Americans by assessing the labor market, determining the needs of industry, opening opportunities for African American workers, and working assiduously to incorporate blacks into trade unions.[31]

In a significant departure from previous African American leaders and organizations, Hill and the NUL supported collective bargaining and black participation in unions. Hill and the Urban League's position on unions clearly contrasted with the majority of African American leaders. For example in 1925, the same year that Hill introduced his plan to familiarize blacks with trade unionism, more than fifty African Americans convened in Washington, D.C. and spoke out vehemently against organized labor.[32] At the national convention of the Improved Benevolent and Protective Order of Elks of the World [African-American Elks or IBPOE], a declaration was announced that "unionism is calculated to do our people all sorts of harm and injure them with the employing class in America...."[33] Nevertheless, Jones and Hill consistently pushed for African American involvement in labor unions and championed unionization for black people. Hill instituted training classes designed to acquaint blacks with unionization in cities ranging from Philadelphia and St. Louis to Cleveland, Richmond, and Atlantic City.[34] Under Jones' direction the NUL developed a relationship with the Dining Hall Employees Union and supported the Brotherhood of Sleeping Car Porters in their fight for union recognition. In November 1926 Jones addressed a labor dinner for black porters. He encouraged the membership to continue organizing for mutual protection and supported their justification in being suspicious of big business.[35]

Jones, Hill, and the League also endorsed, despite its communist sponsorship, the Negro Labor Congress and the New York Trade Union Committee. With a sense of Washingtonian pragmatism and Du Bois' flair in quest of idealistic pursuits, through his Industrial Department, Hill devised a program designed to enhance economic opportunities for the African American worker. In essence, the plan intended to disseminate information about skills possessed by black workers to prospective white employers. Through this effort it was anticipated that blacks would obtain employment. With capable, qualified workers showing an excellent work ethic, employers hopefully would have greater incentive to remove restrictions for hiring and training black workers. This strategy became the manifesto that plotted the direction of industrial relations work into the 1960s.[36]

An emergent black radical movement, known as the African Blood Brotherhood [ABB], forced black leaders like Jones, Hill and others into taking more aggressive stances to ameliorate the black condition. Founded in New York City between 1917 and 1919 by Cyril Valentine Briggs, the ABB endeavored to work for the liberation of African people throughout the world. Briggs, deemed "an angry blond Negro" of West Indian birth, bristled at the discrimination those of African ancestry experienced in the white-dominated world. The radicalized Briggs joined other West Indian dissidents like Wilfred Adolphus Domingo and Richard B. Moore; collectively, they perceived the leftist Du Bois as "a lost leader" and developed an ideology that combined black- nationalism, Marxism, and the revolutionary fervor of Ireland's Sinn Fein movement.[37] Briggs initially published his views when he served as editor of the *Amsterdam News*. Greatly unsettled by his extremism, owners of the *Amsterdam News* forced Briggs to leave the paper and found his own newsmagazine, the *Crusader*. The ABB's message also appeared in *The Messenger*, and for a brief period, Briggs endorsed the black-nationalism espoused by Marcus Garvey.

ABB endorsed self-help and mutual protection against attack, and formulated a plan that stressed "fraternal, economic, educational, physical, social benefits" and protection through "calisthenics, workers' co-operative enterprises, forums, and co-operations with other Darker Peoples."[38] Briggs' background as a colonial enabled him to become interested in the concept of self-determination espoused by Lenin with the intention of liberating Africans, black West Indians, and African Americans. The race riot in Tulsa galvanized the African American community and fostered the creation of mass meetings and ABB posts in many cities. Through Moore, Briggs expressed extreme hostility toward the United States when attendees at an ABB mass meeting held in New York were told: "Get ready—be prepared that you can fight back when attacked."[39]

Despite the radicalism of ABB, the organization maintained a strong sense of purpose and joined other black organizations in a demonstration of unity. In January 1923 the ABB announced that it would attend a meeting convened by the National Equal Rights League to plan an all-Negro conference. Briggs, Domingo, Moore, and the Communist, Otto Huiswoud, represented the ABB and met with Kelly Miller of the National Race Conference, James Weldon Johnson of the NAACP, William Monroe Trotter and Dr. M.A.N. Shaw of the National Equal Rights League, Dr.

David N.E. Campbell of the International Uplift League, and George Schuyler of the Friends of Negro Freedom. The Concordant signed by members representing the six organizations sought "the closest cooperation and the most harmonious relationship possible among all the agencies working for the civil and citizenship rights of Negro Americans."[40] Furthermore, the gathering pledged that each organization would work cooperatively to husband their forces to concentrate against the common enemy and inspire the entire race to achieve united action. The sense of unity and purpose that inspired Briggs and Moore impacted another leader who established an office in Harlem within walking distance of the ABB's *Crusader* at 2299 Seventh Avenue—the nearby office, located at 2305 Seventh Avenue housed A. Philip Randolph's *Messenger*.

The 1920s marked the debut of labor leader A. Philip Randolph, the most fervid black unionist of the twentieth century. Randolph was born to former slaves, an African Methodist Episcopal minister and, as Randolph declared, an "almost white" wife in Crescent City, Florida on April 15, 1889. After receiving private tutoring and learning an appreciation for words and diction, Randolph entered Cookman Institute (later known as Bethune-Cookman College) in 1903. In 1911 he relocated to New York City. While in New York he attended CCNY evening school, and through his wife, Lucille, met Chandler Owen, a graduate student at Columbia. By forging the ideas of Lester Frank Ward's sociological theories with the economic philosophy of Karl Marx, Randolph and Owen developed a budding friendship, embarked upon an intellectual mission, and engaged in activities which shook the foundations of black leadership.

Together Randolph and Owen embraced socialism, attributed racism to capitalism, and searched for the means toward achieving African American amelioration.[41] In November 1917, the pair engaged in a venture to effect positive change for African-Americans through a magazine known as *The Messenger*. With this organ as their voice, Randolph and Owen launched into tirades against established black leadership. Even the great Du Bois, who headed the radical faction against Booker T. Washington, helped create the NAACP, and severely criticized the white power structure, became an object of the "Young Turk's'" wrath. After attacking Du Bois for his "Close Ranks" essay, every black leader of prominence became "fair game." Hardly anyone escaped criticism. The pair accused William Pickens and James Weldon Johnson of the NAACP of engaging in juvenile rhetoric which lulled blacks into a false sense of security.[42] George E. Haynes, Emmett J. Scott, T. Thomas Fortune, and active NUL committeeman Fred R. Moore also fell under attack. They received criticism for complacency and were accused of preaching "the gospel of satisfaction and contentment." Owen and Randolph's caustic remarks extended to Robert Russa Moton who was deemed "a white man's Negro" and Archibald Grimké, a black patriarch labeled as being "an old fossil."[43]

The primary concern Randolph had with his elite contemporaries existed in their indifference toward the masses and dependency on the white establishment. In many respects it became difficult to contest Randolph and Owen's analysis. Black leadership focused primarily on social and political, rather than economic issues. Fear of alienating white philanthropists who provided economic support and leadership to African American colleges and civil rights organizations caused black spokespersons to exercise caution. No one wanted to alienate the proverbial "hand that feeds." This kind of reasoning incensed Randolph and Owen. In reference to the fledgling Urban League, Randolph stated that the organization comprised a "collection of scabs for the industrial capitalists ... [that] cannot represent the working class Negro race."[44]

Randolph also directed his anger toward the black church. As a minister's son, Randolph believed that religion in the black church offered a calming effect, proved entertaining to the parishioners, but failed to encourage the congregation to address pertinent, worldly concerns. He spoke critically of black ministers' reluctance to rouse their flock to confront the issues of disenfranchisement, lynching, and other demeaning aspects of racism that contributed to maintenance of the "color line." Furthermore, Randolph believed that black preachers ignored economic matters essential for the race's survival.

When Chandler Owen deserted New York and *The Messenger* and moved to Chicago, Randolph single-handedly confronted the racism and classism impinging on black Americans. Since *The Messenger* remained popular and subscriptions increased, Randolph realized that his radicalism had a sable following. Yet, Randolph, the opportunist and pragmatist, should have sensed that the First World War, more than fiery rhetoric, contributed to *The Messenger's* success. This Great War, as James Weldon Johnson recalled, fostered black radicalism "motivated by a fierce race consciousness."[45] The limitations of Randolph's popularity appeared immediately during the post war years.

After having failed to develop a successful inter-racial group with the newly established National Association for the Promotion of Labor Unionism Among Negroes or establishing union support among African

Americans with the short-lived United Negro Trades Union, Randolph realized the necessity for changing tactics. Recognizing his livelihood became jeopardized when economic radicalism espoused in *The Messenger* became dated and the magazine's popularity waned, Randolph searched for an alternative means of employment. Familiarity with labor exploitation and popularity gained through *The Messenger* enabled him to recognize the potential gains that could accrue to him through the creation of a black union.

Fortuitously, African Americans employed by the Pullman Company as railroad porters provided the characteristics essential for the creation of a black union. Pullman porters represented the elite of black labor. They were mannerly, well traveled, relatively well educated, presentable, and enjoyed—in the eyes of the larger black community—a lavish lifestyle that enabled them to be viewed as "folk heroes" and "pillars of society."[46] Nevertheless, their work and treatment by the company seemed reminiscent of slavery. Porters worked long hours without compensation, depended largely on tips for income, and were responsible for purchasing their own uniforms and providing for lodging. They also labored without job security, serving at the whim of passengers and employers.

As an intellectual and professional polemicist, Randolph had little knowledge of porters and the work they performed. Circumstances, however, provided Randolph with a unique opportunity to create a black union. First, black porters enjoyed a monopoly as the primary service employees within the Pullman organization. The monopoly evolved from the historical master-servant relationship between blacks and whites in the United States, a relationship that caused privileged whites to customarily expect service from African Americans.[47] Second, exigencies of the era imbued the porters with a sense of race consciousness that heightened possibilities for unionization. Black pride emanating from the Great War permeated the African American community and provided porters with a greater need for self-determination. And finally, Randolph's clairvoyance, charisma, keen intelligence, and penchant for making sound decisions made him the ideal candidate to create a black labor union. Thus by mutual agreement between Pullman porters and Randolph, on August 25, 1925 this son of a Florida preacher man—with support of seasoned porters Billy Bowes and Ashley Trotter—formally established the Brotherhood of Sleeping Car Porters [BSCP].[48] As the head of the BSCP, Randolph found the pragmatic means for promoting unionism, securing his personal finances, and meeting an ideological goal of working incessantly on behalf of the African American working class.

Through the BSCP Randolph displayed enormous talents that not only served as the impetus for a black labor movement, but more importantly, developed skills that eventually would aid the entire African American community. In May, 1925 Randolph spoke as the "Orator of the Day for the Negro Race of the World" at the opening ceremonies at the Philadelphia Sesqui-Centennial celebration. The organizers made a wise, prescient decision in selecting Randolph as the spokesperson for African Americans. Randolph possessed the flair and majesty of Frederick Douglass, the "grass roots" popularity of Booker T. Washington, and the dedication to research comparable to W.E. B. Du Bois. Within a decade he would welcome and transcend the many obstacles posed by an obstinate Pullman Company management, mollify a black press that abhorred unions, and frustrate communist infiltrators intent on singularly championing the working class cause. To attain his goals, Randolph used cunning and guile by threatening strikes, applied political acumen to acquire support, and acquired help from such diverse factions in African American society as the IBPOE, the conservative wing of black leadership as represented by Robert Russa Moton, and representatives of socialist labor unions. Randolph established a legacy that identified him in the estimation of some scholars as founder of the modern Civil Rights Movement.[49]

Other African American leaders and organizations expended enormous amounts of time and energy to improve conditions for their race. Few could doubt the sincerity and earnestness each spokesperson or group brought forward—cultural pride, civil rights, and economic opportunity—to mitigate the harshness of American racism. Still, philosophical differences within black leadership caused the continuation of intra-racial rifts. Just as feelings of cultural pride became manifested in the "New Negro Movement" and omnipresent racism generated an urge for mutual protection, a division within the race occurred which rivaled the Washington-Du Bois controversy in spite and intensity. On a superficial level, problems erupted because of stylistic differences and personality clashes between Marcus Garvey and other black leaders. But in a broader sense the far-reaching implications of this internecine fight manifested a struggle between two distinctly different and divisive philosophic positions. The first matter involved the division between integrationists and black nationalists within the African American community. The second, with even greater potential pejorative consequences for black Americans, involved intra-racial differences attributed to class divisions within the race.

Members of the NAACP, National Bar Association, National Urban League, and Brotherhood of Sleeping Car Porters devoted themselves entirely to activities designed to help blacks integrate into the larger American society. These groups, comprised primarily of the black middle class and elite, took an uncompromising stance against segregation. The Universal Negro Improvement Association, conversely, endorsed a separatist doctrine and essentially represented the alienated, low-income masses who suffered most grievously from the inequality promoted by white racism. To UNIA members, security existed in separation rather than integration. The power struggle that ensued between each leadership faction held significance for African Americans throughout the twentieth century.

Despite the registered successes of the NAACP and National Urban League, the UNIA dominated the headlines before and after the Great War. Since black separatism traditionally had limited appeal within the African American community, Marcus Garvey himself must be credited for the UNIA's success. Garvey's flamboyance and showman like qualities guaranteed publicity for himself and his organization. His appeal to racial self-sufficiency and pride in "Mother African" proved attractive to scores of black Americans. With pomp and circumstance, titled dignitaries comprising a Supreme Potentate and a Lady Commander of the Sublime Order of the Nile, and addresses like "Up You Mighty Race" cascading off the walls in New York City's Liberty Hall, Garvey received enormous acclaim.[50]

More than any other black leader of the era, Garvey understood the political and social climate of America.[51] Although Garvey's commercial ventures proved to be ill conceived and visionary and his style combative and divisive, Garveyism held broad appeal for a disenchanted people seeking a black messiah. Garvey instilled blacks with high self-esteem and visions of a collective unity between "Old" and "New World" Africans that filled thousands of black people with pride and anticipation. He also possessed an instinct for marketing and publicity that gained a receptive audience. Since concerns about race and race relations consumed the American consciousness, Garvey joined the debate by endorsing racial segregation voiced by leaders of the Ku Klux Klan and their "Invisible Empire." Though extreme, Garvey's support of the KKK hardly seemed illogical. Dedicated Garveyites and Klansmen believed strongly in racial purity and pride, and spoke despairingly of integrationists. By giving voice to those who were frustrated by their condition during the 1920s, Marcus Garvey, along with the Klan's Imperial Wizard William J. Simmons and Grand Dragon David C. Stephenson, recognized public dissonance and adroitly directed people into organizations that assuaged their concerns.

The philosophy espoused by the UNIA created a backlash from the more traditional black leaders. Indeed, the enmity Garvey attracted from the black bourgeoisie approached fanaticism. Acid tongued Monroe Trotter referred to Garvey as "an ugly black toad." While Du Bois objectively recognized the legitimacy for the UNIA's existence, he also criticized Garvey for his unfortunate naiveté, woeful lack of business acumen, and irresponsible rhetoric that exceeded the attainable. In Du Bois' estimation, Garvey dashed the hopes and squandered the meager finances of thousands of black Americans.[52]

Ironically, the individual most antagonistic toward Garvey—and for legitimate reasons—proved to be A. Philip Randolph. Although a proponent of radicalism and promoter of anti-black establishment positions, Randolph nevertheless had problems with Garvey and his movement. The initial area of contention pertained to membership recruitment. Garvey and Randolph targeted the same socioeconomic group for membership and support. Although the *Messenger's* economic ideology regarding class struggle and the inequities of wealth spoke directly to progressive minded members of the black middle class, symbolically Randolph coveted support from the low-income masses. Given the window of opportunity to compete for African American support, Garvey easily won the battle. Garvey and the UNIA raised more money in an abbreviated period than any other black movement.[53] Randolph naturally had reasons to abhor Garvey and the UNIA.

Philosophical differences between the two men also promoted mutual antipathy. Profoundly dedicated to uniting the proletariat, Randolph envisioned white and black laborers working collectively as Socialists for economic amelioration. Garvey, in contrast, undermined inter-racial class solidarity by contending that African Americans must operate separate and apart from whites. Randolph used *The Messenger* to blast the UNIA leader in a savage "Garvey Must Go" campaign. Labeling the UNIA leader as "A Supreme Negro Jamaican Jackass," and projecting that Garvey would "set back the clock of Negro progress," Randolph used his newly created Friends of Negro Freedom organization to undermine and bait his West Indian adversary.[54]

Another area of contention involving Randolph and other African American leaders disgusted with Garvey involved nationality and culture. African Americans assumed that Jamaicans were arrogant and failed to understand the race problem in the United States. Jamaicans, in turn, perceived African Americans as being subservient and devoid of ambition. While cultural differences and competing interests led to name calling and other forms of divisiveness, most of the dissenting factions were localized in New York City. However, since the UNIA, the NAACP, the NUL, and Randolph were headquartered in the "Big Apple," in one sense, the rifts would serve to exacerbate the nationalistic differences between native and foreign born blacks.

An equally insidious and complex problem involving African Americans and Jamaicans existed over the issue of color. In the United States everyone of African descent, regardless of skin color, hair texture, or physical features, was deemed a Negro and thereby inferior. Unlike the United States where one drop of Negroid blood classified one as being black, in Jamaica color gradations allowed for differences in social strata. Jamaican mulattos enjoyed higher social position than those of darker hue. Therefore, when Garvey and other West Indians brought their concept of color differentiation to the mainland and attacked blacks of American nationality for being devoid of racial purity and for identifying with the white elite, deep rifts between Jamaicans and African Americans occurred.

Ironically, neither Garvey nor his opponents within the black bourgeoisie were devoid of color consciousness. Both of Garvey's wives—Amy Ashwood and Amy Jacques—could be deemed mulatto. Among African Americans, dark professional men usually married light skinned women. Obviously, each leadership faction maintained a common flaw. Elements of racial self-hatred caused both Garvey and his African American detractors to reveal that light skin color was valued highly in primary relationships, and by default, became a determinant in social status.

Although personal and philosophical differences fostered enmity between Garvey and his opponents, a more insidious factor with dire consequences for the future of black liberation appeared. Clashes between Garvey and his opponents—Du Bois, Randolph and other members of the black intelligentsia— represented divisiveness separating an African American proletariat from the black bourgeoisie. Garvey not only threatened the leadership class in the United States, but equally grave, initiated the first salvos of class divisions between educated, middle class blacks and the distinctly less educated and refined black proletariat. While conflicts between the Bookerites who endorsed Washington and former Niagarites in support of Du Bois had been extremely intense, the clash between Garveyites and the leadership in opposition would prove formidable and prophetic.[55] Du Bois considered Garvey a "Demagogue" who exploited differences within the race—"between our privileged and exploited, our educated and ignorant, our rich and poor, our light and dark"[56]—to destabilize legitimate leadership and gain himself personal acclaim. Fighting back, the black bourgeoisie organized "Marcus Garvey Must Go" protest rallies, excoriated the UNIA declaring it stood for "ugliest Negroes in America," and advocated Garvey's deportation to Jamaica.

The resolution of issues between Garveyites and the more orthodox factions of black leadership came to a head in 1923 when Garvey became indicted, tried, and eventually convicted by the Federal government for mail fraud. Garvey's economic ventures involving the Black Star Line and the prodding of a hostile black bourgeoisie contributed to his demise as a viable black leader. Conceivably, problems between Garvey and African American leadership could have been averted if Garvey had been less flamboyant, contentious, argumentative, and egotistical. By working cooperatively with the KKK on mutual interests of racial purity—Garvey publicly endorsed the Klan's separatist policies—he insulted powerful elements within the African American community.[57] This judgmental error, combined with his air of pomposity, made him appear as a buffoon to staid members of the black elite.

In December 1927, Garvey received a commuted jail sentence and immediate deportation to Jamaica as an undesirable alien. However few black leaders who called for Garvey's downfall relished their victory. Rather, former opponents extolled the Jamaican's virtues. The greatest overtly black champion of the African American masses had been removed but his contribution to African American life endured. The *Amsterdam News* lamented his departure and said: "In a world where black is despised, he taught them that black is beautiful. He taught them to admire and praise black things and black people.... They rallied to him because he heard and responded to the heart beat of his race."[58]

Black leaders of the 1920s missed an opportunity to develop a strong intra-racial bond that would unite different factions within African American society. The black bourgeoisie's historical disdain for the masses prevented them from visualizing or understanding the broad appeal of black-nationalism espoused by Marcus Garvey. Furthermore, many black leaders disdained the earthier, cultural aspects of negritude that Garveyism conveyed—the ostentation, the swagger, and pride in African features and culture. Other traditional intra-racial problems of longstanding also persisted. Regional differences still pitted northern born blacks against African Americans whose origins existed in the South. Divergent philosophies—separation versus integration and soliciting business as opposed to labor support—remained on how best to elevate the race. An incipient intra-racial division between the black bourgeoisie and proletariat surfaced. Of course the persistent clash of egos between strong-willed people rendered consensus building difficult, if not impossible. Yet despite intra-racial dissension, the 1920s represented the decade when black leaders of every class, region, and philosophical persuasion came closest to realizing the necessity for developing unity to achieve racial amelioration.

During the "Roaring Twenties" race conscious cultural giants provided a flair for leadership unparalleled in the annals of African American history. All the primary leaders demonstrated commitment, perseverance, pride, and most uniquely, constantly used literary mediums to promote the African American cause. Langston Hughes' poetry and prose gained white respect for African Americans. He also deepened, temporarily, appreciation of the black elite for the less refined aspects of African American culture. The black Cuban-born bibliophile, Arthur Schomburg, helped convert the 135th Street Branch of the New York Public Library into the cultural center of the Harlem Renaissance.[59] He, along with historian Carter G. Woodson, who established "Negro History Week" in 1926, implanted the importance of African American culture into the minds of the black elite and masses alike. James Weldon Johnson, W.E.B. Du Bois, and Walter White, through magazines like *The Crisis* and *The Nation*, brought race issues and expertise on black culture before the larger American society. A. Philip Randolph expressed his views through *The Messenger*, Marcus Garvey used his newspaper, *The Negro World*, and Eugene Kinkle Jones and Charles S. Johnson offered *Opportunity* magazine to communicate, sermonize, instruct, and instill generations of African Americans with racial pride. Black leadership and literary genius seemed synonymous. Cerebral rather than emotional, steadfast, fearless, and prideful rather than doting and accommodating, black leaders of the 1920s placed the welfare of their entire race first.

The sensitivity and sophistication of James Weldon Johnson, the charisma of Marcus Garvey, doggedness and pragmatism of A. Philip

Randolph, cultural pride of Langston Hughes, organizational skills of Eugene Kinkle Jones, and genius of W.E.B. Du Bois represented leadership at its best. Frederick Douglass would have been proud of the quality, assertiveness, and adventuresome spirit demonstrated by his worthy successors functioning during the "Roaring Twenties." Collectively, these leaders demonstrated an impeccable commitment to elevating the status of blacks in American society. They understood that economic development, civil rights, and cultural pride collectively would provide for the true evolution of the "New Negro." Unfortunately the promise of the 1920s gave way to the Depression of the 1930s and caused African American leadership to reflect on class interests at the expense of race consciousness.

PART II

CONSCIOUSNESS OF CLASS

5

THE GREAT DEPRESSION AND
NEW DIRECTIONS IN BLACK LEADERSHIP

The Great Depression of the 1930s represented a watershed period that significantly altered the role of government and leadership in the history of the United States. Never before had Americans held extreme doubts about the survival of capitalism, political democracy, and individualism, ideologies which enabled United States citizens to feel prideful and secure. The middle and elite class structures that aspiring families spent generations to create and hone were placed in severe jeopardy. Those of less modest means worried about personal survival. Consequently, the public looked toward government for succor and correspondingly, a heightened altruistic role from the nation's leadership cadre. Through the New Deal President Roosevelt assumed the role of a benevolent authority figure who initiated government policies designed to protect the larger American society and its middle class lifestyle. Black leaders also made adjustments to meet the challenges wrought by the Depression. Like Roosevelt and other New Dealers, African American leaders endeavored to use government to protect vital interests for which they had responsibility. The outstanding question posed for black leadership, however, pertained to determining whether race, or rather, class issues would receive greater priority in response to crises caused by the Great Depression.

Initially, African Americans generally, and black leaders in particular had little inkling of the disaster about to befall their race when the stock market fell. According to National Urban League records, the Great Depression began for the African American community during the winter of 1928, nearly a full year before "Black Tuesday." A high rate of black layoffs and subsequent unemployment indicated that a downward spiral in the economy appeared imminent.[1] Few black or white middle class Americans paid attention to these indicators. Since most African Americans remained on the periphery of regular, gainful employment within the larger American economy, hard times visited upon blacks had little consequence for anyone other than those low-income blacks who suffered grievously from poverty.

African American newspapers failed to mention the "Crash" or offer readers insight about the gravity of the economic crisis. Black newspapers in Chicago, Los Angeles, and Philadelphia presented readers with routine news without any discussion about issues that panicked white Americans. The front-page headline appearing in Robert Abbott's *Chicago Defender* immediately after the "Crash" [November 2, 1929] only mentioned the indictment of the African American Bishop, A. J. Carey. In Los Angeles, editor J. B. Bass of the *California Eagle* gave primacy to Moorfield Storey's death and the appearance of "Rising Tenor" Louis Sharp scheduled to appear at the Beaux Arts Theatre [November 1, 1929]. Editor Eugene Rhodes of the *Philadelphia Tribune*, unlike fellow editors, recognized that an economic downturn had occurred but only made the observation in the December 4, 1929 edition of the paper. African American publishers and editors knew their audience did not invest in stocks and therefore had little reason to discuss "the white man's problem." Despite significant strides African American leaders made to eliminate the "color line," the absence of discussion about "Black Tuesday" and its aftermath revealed the blacks and whites existed within two distinct, segregated societies.

By January 1, 1930, African Americans discovered, to their chagrin, the meaning of an economic depression and the hardships that accrue to those caught up in the vortex of a sinking economy. Every black socioeconomic class became affected. Since black professionals served the African American masses and relied upon this clientele for income, unemployment among the masses directly affected the solvency of the black elite. Logically an impoverished black majority contributed to the impecunious condition of the black professional class. Therefore, local affiliates of the National Urban League, in cooperation with the black presses, churches, and organizations from Akron, Toledo, Chicago, Cleveland, Detroit, New

York, Philadelphia, and other cities, endeavored to find gainful employment for the black masses.[2] If the Negro press failed to stress the significance of an economic depression, personal experiences of black readers could attest to the realization of a failed economy that impinged severely upon their personal life and threatened their very survival.

The severity of the depression and its impact upon black leadership could be observed first and foremost in New York City's Harlem, center of the black intelligentsia. In 1927, 2,000 African American families received relief from the municipal government. But three years later 18,000 additional families were placed on the dole.[3] Evidently the only positives gleaned from the sufferings of African Americans in the "Big Apple" existed in the locale of the National Urban League. With the NUL headquartered in New York, local blacks had close proximity to the organization that best understood the plight of disadvantaged blacks and could make immediate steps to mitigate hardships.

More than any other organization or leadership group, officials in the National Urban League established, as a priority, the enhancement of living conditions for migrants recently from the South and assisting other low income African Americans desiring work in industrial cities. To combat impending economic doom, black leaders within the NUL worked assiduously to find employment for the black masses. When the depression initially struck, this dedicated group recognized the difficulty of finding work for unskilled black laborers and launched the Vocational Opportunity Campaign [VOC], a training program designed to improve the marketable skills of the black unemployed. Through the [VOC] the League also endeavored to secure gainful employment for black artisans, but unknown to urban league planners, times had changed. African Americans who embraced vocational education since the era of Booker T. Washington now recognized that industrial training had become passé. Consequently, the NUL's vocational campaign met with hostility from the black middle class—a trend that would appear consistently throughout the decade.

Unlike National Urban League leaders in New York, the better classes of blacks in other cities began to demonstrate coolness toward the NUL objective of training the masses. Evidence that vocational education no longer held relevance for middle class blacks of the depression era appeared in Richmond, Virginia. Located less than 100 miles from Hampton Institute, the birthplace of training for black artisans and Booker T. Washington's alma mater, an appreciation for industrial education had extended to Richmond's white elite. But when trustees of the Julius

Rosenwald Fund, with encouragement from the NUL, offered to build an industrial school in the former capital of the Confederacy, Richmond's Board of Education vetoed the offer. The Board bowed to pressure from black leaders who "tabooed" the idea.[4]

Undeterred by the Richmond rebuff, the NUL continued to press its Vocational Opportunity Campaign. By April 1931, Industrial Secretary T. Arnold Hill and Executive Secretary Eugene Kinkle Jones encouraged 50 cities and 177 employers to endorse the program. The League offered 164 seminars attended by more than 50,000 people. However between 1932 and 1935, the League suspended VOC because of lack of funding needed to sustain staff and prepare meetings for instituting the program, and because of lagging middle class interest in training the poor. Why worry about the poor, the black bourgeoisie reasoned, when faced with their own destitution?

Nevertheless, the NUL hierarchy persisted in working to uplift the race from dire economic straits. More than any other African American civil rights organization of the 1920s, the Urban League focused on economic discrimination that impinged on black communities throughout the nation.[5] The NUL knew of bigotry among white employers, unions, and local governments. Desperation caused by the economic downturn caused frustrated NUL leaders to identify the source of black poverty and acknowledge publicly that the American Federation of Labor held a decided bias toward African Americans. Therefore, Industrial Secretary Hill assumed the responsibility for pressing vigorously to secure work for blacks. He wrote to every state governor and to the Secretaries of Agriculture and Interior in the Hoover Administration to obtain public work for jobless African Americans.

Almost immediately after the Great Depression commenced, NUL Executive Secretary Eugene Kinkle Jones recognized the importance of having blacks appointed to relief boards. Both Jones and Hill targeted the President's Organization of Unemployment Relief as the key to acquiring equal welfare distribution for African Americans. Jones and Hill urged President Hoover to appoint an African American to the unemployment committee. Their efforts enabled John W. Davis, President of West Virginia State College, to gain an appointment to the Committee on Administration of Relief. This endeavor established a pattern that would be applied—and with considerable success—when Franklin Delano Roosevelt became president of the United States. When Roosevelt instituted his first

New Deal, Hill insisted that blacks be placed on the Industrial, Labor, and Consumers Advisory Boards.[6]

Jones' hard work paid dividends when Roosevelt took office. Probably the highlight of Jones' professional career occurred when he received a presidential appointment to serve as Advisor on Negro Affairs in the Department of Commerce. During his tenure at Commerce, Jones performed outstanding service as a federal "insider." By May, 1936 Jones helped place 50 African Americans to high ranking positions within the Roosevelt Administration. Jones himself participated in conferences that addressed African Americans in reference to crime, child welfare, relief, education, homesteads, and NRA violations.[7] It was also through the role of Negro Advisor that Jones, along with Clark Foreman of the Interior Department and Robert C. Weaver, Foreman's assistant, created the nucleus for the formation of the Black Cabinet, an informal advisory group to FDR.

As the acting Executive Secretary in Jones' absence, T. Arnold Hill also performed admirably. As a member of Alpha Phi Alpha Fraternity and fellow graduate of Jones' Alma Mater, Virginia Union, school and fraternity ties made Hill a natural selection as Jones' understudy. Hill made the best of his opportunity by establishing the Emergency Advisory Councils for Negro Workers [EAC], one of the most important selfless endeavors instituted during his tenure as the NUL acting Executive Secretary. Designed to keep blacks cognizant of their rights by acting as advisory agencies, the EAC empowered blacks to take advantage of liberal New Deal policies. To accomplish this end, the organization distributed handbooks to inform the masses about processes used to combat racism practiced by governmental agencies. The handbook listed contacts for public works jobs, revealed how to access federally financed home loans, and cited the steps necessary for acquiring benefits in New Deal programs like the AAA, PWA, NRA, CCC, and TVA. The EAC also served as a mechanism for applying pressure to combat racism practiced by white dominated trade unions. Through the EAC Hill approached Frances Perkins, FDR's Secretary of Labor, to enlist support in the fight against "lily white" union shops. As a black labor lobbying association, the EAC made headway within the African American community. By December 1933, Hill and the NUL were able to establish 196 EAC chapters in 32 states and the District of Columbia.[8] However, the paucity of resources caused by the depression would challenge the ability of Hill and his EAC to fulfill its mandate to help black workers.

The EAC required funding to carry out its objectives. Hill made a direct appeal to the black bourgeoisie for assistance. Given the dire circumstances of middle class blacks, his appeals for support fell on deaf ears. Middle class blacks would no longer think exclusively about encouraging whites to end segregation, respect the humanity of their race, or stress advancement for all African Americans. Instead, the black higher classes and their spokespersons would concentrate upon issues that directly impacted their friends, family, and status.[9] The EAC's desperate financial straits forced Hill to cancel the annual conference of 1933. Three years later the NUL terminated all council activities. While hardly surprising that the depression forced virtually every social service organization to engage in some kind of retrenchment, the demise of the EAC precipitated a diminution of black altruism toward fellow African Americans. Black professionals did not even pretend to harbor an interest in the masses. A disillusioned T. Arnold Hill declared:

> The needs of black Americans demanded the support of that large group of business and professional men who have controlled neither their money nor their intelligence on behalf of these basic factors involved in the adjustment of race relations. It is with difficulty that the National Urban League, with its prestige, its long years of service and practiced program, can secure a thousand dollars from Negroes on any issue. The amount of money and time consumed in raising such an amount equals in money the amount of cash received. Our experience in getting the Emergency Council for Negroes organized ... and in keeping them busy when once organized, is a sad commentary on the willingness of Negroes to support a program which they themselves admit is necessary.[10]

The callous indifference to EAC activities exhibited from those who had long benefited from efforts of the National Urban League would prove exceedingly disappointing. The frustrated Hill possibly reached the nadir of his trust in the "so called" responsible elite when former Fellows of the NUL turned their back on the EAC. Since nearly the turn of the century, the NUL provided professional training and support for scores of aspiring African Americans. But when asked to provide funding for the Emergency Advisory Councils, former fellows contributed a total of $130.87.[11] From the era of the Great Depression forward, black leadership placed middle class interests before the welfare of the race. The response to the needs of the EAC represented a significant change in the direction taken by African American leadership.

Despite being abandoned by the black elite, the NUL continued working to improve conditions for black workers. Recognizing that the black middle class would not help, Hill decided to establish a "federation of workers," a concept designed to raise the consciousness of working class blacks who would draw upon their own strength for solidarity, support, employment, and upward mobility. The NUL established an all black "Committee of One Hundred" to oversee the newly created Workers' Councils. The energetic Lester B. Granger became the NUL official chosen to head the new program.

Lester Blackwell Granger seemed an unlikely candidate for leadership. Born in Newport News, Virginia in 1895, Granger spent his formative years in Newark, New Jersey and became identified as the "black sheep" of the family. The elder Granger and his wife, a physician and public school teacher respectively, were disappointed with their youngest child; five older brothers had become doctors or dentists. Nevertheless, the younger Granger possessed sufficient academic prowess to matriculate to Dartmouth College. After receiving his baccalaureate, Granger earned a commission in the army, and after World War I, became the Industrial Secretary of the New Jersey Urban League where he found employment for returning black veterans. During the late "teens" and early "twenties," Granger served as director of extension work in Bordentown, New Jersey, and as the Executive Secretary of the Los Angeles NUL chapter. Granger returned to New York to become business manager for *Opportunity* magazine and eventually headed the NUL's Workers' Bureau.[12] This latter position enabled Granger to establish his reputation as a dedicated civil rights advocate.

Fearless and committed, Granger traveled throughout the nation in an effort to organize black laborers. Granger ventured south at risk to his life. White racists who were aware of his efforts intended to lynch him. Although Granger's activities north of the Mason Dixon line carried less life-threatening risks, he acquired few kudos from black peers. As Granger recalled: "Blacks—middle class businessmen, white collar workers, civil servants—opposed this activity because they saw the unions as the natural enemy of black workers."[13] By the end of 1936 Granger had organized 73 Workers' Councils. Unfortunately, these successes would be short lived. The NUL decided to continue concentrating on vocational education. But in response to pressures from the fearful African American middle class, black leaders sought secure civil service jobs primarily for the black bourgeoisie.[14] Only efforts of the Communist Party of the United States

[CPUSA] prevented black leadership from eschewing entirely concern for the African American masses.

Like the NAACP and National Urban League, the genesis for communism in relation to African American leadership evolved from efforts instituted by altruistic white men and women. Idealistic rather than wealthy, and intellectual ideologues rather than "noblesse oblige" devotees, whites who belonged to the CPUSA would eventually risk life and limb on behalf of African Americans. With the zealousness of the martyred John Brown, the communists ventured forth using every means necessary to free oppressed blacks from the shackles of white racism. In capitalistic America, communism, an ideology that emphasized the righteousness of the worker over the industrialist, was anathema. Moreover, communism, as espoused by Russian Bolsheviks, advocated international revolution and the destruction of western capitalism. Their messianic fervor instilled Americans with a loathing for unions and an organized working class.[15] The CPUSA would face considerable obstacles in its effort to gain African American converts to a European ideology conceived by the German, Karl Marx, and disseminated to the West at the direction of Russian visionaries like Vladimir Ulianov [Lenin]. Nevertheless, historians Philip S. Foner and Herbert Shapiro frankly acknowledge that "despite all of its weaknesses ... the Communist Party of the United States occupied the vanguard position in the entire country on the crucial issue of African American liberation.[16]

In September 1919 the first "Program of the Communist Party" mentioned the political, economic and racial oppression of Negroes as something that should be addressed. Under the guise of the Trade Union Educational League, the CPUSA adopted a policy to "bore from within" and gain inroads into the black organizational structure. After finding the NAACP hostile to CPUSA entreaties, the Party founded the American Negro Labor Congress [ANLC] in October, 1925 and selected James W. Ford to head the organization. Under Ford's direction the ANLC endeavored to infiltrate the black labor movement through the Brotherhood of Sleeping Car Porters. Randolph, a dedicated Socialist, viewed communism as an enemy ideology. He protected the BSCP from communist incursions but had little cause for worry. Porters, for the most part, were middle class conservatives; initial forays to wrest leadership from Randolph failed.[17]

Encouraged rather than daunted by the inability of the CPUSA to play a dominant role in directing the black masses, the Communist Party's concern for African Americans began in earnest during the Fourth Congress of the Communist International held in Moscow in 1922. At this time Otto

Huiswoud introduced the "Negro Question" before the delegates when he served as chairman of the Negro Commission. Huiswoud was joined by fellow black Americans Claude McKay and Richard B. Moore of Harlem. The efforts of Huiswoud and McKay caused the gathering to identify the Negro problem as "a vital question of the world revolution, and tied the world struggle of the Negro race to the struggle against capitalism and imperialism.[18] Dogmatic communists recognized that African Americans who comprised a large, visible working class were ripe for recruitment and thereby became "potential allies of the revolutionary proletariat." To realize the International's goal, members of the CPUSA decided upon multiple strategies to ingratiate themselves with black Americans. They attacked all manifestations of racism, voiced specific objections to racial discrimination in trade unions, and supported the black working class at the expense of the black bourgeoisie.[19] In order to promote the hegemony of the black worker over the African American middle class, members of the CPUSA saw a need to recruit, promote, and place blacks in responsible positions within the Party.

As early as 1929, the CPUSA elected African Americans to influential committees within the Party, selected a black district organizer, and established a Negro Commission with a black man—Otto Huiswoud—as the director. These aggressive actions contributed to the increase of black party members from approximately 200 in March 1929, to some 1,300 the following year. By identifying unemployment, lynching, racial discrimination, and supporting defenseless blacks, the CPUSA established the League of Struggle for Negro Rights in Harlem. It also acquired support from nationally renowned poet Langston Hughes, who became the League's first president.[20]

During the Great Depression, the CPUSA would use race, class, and any means necessary to heighten their Party's possibilities for success among African Americans. In order for their ideology to gain credence within the black community, the Communist Party decided to discredit the NAACP and National Urban League. By attacking the middle class orientation of these venerable agencies, party members endeavored to convince the unemployed masses that the only people sincerely committed to their well being belonged to the CPUSA. To promote an identity with the lower class, party members organized mass demonstrations against municipal and state agencies. The CPUSA also received notoriety by organizing rent strikes on behalf of black tenants. In these instances communists willingly resorted to violence to prevent landlords from forcibly evicting tenants. With daring and elan bordering on fanaticism, communists accused black leaders in established organizations of lacking aggressiveness. Contemptuously, the communists labeled traditional black leaders as "misleaders" and "Judases."[21]

A murder trial celebrated as the Scottsboro Boys case propelled the Communist Party into prominence within the African American community. In the spring of 1931 nine innocent young black males ranging in age from 14 to 20 were wrongly accused of raping two white women in a railroad car located near Scottsboro, Alabama. After an all-white jury convicted every defendant, sentencing eight to death and the youngest to life imprisonment, the Communist Party entered the fray. With support from the International Labor Defense [ILD]—legal arm of the American communists—the CPUSA gained a stay of execution, acquired national and international support for the defendants, and received praise from the larger African American community. Previously unknown black communists like William L. Patterson, National Secretary of the ILD, James W. Ford, CPUSA national Vice Presidential nominee, and Benjamin Davis, Jr., a prominent attorney with Morehouse, Amherst, and Harvard credentials who defended the party faithful, acquired the opportunity to rival conservative black leaders and their organizations. Walter White realized that communist advocacy on behalf of the Scottsboro Boys placed the primacy of the NAACP as legal defender of African American rights in jeopardy. Though the National Association worked jointly with the CPUSA and helped the Scottsboro Boys eventually gain freedom, the case enabled American communists to rival the black establishment and enhance the Party's role as leaders devoted to liberating African Americans from racism and capitalistic exploitation.

Communist radicalism forced conservative black leaders into more aggressive action as representatives of their race. Committed to improving life for laborers generally and poor blacks specifically, members of the CPUSA ventured into the "deep South" at the risk of death to organize black laborers, sharecroppers, and farmers. To retain their influence as African American leaders, black spokespersons became more inclined to adopt a more radical and comprehensive stance toward achieving racial amelioration.

Among the first blacks of some stature to gravitate toward left-wing politics was the Washington, D.C. native, John P. Davis. Davis emulated the aggressiveness evidenced by the Communist Party and founded an organization that personified the apogee of unified race leadership. The organization, known as the National Negro Congress [NNC], would represent the most concerted effort of black leadership to address every conceivable problem concerning African Americans. In 1935 Davis published and distributed 65,000 pamphlets entitled, "Let Us Build a NATIONAL NEGRO CONGRESS." This 31 page disquisition explained the reasons for establishing the NNC. It described the fledgling Congress' objectives and invited established secular and religious organizations to attend the first national conference, a meeting held in Chicago on February 14, 1936.[22]

The initial convention proved successful when 817 delegates, representing 27 states and the District of Columbia answered Davis' "Call." Lester B. Granger and T. Arnold Hill of the National Urban League; Augustus Hawkins of the California Legislature; B.B. McKinney, Vice-President of the Southern Tenant Farmers Union; and Rufus Atwood, President of Kentucky State College were included among the conferees. The NAACP also sent delegates. Snow Grigsby, President of the Detroit chapter and Arthur Huff Fauset (author Jesse Fauset's younger sibling) of Philadelphia represented their respective chapters, and Marian Cuthbert attended on behalf of the National Office. Conservative religious leaders and radicals from the CPUSA went to Chicago as well. The Congress' future looked promising when the diverse array of delegates elected A. Philip Randolph, President, John P. Davis, Executive Secretary, and honored the NAACP by selecting Miss Cuthbert as the NNC's National Treasurer.

In the business meeting delegates discussed methods for attaining NNC objectives. They debated issues ranging from the right of "Negroes to jobs," "aid to the Negro farm population," and the "fight against lynching (and) mob violence," to "complete equality for Negro women." Delegates also passed several resolutions. They voiced the black community's objection to the Italian invasion of Ethiopia; and in a precedent-setting declaration, demanded that black churches engage in social action to support and protect African Americans. The strong contingent of black and white communists encouraged delegates to oppose "war and fascism" and advocated extension of the United States neutrality act.[23] However, the most promising goal holding the greatest prospect for success was something African American leaders alone could achieve—the attainment of racial unity. To enable blacks to survive the existing economic crisis, the NNC stated: "By unity of action we can create a nation-wide public opinion which will force real consideration from public officials, such as no single organization can hope to muster."[24] After being briefed about the NNC convention, Roy Wilkins, Assistant Secretary of the NAACP, concurred with prospects for unified leadership. On behalf of the Association Wilkins declared: "... all the objectives set up by the Congress are the objectives of the NAACP ... it would be better for the Association to be a participant.... It seems to me that the only way we can see that this remains the objective is to go in and have a voice in the making of policies."[25] Given the success of the initial convention, prospects for the second National Negro Congress convention destined for Philadelphia in 1937 seemed promising.

The Philadelphia Conference contained enthusiastic delegates energized and optimistic about the race's future. The Philadelphia organizing committee headed by educator Arthur Huff Fauset, in conjunction with the national officers, prepared an outstanding program. From Friday, October 15 through Sunday the 18th, a comprehensive agenda stressing social, economic, religious, secular, political, educational, and regional issues commanded the attention of those in attendance. Every significant black organization sent representatives. Presenters and delegates participated in seminars about many aspects of African American life. Discussions concerning youth, the church, trade unions, civil liberties, rural living, unemployment, health, housing, women, fraternal organizations, education, the foreign born, and culture provided delegates with information on the current condition of the black race.[26]

African American leaders had reason for being sanguine about their ability to work collectively for a better future. James W. Ford, one of the ranking black communists said: "We Communists desire to do everything possible in building and broadening the movement of the Negro people in cooperation with the NAACP, the National Negro Congress, the Urban League, and other organizations."[27] As the organization most critical of black leadership, Ford's words represented a sincere quest for black unification. Despite Ford's encouraging words, inter-organizational suspicion and the doctrinaire positions of the International adopted by the Communist Party in America brought about the demise of the NNC, and forever threatened the legitimacy of a leftist ideology—concern about the lower class elements of the race—in the pursuit of civil rights.

Seeds for dissension existed among organizations that formed the NNC coalition at the inception of the Congress. Amherst College and Harvard Law graduate Charles H. Houston, the NAACP's lead counsel, voiced his reservations about African-Americans who would support the NNC. With a sense of hauteur expected from an accomplished Harvard man, Houston stated: "From what I can figure out of the persons paying most attention to the Congress are the emotional beings who go off in sympathy for anything labeled Negro progress ... chiefly a lot of second-string folk...."[28] The ever cautious Walter White informed Randolph that a scheduling conflict made it impossible for him to attend the Chicago conference. White then voiced an admonition to Randolph about the NNC, adding: "I do hope the Congress is not permitted to be 'sold down the river' to any political [Communist] group." Randolph informed White not to despair, declaring: "... so far as I have any power, the Congress will not be 'sold down the river...."[29] Events would demonstrate that Randolph was far too trusting and naive.

Soon after the Philadelphia convention ended, American Communists decided that the NNC could be used effectively to gain influence over the black proletariat. They encouraged the NNC to renew the fight against lynching. Skeptical and suspicious of NNC motives, Walter White informed Fauset that the NNC's anti-lynching campaign duplicated efforts of the NAACP. White's concerns about NNC intentions increased when John P. Davis asked the NAACP's Executive Secretary to issue calls to National Association Branches to rally support for two anti-lynching Congressional bills. Davis' appeal went unheeded. Regardless of the earnestness of the cause and the significance of issues raised, White never allowed the NAACP to act at the behest of any other organization.[30]

Events proved NAACP doubts about prospects for NNC success justified. Arthur Huff Fauset, president of the Philadelphia Council of the NNC and arguably the organization's most ardent member, observed that communists had attained control of important subcommittees and held key positions in the NNC hierarchy. Alarmed, Fauset informed Randolph about communist infiltration and encouraged the NNC president to purge the organization of "Fellow Travelers."[31] Randolph ignored the admonition. Although promising Walter White he would be vigilant in regard to the CPUSA, Randolph waited far too long to control fanatical members of the Communist Party. Consequently, a disillusioned Arthur Fauset resigned from the National Negro Congress.

Unlike other black organizations that declined because of internecine fighting, the NNC's demise could be attributed primarily to discord generated by whites with the assistance from black leftist Max Yergan.[32] Though instrumental in promoting the NNC, the white communist contingent undermined the organization. These whites, like others befriending African Americans, succumbed to the accepted racist norms mandating that white people were ordained to control and lead blacks. Communist attempts to dominate sessions at NNC conventions, gain key positions on local councils, and dominate the national board deeply alienated black middle class leaders. Proud members of the black bourgeoisie resented communist paternalism. People like Fauset and eventually Randolph, who placed greater emphasis on organizational goals and objectives than the means for attaining success, were destined to become frustrated and disappointed.

The demise of the National Negro Congress as a viable, coalescing civil rights organization had far reaching implications on the future direction of black leadership. The first inkling of a shift in focus occurred when the NNC forced A. Philip Randolph into the awkward role of eschewing radicalism. As a leftist who strongly identified with the working class and who devoted his life to aiding the African American masses, Randolph maintained a profound trust in those who held similar principles. Since most middle class black leaders were conservative, opposed unions, and maintained a superior air in relation to disadvantaged African Americans, Randolph found the alliance with white communists convenient. Moreover, his fame enticed members of the conservative, black "old guard" into the NNC. Strong-willed, egotistical, idealistic, and pleased that the organization selected him as president—though Randolph held reservations about the scores of communists entrenched within the NNC—he seemed to be taken in by the potential advantages to be gained from a unified front against racism. He sincerely believed that conservatives and liberals, Jews and Gentiles, and blacks and whites could join hands and fight collectively for the rights of African Americans. This explained his reluctance to act when warning signs of communist manipulation appeared.

The ramifications of Randolph's "blind eye" in relation to communists caused the black middle class to terminate its momentary flirtation with the left and feel justified in their persistent cautious, conservatism. They would continue distrusting liberal or radical proposals designed to uplift African Americans. Only Randolph's "popularity and cult of personality" prevented an earlier schism between the black bourgeoisie and communists within the NNC.[33] Furthermore, the collapse of the NNC raised additional questions. Dogmatic behavior displayed by members of the CPUSA cast doubts on the sincerity of white radicals to further the African American cause.

An irrevocable breach between the black middle class and the Communist Party, in regard to the NNC, commenced in the summer of 1939. Obedient to the direction of leadership in Moscow, American communists who now controlled the NNC betrayed black leadership and abandoned the African-American community. When the Soviet Union signed the Molotov-Ribbentrop non-aggression pact with Germany in August 1939, members of the CPUSA supported the Russian alliance with Germany and attacked Roosevelt's pro-Allied stance against the NAZIS. But more significantly for African Americans, the CPUSA encouraged blacks to forgo civil rights and follow the dictates of Moscow. This reversal by the communists undermined the credibility of the NNC, alienated the African American majority who supported Roosevelt, and made Randolph appear a duped puppet.

Still oblivious of communist treachery, Randolph addressed the third NNC Conference in April 1940 and absolved the organization of being a communist front. When communist backed resolutions which had little relevance for African Americans received approval at the convention, Randolph eventually realized that the CPUSA controlled his beloved National Negro Congress. Only then did Randolph refuse to stand for reelection as the NNC president. Now angry and embittered, Randolph verbalized his distrust for white people when he said: "The American Negro will not long follow any organization that accepts dictation and control from any white organization."[34] Fortunately for Randolph, the stature he acquired as a leader of the common people remained strong; this enabled him to retain the adulation of an adoring African American public.

Randolph's disenchantment with NNC politics ended the coalescence of African American organizations. Without his support the NNC was doomed. However, reasons for the NNC's dissolution could not be placed entirely on the communists, organizational jealousies, or the political epiphany of Randolph. Even before the inception of the NNC, trends had been developing that suggested intra-racial harmony could not prevail. Efforts of the National Urban League, NAACP, and National Negro Congress to develop comprehensive strategies to ameliorate the African American condition under the guise of racial unity were tenuous and short-lived. Class differences within the race were too vast to bridge. Equally important, bitterness related to the demise of the National Negro Congress made future prospects for unifying distinctly different African American groups virtually impossible.

With the inception of the New Deal, the need to protect, defend, and aid African Americans under one leader, organization, or philosophy ended. By 1936, the responsibility of caring for the entire African American race shifted from the shoulders of black leaders and organizations to the federal government. Northern black leaders, particularly, endeavored to encourage the government to treat African Americans with greater beneficence. Since the New Deal coalition demanded the retention of black voters, African American leaders pressured Roosevelt New Dealers to provide welfare and jobs for indigent members of the race. Largess necessary for black survival required enormous efforts on the part of concerned black leaders. Historian Raymond Wolters found that regionalism dictated whether or not destitute blacks would receive ample federal assistance.[35] This realization proved particularly true in the South where restrictive racial codes eliminated blacks from welfare rolls and forced destitute African Americans into starvation. Inequities notwithstanding, the sense of responsibility the Roosevelt Administration had for assisting all Americans "trickled down" to the nation's black citizenry. Desperation that drove disparate black organizations to coalesce under the NNC banner would abate somewhat owing to the expanded role of government in the lives of average African Americans.

Mary McLeod Bethune emerged as one of the most adroit black leaders capable of appealing to the federal government to assist African Americans. Born on July 10, 1875 near Maysville, South Carolina as the 15th of 17 children, young Mary McLeod entered a proud but impoverished family. Despite her hardscrabble background—her parents were former slaves—Mary McLeod gained the opportunity to attend Trinity Presbyterian Mission School, Scotia Seminary, and Dwight Moody's Chicago based Institute for Home and Foreign Missions. During these formative years she acquired Victorian principles and Christian values, qualities which served as the foundation and catalysts for her life's work as a humanitarian, civil rights activists, and leader. In 1898 she married Albertus Bethune, moved to Daytona, Florida, and in 1904, founded the Daytona Industrial and Educational Institute for Negro Girls. During the first two decades of the century, Mary McLeod Bethune worked tirelessly to establish the Institute by serving chicken dinners, arranging for student recitals featuring Negro Spirituals, and enlisting support from white philanthropists. Her dedication made the school solvent. By 1923 she had created a debt free institution with property valued at $250,000 which instructed more than 300 students. That same year her school merged with Cookman Institute in Jacksonville to create Bethune-Cookman College, a coeducational institution dedicated to training young African American men and women.

Bethune's prowess as an educator and social activist grew, enabling her to acquire respect and name recognition from leading national politicians.

Bethune initially gained fame when she served as president of the Florida Federation of Colored Women's Clubs in 1917. By 1924 she became president of the National Association of Colored Women [NACW], the highest national position attained by an African American female. During her tenure as president she worked cooperatively with white women to benefit blacks, initiated the eradication of segregation in women's organizations, and established a national headquarters for NACW in Washington, D.C. By the early 1930s, the perseverance and positive attitude she displayed to keep Bethune-Cookman in operation, while simultaneously raising its academic standards and acting as a guiding force in a myriad of organizations, provided inspiration to many dispirited African Americans. In 1935 she received the Spingarn Medal, the highest award granted by the NAACP. With this accolade Mary McLeod Bethune firmly established herself as the foremost African-American female in the United States.

Although this formidable woman garnered many successes as a college president and head of the most prominent black women's organizations, Bethune's crowning achievement occurred when she served as director of the Negro Division of the National Youth Administration. From this lofty position Bethune became the titular head of the Federal Council of Negro Affairs, or the Black Cabinet, a group comprising some 30 influential African American appointees serving in the Roosevelt Administration. Under her direction, these black New Dealers functioned effectively as bureaucrats laboring on behalf of the African American majority. With Bethune's initiative and support from the Black Cabinet, a federally sponsored National Conference on the Problems of the Negro and Negro Youth occurred on January 6-8, 1937 at the Department of Labor. The Conference addressed and offered recommendations to resolve problems dealing with security and legal protection, health and housing conditions, educational and recreational opportunities, and economic issues ranging from the termination of discrimination in all branches of the federal government and social security to decent wages for black employees.[36]

The work of Mary McLeod Bethune and the Black Cabinet had far reaching consequences for subsequent African American leaders and the black majority whom they served. The harsh economic conditions visited upon all Americans during the Great Depression fostered public reliance on the federal government for survival. This reality became particularly telling for African Americans who—unlike whites who used New Deal programs as "stop-gap" measures—had needs that made them entirely dependent upon federal relief. This development meant that the government, rather than black leaders, would be looked upon to assume responsibility for the impoverished black majority.

While black leaders continued promoting human rights for African Americans, the depression directed them toward a different responsibility. Black leaders now found themselves functioning as advocates for government largess. Through the good offices of Bethune and other black leaders, demands were made for equitable distribution of welfare and equal access to federal work relief jobs. Their efforts would prove productive. The federal government accepted responsibility for providing the masses with the means for survival, but ironically, black leadership's success as a pressure group also enabled them to abdicate their role as leaders of the entire race. With the basic needs of the masses provided for by the federal government, black leaders began focusing exclusively on improving conditions for the black bourgeoisie.[37] From this period forward, black leadership represented middle class interests far more than the concerns of the African American majority.

Black leadership's focus on class rather than race interests evolved naturally. Early signs of this change occurred between 1930 and 1932. The black press, for example, placed more emphasis on finding work for white-collar than blue-collar workers. In Philadelphia, black newspaper editors of the *Tribune* and the *Independent* shifted their papers' emphasis from demanding jobs for "anyone who wants work" to stressing employment for specific "respectable" positions—judges, librarians, police officers, firefighters, school board members, and supervisors.[38] Leadership's shift from race to class evolved in other cities as well. In Harlem the National Urban League documented the plight of black professionals when it discovered that 60 percent of the African American physicians in Harlem required relief to survive.[39] Therefore if black physicians in Harlem, the "Mecca of the African American elite," faced a doubtful existence, the plight of African American professionals elsewhere would be exceedingly dire. Black professionals responded to the Great Depression with a single mindedness that would ensure the survival of the black middle class. The shock of facing destitution proved more than the hard-working black bourgeoisie could bear without focusing entirely on personal middle class interests.

Civil Rights organizations like the National Urban League reflected the altered focus within black leadership that deviated from the broader aspects of race consciousness to concentrate on middle class concerns. For example the aforementioned black bourgeoisie's indifference to the NUL's vocational training proposal, and the League's inability to obtain financial support from the African American elite underscored the declining support for the impoverished masses. National Urban League leaders recognized these changes and directed attention toward "friendly" middle class activities like the long established "Negro and Civic League" clean block campaign that occurred annually in St. Louis. League officials would join the ranks of others looking increasingly to agencies within the Federal Government to care for the African American masses.[40]

Leaders within the NAACP pursued a course similar to that of the National Urban League. This shift in emphasis could be observed in the diminished role Du Bois played in the Association's affairs. Du Bois believed that racial solidarity, self-help, and the concept of group economy would lift African Americans from the throes of depression. In a major departure from long held integrationist beliefs, Du Bois now believed the exigencies of the times dictated the acceptance of segregation. Through mutual support efforts he decided to use racial discrimination advantageously to advance the black economy. To accomplish these ends, Du Bois recognized that the higher black classes would have to become more race conscious, eliminate hauteur directed toward the masses, and eschew their unequivocal acceptance of white values and culture.[41] This would prove a daunting task since, as Du Bois observed, "the younger and more prosperous Negro professional men ... were clinging to the older ideals of property, ownership, and profits even more firmly than the whites...."[42] Du Bois also noticed that "The Association had attracted the higher income group of colored people, who regarded it as a weapon to attack the sort of social discrimination which especially irked them; rather than as an organization to improve the status and power of the whole Negro group."[43] With his separatist inclinations and critical stance against bourgeois values, Du Bois found himself at odds with the NAACP hierarchy. Views printed in *The Crisis* favoring segregation, coupled with personal conflicts with Walter White (Du Bois declared that the blond and blue eyed White was actually a white man) and Roy Wilkins resulted in Du Bois' resignation as *Crisis* editor and departure from the NAACP in 1934.[44] A great voice speaking on behalf of the African American masses had become muted.

Du Bois' admonition about black leadership's growing obsession with class interests over race consciousness would prove prophetic. Given the economic pressures middle class blacks experienced during the 1930s, economic security became a priority for those of higher station.

The decline of black leadership's concern with race and the decided stress on promoting middle class interests emerged almost simultaneously with the application of New Deal policies. Since the only proper and relatively secure jobs available to the black middle class during the Great Depression existed in the federal government, the black elite acquired knowledge about fledgling New Deal jobs and eagerly filled those positions. Opportunities created by liberal New Dealers enabled African Americans to gain positions in municipal, state, and federal boards and agencies. These opportunities enabled the black bourgeoisie to maintain its lofty position in black society, assure its continuation as a viable class, and elevate its socioeconomic status in the larger American society. Thanks to the New Deal middle class blacks acquired positions of authority and re- sponsibility that assured the black bourgeoisie's survival.

Since hardships created by the Great Depression proved to be a leveler of society, black leaders recognized an opportunity existed to promote the integration of African Americans of stature into mainstream society. One means for attaining this objective appeared through efforts designed to upgrade black living conditions. Most urban blacks were confined to living in black ghettoes. Because African American leaders resided in the African American community, aesthetic improvements in black occupied housing became imperative. As early as December 1931 a blue ribbon committee of African Americans headed by Nannie H. Burroughs of Washington, D.C. endeavored to ameliorate housing conditions for black Americans.

Like Mary McLeod Bethune, Burroughs used the federal government in her crusade to assist members of her race. Born in Orange, Virginia in 1879 to John and Jennie (Poindexter) Burroughs, Nannie Helen Burroughs came to maturity in Washington, D.C. She studied at the M Street School where she came under the influence of Mary Church Terrell and Anna J. Cooper. She also became affiliated with the Nineteenth Street Baptist Church and developed an interest in helping low income black women and empowering them to fight for social justice. As one of the founders of the women's movement in the National Baptist Convention, Burroughs diligently worked for racial and gender equity. A brilliant orator, member of the Urban League and NAACP, and founder of the National League of Republican Colored Women, Burroughs' visibility propelled her into a national celebrity. As chair of President Hoover's housing committee, Burroughs presented the housing needs of African Americans in a book published in 1932 entitled, "Negro Housing Report on the Committee on

Negro Housing." The report spoke generically of housing conditions for the entire black community.

The Burroughs report served as only the precursor to several housing studies on blacks undertaken during the New Deal. All were designed to address and rectify poor housing conditions existing within the black community. In cities ranging from Omaha and Richmond to Chicago, Washington, and New York, black leaders investigated and sought to improve black housing conditions.[45] Studies on black housing eventually bore fruit, providing Burroughs and other influential African American leaders with sufficient clout to acquire positions on municipal housing boards. Throughout the decade these representatives had responsibility for determining that new housing units were constructed for black occupancy.

Black leadership's interest in housing reform served several purposes beyond sheltering impoverished African Americans. First, by acquiring positions on municipal housing boards, black leaders gained visibility and, in turn, respect from white peers. The opportunity to work jointly with influential whites helped middle class blacks remove the stigma of racial inferiority and provided a foundation for future inter-racial discourse. A second advantage derived from blacks gaining seats on housing boards occurred when African American representatives directed funds to host excursions into the black community. Through "Reconciliation Trips" (a name given to these excursions in Philadelphia), prominent African Americans entertained white peers visiting selected neighborhoods to enable them to observe lifestyles of the black elite. Third, by determining where money for housing reform would be spent in the African American community, black leaders enhanced the aesthetics of black neighborhoods. And finally, African American housing administrators preyed upon the fears of whites who sought to keep the wealthier blacks confined to black neighborhoods. These fears enabled black board members to channel funds to "the upper level of Negroes;" the recipients subsequently upgraded their personal property and lived comfortably in the black community.[46]

In order to acquire or sustain government largess, black leaders had to make certain that African Americans capable of voting remained active in the national political process to ensure the black bourgeoisie's survival. The 1936 presidential election marked a time when the political interests of middle class blacks diverged. Traditional black Republicans attended the national convention in Cleveland confirmed in their belief that the G.O.P., the party of Abraham Lincoln, best served African Americans. They believed that Southern Democrats, the racists within the Democratic Party who made "Negro baiting" a favorite pastime, diminished the beneficence of the New Deal. Black Republicans also opposed New Deal policies that undermined individual initiative and made blacks dependent on welfare. And finally, they believed the G.O.P. platform committee should address issues pertinent to the black middle class—the eradication of "Jim Crow"—rather than the more immediate concerns about economic survival that would be of greater relevance to the masses.[47] In opposition, a new but equally earnest contingent of prominent blacks would attend the Democratic National Convention in Philadelphia and support Roosevelt and the New Deal. Recognizing that the Democratic Party offered opportunities for ambitious black professionals and provided needed support for the jobless masses, they appealed to every black socioeconomic class within the United States. Through the auspices of the National Colored Committee, black Democrats prepared a document "Has the Roosevelt New Deal Helped the Colored Citizen?" that outlined strategies used to win black support for FDR. Each page provided information about a prominent Negro appointed to a responsible position and cited the professional jobs available to blacks within specific departments. Alfred Edgar Smith, the Colored Administrative Assistant in the Labor Relations Division, for example, cited nearly 70,000 jobs available for white collar professionals, skilled workers, artists, social workers, supervisors, and recreational leaders. Presumably, this information held especial appeal to ambitious African Americans and enticed them to vote for Roosevelt and his New Deal.

After the successful election and through the course of the New Deal, the Democratic Party boasted about the many prominent African Americans who acquired power and prestige in the Roosevelt Administration. They included Eugene Kinkle Jones of the National Urban League; Dr. William J. Thompkins, Recorder of the Deeds for Washington, D.C.; Lester A. Walton, Minister to Liberia; Dr. Robert C. Weaver and Edgar O. Brown, Advisors on Negro Affairs; and Mrs. Mary McLeod Bethune, Director of Negro Activities and Member of the President's Advisory Committee of the NYA.[48] Members of the black elite who joined the New Deal team, found dignity and respect long coveted by the "accomplished classes" within African American society.

When New Deal Democrats appealed to the African American vote and placed blacks in responsible and authoritative positions, the political landscape changed favorably for northern black leadership. At this time most African Americans still resided in the South. Since most southern blacks were poor and denied the franchise, black professionals of the

South—those who comprised the leadership class—remained impotent and insignificant nationally. The only visible effective black leadership existed in the urban North. Sophisticated and gaining ascendancy in political affairs, these urbane black northerners established precedents that immensely benefited the African American middle class. In their capacity as leaders, they sought full entitlement for moderately comfortable northern black constituents who coveted respect as middle class citizens. A generation would pass before a prominent black southerner would assume the mantle of national leadership reminiscent of Booker T. Washington.

In many respects, the Great Depression established precedents for modern black leadership's political behavior. First, black politicos learned to place greater emphasis on self-preservation than race consciousness, a trait that extended throughout the entire twentieth century.[49] Second, black leaders who established themselves through politics also mastered the art of compromise. As men and women who spoke for their race, black politicians learned that success depended on their ability to follow dictates of party leaders and declare, through act and deed, allegiance to the party hierarchy. And finally, black politicians, like the middle class constituency they represented, avoided taking risks. Rarely extending themselves to argue vehemently on behalf of the masses, to these new black Democrats, party transcended race. Black leaders adhered to the New Deal objective of bolstering the American middle class and correspondingly, contributed to the maintenance of the black bourgeoisie.

Perhaps the most striking evidence of African American leadership at work on behalf of middle class blacks occurred in the realm of education. Black educational issues proved unique, of long duration, and complicated. Formal education had been denied to all but the most exceptional blacks until the era of Reconstruction. During the late nineteenth and early twentieth centuries, ambitious African Americans realized that education enhanced prospects for higher socioeconomic status. Unfortunately, *Plessy v. Ferguson* legalized segregation and meant that blacks with academic potential would be denied access to competitive white primary and secondary schools. Without the ability to attend quality schools attended by white youths, the children of middle class blacks faced the possibility of status regression. Black leaders of the 1930s, therefore, would embark on a long crusade to integrate public education.

Initially, African American leadership's response to segregated schools appeared eclectic and inconsistent. Ever mindful of their middle class constituency, black leaders of the Depression era proceeded with caution because segregated schools ensured work for African American teachers, the largest black professional group in the nation. In cities that contained an excellent African American staff like the M Street School in Washington, D.C., Howard High in Wilmington, Delaware, Maggie Walker High in Richmond, Virginia, the Paul Lawrence Dunbar High School in Dayton, Ohio, and in numerous black grammar and secondary schools, segregation proved beneficial. Highly motivated and race conscious, dedicated African American teachers made certain black children acquired racial pride and appreciated the importance of education. However, in most black schools, segregation carried the stigma of inferiority notwithstanding the quality of instruction. African Americans attending separate black schools never received funding comparable to their white counterparts, and the physical plants attended by blacks versus whites were decidedly "separate and unequal."

Each city or region faced different educational problems associated with segregation. Nevertheless, uniformity existed in targeting adult employees rather than students as the object of black leadership's concerns. Black Philadelphians fought to have African American faculty integrated into schools containing mixed or predominantly white student populations. In Detroit black leaders demanded the hiring of additional black faculty to teach the burgeoning black student population. African Americans in Los Angeles sought to have blacks hired as substitute teachers. And in Omaha, Nebraska, an African American employed in any capacity from teacher to janitor would be hailed as an accomplishment.[50] Because African American educators comprised the largest black professional class in the nation and the Depression placed their jobs in jeopardy, they possessed sufficient influence to engage lawyers to protect their interests. So naturally, one of the initial successful Supreme Court decisions concerned black educators. In December, 1936, the case of Gibbs v. Board of Education of Montgomery County, Maryland declared that the salaries of black and white teachers must be equalized.

When African American leaders decided to focus on broadening black educational opportunities, they concentrated on desegregating graduate and professional schools.[51] As early as 1935 when Charles H. Houston became Special Council for the NAACP, a strategy became instituted to make educational opportunities available for an aspiring black professional middle class. Confident that a severe blow against segregation could be struck against states without separate graduate and professional schools, the NAACP carefully prepared legal briefs against what Houston deemed "the soft underbelly of Jim Crow" in graduate education. The NAACP selected an African American graduate of Amherst, Donald Murray, to test the constitutionality of segregation in higher education. When Murray attempted to gain admission into the University of Maryland School of Law, the Supreme Court ruled that Murray must be admitted since no separate state law school existed for blacks.

Houston knew that practical economics would determine that states legally obligated to provide educational opportunities for all residents would find it more prudent to integrate than build separate black law and medical schools. When Murray graduated in 1938 the NAACP proved that its strategy worked. That same year the National Association won another monumental Supreme Court judgment in the case of Missouri ex rel. Gaines. The Court ruled that states must provide equal, if separate, educational professional schools for African Americans. In October 1939, Charles Houston and the NAACP created the Legal Defense and Educational Fund, a measure indicating that equal access to higher education would be a major priority. To demonstrate the earnestness of its cause, the Association prepared nine cases for court decisions that demanded the right of African American students to attend tax-supported state universities.[52]

Only by June 1939 did the initial effort to address the concern of black youths appear. Thurgood Marshall, Houston's successor as Special Council for the NAACP, prepared to terminate racial segregation in public schools. In his "Procedure to Equalize Educational Opportunities," Marshall outlined the means for attack. He instructed leaders in local communities to observe and collect information that documented segregation in elementary and secondary schools.[53] African American leaders heeded Marshall's advice and maintained records of racial discrimination. Their relatives and associates would be the beneficiaries of his cautious, but highly effective approach, an approach that eventually attained fruition in the Brown decision of 1954. Children primarily from middle class families who could defer gratification, attend college, and obtain graduate and professional degrees profited from integration. Unfortunately, few disadvantaged children enjoyed the immediate or deferred benefits of desegregation. African American leaders concentrated almost exclusively on protecting black educators by strategizing to terminate segregation; they would endeavor to place black teachers and guidance counselors in white schools and having black representation on boards of education.[54] Unfortunately, the black masses would remain far behind middle class blacks and the larger white society in educational achievement.

Black leaders of the 1930s joined President Roosevelt in helping to maintain the American middle class. Demonstrating a resilience which epitomized the industrious roots which spawned them, African American representatives focused their attention upon those areas meaningful to their class—white collar employment, respect from white power brokers, and affinity for education—which advanced the better elements of their race. When the federal government, under the aegis of the New Deal, provided welfare, and welfare related support enabling the disadvantaged black masses to survive, it lifted the burden of protecting the masses from the shoulders of the black bourgeoisie. African American leaders proceeded to concentrate, almost exclusively, upon issues beneficial to blacks of higher station.

6

WORLD WAR II AND THE
GENESIS OF MODERN LEADERSHIP

Two striking realities dominated the decade of the 1940s that determined the future path taken by African American leadership—World War II and prosperity of the post-war years. However the war enabled African American leaders to present an additional reality before the American public; they drew comparisons between Fascism abroad and racism at home, showing the contradiction between American platitudes and the inhumane treatment accorded citizens of African ancestry. During the war black leaders appealed to the conscience of fair-minded whites and encouraged public officials to address and resolve African American grievances. After the war, black leaders continued the fight against entrenched racism with increased vigor by demanding that hard-working, upwardly mobile blacks should enjoy post-war prosperity like their white counterparts. Therefore, desegregation of public establishments, equal protection under the law, and the elimination of restrictive housing covenants became primary objectives of black leaders. Collectively, circumstances during and immediately after the war enabled black leaders to provide the foundation for future civil rights gains in the United States and channel those gains to promote and serve the interests of a burgeoning black middle class.

Even before the war began a significant event occurred that placed African Americans in the limelight of international politics and provided black leaders with an opportunity to use race advantageously. Questions about the legitimacy of racial superiority swirled around the 1936 Olympic Games held in Berlin, Germany. The infamous racial theories of German Fuhrer Adolph Hitler were known throughout the United States. Hitler's boasts of Aryan superiority angered patriotic Americans. Therefore, American pride dictated that the nation find athletes capable of besting the Germans and debunking the Aryan myth. The black auxiliary on the United States Olympic team, ironically, would be looked upon to disprove theories of racial superiority so that Americans could celebrate democracy, take pride in their nationality, and prepare for the darkening war clouds hovering over Europe. The stage appeared ready for the heroic performance of a college undergraduate named Jesse Owens.

On September 12, 1913 Henry and Emma Owens became the proud parents of James Cleveland Owens. Born in Oakville, Alabama, Owens, like his parents, became subjected to racial slights common to the South. In the 1920s the family moved to Cleveland, Ohio where young James Cleveland attended Bolton Elementary School where he acquired, by slurring his first and middle initials J and C, the name Jesse. But it was at East Technical High School where Owens distinguished himself as a world class athlete. In a National Interscholastic meet held at Stagg Field in Chicago, Owens tied the world mark in the 100 yard dash and established a new world record in the 220 yard sprint.[1] These athletic exploits attracted college recruiters. So despite the existence of racial prejudice at Ohio State University, Owens enrolled at the Columbus, Ohio campus on a work scholarship in 1933. As a collegian, Owens established three additional world records and tied a fourth on May 25, 1935. However the highlight of his career occurred during the Berlin Olympic Games the following year.

Though not the first black Olympic champion, Owens garnered acclaim because his Herculean effort in winning three individual gold medals [100 meters, 200 meters, and long jump] and receiving a fourth as a member of the winning 400 meter relay team. Though practicing racism and anti-Semitism at home, Americans disputed Hitler's claim of German superiority and conveniently used Owens' feat to discredit the Aryan myth. This marked the first time white Americans treated an African American as royalty. Upon his return to the United States, Owens received a "ticker tape" parade through New York City. The Republican Party aggressively courted Owens and encouraged him to speak before black audiences to endorse the candidacy of Alfred M. Landon in the 1936 presidential election. For a rare interlude in United States history, a black man became lauded as a national hero and proclaimed a representative of American democracy.

Unfortunately, Owens' exploits proved convenient and his notoriety short lived within the white athletic establishment. Soon after the applause for his extraordinary performance in Berlin abated Owens fell from grace. Exhausted and homesick, Owens refused to participate in post Olympic races in Europe at the behest of the United States Olympic Committee. In retribution, powerful elements within American amateur athletics bestowed the Sullivan Award for the outstanding amateur athlete of the year to Glenn Morris, a white man who won a gold medal in the Olympic Decathlon. Disappointed and facing destitution because of family responsibilities, Owens withdrew from Ohio State. Despite his exploits and ingratiating personality, Owens was reduced to racing against horses and automobiles to earn a living. The United States refused to honor blacks failing to follow directions and forgetting their place.

African Americans, like white people, reveled in the glory achieved by Owens and other black Olympians, but blacks also resembled white Americans and displayed a lamentable lack of support for Owens after he had fallen on hard times. Nevertheless, Owens represented a new kind of leader—a black man whose popularity crossed racial lines and whose celebrity made white America more receptive to civil rights entreaties. While black leaders failed to take full advantage of Owens' popularity by using his exploits to generate renewed support for an anti-lynching bill or encourage him to speak out about correlations between Nazis and white American bigots, they would learn that the path toward racial justice and black opportunity could be carried on the shoulders of the African American athlete.

Fortunately, Owens' achievements served as a prelude to another African American whose exploits had favorable international and domestic implications for blacks. This time, a heavyweight boxing champion named Joe Louis entered the world stage as a positive representative of American democracy. Like Owens, Louis also had a predecessor—the first heavyweight boxing champion was the Galveston, Texas native, Jack Johnson. Johnson reigned between 1908 and 1915. While no one disputed Johnson's prowess in the ring, his personal life infuriated white Americans because Johnson dated and married white women. Moreover, Johnson flaunted his taste in white women before the American public, causing him to become the object for a myriad of criminal charges that forced him to live as an exile in France. By contrast, Louis was quiet, modest, and physically attractive. Nicknamed "the Brown Bomber," Louis represented the kind of person black and white America easily embraced.

Joe Louis was born with the surname Barrow in Lafayette, Alabama on May 13, 1914. His father, Munro, after being diagnosed as mentally ill, was committed to a state hospital where he eventually died. After his father's death Louis' mother Lily married Patrick Brooks who moved the entire family to Detroit. Never a good student, young Louis, though twelve years old, had been placed in the fifth grade. By age 17 Louis quit school and found employment in the Briggs Automobile Factory. In his spare time he took violin lessons (evidence of a family striving for upward mobility during the Great Depression), and on a dare from a friend, took up boxing. Louis enjoyed the sport, won 54 amateur fights, and eventually acquired American Amateur Union and Golden Gloves national boxing championships. Having achieved the highest possible levels as an amateur, Louis decided to become a professional pugilist.

As a professional boxer Louis enjoyed meteoric success. En route toward the heavyweight championship of the world, Louis suffered only one defeat—a knockout at the hands of Germany's Max Schmeling. But in the return bout held on June 22, 1938, Louis destroyed Schmeling in two minutes, four seconds of the first round. Louis' victory was celebrated by blacks and whites and represented the second major blow an African American registered against Hitler's theory of Aryan supremacy.

Once again African Americans took pride in the physical prowess of a champion athlete and repeated their inability to exploit athletic heroics to enhance the race. Though not leaders in the classical sense as ideologues, politicos, or power brokers, Owens and Louis brought dignity to their race and received deserved recognition for their exploits from black and white Americans. As Owens and Louis' successes hastened white acceptance of African American humanity, black leaders had a greater opportunity to press for racial equality. Directly or indirectly, Owens and Louis would enable talented African Americans to make inroads in business, law, education, and other professions denied accessibility to blacks prior to World War II.

While Owens and Louis helped instill confidence in the nation preparing for a foreign war against Fascism, racism and intolerance, Swedish national Gunnar Myrdal would prepare whites about the African American condition at home. In 1937 Trustees of the Carnegie Corporation of New York commissioned Myrdal to perform "a comprehensive study of the Negro in the United States." Recognizing that as a foreigner he did not have a profound understanding of African Americans and the relationship between blacks and whites, Myrdal added knowledgeable blacks to his research team. Counted among the African American scholars and experts were Ralph J. Bunche, Horace Cayton, E. Franklin Frazier, Charles S. Johnson, Eugene Kinkle Jones, Alain Locke, Ira DeA. Reid, Walter White, and W.E.B. Du Bois. Myrdal also sought the expertise of agencies like the NAACP, the National Urban League, and the Commission for Interracial Cooperation. Since these scholars, experts, and agencies enabled Myrdal to delve into virtually every aspect of African American life, his interpretation of black life and the means for ameliorating the status of blacks would be influenced largely by the African Americans on his staff.

When Myrdal published *An American Dilemma* during the height of World War II, African American leaders had taken the opportunity to plead the Negro's case. In many respects, the Myrdal study charted the direction black leadership wanted the nation to pursue to enhance the condition of African Americans. The last chapter in the book proved particularly telling. Myrdal and his associates correctly surmised that when the study was completed in October 1942, the war would redefine the status of African Americans in the United States. To underscore his point, Myrdal quoted Wendell Willkie, the Republican presidential nominee in the 1940 election and G.O.P. Party leader who declared:

> Today it is becoming increasingly apparent to thoughtful Americans that we cannot fight the forces and ideas of imperialism abroad and maintain a form of imperialism at home.... Our very proclamations of what we are fighting for have rendered our own inequities self-evident when we talk of freedom and opportunity for all nations the mocking paradoxes in our own society become so clear they can no longer be ignored.[2]

Most white Americans would not agree with Willkie's observations. They would rather ignore the contradiction between American ideals and racial practices. But among blacks Willkie's statement reflected the view of African American leadership. Black leaders would present this theme continuously, reminding white Americans about the inconsistency between fighting a foreign war to protect American democracy while according its Negro citizenry inequitable treatment at home.

Early in 1940 President Roosevelt recognized the need to establish the United States as the "Arsenal of Democracy." In preparation for war, plants designed for manufacturing domestic products were converted into factories producing war materials. Jobless Americans gradually returned to work as limited defense spending enabled the despair of the Great Depression to fade before the euphoria derived from gainful employment. Unfortunately, Roosevelt and those who supervised war production in defense industries overlooked African Americans desperately in need of work. Myrdal found that the percentage of blacks in employment service placements actually declined, a reality understood by black leaders and workers.[3] African Americans were hired in defense industries at a slower pace than whites. They were also denied equal access to training opportunities, and when hired, occupied low paying menial jobs. During the depression signs read "No Help Wanted." But during the early 1940s overt discrimination appeared as signs read: "Help Wanted, White."[4] Few large factories contained black workers, and as late as December 1940 less than 2 percent of the trainees geared for work in defense industries were African American. Black spokespersons realized that African Americans bore the brunt of racial discrimination. The black press publicized information citing that ¼ million new defense jobs were closed to African Americans. Equally important, black leaders knew that racial discrimination excluded blacks from jobs even at the expense of preparing for war.

While most black leaders supported Roosevelt because of his New Deal, even the most rabid black Democrats became angered by racial discrimination that limited economic opportunities for their race. Equally important, the patriotism blacks willingly displayed to defend their country was at best ignored, and more commonly, discouraged. Racism experienced by African Americans in 1940 propelled black leaders into action. The contradictions of white leadership speaking derisively of Fascism abroad while ignoring bigotry at home proved far more than any self-respecting black leader or organization could accept. Unlike the "Close Ranks" philosophy voiced on the eve of World War I, black spokespersons decried fighting a war abroad while racism existed in the United States.

Even before the United States entered the war, African American representatives prepared to pressure the federal government and high-ranking authorities to eradicate racial discrimination. Early in 1939 black leaders created the Committee for Participation of Negroes in the National Defense. With endorsement from the *Pittsburgh Courier*, and with *Courier* editor Robert Vann and Howard University Professor Rayford W. Logan as primary spokespersons, the Committee encouraged the White House and Congress to pass legislation designed to terminate racial discrimination against African Americans. Concomitantly, the NAACP and National

Urban League advocated the end of "Jim Crow" in defense plants and in the Armed Services.[5] Despite the earnest work of black leaders and their organizations, the only concession granted by the Roosevelt administration appeared in a clause inserted into the Selective Service Act, declaring "no person should be admitted into the Army or Navy unless he were acceptable to high executives within the Army and Navy ... a declaration that essentially negated the non-discrimination clause."[6] In response to the President's weak directive, on January 26, 1941 the NAACP launched National Defense Day and organized protest meetings in 23 states to dramatize black annoyance with employment discrimination. The Association also asked its supporters to picket national defense plants in designated cities to demonstrate African American displeasure with "Jim Crow" policies that excluded deserving blacks from work.[7]

By 1940 A. Philip Randolph of the Brotherhood for Sleeping Car Porters, Walter White of the NAACP, and T. Arnold Hill of the National Urban League decided to take Roosevelt to task. They reasoned Roosevelt must do more to provide blacks with the opportunity to acquire dignity through gainful employment in defense industries. Therefore, in September the leaders assembled to meet with Roosevelt and voice their concern about the dearth of employment opportunities for African Americans. They also intended to address segregation in the Armed Services. Given the pride blacks had in fighting heroically in every American war, they intended to stress that restrictions imposed upon blacks who desired to enlist in the Armed Services were extremely demeaning and insulting. The meeting with President Roosevelt proved cordial but uneventful. However, when a subsequent press release indicated that this African American vanguard accepted the War Department's segregationist policies, the three spokesmen found themselves in an embarrassing predicament. The black press excoriated them for being race traitors. Irate for having their reputations besmirched, Randolph, White, and Hill decided upon desperate measures to clear their names. Randolph decided upon an ingenious strategy to ingratiate themselves with black Americans while simultaneously pressuring Roosevelt to end racist hiring practices in defense industries. By reversing the union tactic of the strike—walking off the job to pressure management into making favorable concessions—Randolph recommended that 10,000 African Americans approach the employer, the federal government, an idea that gave birth to the March on Washington Movement [MOWM].

In an extreme departure from most civil rights movements, Randolph, the leader of the newly formed MOWM, decided that white people would be excluded from the organization. Disillusionment with white communists who undermined the National Negro Congress certainly contributed to Randolph's controversial decision. However his aversion to white participation in a black movement was also derived from the desertion of white allies who traditionally befriended African Americans. The declaration of war in Europe and the bellicose behavior of Japan in Asia caused former white associates to focus on foreign crises rather than the woeful status of African Americans in the United States. Consequently, Randolph reasoned that blacks would have to act singularly to advance their race.

The MOWM represented the first time in the twentieth century that traditionally conservative black leadership fired the imagination of the African American masses. Working class blacks desiring employment deeply resented being overlooked for prospective jobs in defense plants. These feelings corresponded to the sentiments of the black elite and middle class. Every black socioeconomic class grated at the platitudes voiced by Americans who spoke of freedom, democracy, and equality in response to Nazism while the nation practiced bigotry at home.

As Roy Wilkins wrote in *The Crisis*:

> No agitators were needed to point out … what we were fighting for, and what we did…. [The typical black] did not need [to be shown] that it sounds pretty foolish to be against park benches marked 'Jude' in Berlin, but to be for park benches marked 'colored' in Tallahassee, Florida.[8]

Randolph devoted six months to organize and promote the protest movement that would march on the nation's capital. NUL Executive Secretary Lester Granger credited Randolph for being the "heart and soul" of the movement when he declared: "It was Randolph's immense prestige among all classes of Negroes that made the idea something more than a pretentious notion."[9] Although Roosevelt could call Randolph's bluff, the President had to prepare the nation for war and decided to take Randolph and his March on Washington Movement seriously.

Eventually, pressure applied by Randolph and the MOWM brain trust forced Roosevelt to accede to black leadership's demands. In order to head off the threatened march scheduled for June 25, 1941, Roosevelt issued Executive Order 8802. The presidential decree proclaimed that blacks must be admitted to job training programs and declared that discrimination against African American workers must be eliminated from companies holding defense contracts. However the most far-reaching aspect of the Executive Order existed in the creation of the Fair Employment Practices Committee [FEPC]. Designed as a body to investigate charges of racial discrimination, FEPC served as the key item in the Executive Order that appeased black leadership. Roosevelt's concessions enabled Randolph to call off the march.

Initially FEPC appeared as an empty gesture designed to quell the MOWM. But after a tentative start, FEPC became reorganized, had its budget augmented, conducted hearings about complaints, and enforced anti-discrimination contract clauses. With the government now dedicated to ending discrimination in defense industries, Randolph deserved credit for initiating the first step to erode discriminatory practices against black workers. Eventually, FEPC would be remembered as the launching pad that made an expanded black middle class possible. Through FEPC respectable government and government related jobs would be made available to ambitious African Americans.

Aside from serving as the impetus for African American employment opportunities, the MOWM proved successful primarily because of the fortitude of A. Philip Randolph. Although the June march had been canceled, Randolph decided to keep the MOWM alive. Using the veiled threat of the march as a utilitarian strategy, Randolph believed he could force Roosevelt to honor his commitment to force industries to contract African Americans for defense work. While no black leader openly opposed Randolph, historian Herbert Garfinkel declared that Randolph virtually acted alone to sustain the movement. The black bourgeoisie and the organizations they supported—even the NUL headed by Hill and White's NAACP—remained conservative and displayed disinterest in the black laboring class.[10] Astonishingly, African American editors of the Negro press failed to lend support to the MOWM. With Du Bois no longer at the helm, *The Crisis* remained mute, displaying an unmistakable reluctance to support Randolph by confronting the Roosevelt Administration.

Reluctance on the part of black leaders to endorse the MOWM may be attributed directly to their wariness about involving the masses in civil rights activities. Among traditional black leaders the pejorative residue of Garveyism remained. They resented the masses' support for Garvey and his gaudy ostentation. Middle class leaders, therefore, distrusted the masses' ability to follow their directions and become a dependable, dignified ally in the struggle for civil rights. Middle class leaders, therefore, decided to use the masses for the march only as a last resort.[11] While Randolph genuinely believed the MOWM could prove instrumental in aiding the masses, others among the leadership cadre endorsed the movement solely because of the desire to oppose "Jim Crow." They appeared to hate racial discrimination that impinged on their freedom far more than the drudgery and degradation the masses experienced daily as a penalty for being poor and black.

From the inception of the United States entry into the global conflict, most black leaders expressed disenchantment with war policy directives in relation to "the Negro." Robert L. Vann of the *Pittsburgh Courier* emerged as the individual who pointedly expressed African American aversion to white bigotry in the armed services. Born on August 20, 1879 near Ahoskie, North Carolina, Vann's mother, Lucy Peoples worked as a cook for the Albert Vann family, one of the most prominent white families in rural Hertford County. As an only child of a single mother, Vann enjoyed a fairly comfortable childhood. His mother's fair complexion and relatively high status as a cook enabled young Vann to be in close proximity to wealthy whites and motivated him to seek personal acclaim.[12] Six years of field hand drudgery under the tutelage of a recently acquired stepfather named John Simon augmented Vann's desire to acquire an education and become successful. After gaining access to the black Waters Training School in Winton, North Carolina and traveling to Boston where he gained sophistication, Vann eventually entered Virginia Union University. He graduated from "Union" in 1903, migrated to Pittsburgh to escape encroaching southern racism, and received a bachelor's degree from the Western University of Pennsylvania (later, the University of Pittsburgh) in 1906. By 1909 Vann returned to the University to earn a degree in law. And in 1910, Vann became involved with Pittsburgh's black newspaper, the *Courier*, and soon became its editor—a position he held through the remainder of his life.

A fastidious dresser and conservative Victorian, Vann used the newspaper to advocate for African American rights. As early as 1926 Vann proposed that a monument be dedicated to black soldiers who fought in the Great War. Although the initiative failed, Vann retained interest in the welfare of black armed service personnel. In 1934 he instructed *Courier* reporters to investigate duties assigned to black soldiers. Vann's curiosity caused him to designate staff to investigate the entire military where he found black enlisted men in the army confined to performing menial tasks. Vann's team of reporters also found that blacks were excluded from the Artillery, Coast Guard, Army Air Corps, Signal and Tank Corps, Corps of Engineers, and the Marines. Vann's investigators discovered that the navy accepted blacks, but limited them to serving as cooks, stewards, and waiters. As late as 1940 Vann reported that only five African American officers could be found in the regular army and only two had received combat training.[13]

In February 1938 Vann published an open letter to President Roosevelt citing ten reasons why blacks deserved equal treatment in the Armed Services. Vann adopted the customary African American view that blacks measuring arms in national wars would enhance the race's ability to acquire all the rights entitled to citizens of the United States. He wanted his race to have access to jobs and education, and have the opportunity to shatter prejudice by displaying a patriotic fervor within the Armed Services to inspire future generations of black Americans. Vann canvassed his African American readers, asking whether black troops should be integrated into armed service branches or confined to segregated units. Research led him to conclude that segregated black units should be formed. Vann concurred with the results; he merely wanted African Americans to be given the opportunity to serve their country.[14]

Soon after Vann endorsed the concept of a segregated black army division, he met a challenge from Walter White, a man who uncompromisingly opposed segregation. Undeterred by White's opposition, Vann continued working strenuously to gain blacks greater access into the military. He financed the Committee for Participation of Negroes in the National Defense with the avowed purpose of attaining racial equality in the military. Through letters, telegrams, and delegations, Vann's organization pressured Congress, the President, and the War Department to end discrimination in the Armed Services of the United States. Vann punctuated his thinking by requesting that Colonel Benjamin O. Davis, Sr. be promoted to general.

Although Vann died fourteen months prior to America's entry into war, he established the "Double V for Victory"—representing victory at home and abroad, a concept that transcended his death. Not long after the Japanese attacked Pearl Harbor, the Urban League convened seventeen national African American organizations and resolved "that the Negro was 'not whole-heartedly and unreservedly' behind the government's program." Archibald MacLeish, who headed the Office of Facts and Figures, received confirmation of these beliefs. Delegates representing fifty black organizations bluntly told MacLeish that "the Negro people were cool to the war effort and that there could be no national unity nor high morale among Negroes unless they were given their rights."[15] The "Double V for Victory" idea that Vann introduced proved one of his lasting legacies. Perhaps inadvertently, Vann's actions heightened another legacy. His endorsement of segregation perpetuated a controversy between pragmatic segregationists and idealistic integrationists that divided black leaders until the Civil Rights Movement of the 1960s.

In keeping with Vann's desire to ensure an African American victory at home, Randolph organized a series of MOWM rallies in major cities. Just as United States Armed Forces faced defeat on foreign battlefields, Randolph experienced wavering enthusiasm for a victorious march at home. A crack in African American resolve, evidenced continuously by black leadership that never shared Randolph's enthusiasm for aiding the laboring masses, occurred at a Madison Square Garden rally held in New York on June 16, 1942. As the creator of MOWM and most acclaimed leader on the dais, Randolph had been scheduled to give the keynote address. Unfortunately, previous speakers took the opportunity to engage in self aggrandizing orations to elevate their status and consumed five hours of precious time. As a reporter covering the rally observed: "Speaker after speaker read prepared speeches and in the end there was not time enough for A. Philip Randolph to make the principal address."[16] Randolph did not speak, a failure, according to historian Herbert Garfinkel that served as a "portent of incipient decline."

Although the black masses gravitated to Randolph, it became evident that fewer and fewer middle class blacks maintained Randolph's enthusiasm for broad racial uplift. Conservative black leaders feared that criticism hurled at white America during a time of war would create a backlash against their race. They found additional justification for their beliefs because Randolph excluded white people from participating in the MOWM, a segregationist position anathema to the integration minded black bourgeoisie. Moreover, the masses that served as Randolph's support base became appeased through steady job placement in defense industries. In this instance, Randolph's years of work on behalf of black labor ironically caused him to become a victim of his own success. African Americans had been hired in sufficient numbers to dampen the desire for protest.[17] Thus, Randolph's "We Don't Give A Damn" speech—the moniker applied to the Chicago rally which stirred emotional passions—failed to inspire listeners into aggressive action. African Americans, middle class and poor, urban and rural, elected to go along, get along, and enjoy the bountiful changes in their life. Blacks simply lost their enthusiasm for protest during these prosperous times. The MOWM became a moribund organization.

Despite the demise of the MOWM, Randolph retained his prestige among the masses and maintained a grudging respect from black leaders. Black loyalty toward Randolph continued with good reason. Racism toward blacks remained throughout the war and post-war years. Although Randolph and other black leaders effectively used the MOWM to gain employment opportunities on the domestic front, little headway had been achieved in integrating the military. Blacks rarely received training or opportunities for advancement that would enable African Americans to achieve success and gain respect within the branches of the Armed Services.

Soon after Randolph conceived of the MOWM, Roosevelt revealed the focus of his presidency shifted from "Dr. New Deal" to "Dr. Win the War." Roosevelt proclaimed to every citizen that the war held primacy over domestic concerns. For African Americans, however, Roosevelt's concentration on preparing the nation for war would have ominous repercussions. Since military necessity took precedence over appeasing disgruntled blacks, white southern mores maintained in the Armed Services—segregation and discrimination—would continue at the expense of the Negro. Neither Roosevelt nor members of the Joint Chiefs of Staff cared about American hypocrisy. They condemned the concept of Aryan superiority abroad and ignored white supremacy at home. Black leaders had to decide whether to embrace American nationalism by joining Roosevelt in the fight against Fascism and imperialism abroad or seize the opportunity to fight the horrors of "home-grown" American racism and risk criticism for being unpatriotic.

While black leaders proved reluctant to support Randolph and directly confront breaches in the enforcement of FEPC, they refused to allow American hypocrisy to exist with impunity. Publicity attracting race riots in Mobile, Detroit, Harlem in New York, Beaumont, Texas, and in other cities dictated that black leaders must act. Black newspapers led the attack. Because the black press headlined stories about racial injustice in the Armed Services, the Justice Department considered bringing forward sedition charges against the editors. In 1942 the NAACP convened a conference among Negro editors to establish guidelines for criticism and thereby prevent the government from suppressing access to newsprint and paper.[18] While Walter White used his influence to keep the black press operating, at every opportunity he observed and forwarded information to various Defense Department and Armed Service agencies to illustrate the inconsistency between pronouncements of American democracy and practiced bigotry. White found sufficient evidence to amplify his point. For example in June, 1943, 25,000 white employees at the Packard plant in Detroit that manufactured engines for American bombers and P. T. boats went on strike in protest of the hiring of African American workers. White reported that he heard one fiery orator proclaim: "I'd rather see Hitler and Hirohito win the war than work beside a nigger on the assembly line.[19] This kind of "redneck" resistance provided the black press with ample information to raise black racial consciousness and goad the Administration into broadening democracy to benefit African Americans.

Eventually the War Department and Roosevelt Administration capitulated to pressure applied by black leaders. To mitigate criticism and raise black morale on behalf of the war effort, the War Department permitted twenty African American correspondents to report on the various theaters of operation. Walter White, along with Lem Graves of the *Norfolk Journal and Guide*, Ollie Stewart of the *Baltimore Afro-American*, Lester B. Granger of the Urban League, and others spoke of black heroism at the front but also reported on racist incidents in the armed services. For the War Department and Roosevelt, concessions to black leaders had varied results. The African American public relished being informed about the active black participation in the war effort and took pride in the black fighting phalanx, but they also learned first-hand of repression and inequities visited upon blacks in the Armed Services.[20] An enlightened and aggrieved black public could only heighten black demands for civil rights.

Walter White, perhaps more than any other African American leader during the Second World War, worked assiduously to release blacks from the bonds of bigotry to enable his race to enjoy the fruits of United States citizenship. White entered the world on July 1, 1893 in Atlanta, Georgia. His father carried mail and mother taught school. Like both parents, White was extremely fair, and as a blond, blue eyed, person, was capable of passing for white. Although extremely poor by white middle class family standards, the Whites managed, by frugality and perseverance, to remain respectful and proud. Equally important, White's parents instilled him with a desire to succeed and to work to ameliorate the condition of African Americans.

After graduating from Atlanta University where he participated on the football team and served as class president, White joined the NAACP, and by World War II, functioned as the Association's Executive Secretary. He staunchly supported Randolph's March on Washington and the MOWM movement. White also defended the black press against aforementioned sedition charges, argued to end segregation in the armed services, and agitated to end discrimination in government financed war industries.[21] Although fear of racial conflicts within the military prevented the War Department from allowing White's efforts to integrate the military reach immediate fruition, the embarrassment he created as a war correspondent eventually forced the government to modify its racist policies.[22]

Dr. Charles H. Wesley, a prominent historian during the 1940s, also spoke for the larger African American community in a paraphrase of FDR's justification for defending the West in "the Negro Has Always Wanted the Four Freedoms." Echoing Roosevelt's principles, Wesley observed that "Negroes would willingly fight for democracy abroad, but had equal, if not greater, desire to fight for democracy at home. Blacks sought freedom from color restrictions and white supremacy.[23] Since the military brass could hardly care what Vann, Randolph, Wilkins, White, Wesley, or other black leaders thought, black leadership would face a daunting task.[24]

Mindful of the late Robert Vann's Double V slogan, Dr. Wesley pushed the Administration relentlessly to garner respect for his race. To appease Dr. Wesley, Walter White, Dr. Rayford Logan, Judge Charles H. Houston, and others, Secretary of War Henry L. Stimson, with prodding from Franklin and Eleanor Roosevelt, appointed William Hastie, Dean of the Howard University School of Law, to be the Civilian Aide On Negro Affairs. Politics also compelled the Secretary to promote Colonel Benjamin O. Davis, Sr. to Brigadier General. And to mollify concerned black leaders further, the War Department established a training facility for a "Negro pursuit squadron" at Tuskegee Institute, Alabama. This proved to be a long-overdo concession. As early as 1931 Walter White of the NAACP and Robert Russa Moton of Tuskegee requested a training site for black pilots in the Army Air Corps. In a rare concession to pragmatic rather than idealistic tendencies, White restrained his anathema toward segregation so that African Americans could demonstrate their bravery, competence, and intelligence by mastering the intricacies of aerial combat. With help from friends in Congress, black leaders forced the War Department to create a flight-training center for African Americans. Thus, with pressure applied by Judge Hastie and other black leaders, an Army Air Corps training school opened at Tuskegee on July 19, 1941.

The young men who volunteered to serve in the Army Air Corps represented an ambitious coterie of African Americans dedicated to serving their country and demanding respect and equality for their race. They faced enormous obstacles. Unfortunately for the black volunteers, the Tuskegee training school existed primarily for "window dressing." Fearing that integration and other liberal racial policies would disrupt the war effort, the War Department refused to end discrimination imposed on African Americans in the United States military and would send black airmen to the front with great reluctance. Racist white officers went to extraordinary lengths to prevent qualified black pilots from joining their countrymen at the front. Problems encountered by the 477th Bombardment group proved particularly revealing. Like the 9th and 10th Cavalries, this combat ready group had been scheduled for disbandment even before it saw action. Only the concerted efforts of black leaders enabled African American officers and men in the 477th to remain on active duty despite suffering the ignominy of being denied the opportunity to fight.[25]

Despite obstacles, when the Tuskegee airmen finally engaged in combat they performed heroically. Colonel Benjamin O. Davis, Jr. served as the ranking African American officer.[26] Of the 992 pilots graduated from Tuskegee, 450 served abroad. They participated in 1,578 missions and destroyed 261 enemy airplanes. For meritorious action, the men received 744 air medals and clusters, 150 distinguished Flying Crosses, two Soldier Medals, a Silver Star, and a Legion of Merit.[27]

One of the lasting legacies the Tuskegee Airmen and other members of the Armed Services contributed to the larger African American society appeared in their contribution to destroy segregation in the Armed Services. When the Army Air Corps prohibited blacks from entering an officers club at Freeman Field in Seymour, Indiana, prideful African American officers decided to take on the War Department. Black officers knew that War Regulation A-R 210-10 stated that officers clubs were open to all qualified personnel and prepared to face courts-martial to gain full equality. Civil disobedience occurred when 100 blacks stormed the officers club and refused to leave. The protest occurred at considerable expense to Lieutenants Shirly R. Clifton, Marsden A. Thompson and Roger C. Terry. Clifton and Thompson were eventually acquitted of all charges. However Terry, a UCLA graduate, received a guilty verdict for resisting arrest and served three months in jail.[28]

Actions of the protesting officers served as a prelude to future civil rights demonstrations as blacks purposefully broke segregation laws to achieve human dignity. Protesters at Freeman Field forced the Air Force to conduct a hearing and launch an investigation of its regulatory policies in regard to African Americans. Under the auspices of the Secretary of War, General Alvan Gillem convened a board in the summer of 1945 to assess the treatment of blacks in the Armed Services during the post-war era. Black and white leaders throughout the nation were called to testify. In order to buttress its position, the War Department found Truman Gibson, an African American willing to endorse segregation within the Armed Services. Gibson, an aid to Judge William Hastie, succeeded the Judge after the latter's resignation as Civilian Aid to the Secretary of War. Thinking in the same mode as the accommodationist Booker T. Washington, Gibson defended the War Department and declared that certain African American leaders and their organizations like the NAACP were more disruptive than helpful when inferring that shortcomings of black servicemen "should be rationalized and not publicly discussed."[29] Roy Wilkins of the NAACP declared Gibson's defense of the War Department "indefensible by any standard." Grant Reynolds, President of the Committee Against Jim Crow, labeled Gibson as "the War Department's mouthpiece," and Congressional Representative Adam Clayton Powell, Jr. identified Gibson "as the rubber stamp Uncle Tom who was used by the War Department."[30] While Truman Gibson contended that full integration would not work, black leaders like Walter White, Judge Hastie, and General Benjamin O. Davis Sr. spoke uncompromisingly in favor of integrating the Armed Services. When the Gillem Board recommended that blacks in the military should be used in a broader professional basis, the opening salvo for desegregation nationally had been sounded. The military establishment concurred with black leadership and agreed that integration must move forward in the best interest of the Armed Services and eventually, the nation.[31]

In the future, self-serving people like Gibson would continue to undermine their race. However, unlike the conservative Booker Washington who sincerely worked to benefit his race, people like Gibson would be perceived as active participants in self-aggrandizement and precursors to blacks who willingly served as tools for the conservative white establishment.

President Harry S. Truman finalized the debate over integration in the military. Pressure generated by Randolph's admonition that blacks would ignore the military draft, and fear of losing the black vote in the forthcoming presidential election, pressed Truman into action.[32] First, on December 5, 1946 Truman created the President's Committee on Civil Rights to investigate and enhance enforcement measures to protect the rights of African Americans. Next, in October 1947 the Committee released its report in a declaration "To Secure These Rights," which urged Congress to end immediately, all discrimination and segregation in the Armed Services. And finally, on February 2, 1948 Truman submitted a "Special Message on Civil Rights" to Congress. The President's message unequivocally declared that the equality of opportunity must occur within the Armed Services "without regard to race, color, religion, or national origin." The military would integrate. It now became incumbent for black leaders to achieve integration in civilian life.[33]

During the Roosevelt and Truman administrations economic opportunities attributed to the War contributed significantly to African American advancement, a fact proven through research performed by the National Urban League. Early in 1944 the NUL conducted an industrial relations experiment. The League selected 300 war plants in twenty-five states that employed African American workers. By prior agreement the plants accepted NUL counseling to aid the performance of black employees. The experiment convinced the majority of participating industrial plants that black workers should be retained after the war. This favorable assessment enabled the NUL to place scores of blacks in American industries. At the same time, the League also encouraged blacks to enter civil service and join the labor movement. Circumstances attributed to NUL efforts and World War II allowed the number of black union members to rise from 180,000 in 1935 to 1,250,000 by 1945.

The war also enabled the National Urban League to experience an augmentation of its Vocational Opportunity Campaign. Using the theme "The Future is Yours," the League established a means for helping college trained blacks enter professions in greater numbers than in any prior generation.[34] Simultaneously, the NUL also placed African Americans in executive positions through a Pilot Placement Project. Between 1944 and 1950, the League helped thousands of African Americans find work in visible, prestigious professional occupations. These represented a subtle, but continuous NUL shift from securing employment for the destitute masses to finding work for the black middle class.

In many respects black leaders should be credited for sensing the shifting occupational requirements in a post-war economy. War-time efficiency led to heightened mechanization and limited the need for unskilled labor—jobs that traditionally contained a high concentration of low-income blacks. Key administrators within the NUL's Commerce and Industry Council wisely cultivated relationships with the giants of corporate America. By the end of the decade the League gained influence with and placed African Americans in a myriad of positions with Fortune 500 companies like General Electric, General Motors, Ford, Du Pont, Standard Oil, RCA, Allied Stores, U.S. Steel, Safeway Stores, NBC, CBS, Metropolitan Life, and *Time* and *Life* magazines. The League also enlisted the support of corporate heads to investigate and diminish "discriminatory or otherwise unsatisfactory employment conditions in any and all of the company's plants throughout the country." [35] Urban League chroniclers Parris and Brooks found these changes to be revolutionary, given employment restrictions toward blacks less than a decade earlier.[36] Naturally, as economic opportunities for middle class African Americans became crystallized, black leadership made certain that the black bourgeoisie would attain respect worthy of their ambition and station.

The war and post-war era created positive changes in American society and offered opportunities for African Americans that exceeded anything previous black leaders could have imagined. One of the most significant changes could be observed through the growth of black income and the resultant augmentation of the black middle class. Between 1937 and 1950 black income increased approximately 80 percent faster than for whites and black median family income rose from a pre-war level of 41 percent to 57 percent of white families. In short, blacks acquired respectable work and found higher paying jobs that significantly enhanced the lifestyle of African Americans. Social scientist Robert Weaver found that in 1946, 85,000 urban black families in the northeast and north central states earned an estimated $5,000 (approximately $35,000 given inflation in 1996).[37] Weaver also found that the number of African Americans living below the subsistence level declined, and that a greater number of blacks— specifically G.I.'s—were prepared to purchase homes and/or rent housing in more attractive white neighborhoods.[38]

Given the economic advances made by African Americans generally and the black bourgeoisie in particular, black leaders had little reason for demanding a fairer distribution of resources. The unprecedented growth of the NAACP from 50,000 members in 1940 to 350,000 in 1945 and a consistent core of members who maintained affiliation throughout the decade, dictated that black leaders would focus upon enhancing the quality of life for the rising black middle class. Thus, African American leadership envisioned white prejudice as the most immediate problem and devoted considerable attention to addressing civil rights issues rather than working to minimize economic hardships still encountered by the black majority.[39]

Unlike the close of World War I, extensive white hostility toward African Americans failed to materialize after the Second World War. Conversion to a peace-time economy during a period when the nation experienced unparalleled access to material goods enabled white Americans to look to the future with optimism. African Americans who possessed technical skills and acquired professional training, therefore, appeared non-threatening. During this unique era of United States history, blacks could consolidate gains made during the war and become an integral part of the post-war economy. Never before had such a large contingent of African Americans felt sufficiently secure economically and socially to approximate "the American Dream."[40]

Access to better housing had long been an objective of the black leadership class. In northern and mid-western cities residential segregation in an imposed ghetto impinged severely on all African Americans, the economically advantaged and ambitious as well as the poor. During the war ghetto life proved particularly difficult for enterprising blacks to endure because of the extreme overcrowding that contributed to unsanitary conditions and threats to public health. With higher incomes, steady work, greater incorporation into the national economy, and backing from the federal government, accomplished blacks endeavored to break down racial covenants that restricted African Americans to living in black neighborhoods. Two Supreme Court Cases—Shelley v. Kraemer and Hurd v. Hodge declared restrictive covenants unconstitutional and suggested that moral suasion used by outspoken blacks could have a favorable impression on the Judiciary. Prospects for outward residential expansion were further enhanced when studies proved that the quality of home maintenance depended largely on class rather than race. Consequently, when members of the black bourgeoisie who trickled into white neighborhoods proved they could maintain property similarly to whites, racial barriers slowly began to erode. Also, realtors realized enormous profits when selling to blacks because the scarcity of homes enabled them to sell property to African Americans at an inflated price.[41] These developments were enhanced by returning veterans who had the ability to purchase homes through the G.I. Bill. Thus, a primary indication of positive relationships between blacks and whites could be observed through the diminution of segregated housing.

During the 1940s African Americans collectively enjoyed more prosperity than at any previous time in history. Therefore, black leadership would find the greatest encouragement within the race—since the anti-slavery movement of the nineteenth century—to fight racial discrimination and strive for full equality as citizens of the United States. While Randolph lapsed into being a "leader without a movement" as the MOWM waned, a new, viable civil rights organization evolved. This organization adopted Randolph's aggressive stance and created a new kind of activism; it would be known as the Committee (later Congress) of Racial Equality [CORE].

CORE, representing a blend of the idealism of a new bourgeoisie with the active race consciousness of youth evolved as the first wartime organization that agitated for black civil rights. Middle class black students, with assistance from white peers, decided to assert their rights as American citizens. Founded in Chicago in 1942 as a bi-racial organization, CORE derived its membership from the young, collegiate intelligentsia. James Forman, son of an African American professor and Bayard Rustin, a former CCNY student, humanitarian, and pacifist, along with two white men, George Houser, a white minister's son and James R. Robinson, served as early leaders of the organization. As disciples of the Gandhian concept of civil disobedience, members of CORE studied Krishnalal Shidharani's book, *War Without Violence*, and practiced passive aggression through direct, non-violent action. After gaining confidence by using "sit-in" tactics to desegregate a restaurant in Chicago, CORE expanded its operations. The organization used direct action to desegregate theaters and restaurants in Baltimore, the District of Columbia, Syracuse, Detroit, and Denver. Even at the federal prison in Danbury, Connecticut, CORE succeeded in eliminating segregation. In 1947 CORE ventured into the "deep South," and sent the first "freedom riders" into "Dixie" to test the Supreme Court's June 3, 1946 decision that banned segregation in interstate bus travel.[42] CORE activities served as a prelude to later concerted civil rights efforts.

Rhetoric about democracy during World War II shamed black and white leaders in both the Young Men and Young Women's Christian Associations into desegregating their respective organizations. The YMCA in the United States had been divided by race since its inception in 1852. In 1853 the first black YMCA appeared in Washington, D.C. and established a trend that continued throughout the nineteenth and into the early twentieth centuries. By the decade of the 1920s black YMCAs had been constructed in most major cities, functioned as black controlled community centers, and operated as autonomous, segregated associations. The segregated black "Y" troubled integrationists within the NAACP.[43] But segregation also allowed the YMCA directors generally, and Secretary Channing H. Tobias in particular to play an invaluable role as mentors and caretakers of the African American community.

Channing Tobias seemed destined to serve as the catalyst for institutional change in the YMCA. Born in Augusta, Georgia on February, 1, 1882, Tobias received a Bachelor of Arts degree from Paine Institute in 1902, a baccalaureate in divinity from Drew University in 1905, and joined the YMCA's International Committee in 1911. By 1923 Tobias became the senior African American secretary and served as the head of all black YMCAs through World War II. As the head of black "Y's," Tobias functioned as an anomaly. He believed in intra-racial dialogue but supported separate black associations in order to "develop leadership in a way and to an extent that would never be possible ... in branches made up largely of white people." [44] Yet at the same time he unalterably opposed segregation.

When the World War caused Tobias and other black association leaders to organize joint conferences with the NAACP, National Urban League, National Negro Congress, Brotherhood of Sleeping Car Porters and other black organizations to decide on how best to achieve racial equality, the ideological problem associated with the existence of segregated black YMCAs demanded resolution. After meeting with A. Philip Randolph, Walter White, Roy Wilkins, Lester Granger, Judge William H. Hastie, Adam Clayton Powell, Jr., Paul Robeson, and other black leaders to discuss the black American role in the war effort and equal opportunity in the military and defense plants, Tobias had to demand that white colleagues live by the Christian ideals they professed. Tobias attracted the attention of Eugene Barnett, a white man who served as General Secretary over all white YMCAs in the United States. In 1944 Barnett announced that racial discrimination was incompatible with the YMCA's Christian ideals and advocated the desegregation of all associations. And in 1946 the National Council declared that all local associations must eliminate racial discrimination. That same year Tobias followed predecessors like George E. Haynes of the Urban League and Mordecai Johnson, the President of Howard University, and used leadership in the black YMCA to advance his career and receive an appointment to President Truman's Committee on Civil Rights.[45]

African American women who headed the black YWCA mirrored the role of their male counterparts. Four years after the first YWCA was formed in Boston in 1866, black women established a Negro "Y" in Philadelphia. Black and white YWCA members worked jointly but separately to meet the needs for lodging and social services in urban America. A national YWCA board allowed for separate black associations known as branches. These branches reported to the local white dominated board, and, in turn, received financial assistance to administer to the needs of the African American community. From the 1920s through World War II, several women controlled the black branches of the YWCA, the most prominent being Eva Bowles, Elizabeth Ross Haynes, Anna Arnold Hedgeman, and Dorothy Height.

Eva Del Vakia Bowles served as the first prominent black official of the YWCA. Born on January 24, 1875 in Albany, Ohio, Bowles began her career as a teacher. After having taken courses at Ohio State University and the Columbia University School of Philanthropy, in 1905 Bowles became Secretary of the Colored Young Women's Christian Association in Harlem. By 1913 she became Secretary of the newly formed YWCA National Board Subcommittee for Colored Work. In this capacity Bowles worked assiduously to improve living conditions of black women in urban America and championed both the independence of a "colored" YWCA department and strengthening inter-racial ties with white women in the Central Association. From World War I to her retirement in 1932, Bowles significantly increased the number of black branches and the volume of African American women participating in YWCA activities. She also cemented relationships between the YWCA and civil rights agencies like the NAACP and the National Urban League.[46] Therefore, when her successors—Haynes, Hedgeman, Height, and others—came to prominence, the leadership role of black women in the YWCA had been firmly established.

Prior to World War II Haynes, Hedgeman, and Height encouraged the "Y's" white hierarchy to hold intra-racial meetings and broaden the relationship between black branches and white associations. Elizabeth Ross Haynes, the first black to serve on the National Board (1924-1932), functioned as the link between reformist whites and leaders of African American branches. Anna Hedgeman, director of the Brooklyn YWCA, challenged the white establishment by using her position to expand job opportunities for black women. Dorothy Irene Height—a national leader in both the YWCA and the National Council of Negro Women, labored successfully with Vivian Carter Mason, Juanita Saddler, and Cecelia Cabaniss Saunders to integrate the YWCA. Eventually, the pressure to end the practice of separating the YWCAs by race proved successful. By 1946 directors of the Young Women's Christian Association joined their male counterparts and announced the official end to segregation.[47]

During the post war era religious organizations joined black leaders in support of civil rights endeavors. In March 1946, the Federal Council of the Churches of Christ in America examined segregationist patterns of racism in the United States and decided that the practices were anti-Christian and inimical to the larger society. The Church declared that racism, "results in economic discrimination, retarded mobilization of manpower during the war, creates grave psychological problems, handicaps the nation in its international relationships, occasions disfranchisement of a larger number of citizens, and increases and accentuates racial tensions."[48] Offering proof of their sincerity, the Federal Council agreed to "work for a non-segregated Church and a non-segregated society."[49] The National Catholic Welfare Conference, representing the Catholic Church, concurred with the findings of its Protestant counterpart. The Conference denounced segregation, declaring these nefarious acts "must be exposed as an un-American institution, contrary not only to Christian laws of charity and justice but also to the fundamental principle of democratic rights guaranteed by the Constitution of the United States."[50]

Despite support for civil rights generated nationally by black leaders during the war, Major League Baseball, an important segment of Americana remained untouched. The owners of major league baseball teams kept the nation's national pastime "lily white." Only when the racial schism that separated black and white professional players was breached would the average white American recognize that the war changed race relations in the United States. It would take a special talent to integrate professional baseball. Jackie Robinson would evolve as the athlete selected with the athleticism, intelligence, and temperament to force America's white, mainstream population to commence respecting blacks as citizens of the United States.

At approximately 6:00 PM. on January 31, 1919 in a town near Cairo, Georgia, future Hall of Fame baseball star Jack Roosevelt Robinson entered the world. As the youngest among five siblings, Jack never knew his father, a shiftless man who deserted the family. Alone and desperate to leave the poverty and degradation of the South, Jackie's mother, Mallie Robinson gathered her children, and in May 1921, headed for her half brother's home in Pasadena, California. Pasadena hardly proved a transition from hell to heaven for the Robinson family. Although white Californians did not engage in racial violence like white southerners, racism limited prospects for economic advancement. Consequently, the Robinsons found survival enormously challenging during Jackie's early years. Fortunately, his mother's fortitude and the extraordinary athletic gifts of Jackie, and his older brother Mac—a silver medallist at the 1936 Olympic Games—enabled the Robinson family to receive respect within the Pasadena community.

In high school Jackie Robinson distinguished himself as a multi-talented athlete in five sports—football, basketball, track and field, tennis, and baseball.[51] His athletic gifts extended into higher education at Pasadena Junior College and eventually at UCLA where he earned varsity letters in four sports and won an NCAA championship in the broad (long) jump.

After leaving UCLA only months before graduation to find work and reduce his mother's life of drudgery, Robinson joined the army and befriended Joe Louis at the army base in Fort Riley, Kansas. While there, Robinson entered the Officers Candidate School [OCS] program. As a prelude to gaining his lasting reputation as the man who ended segregation in major league baseball, Robinson attended the very first integrated OCS training unit. Despite conflicting stories about his fiery temper and inability to accept racial slights from drill instructors and white officers, Robinson earned a commission as a lieutenant in the cavalry division of the United States Army.

Robinson's years in the service proved difficult but representative of the new and prideful African American who preferred defiance to accommodation. While he displayed unquestionable leadership ability, the army's racist policies denigrated African American officers. Events came to a head with Robinson on July 6, 1944. On that date he fell into a dispute with local authorities outside Fort Hood in the nearby town of Temple, Texas. After being arrested for refusing to move to the back of a bus and creating a scene when called a "nigger," Robinson faced court martial. In the ensuing trial, Robinson defended himself against racial slurs and disrespect accorded him as an officer in the army, proclaimed his abhorrence for southern racial practices, and achieved exoneration by being found innocent.

After gaining an honorable discharge from the army and playing briefly with the Kansas City Monarch of the Negro Baseball League, the Dodger organization—headed by Branch Rickey—decided to break the color barrier by bringing black players into their organization. Therefore, on October 23, 1945, the Brooklyn Dodgers took the first step in integrating major league baseball by signing Jackie Robinson to a contract with the Dodgers' minor league affiliate, the Montreal Royals. After a stellar year with Montreal, Robinson signed a contract with the parent club on April 11, 1946. A new era in baseball and in the status of blacks in America commenced.

When Jackie Robinson became promoted to the major leagues he carried an entire race on his shoulders because the integration of baseball represented a major cultural breakthrough for African Americans. Every black socioeconomic class stood united behind Robinson. His failure to remain with the Dodgers would suggest in white and black minds that blacks remained outside the pale of American society. And if he succeeded, Americans would realize that integration, particularly in a sport dominated by white southerners, should occur nationwide.

Robinson represented many aspects of African American life. Southern-born, poor, and fatherless, his origins proved similar to many blacks of that era. However, by being college trained, articulate, reserved, and with his commission in the army as an officer and a gentleman, black aristocrats could embrace him as one of their own. Thus, by winning a place on the Dodger roster, Robinson performed two invaluable roles for his race. First, he proved himself an excellent representative of black America by carrying himself with dignity and pride. And second, his presence on the baseball diamond required black leadership to engage in an uncompromising, relentless effort to integrate blacks into the larger American society.

As a sensitive, prideful, determined, and gifted young man who came to prominence during the post-war era, Robinson anticipated the objectives of late twentieth century black leaders. This leadership class not only demanded equal rights, but also began to acquire wealth comparable to white peers. When Robinson retired from baseball, he became a corporate vice president of the "Chock Full o' Nuts" coffee corporation. Robinson's success gave rise to a new kind of conservative leadership that represented a "rags to riches" story emulated by subsequent black Republicans. For gifted and talented African Americans, Robinson demonstrated that the race could become a more integral part of the post-war world's leading democracy.

By the end of the decade the observations in *An American Dilemma* made by Swedish social scientist Gunnar Myrdal and his associates left an indelible mark on America's psyche that impacted the entire nation. The book spoke to the divisiveness caused by racism in America and the timing of its publication during a war to preserve American Democracy worked to the advantage of African Americans. Because of democratization attributed to the war, the black middle class experienced great tolerance from white Americans in the North. Enterprising blacks with money were no longer precluded from leaving the ghetto and moving into more attractive suburban homes in white suburban neighborhoods. White northerners would be more inclined to accept middle class blacks into their ranks and African Americans of "higher station" began to enjoy long coveted social respect. On the other hand, factors inimical for the African American masses—unemployment, overcrowded housing, crime, and vice—also identified in Myrdal's study were overlooked and ignored both by white society and black leadership.

Black intellectuals on Myrdal's staff helped him understand that the greatest obstacle to racial progress existed in the South. Myrdal reported that 50 southern African American leaders convened to mitigate racial animosity within their region. He also found that the groundswell for black racial justice during the war and post-war era appeared to originate with the masses in the South rather than the North. Black clergyman Dr. J.S. Nathaniel Tross gave credence to the restiveness of the masses when he lamented: "I am afraid for my people. They have grown restless. They are not happy. They no longer laugh. There is a new policy among them—something strange, perhaps terrible."[52] Tross' fears would be visited decades later through the work of a southern born, northern educated black intellectual, Martin Luther King, Jr.

The war decade demonstrated that black leaders from Jesse Owens, Joe Lewis and Jackie Robinson to A. Philip Randolph, Walter White, and Benjamin O. Davis Sr. and Jr. had earned grudging admiration for their race from the white establishment. More precisely, a basis for equality had been established for the black bourgeoisie—those blacks with sufficient industry, intelligence, talent, and bearing to be recognized as contributors to the larger American society. Black leaders and middle class African Americans, in turn, reflected the imagery of their white counterparts and helped their race become closer than ever before to meeting the standard norms established by middle class white America. Despite the heroics of black leaders and the work they performed to further the cause of African Americans, the war, and the war alone, determined the direction sable leaders would take as standard bearers for their race. Few at the time took into consideration the long-range impact of World War II. Southern black migration to the North, steady black employment and rising income, and the corresponding "knowledge of wants" acted as change agents in black and white society and hastened the black bourgeoisie's quest for civil rights. While the immediate changes provided comfort and solace, the over-reaching impact provided something different. As historian James MacGregor Burns observed: "The burning cities of 1967 and 1968 were not wholly unrelated to steps not taken, visions not glimpsed, priorities not established, in the federal agenda of 1943-1944.[53] Burns might have added an additional clause; black leaders underestimated the impact of World War II upon the African American masses—leaving the black majority hopeful but unfulfilled.

7

THE 1950s: CIVIL RIGHTS
AS A MIDDLE CLASS PANACEA

Having survived the Great Depression and escaped from the ravages of war, middle class blacks resembled the larger American society and sought a relief from crises in order to enjoy peace and prosperity. These desires remained unfulfilled. With the evolution of the Cold War—the uncontested hegemony of the Soviet Union in Eastern Europe and a western fear of messianic communism rising in Asia, Africa, and Latin America—Americans felt uneasy about the future. They became particularly concerned about critiques of the United States and savaged any citizen who challenged domestic practices in regard to race relations. These realities placed black leaders on the horns of a dilemma. African Americans who earnestly sought to ameliorate conditions for the masses by openly challenging existing racist policies faced the ignominy of being branded ungrateful at best, and at the very worst, a communist. On the other hand, sable leaders who charted a cautious course intent on acquiring rights for the black middle class could garner enormous successes. The challenge facing African American leadership, therefore, would be in determining whether to consolidate middle class gains or engage in risky political and social action with the ulterior motive of elevating the entire race.

Understandably, most African American leaders would be expected to tread cautiously and offer few challenges to the white power elite in American society. Like most United States citizens, blacks obviously coveted the prospects for enjoying prosperity in the post-war society. But unlike white Americans, blacks questioned the self-righteousness and sense of moral superiority extolled by anyone who believed that victory in war suggested that the American way of life had been vindicated. Instead, given the hypocrisy evident in American racism, African Americans appeared as the people most inclined to question and challenge domestic folkways, mores, and platitudes. More than anyone, they knew that racial discrimination existed as the antithesis to American principles of freedom and equality. These inconsistencies demanded a response from African American leadership—a response that would be heard nationally and internationally.

W.E.B. Du Bois became one of the first eminent blacks to take on the establishment, speak out vociferously against the America's non-democratic treatment of blacks, and embrace the Soviet Union as a paragon of virtue in its treatment of colored people. By 1950, the eighty-two year old Du Bois remained unparalleled as a researcher, scholar, and propagandist on behalf of his people. Fatigued by the relentless struggle for equal rights and embittered by the increasingly bourgeois leanings of the "talented tenth" and sanctimoniousness of American democracy, Du Bois gravitated toward socialism and internationalism. Du Bois also spoke openly in support of segregation and created an irrevocable split with Walter White, leading to his resignation from the NAACP and return to Atlanta in 1934. After retiring from his professorship at Atlanta University, he rejoined the NAACP in 1943 and promoted a relationship between the Association and the United Nations. The "good graces" Du Bois enjoyed with the black bourgeoisie and the NAACP, however, would be short lived. First, he publicly criticized the Boulé, the organization emblematic of black America's "talented tenth." This, added to subsequent disagreements with Walter White on a myriad of issues—among them, White's abhorrence to Du Bois' declaration that the Soviet Union was the "most hopeful country on earth"—led to Du Bois' ouster from the NAACP and alienation from the black establishment.[1] Thus when Du Bois became the object of State Department investigations in 1950 because of left wing leanings, he found himself shunned by black peers and a pariah in the United States. After reclaiming his passport, Du Bois would emigrate and spend his final years as an expatriate in Ghana.

Entertainer Paul Robeson, arguably the most renowned African American in the world, became another prominent black leader to raise embarrassing questions about America's racial practices. Like Du Bois,

Robeson would expose America's contradictory practices before the entire world and embrace radical concepts to free his race from degradation. On April 9, 1898 in Princeton, New Jersey, Paul Leroy Robeson entered the world. His father, William Drew Robeson had been a runaway slave who graduated from Lincoln University in Pennsylvania with a Bachelor of Sacred Theology degree. Paul's mother, Maria Louisa Bustill, hailed from one of the most prominent African American families in Philadelphia. As the youngest of seven children, young Robeson acquired the most positive attributes of his older siblings and would eventually establish himself as one of the most multi-talented men of his era. During his formative years growing up in a predominantly white society, Robeson honed his coping skills, accepted his father's sense of "obligation to the race," and acquired the determination to succeed with a quiet, regal dignity.[2] In 1915 Robeson enrolled at Rutgers College where he garnered numerous awards as an athlete and scholar. After his graduation from Rutgers as the class vale-dictorian, Robeson matriculated to Columbia Law School and, in 1923, received a degree in jurisprudence. However even before completing Law School, the multi-talented Robeson became recognized as a vocalist and actor, giving enthralling performances in concerts, on stage, and on the screen that gained him national and international acclaim.

During the early stages of Robeson's artistic career he became intro-duced to politics. Quietly smoldering from the insults hurled at him and his race, Robeson easily identified with the thoughts and deeds of liberal friends within the entertainment industry. His travels brought him in contact with the radical thinking European Emma Goldman, a woman of great intellect possessing enormous political energy and insight that profoundly influenced Robeson. Also included among his many friends were militant West Indian poet, Claude McKay, Walter White, W.E.B. Du Bois, and William L. Patterson, a young black lawyer who would become a leader in the Communist Party. Eventually, an association between communism and Russia developed in Robeson. He learned to speak that language fluently with the belief that Russian music suited his voice and because be believed "there is a kinship between the Russians and the Negroes. They were both serfs, and in the music there is the same note of melancholy touched with mysticism."[3] When Robeson made his initial trip to the Soviet Union in 1934, he had been prepared to become immediately enamored with the Russian language and culture, and primed to accept the Soviet political perspective unconditionally.[4]

By having sympathetic feelings for communism, Robeson jeopardized his leadership status and sounded the death knell for any African American or critically aggressive movement designed to aid poor, dispossessed, and disadvantaged blacks. Within certain circles, anyone championing the cause of the poor and attributing the root cause to capitalism would be held suspect, a factor in American society that Robeson ignored. Indeed, fears about appeals to the working class originated with the Bolshevik Revolution of 1917. Although the American public had little knowledge or interest in Russia's domestic affairs and were captivated more by the Great War raging in Europe, the captains of American industry had different concerns. American capitalists had great reservations about the repercussions of the Russian Revolution, a "revolt of the proletariat"—the masses of workers—and its impact upon the American labor force. Unlike Fascism driven by nationalism, Communism presented a messianic philosophy that threatened the status quo in capitalistic nations, a concept that chilled the blood of America's business establishment.[5]

Given the travail of African Americans, most of whom would be deemed working class, Robeson's support of communism seemed appropriate. Since the CPUSA perceived the majority of African Americans as members of the proletariat, Robeson respected American communists because members risked life and limb to defend the rights of the black masses.[6] Because Robeson retained a profound empathy for the suffering of his people, he appreciated the communist commitment to his race. And because no other white dominated party, organization, or group exceeded the communists in their zeal to help disadvantaged blacks, he welcomed CPUSA support.

Robeson's unremitting admiration for Russia and appreciation for Soviet politics and communism continued during the 1930s through World War II. Post-war politics in the United States, however, placed Robeson in a precarious situation. Before, only conservative Americans expressed concern about Robeson's leftist leanings. Suspicions about the Soviet Union and communism, however, alarmed a broader array of people and caused Robeson to become the focus of considerable public discontent. As early as 1947 Robeson became the object of FBI surveillance to prove directly or indirectly his relationship with the Communist Party. J. Edgar Hoover and gossip columnist Hedda Hopper promoted attacks against Robeson as he engaged on a national speaking tour. The House Un-American Activities Committee [HUAC] cited Robeson as being a supporter or member of CPUSA.[7]

During the remainder of the 1940s and into the 1950s, Robeson perceived the issue at hand as being a fight between Fascists—racists and bigots who attacked African Americans and working people—and anti-Fascists, progressives who would defend the civil and human rights of the downtrodden. Although Robeson spoke primarily about injustices accorded blacks in the South, he, along with the increasingly left-leaning W.E.B. Du Bois, became pariahs among the black leadership cadre. Even the most progressive minded black leaders believed Robeson had gone too far. The progressive thinking Bayard Rustin and A. Philip Randolph, along with Roy Wilkins, Mary McLeod Bethune, Charles H. Houston, and Congressman Adam Clayton Powell Jr., met and decided upon a united strategy to combat Robeson's "heresy." They knew that any American deemed a "fellow traveler" would find life in the United States difficult for himself and his associates. Therefore they believed that Robeson's "brand" of support for the masses, regardless of the provocation that inspired his passion for justice, would prove dangerous and ineffective.

A misquote attributed to Robeson in April, 1949 established a precedent that revealed black leadership's willingness to distance itself from the black working class community's most strident advocate. Robeson's frustration with American racial policies goaded him into making the intemperate and indefensible statement that blacks would not fight against anyone generally and the Soviet Union in particular. This remark became repeated and embellished by the American media, and enabled detractors of racial equality to suggest that blacks were "un-American." This elicited an immediate uproar from black leadership. Nearly every prominent African American voiced the opinion that Robeson spoke only for himself. Furthermore, believing the key to racial ameliora-tion existed in placating rather than insulting the white establishment, black leaders discredited and isolated themselves from a man they deemed a threat to the representative class of African Americans.[8] Equally important, black leadership reacted to Robeson's alleged utterance without verifying the accuracy of the remarks attributed to him. Frightened leaders com-pounded their rush to judgement by insinuating that Robeson did not speak for "ordinary" black citizens. The *Crisis* magazine declared that "Robeson has none except sentimental roots among American Negroes. He is one of them, but not with them."[9] Once again they failed to recognize that the masses bore the brunt of white violence and second-class citizenship that Robeson addressed. When chided by black peers and asked to mitigate his statement, Robeson spoke as a man who believed in equality for the masses and resented deeply the second class status of African Americans when he declared: "I'm looking for freedom—full freedom, not an inferior brand."[10]

Life for Paul Robeson worsened during the 1950s. Paranoia about communism, combined with Robeson's public admiration for the Soviet Union, closed the domestic market to his services. The federal government decided to silence him by confiscating his passport and preventing him from working abroad. These actions severely limited Robeson's ability to make a living. Consequently, a protracted legal fight commenced between Robeson and the government. Robeson sought to regain his rights as an American citizen to visit foreign countries while the government endeavored to reduce Robeson's popularity abroad and confine him to a life of penury and anonymity at home.

Prominent blacks embraced the State Department position and attacked Robeson. Former friend Walter White spoke patronizingly of the great virtuoso, suggesting that he was to be pitied more than damned, and declaring that he was overly sensitive to racial slights. Attacks against Robeson appeared in *The Crisis* and the black press. NAACP officials labeled Robeson as being a Kremlin Stooge, and the black press excoriated him for being a supporter of Russia. Even the most loyal of Robeson's support—the black church—retreated. Black ministers would rather disdain Robeson's melodious renditions of Negro spirituals than take risks that threatened the welfare of their congregations. Clearly the State Department and the conservative black leadership class systematically dismantled Robeson's effectiveness as a race leader and advocate for the African American masses.

Robeson could hardly be perceived as blameless for his isolation and fall from grace. Ego vested and unwilling to distance himself from the Soviet Union—America's Cold War enemy—Robeson's stubborn stance allowed his effectiveness as a race leader to be diminished. Though courageously committed to voicing his opinions, adulation for Stalin and the Soviet system militated against any assistance he could provide his race. Robeson's acts and deeds suggested that he would rather be idealistic and lose his effectiveness as a leader than become politically pragmatic and acquire some redress for African Americans. Robeson decided to pursue a singular path of self-righteousness and operate as an isolate. His sense of nobility in criticizing the United States while simultaneously praising the Soviet Union made him an outcast in American society.

Robeson failed to sense reasons for black middle class timidity during the time of McCarthyism, the tragic era that represented America's nadir as a free society. He allowed his fight with the government to become so personal that it imbued him with the notion that he spoke for every defenseless black man and woman in the African American community. When once baited by reporters who accused him of hurting his cause by allying himself with communism, Robeson expressed his anger by exclaiming: "Is this what you want? For me to bend and bow and shuffle along and be a nice, kindly colored man and say please when I ask for better treatment for my people? Well, it doesn't work."[11] Both blessed and cursed with the proud temperament of an artist, Robeson played in a political arena but ignored the "give and take" style of political games involving compromise, defeats, and victories. Instead, his actions made him appear less interested in improving the African American condition than furthering his personal vendetta against reactionary forces within the United States. Robeson simply refused moderation. When a nascent civil rights movement began at mid decade, Robeson had become inconsequential, rendering his remarks on behalf of African Americans irrelevant.

Despite the mistakes Robeson made in linking black liberation with the alleged class egalitarianism of Soviet Russia, he inadvertently expanded the vision of black leadership. Robeson's actions determined that prominent African Americans must think internationally to broaden support for an agenda designed to integrate blacks into mainstream America. Robeson's behavior also enabled black leaders to realize that to advance the African American cause by playing to an international audience, one must act with decorum, sensitivity, and show appreciation for the United States as the democratic leader of the Free World.

A man who learned from the mistakes of Paul Robeson was Ralph Johnson Bunche, a scholarly man who would demonstrate that he possessed the class, sobriety and prowess necessary to provide an African American presence on the stage of world politics. Born in Detroit to Frederick and Olive Johnson Bunche on August 7, 1903, young Ralph entered the household of a warm and talented family. Fred Bunche, who possessed a profound wanderlust, made his living as a barber and moved his family to various cities in the mid-west and South—from Cleveland and Toledo, Ohio to Knoxville, Tennessee. By 1915 tuberculosis contracted by Olive Bunche caused the family to uproot itself once again and move to Albuquerque, New Mexico. After his mother's death in 1917, Bunche came under the care of California relatives who raised Ralph and his siblings in Los Angeles. During his late adolescence Bunche developed a fierce academic and athletic competitiveness and earned a scholarship to UCLA.

He starred on the basketball team that won three conference champion-ships, majored in political science, and graduated in 1927 as the valedicto-rian of his class.

Bunche's academic prowess at UCLA earned him a scholarship to Harvard University where he continued his study in political science. After earning a Masters Degree, Bunche took leave from Harvard to become a professor at Howard University in Washington, D.C. Unfamiliar with segregation, Bunche found racism in the nation's capital appalling. Washington and Howard proved extremely confining, for as Bunche recalled: "Living in the nation's capital is like serving out a sentence. It's extremely difficult for a Negro to maintain even a semblance of human dignity in Washington."[12] It was at this time that he acquired a sense of "calculated" radicalism. Already prideful of his race, the sojourn to Howard under the conservative leadership of President Mordecai Johnson instilled Bunche with determination to use his social science training to champion the rights of the African American masses and colonized people throughout the world. In 1929 Bunche returned to Harvard to complete his Ph.D. and prepared a dissertation that served as a foundation for United Nations policies on trusteeship and de-colonization.[13]

Throughout the 1930s Bunche's radicalism held sway. He found himself outside the standard norms of black intellectual thought and believed that the NAACP and National Urban League were excessively middle class and elitist. In his estimation, these organizations failed to meet the needs of the disadvantaged African American majority. Recognizing the wretched condition of African Americans, Bunche decided to dedicate his life to advance the cause of his race. He organized conferences, sharpened his political thinking by traveling and studying abroad, and served as a primary researcher and investigator for Myrdal's classic, *An American Dilemma*. Myrdal's influence shaped Bunche's career, for under his tutelage, Bunche tempered his socialistic concepts and endorsed the social-engineering prospective that suggested blacks should adopt the norms of middle class white society.[14] This shift in thought and deed earned Bunche the reputation as a moderate, temperate intellectual who could be trusted to serve his country—and race—on the international stage.

Bunche's venture into internationalism may in part be derived from his frustration with African American leadership. "Because of the extreme provincialism of its organizations and leaders, he reasoned, "the Negro population suffers from stagnation in its social thought."[15] Since Bunche thought outside the confines of the American political and social structure, he seemed primed to venture into an uncharted career as an internationalist. Bunche's intellectual interests, coupled with his sensitivity to disadvantaged minorities throughout the world, attracted the attention of the Office of Strategic Services [OSS], an agency established during World War II that served as the precursor to the Central Intelligence Agency. The value of Bunche's expertise in OSS became immediately apparent to the Department of State, the federal agency that retained his services throughout the duration of the war. Because of the excellent work Bunche provided the State Department, he was selected to represent the United States as a delegate to the San Francisco conference that created the United Nations.

Ironically, Bunche found it easier to work effectively as an internationalist than to agitate for reform in race relations at home. Robeson's trials and tribulations made Bunche realize that conservatism in post-war American society prevented a direct attack on black colonization in the American South. Indirect attacks on American racism, however, became possible through the United Nations [UN]. Delegates to the San Francisco conference proved receptive to the decolonization plans Bunche devised for the UN. Eventually, Bunche's work at the UN would make the United States more receptive to addressing the plight of blacks in the American South. As a pioneering senior official in the fledgling United Nations, Bunche presented a moderating, positive image of America which white leaders in the United States appreciated and extolled. Bunche would gain comfort knowing that his earlier work and progressive ideas could attain fruition by making white Americans more amenable to granting blacks civil rights. Ralph Johnson Bunche represented a perfect foil to the militancy of Paul Robeson.

Bunche's expertise as a writer and negotiator gained him an appointment as Chief Representative of the Secretary-General in Palestine. As the deputy and chief advisor to Count Folke Bernadotte of Sweden who headed the UN delegation, Bunche acquired intimate knowledge of the Arab-Israeli crisis. Soon after the assassination of Bernadotte by Israeli terrorists, the UN appointed Bunche to head the peace delegation. In this capacity he brought negotiations between the Arabs and Israelis to a positive conclusion and received the Nobel Peace Prize in December, 1950.

Although Ralph Bunche may be deemed one of the greatest, consistently decent, and most sincere African American leaders dedicated to lifting blacks from degradation, success occurred at a considerable price. Jealous of Bunche's achievements, W.E.B. Du Bois publicly criticized him for the "disgraceful betrayal" of Jewish interests over the Palestine question, and implied that Bunche "sold out" to acquire money and power.[16] Self-hating blacks also shunned Bunche and stung him by their rebuff. After receiving the Nobel Prize, Bunche underscored the need for peace and justice—at home and abroad—in his public addresses. While recognizing that his work received positive notoriety in the South, Bunche wrote the added phrase "except for Negroes of course." Black people at the time simply had difficulty lauding a deserving member of their race.[17]

Bunche's internationalism, staunch support for the UN, and pride in his racial heritage earned him the opprobrium of conservative white Americans. When he used the prestige acquired as a Nobel laureate to denounce American racism, he angered none other than President Dwight David Eisenhower. Eisenhower believed that Bunche should refrain from speaking out about the "Negro problem" and leave the race struggle to others. Predictably, Bunche also became an object for attack by McCarthyites. The most unfortunate aspect of the "witch hunt" against Bunche, however, involved blacks who colluded against him with right-wing whites. Max Yergan, former president of the National Negro Congress, along with Manning Johnson and Leonard Patterson—two former black communists—plotted against Bunche to sully his reputation. These men fabricated stories about Bunche's efforts to uplift the black masses and accused him of being a communist.[18] Although Bunche eagerly testified before the Loyalty Board and was exonerated of all charges, a precedent had been established. As with Robeson, any prominent African American who spoke before an international audience against American racism would become an object for right-wing harassment and be labeled a communist.

The treatment accorded Bunche must be understood as a backdrop to American domestic politics of the 1950s. The Truman legacy that enabled progressive black leadership to access the Chief Executive ended with the election of Eisenhower to the White House. An affable war hero, "Ike" (an affectation directed toward him by the fawning public) possessed an opportunity to move toward ending racial discord within the United States by striking down the vestiges of racial discrimination. Unfortunately, Eisenhower followed the dictates of his conservative advisors. When Eisenhower failed to defend his friend and former boss General George Marshall against anti-Communist zealots, blacks could hardly expect presidential support for their grievances. Eisenhower not only opposed the civil rights movement, but also identified far more with whites who engaged in discriminatory practices against blacks than for African

Americans seeking deliverance from the degradation of second class citizenship.

The hegemony of communism in China, the Korean War, and the Soviet Union's aggressive efforts to entice uncommitted nations to reject democratic capitalism forced Eisenhower to devise a means for combating the so called Communist menace. To mitigate the contradiction between segregation and democracy, Eisenhower incorporated blacks into his administration. By searching for and convening a "Black Cabinet" and placing African Americans in administrative positions, Eisenhower muted criticism from black leadership, perfected the concept of "visible tokenism,"—a policy evidently acceptable to the black middle class—and endeavored to counter communist accusations of American hypocrisy.

By sprinkling blacks throughout the State Department, Eisenhower elevated the concept of the black appointee to a high science. The State Department appointed Frank Snowden to be the Cultural Attaché in Rome. Clifton Wharton became the first black to head a foreign mission in a white country by serving as the American ambassador to Rumania. Other blacks serving on foreign missions included Robert Lee Brokenburr, Charles H. Mahoney, and Archibald J. Carey. Another unique appointment involved John B. Eubanks, a man designated to head the Rural Improvements Staff for the United States Operations Mission of the International Cooperation Administration. The Administration placed blacks in visible domestic positions as well. E. Frederic Morrow became the first black administrative assistant to work for a President of the United States. To bolster black visibility in the judiciary arm of government, the Administration selected Jewell Stratford Rogers to serve as an assistant U.S. attorney while Julia Cooper became the Administration's choice to serve as an attorney in the Criminal Division of the Justice Department. And finally, with ominous but perhaps pragmatic reasoning given the disproportionate number of African Americans incarcerated in prisons, Eisenhower appointed Scovel Richardson to chair the Board of Parole.[19]

Blacks who received positions in the Eisenhower Administration seemed pleased with their good fortune. These feelings seemed best exemplified by E. Frederic Morrow, a minister's son born on April 20, 1909 in Hackensack, New Jersey. Reverend John and Mamie Morrow enabled young Frederic to enjoy a serene early life. One of five siblings, Morrow inherited a burning desire to succeed despite racial obstacles strewn in his path. As a youngster he accepted racial discrimination as a fait accomplis and relied upon his deep faith in God for deliverance. In 1926

Morrow entered Bowdoin College and perfected his ability to deal effectively with white prejudice. As one of only two black students attending Bowdoin that year, Morrow accepted racial slights as the norm. He relied upon a simple axiom: "One must make oneself available to those who want to extend the right hand of fellowship and ignore with dignified pride and self-assurance those who do not."[20] Imbued with a profound faith in a benevolent God who would "open the way," Morrow revealed an industrious nature, a desire to excel, and a commitment to work silently toward establishing a positive example for his race.

After graduation from Bowdoin, social connections enabled Morrow to find employment in a Wall Street bank. As the only black trainee, Morrow met constant rebuffs. The sobering experience of racism within the bowels of capitalist America encouraged him to seek employment elsewhere. With support from a black fraternity friend, Morrow found work with the National Urban League as a staff member for *Opportunity* magazine. Seeking to achieve even greater advances for his race, Morrow eventually left *Opportunity* in 1937 and began working for the NAACP. As a member of the NAACP hierarchy, Morrow visited branches throughout the country, mitigated internal bickering, and demonstrated some concern about the welfare of the masses.[21] Induction into the army during World War II further convinced Morrow about the necessity for using his intelligence and training to pursue a career in civil rights. Recalling his harrowing military experience, Morrow said: "I left the service bitter and angry about the sacrifice of four years to ignominy and personal shame. I knew without contradiction that as long as I lived, I would never escape from America's shameful method of dealing with race and color."[22] Yet despite his anger attributed to the ill treatment he received, Morrow remained a steadfast, loyal American.

After mustering out of the service and attending the Rutgers University Law School, Morrow served as a writer for CBS in the Public Affairs Division. There, he caught the eye of Val Washington, Assistant to the Chairman of the Republican National Committee for Negro Affairs. As a leader among young Republicans in Hackensack, Morrow eagerly rekindled his association with the G.O.P. With Washington's assistance, Morrow was selected to be an advisor and consultant to General Eisenhower's presidential campaign of 1952. Morrow's demeanor and work ethic impressed Eisenhower's campaign directors. After the election, Sherman Adams, the newly elected president's Chief Executive, invited Morrow to join the White House staff.

Morrow soon learned that race would inhibit prospects for his success as an administrative "insider." Nearly two years elapsed before Morrow acquired a job as Administrative Officer for the Special Projects Group in the White House. When he finally became a member of the White House—where he became the first black executive assistant to serve the President—he found himself scorned by the Republican hierarchy. Nevertheless, Morrow remained an unequivocal supporter of the Eisenhower Administration. Not even criticism from a trusted black Republican who detailed the African American community's frustration for Eisenhower's insensitivity toward blacks deterred Morrow from being absolutely loyal to Ike.[23]

Morrow remained with Eisenhower and even offered the administration advice contrary to the interests of black people. Evidence of Morrow's questionable role as a black spokesperson occurred during the crisis concerning the integration of Central High School in Little Rock, Arkansas. In October 1957 black organizers sought an audience with President Eisenhower to enlist his support for their cause. Morrow recommended that the President avoid an audience with Daisy Bates and students known as the "Little Rock Nine," suggesting that the meeting would not be in the Chief Executive's best interest. Morrow also advised Jackie Robinson to avoid participating in a march on Washington to dramatize African American concerns about the Little Rock affair.[24] In response to his blind loyalty to Eisenhower, Morrow defended himself by saying: "Negroes look upon me as a symbol of disloyalty and a kind of benevolent traitor." Nevertheless, Morrow remained steadfast in the righteousness of his position, convinced that his actions served the best interests of his nation and race.[25]

In many respects Frederic Morrow anticipated the thinking of conservative African Americans at the dawn of the new millennium. He did the bidding for the establishment, accepted personal and racial slights with dignity, and remained loyal to a party whose actions proved inimical to the larger African American community. Moreover, Morrow convinced himself that the insults he endured were necessary sacrifices made on behalf of his race. He dismissed entirely the notion that he accepted insults and became a "toady" to remain a member on Eisenhower's team of presidential advisors. Morrow also perceived himself as being an elite representative of his race rather than a racial advocate. In his memoirs Morrow proudly declared:

I refused to be his [Eisenhower's] advisor on Black affairs. I said I would go to Washington to assist him if I were given the same recognition, responsibilities, and privileges of any other staff members. There was something abhorrent to me in being a professional "race-saver."[26]

In his capacity as White House advisor, Morrow appeared loath to address the needs of the masses. Though treated with disdain by the Republican establishment and Eisenhower cronies, Morrow declared: "I could never be disloyal to Dwight Eisenhower." Polemicist Frantz Fanon could easily classify Morrow as a prototype for the subjects described in his book, *Black Skin, White Masks*. Politics required loyalty, but Morrow's acquiescence seemed extreme even for the most class-conscious black leaders. But again, no other black leader at that time had a presidential appointment in the White House to protect.

Individuals like Morrow claimed to be proponents of civil rights, but they defined those "rights" within strict middle class guidelines. This could be observed in their avoidance of the larger African American community's need for decent housing. Post-war America required thousands of new housing units to satisfy the needs of burgeoning families.[27] As millions moved into newly created suburbs, two significant realities emerged; access to outlying urban districts required massive highway construction, and cities demanded urban renewal to meet the needs of an ever expanding, prosperous population. Under the aegis of the Urban Renewal Administration of 1954 the federal government displaced scores of blacks for highway construction and urban renewal projects. Although those who lost property through the right of eminent domain received credit extensions to purchase new homes, few impacted African Americans possessed the resources to qualify for federal funds.[28] Earl W. Schwulst of the National Commission on Race and Housing candidly stated: "Housing is apparently the only commodity in the American market which is not freely available to those minority groups who are non-white."[29]

Mainstream middle class black leadership had little to offer regarding the displacement of the urban black masses. Rather, they became comfortably ensconced in the security of aesthetic, serene black enclaves inhabited by the "better class" of African Americans.[30] Those desperately in need of housing were not of their class, and therefore received little concern from the black elite. For example when questions arose in Chicago about Negro housing, the issue involved pertained to segregation in middle class zones which prevented the black bourgeoisie from moving into upscale white neighborhoods. Housing for the working class who suffered grievously in unseemly, decaying structures never received consideration. Between 1950 and 1960, the percentage of non-whites in the United States (primarily blacks) occupying substandard housing increased from 19 to 27 percent.[31]

With the exception of Reverend Adam Clayton Powell Jr., no black leader of the early 1950s championed the cause of homeless, destitute African Americans. Born in New Haven, Connecticut on November 29, 1908, young Adam grew up in luxury in the household of Adam Sr. and Matte Powell. Soon after Adam Jr.'s birth, the elder Powell moved to New York City to serve as pastor of the Abyssinian Baptist Church. Though both parents could easily pass for white, they instilled Adam, Jr. with a profound sense of racial pride. In 1922 Powell attended the prestigious Townsend Harris Hall High School in Manhattan, matriculated to City College and eventually Colgate University where he earned his undergraduate degree in 1930. At Colgate Powell distinguished himself as an independent thinker and a serious, but hedonistic student. After graduating from Colgate, Powell attended the Union Theological Seminary in preparation for succeeding his father as minister of Abyssinian. Before taking the place of his father Powell served as the church's business manager and became deeply affected by the suffering black people experienced during the Great Depression.[32] The hardships endured by black Harlemites left a profound impression on Powell and caused him to devote his professional career to ameliorating the suffering of downtrodden blacks.

Tall, engaging, and extremely handsome, Powell exhibited a talent for oratory and love for politics. New York City became the ideal locale for Powell, enabling him to exhibit his many talents in anticipation of a political career. Progressive minded New York politicians and machine run Tammany Hall provided Powell with stimulation he could not ignore. He used the "Bully" pulpit of Abyssinian to satisfy his political ambitions. From the inception of his foray into politics, Powell contested strong and powerful forces to support the weak, but Powell was no fool. Intent on winning every contest he entered, every fight he initiated was always calculated. He knew how to use people effectively, how to mend political fences, and possessed an uncanny knack for extricating himself from difficult situations. He also proved adroit at organizing rallies and achieving the expected objectives through direct action. These qualities made him a consistent winner, enabled him to gain largess for his constituents, and enhanced his prestige in black and white America sufficiently to become a national leader.

Elected to Congress in 1942, Powell established a reputation for being shrewd, creative, brilliant, colorful, and arrogant. By 1950 Powell had established himself as the most race conscious black politician to serve in Congress since Reconstruction. Unlike Oscar De Priest, Arthur Mitchell, and William Dawson, ineffective congressional predecessors who represented the black congressional district in Chicago, Powell exhibited a combative style in the House. He referred to the black Chicago House members as "Uncle Toms." Unlike the Chicago cadre, Powell refused to accept racial slights, gleefully took on bigoted southern whites, and aggressively challenged anyone with whom he disagreed. An opportunist and a maverick Democrat, Powell vociferously attacked liberals and conservatives, Republicans and Democrats, and blacks and whites with equal fervor in order to satiate his ambition and derive opportunities for his race.

On the eve of the 1952 election Powell firmly established himself as a political power broker. Known as "Mr. Civil Rights," he attacked the Democratic National Convention and made his presence felt within the Party hierarchy. He denounced Alabama Senator John Sparkman as the Democratic Party's vice presidential nominee and vilified the weak civil rights plank contained in the Democratic platform. After the convention Powell forced the Democratic presidential nominee, Adlai Stevenson to make a New York City pilgrimage. Powell not only required Stevenson to pay homage to him, but also exacted concessions beneficial to African Americans. If elected, Stevenson agreed to eradicate segregation in Washington, D.C. and fight segregation nationally.[33] Stevenson's concession to Powell's civil rights demands made Powell the most influential black political figure in the nation.

Although Eisenhower won the election, the Democrats retained control in both houses of Congress. When the Eisenhower Administration reneged on its promise to desegregate military bases, Powell charged the White House staff of being insubordinate and responsible for sabotaging integration. The Administration immediately responded to Powell by sending Secretary of the Cabinet Max Rabb to placate the powerful congressman. Powell's outburst paid dividends for Powell, the Administration, and for African Americans. Given the responsibility for traveling to American military bases, Powell became the Administration's watchdog for the integration of American military bases throughout the world. After he visited a segregated base, Powell informed the Administration about his "discovery," causing "Jim Crow" signs to disappear immediately. Thus,

Adam Clayton Powell, Jr. became the first African American leader of national repute since Booker T. Washington to have direct access to and influence with the White House. The crafty Powell also knew how to remain within the good graces of the Administration by extolling, whenever possible, the virtues of American democracy before the international community. In this way he avoided any possibility of being deemed a disloyal American. Obviously, Powell earned the Administration's grudging respect, for as Sherman Adams recalled: "Powell ... was a political asset and we treated him as such."[34]

The Eisenhower White House learned how to control Powell by playing to his ego, a strategy that paid dividends for the G.O.P. in 1954. In February of that year, Powell addressed a union rally in Chicago and declared that Eisenhower "had done more to restore the Negro "to the status of first-class citizenship' than anyone since Lincoln."[35] When the White House staff arranged to have Powell write a positive article about Eisenhower in relation to blacks in *Readers Digest*, the ego driven Congressman complied. The article appeared in October 1954 on the eve of mid-term elections, an act that outraged leaders within the Democratic Party. To loyal Democrats, Powell reached the apex of political "double-dealing" two years later when he endorsed Eisenhower over Stevenson in the presidential election. Powell's action placed scores of African Americans on the Eisenhower bandwagon. Although he became a pariah within the Democratic Party, the Congressman hardly cared. For endorsing Eisenhower, Powell received between $50,000 and $100,000 to augment his personal "war chest."[36]

Powell maintained the loyalty of his constituents despite exhibiting an unconventional political style. He possessed an uncanny sense of knowing which specific issues held most relevance to the African American public. By the-mid 1950s, school integration became the primary focus of civil rights activists, and here, Powell claimed his most noteworthy success. In 1956 the Eisenhower Administration announced a school construction plan. The proposed education bill created a maelstrom. Because the Brown decision mandated that schools must be integrated, southerners and northerners clashed over whether or not segregated schools could be built with federal funds. Eisenhower believed that pragmatic necessity, the desperate need for new schools, took precedent over social reform. In his estimation, the building program should proceed with segregation. At that time Powell served as a ranking member on the House Committee of Education and Labor. He objected to the construction of segregated schools with federal money. As an influential member of the House Committee,

Powell presented a forceful amendment that could defeat the Administration's building program. Characteristically, Frederic Morrow opposed the Powell amendment, declaring his unqualified faith and trust in the President's judgement,[37] but in the end the Administration capitulated and Powell won. Segregated schools would never be constructed with federal funds.

Powell and Morrow represented two contrasting styles that served as precedents for future generations of African American leaders. The Powell style proved efficacious during the late 1950s and extended into the 1960s. Powell would prove one of the last prominent leaders who worked almost exclusively on behalf of the entire race rather than the black middle class. He renounced the haughty mannerisms of the black bourgeoisie, befriended people of darker hue, and gladly alienated the African American elite to curry favor with the masses. Brusque, boisterous, and representative of the "earthier" aspects of African American culture, he chose to be known as a proud, conspicuous black man rather than as a token "Negro." Morrow, conversely, represented the opposite end of the political and social spectrum. Always proper and dignified, he manifested all the characteristics of an African American pioneer, and epitomized the Myrdal concept of social engineering. Morrow identified strongly with whites—even at the expense of his race—in order to be accepted by the white power structure. Being the first and only member of his race to play a role in decision making with the most powerful white leader of the nation, Morrow received personal gratification that transcended accusations that deemed him a "race traitor" by contentious black opponents. Morrow's style, reminiscent of the accommodationist role of Booker T. Washington, would gain adherents after the social and political controversies regarding school integration had abated. An amalgam of the two styles—confrontational versus passive—would be applied during the African American quest for equality in the efforts to integrate public schools.

For several decades black leadership perceived education as the key to acquiring civil rights for African Americans. As early as 1939 the NAACP prepared to gain black admittance into higher quality, white public elementary and secondary schools in southern and border-states, and had mapped out an excellent strategy to achieve success.[38] Theoretically, with access to equal educational opportunities, aspiring blacks would be able to demonstrate their intellectual abilities before skeptical whites, gain access to any position for which they qualified, and thereby contribute to the eradication of American racism. In addition, the black bourgeoisie felt confident that education enabled the middle class to maintain its existence and expand because education assured their progeny a worthy place in society. Through a series of attacks launched against the bastions of segregation in graduate and professional schools in Gaines v. Canada, Sweatt v. Painter and other Supreme Court cases, the stage had been carefully prepared for Brown and the reversal of the "separate but equal" doctrine contained in Plessy v. Ferguson.

With the NAACP victory in the Brown decision of 1954, middle class blacks and liberal whites sincerely believed a panacea for resolving the race problem in the United States had been found through the Supreme Court mandate. Thurgood Marshall mobilized the integrationist forces and formulated the strategy that culminated in the most powerful blow against segregation in United States history. Born in Baltimore, Maryland on July 2, 1908 to William and Norma Marshall, young Thurgood enjoyed a comfortable, middle class lifestyle. His father held a prestigious job in the black community as a Pullman-car waiter and his mother worked as an elementary school teacher. After enjoying a relatively comfortable childhood, Marshall enrolled at Lincoln University, Pennsylvania in 1925 with thoughts of becoming a dentist. By his senior year, however, he decided upon a career in law. After graduating from Lincoln with honors in 1930, Marshall enrolled at the Howard University School of Law where he came under the influence of Vice-Dean Charles H. Houston. Houston became Marshall's most influential mentor and directed his young charge toward a career in civil rights litigation.

In 1934 Marshall became the primary attorney for the Baltimore branch of the NAACP. When the national headquarters in New York selected Houston to serve as the NAACP's Special Council, he hired his protégé as an assistant. Marshall accepted the position and began a life-long career as an advocate for African American civil rights. By 1940 Marshall became the NAACP's Director-Council and became responsible for coordinating the Association's entire legal program. Therefore, prior to his appearance before the Supreme Court to argue the Brown case, Marshall had acquired twenty years of invaluable experience as a civil rights attorney.

With support from Walter White and Howard Law School Dean William H. Hastie, Marshall decided to launch a frontal assault against the "separate but equal" dictum. Using arguments proposed and documented by social scientists, Marshall endeavored to prove that the "'separate but equal' doctrine was devoid of legal foundation or social justification." He also argued that "classification and distinctions based on race or color have no moral or legal validity in our society."[39] Furthermore, Marshall contended that both Negroes and whites suffered from imposed segregation. Black pathos, he insisted, seemed self-evident given the stigma of inferiority attributed to all African Americans. However, he reasoned that white people who insisted on maintaining segregation expended enormous efforts that taxed the economic, political, legal, and moral standards of society. In conclusion, Marshall argued that an atmosphere of mutual distrust and hatred resulted that kept blacks and whites divided.[40]

The attack against separate public schools began in earnest during the summer of 1950. Five sites were targeted for litigation—Clarendon County, South Carolina; Topeka, Kansas; Farmville, Prince Edward County, Virginia; the Chancery Court of the State of Delaware; and Washington, D.C. Marshall vigorously argued that racial segregation undermined the principles of American democracy, and that the nefarious practice of segregating children in schools should be declared unconstitutional. The Supreme Court concurred with Marshall's position and endorsed his argument unanimously. Unfortunately, decades would pass before stubborn forces within the South complied with "Brown" and overt segregation became eliminated from American society. Nevertheless, the first major breakthrough against segregation had been achieved. The quest for civil rights from the middle class black perspective neared completion.

The Brown vs. Board of Education Supreme Court case easily ranked as the most far-reaching accomplishment achieved by black leadership during the twentieth century. Unfortunately, the decision had limited, if any effect on the masses. Although articulate, suave, debonair, and intelligent, Marshall and Congressman Powell collectively could hardly address the problems inherent in a profoundly racist American society through school integration alone. With Walter White deceased (he died in 1955) and Du Bois and Robeson discredited because of flirtations with communism, blacks required new leadership. Embarrassingly, novelist I.F. Stone raised the question in October 1955 when he opined: "The American Negro needs a Ghandi to lead him, and we need the American Negro to lead us."[41]

After the Brown case declared segregation in public schools unconstitutional, black leaders received encouragement to attack other manifestations of institutional segregation. The individual selected to destroy bastions of racism was a southern born minister named Martin Luther King, Jr. Unlike Powell and Marshall who operated primarily from the comfortable confines of Harlem in New York City, King began his career in Montgomery, Alabama, one of the most virulent, racist cities in America. While Powell's father prepared his son to become a spiritual altruist and Marshall's paternal mentor directed him to care for people through legal redress, King's role as a leader occurred accidentally. When Mrs. Rosa Parks refused to move to the back of the bus on December 5, 1955, she inadvertently launched the career of America's foremost civil rights leader.

Initially, King played no role in formulating a strategy to combat discrimination. Rather, E.D. Nixon, a Pullman porter, president of the Montgomery NAACP, and a close friend of Parks, along with Professor Jo Ann Robinson of Alabama State College, prepared to combat the Bus Company and white cultural norms. Only bullying by Nixon, who invoked support for powerless domestics who comprised the majority of bus riders, shamed the ministers and propelled King into action. King proved more than equal to the task. With brilliant oratory and exemplary leadership skills, King united Montgomery's African American community.

Black leaders selected King to head the Montgomery Improvement Association [MIA], the organization responsible for spearheading the boycott. The MIA established car pools and purchased fifteen station wagons to transport blacks throughout the city. Despite the inconveniences to black commuters and threats of white reprisals, the boycott continued. Finally, on November 13, 1956, nearly one year after Rosa Parks' arrest, the Supreme Court declared the Montgomery bus segregation law unconstitutional.[42] The Montgomery bus boycott represented one of those rare instances in the civil rights movement where blacks of all socioeconomic levels joined collectively to achieve mutual goals.

Ironically, one of the most significant civil rights achievements during the 1950s emanated from a most unlikely source—the administration of President Dwight David Eisenhower. Eisenhower sought tranquility during his second term in office, an unlikely probability given the burgeoning civil rights activities in the South. As a confirmed states rights advocate, Eisenhower fervently believed that the resolution of civil rights issues remained entirely within the purview of states rights. Blacks and liberal whites, however, looked to the federal government for support and protection. Attorney General Herbert Brownell sought a means for avoiding a clash between the federal government and the states. Brownell reasoned that the Administration could avoid using direct federal intervention in the South—a policy Eisenhower deemed politically risky and philosophically objectionable—if blacks were granted suffrage. The Brownell strategy appeared uncanny for several reasons. First, by having black people focus on voting rather than school integration, implementation of the Brown decision could be stalled without forcing the Administration's hand. Second, African American suffrage would occur without risk to the Republican Party because white southerners voted overwhelmingly Democratic. Moreover, the G.O.P. could retain black middle class voters and incorporate newly enfranchised African Americans into Republican ranks because the executive branch endorsed black suffrage. Third, by focusing on voting in the South, the G.O.P. could avoid addressing jobs and housing—issues of significant importance to the black masses in all regions of the nation. And finally, national support of the civil rights voting bill would presumably keep Republicans in the White House. Thus with the passage of the Civil Rights Bill of 1957, the G.O.P. played a carefully crafted hand.

Black leaders knew nothing of the wily Republican strategy. Brownell masked the subterfuge by enlisting the assistance of African Americans expected to guide the legislative process like attorney Maceo Hubbard of Philadelphia, Clarence Mitchell of the NAACP, and White House consultant E. Frederic Morrow.[43] While Brownell enabled the Eisenhower administration to establish a positive image for the Republican Party, the President also took steps to enhance his image within the black community. The President established a Commission on Civil Rights [CCR], the watchdog agency responsible for overseeing voting in the South. Ever the cautious conservative, Eisenhower found a means for avoiding public pronouncements about racial discrimination. Instead, he reasoned, the CCR would do all the talking. Eisenhower and the Republicans presumably placed themselves in a "no lose" situation in regard to African Americans and the entire American electorate.

The Eisenhower Administration's ploy to appease African Americans occurred out of necessity rather than by design. While American paranoia about communism during the early 1950s revealed limited white tolerance for outspoken blacks, by the decade's end the national and international political landscape had changed. Previously, black leadership was of so little consequence that Eisenhower refused to meet any emissary officially from the African American community. But with the public humiliation of "red baiting" Senator Joseph McCarthy, the 1954 Brown judgement, and the reversal of Eisenhower's "states rights" position when Arkansas Governor Orville Faubus embarrassed the President by refusing a federal mandate to integrate Little Rock High School, ascension for black rights occurred. Likewise, inroads made by international communism—the rise of Castro in Cuba and the pejorative impact of United States racial policies upon "uncommitted nations" exploited by the Soviet Union—had a demonstrable effect on the President. In a public gaffe, Eisenhower suggested that blacks exercise patience in their quest for equal citizenship. Eisenhower's rhetorical error served as the final factor that compelled the President to relent and meet with black leadership.

On June 23, 1958 Eisenhower met with Roy Wilkins of the NAACP, A. Philip Randolph, and Martin Luther King, Jr. [Fredric Morrow made certain that Powell would be excluded], a meeting that reflected accurately the cautious thinking of sable leaders of the 1950s. The men asked Eisenhower to help African Americans acquire basic constitutional rights—freedom of speech, association, assembly, and the redress of grievances. Maltreatment accorded African Americans, they argued, diminished the status of the United States internationally. As patriotic Americans, they provided Eisenhower with an opportunity to redress legitimate black grievances. The triumvirate also lamented the disrespect for law exhibited by state and local office holders sworn to uphold rights inherent in the Constitution.

At first glance, requests Wilkins, Randolph, and King made of President Eisenhower were all encompassing and designed to benefit the entire African American community. No civil rights advocate would disagree with the black triumvirate's desire to have the Department of Justice investigate brutality inflicted upon African Americans and have the perpetrators brought to justice. And yet certain underlying unspoken assumptions may be gleaned about the intentions of Wilkins, Randolph, and King. Black leadership certainly demanded security for their race; simple protection under the aegis of the federal government; fair treatment for African Americans; and the opportunity for blacks to enjoy all legal rights extended to United States citizens.[44] However, the issues that rose pertained primarily to rights that should have been accorded specifically to the black middle class. Civil rights, though extremely important, would hold less relevance for the masses that focused essentially on survival. Employment, food, health care, and adequate housing existed as the fundamental needs coveted by the black majority.

The primary concerns of the African American middle class as voiced by the black envoys appeared in a formal statement presented to the President. After the triumvirate outlined their nine major areas of concern, only brief mention was made of the most relevant desire of working class blacks; namely, fairness in employment. The statement declared:

Widespread discrimination against Negroes in employment persists in industry, business, government, and has been underscored by the general rise in unemployment. The problem is highlighted by repeated failures of efforts to enact national fair employment legislation and by the demonstrated ineffectiveness of administrative directives.[45]

But even then, the thrust of black leadership's thinking in regard to its middle class orientation occurred in regard to black employment when the leaders concluded their requests in a statement that read:

The need continues for vigorous enforcement of the Federal policy of non-discrimination in government employment. The national government can set an example by removing the barriers which have limited the employment of Negro citizens in all U.S. installations abroad, including the foreign service.[46]

Presumably, the black masses never contemplated employment abroad. Equally apparent, a specific request demanding greater job accessibility for working class African Americans within the United States was never raised.

Black leaders recognized that their race experienced extraordinarily trying times during the 1950s. Lester Granger spoke truthfully and accurately when he told President Eisenhower that bitterness on the part of the Negro people never showed "more signs of congealing" than at present.[47] Murderous rampages in the South, the withholding of Federal protection for civil rights activists, unscrupulous politicians who incited racial hatred and a Chief Executive reluctant to appeal to the better instincts of democratic thinking Americans dictated the direction taken by black leadership. However, the concerns they addressed, even when fulfilled, would fall far short of meeting the needs of the larger African American community. Obviously, human rights had to be guaranteed to southern blacks, but not at the expense of an equally large number of poor, urban, northern blacks for whom civil rights had little meaning. Destitute African Americans wanted a job and a decent place to live.

Changes evident at the decade's end presented black leadership with an agenda replete with both hope and foreboding. The mid term elections held in November, 1958 represented a crushing defeat for a Republican Party that had restricted the movement toward black progress. The conservative but realistic E. Frederic Morrow recognized that blacks played a considerable role in aiding the Democratic victory, a development that gave black political observers reason for optimism. "Their [the black electorate] role," he noted, "indicated that besides civil rights, they were interested in economics first and foremost."[48] Few black leaders seemed aware of Morrow's astute observation or concerned about the wretched conditions and anger rising within the impoverished black masses. Concerns before downtrodden blacks hardly pertained to civil rights, political opportunities or social aspirations denied them because of race. Rather, these people looked toward a future that offered the basic necessities of life—food, clothing, shelter, and prospects for human dignity achieved through gainful employment. Therefore, the 1960s would present enormous differences between region and class that affected black leaders responsible for charting the course of the Civil Rights Movement.

8

THE 1960S: A DECADE OF CONTENTIOUS LEADERSHIP

Traditional black leaders became surprised, baffled, and controlled by events unfolding during the civil rights decade of the 1960s. The uncertainty seemed ironic. Americans generally recognized that blacks had legitimate grievances demanding redress. The executive and legislative branches of government realized the necessity for correcting past abuses and enacting policies to hasten the integration of blacks into mainstream America. Restrictive barriers based upon race eroded as African Americans became recognized as a group with economic power, as a race worthy of consideration for political largess, and as humans rightfully entitled to social equality. But as federal concerns about the welfare of African Americans increased, bitterness and anger erupted from within the bowels of the black masses in a manner that shocked the nation. Furthermore, concerns about the direction of the Civil Rights Movement became heightened as the masses' respect for African American leaders deteriorated, rendering the traditional black organizations and their spokespersons irrelevant, powerless, and obsolete.

For African Americans generally, and black leaders in particular, the decade began with a sense of determination and expectation. Yet unlike previous African American efforts to acquire civil rights, the decade would be largely influenced by people devoid of influence or prominence. On February 1, 1960 the first sign of a new leadership cadre emerging appeared when North Carolina A & T College students David Richmond, Franklin McCain, Ezell Blair, Jr., and Joseph McNeil applied Martin Luther King, Jr.'s tactic of non-violence by "sitting in" at a Woolworth lunch counter in Greensboro. The intrepid action of these young men forced management to desegregate the lunch counter and precipitated a massive movement that inspired scores of black students to engage in similar protest actions. From Hampton Institute in Virginia to Fayetteville State Teachers College in Arkansas, and Fisk in Nashville, Tennessee, students participated in a ground swell movement on behalf of civil rights.[1]

Interestingly, the "sit-in" movement initiated by the college students represented a continuous example of black middle class demands for equality and dignity worthy of their station. However the activist role black students played was unanticipated. Students attending black colleges traditionally exhibited a conservative and passive demeanor. As Milton Viorst observed: "students on these campuses were encouraged to pursue status, income, and consumption, not culture or learning, and certainly not the well-being of the race." He then added: "For generations, the graduates of these colleges were notorious for their social indifference."[2] However, the "Brown Decision," complemented by the courage displayed by blacks in Montgomery and Little Rock, spurred black college undergraduates into action. Students who matriculated to black colleges—the future physicians, lawyers, educators, ministers, and businessmen—now sensed the time was propitious for taking risks to guarantee their rights as professionals.[3] Previous generations of middle class blacks provided the foundation for freedom. College students of the 1960s intended to fulfill expectations initiated by their predecessors by risking their lives and demanding the inalienable rights accorded all American citizens.

John Lewis emerged as the era's most prominent student activist. Born on an Alabama farm in 1940 as one of ten children, Lewis suffered grievously from poverty during childhood years. Nevertheless, fired by ambition, he was determined to succeed and enjoy a more prosperous lifestyle. Lewis' probing mind searched for a means to extricate him from predestined poverty; he found solutions to his plight by exhibiting a fanatic desire for education.[4] Lewis' thirst for reading enabled him to learn of the Supreme Court's ruling against segregation in Brown v. The Board of Education, and with great expectation, he prepared to broaden his education by attending competitive integrated white schools. When die-hard segregationists refused to follow the dictates of the law and forcefully maintained "Jim Crow" schools, Lewis looked for additional inspiration to achieve personal goals. He found answers in the words and deeds of Dr. Martin Luther King.[5]

In 1957 Lewis enrolled at the American Baptist Theological Seminary in Nashville, Tennessee. While there, he joined the Nashville Chapter of the NAACP and came under the influence of James M. Lawson, Jr., a graduate student familiar with Gandhi, and an undergraduate named Diane Nash, a person Lewis deemed "the most daring of our leaders." Uncompromising, intense, and extremely dedicated to racial amelioration, Nash, along with Lawson and Lewis, made Nashville the most efficient and effective student-run civil rights center in the nation. The students' courage caused Fisk University president Dr. Stephen J. Wright to become the first chief executive of a black college to take a stand in support of civil rights. Dr. King even paid homage to the Nashville movement, describing it as "the best organized and the most disciplined in the Southland." Almost single handedly, Lewis, Nash, and other black students attending Nashville colleges integrated the Greyhound bus terminal and desegregated downtown department stores. They also led a march on City Hall demanding civil rights.[6]

Lewis' involvement in the Nashville Civil Rights Movement conveyed far more than opposition to "Jim Crow." He and other students lost faith in traditional black leaders and organizations. Their wariness became initially raised by Myles Horton, a fifty-year old white man who founded the Highlander Folk School. Highlander served as a training ground for social justice activists. Horton warned the students, as Lewis remembered: "... not to allow ourselves to become the slaves of any of the old, established civil rights organizations." Lewis finally recalled that Horton reminded his charges: "Don't let anyone else, specially the older folks, tell you what to do."[7] These admonitions proved prophetic when Dr. Wright, along with Tennessee State University President W.S. Davis, endeavored to undercut the students by independently reaching a compromise with city merchants over segregated seating in restaurants. Further evidence of traditional black leaders' naiveté about student motives occurred when Thurgood Marshall visited Fisk at the height of the "sit-in" movement and admonished the students for getting arrested and refusing bail. Marshall advised: "Once you've been arrested you've made your point. If someone offers to get you out, man, get out." Marshall's suggestion fell on unreceptive ears. In response to the warning, Lewis recalled: "Thurgood Marshall was a good man ... but watching him speak on the April evening in Nashville convinced me more than ever that our revolt was as much against this nation's traditional black leadership structure as it was against racial segregation and discrimination."[8]

Throughout the spring of 1960 the "sit-in" movement comprised approximately 75,000 active participants. These efforts met with success. Eventually sixty-nine cities throughout the nation terminated segregation, including twenty-seven southern municipalities that integrated lunch counters. While the "deep South" remained bitterly opposed to integration, student leaders convinced most white Americans, including pragmatic, progressive southerners, about the righteousness of their cause.

Realizing that "sit-ins" alone would be unable to end segregation, student activists decided to hold a strategy meeting to complete the task at hand. Ella Baker, a woman who devoted her life to the civil rights struggle, served as the conference catalyst. As the Executive Secretary of the Southern Christian Leadership Conference [SCLC], Baker convinced the organization to host the event. Approximately one hundred student "sit-in" veterans representing sixty-five colleges and universities convened at Shaw University in Raleigh, North Carolina to expand the movement and enhance its effectiveness. The students wanted to pursue an independent path in the Civil Rights Movement. Although the assemblage accepted non-violence as a tactic, student leaders found it difficult, if not impossible, to adhere to non-violence as a way of life and eschewed the passive aggressiveness of Martin Luther King. Nevertheless, in deference to Lawson, students accepted non-violence and astutely invoked this principle by naming their fledgling organization the Student Non-Violent Coordinating Committee [SNCC].[9]

An additional and uniquely striking principle invoked by students attending the Raleigh conference pertained to the importance of economics in the Civil Rights Movement. The students' perception that economics served as the driving force underlying segregation served as a primary wedge that separated SNCC from SCLC, the parent organization. At that time, King failed to comprehend the relationship between racism and classism, or appreciate the degree to which students understood class and race issues. He ignored entirely the possibility that segregation and other forms of discrimination had economic underpinnings. Instead, as a moralist and man of the cloth, he believed in the goodness of humankind and sensed that moral suasion, in the end, would prevail. Ella Baker disagreed with King's contention that civil rights must inspire white Americans to achieve a higher level of morality. Rather, Baker recognized that elevating the moral understanding of whites toward blacks was irrelevant when she posed the question: "What's the use of integrating lunch counters when Negroes can't afford to sit down and buy a hamburger?"[10] King refused to adopt Baker's reasoning and the opinion of students and eventually had Baker fired. King's recalcitrance unwittingly created dire consequences for the Civil Rights Movement. Without access to economic equality, blacks could never become completely free. Although economic equity would become more and more feasible for the black middle class, the black masses would remain unrequited, surly, and inclined toward violent outbursts in protest against their condition.

When SNCC became officially established in the fall of 1960, it predicated a transformation in the Civil Rights Movement. The organization would represent the restive element of civil rights activists. Imbued with strong Christian principles, students involved with SNCC professed a broader construct; they presumed to have a better understanding of the means for achieving black freedom than their mentors. Using firebrand rhetoric reminiscent of the Black Muslims, the courage of SCLC pacifists, and the urgency of youth, SNCC would momentarily wrest a portion of the leadership role from the black establishment and help push the federal government into a more aggressive stance on behalf of black civil rights.

On the eve of the 1960 presidential election astute white politicians recognized that blacks could play a pivotal role in the election. Events since "Brown" dictated that blacks would make greater demands from leaders—black and white—to secure rights outlined in the United States Constitution. Presidential candidates Nixon and Kennedy sensed the winds of change. Although black people did not know Vice President Nixon well, he had name recognition and proved to be a far greater friend to African Americans than President Eisenhower. Nixon offered positive council on civil rights issues and gained accessibility to influential black leaders.[11] Kennedy, on the other hand, had no discernable civil rights record and presented a less than stellar resume as a United States Senator. To Americans generally, and African Americans specifically, gaining the White House seemed more like an election for Nixon to lose than for Kennedy, an Irish Catholic, to win.

Fortunately for Kennedy, an African American leader played an instrumental role in the outcome of the election and precipitated a change in the federal government's role in civil rights. A Georgia judge incarcerated Martin Luther King, Jr. in the Reidsville Prison for an alleged parole violation and sentenced him to four months hard labor. Both Nixon and Kennedy had an opportunity to make a humanitarian gesture to extricate

King from jail. Only Kennedy acted. He called Correta King, expressed concern about her husband's incarceration, and had his brother Robert contact the judge to secure King's release. News of Kennedy's gesture reverberated throughout black America. Black voters swarmed to the polls in unprecedented numbers. The black vote in pivotal states like Michigan, Texas, South Carolina, Louisiana, and Illinois provided Kennedy with a narrow margin of victory. African Americans rejoiced in knowing that Kennedy's triumph also served as a victory for King and for the larger black society. African Americans, the leaders and masses alike, looked with great anticipation to a federal government headed by a sympathetic John Fitzgerald Kennedy.

Realizing that blacks played a major role in his victory, Kennedy made appreciative gestures toward the African American community. He issued an Executive Order that denounced discrimination in federal employment and placed blacks in key administrative positions. Nevertheless, an essential question remained. How would black leaders capitalize on Kennedy's victory by encouraging the new administration to benefit African Americans?

Demanding blacks expected far more from the Administration than political appointments and Executive Orders denouncing racism. Almost immediately after Kennedy took office, James Farmer decided to test Kennedy's commitment to civil rights. On February 1, 1961, Farmer became the national director of the CORE. A graduate of Wiley College in Marshall, Texas and the School of Divinity at Howard University, Farmer had familiarity with Gandhi's tactics and decided to apply the concept of non-violent protest in a Freedom Ride through the "deep South." The "Ride" had a two-fold purpose—to expose the nation and world to the excesses of southern bigotry and to test the resolve of President Kennedy in ending southern racism. Farmer selected a mixed racial group—eleven men and two women—to join him in a challenge to southerners and the Administration. Thus, on May 4, 1961 Farmer, along with John Lewis and other brave young men and women ventured forth from Atlanta, Georgia [with the final destination New Orleans] to engage the opponents of human rights.

Freedom Riders did far more than test Kennedy's stance on civil rights; participants also tested the courage of established black leaders. The first violent response to the Freedom Riders occurred in Rock Hill, South Carolina. There, Lewis and Albert Bigelow, a white man and former navy captain who served in World War II, received beatings at the hands of white toughs. The situation became even more critical for the Riders in Anniston and Birmingham, Alabama. In these cities Freedom Riders suffered grievously at the hands of mobs and barely escaped death. The violent response caused Farmer to terminate the venture. When Farmer's decision became public, Nashville students insisted on continuing the operation. Despite the omnipresent aura of danger, Diane Nash called Farmer, asked for his support, resolutely declared that students would continue the "Rides," and declared that members of the Nashville Student Movement "would take their chances on getting massacred."[12]

Lewis and the second tier of Riders continued the Freedom Rides and established a prelude to the future. Subsequent civil rights activists became fearless and transcended the caution of traditional black leaders. Thurgood Marshall, though well intended, again appeared as a reactionary force to youthful civil rights enthusiasts when he advised southern blacks to keep away from the "well-meaning" radical groups.[13] He also told SNCC members to refrain from their actions declaring: "It's a waste ... you'll get people hurt ... you'll get people killed." Events, however, would suggest that the "Young Turks" had a better strategy for combating southern racism than the "old guard." No freedom rider died. Equally important, the vitriol, hatred, and violence displayed by southern whites pressed the Kennedy Administration into action. Farmer's gamble paid dividends when Attorney General Robert Kennedy decided the federal government would escort the riders from Birmingham to Montgomery, Alabama. Freedom Riders succeeded in forcing the federal government to take another step toward endorsing civil rights.

The younger generation of African American "Riders" forced Farmer to announce that "Freedom Riders" would continue their destination to Mississippi. To Farmer, the ride into Mississippi was a frightful prospect. Farmer initially excused himself from the trip and admitted he "was scared shitless." A patronizing glare and statement from one of the young female students shamed Farmer into boarding the bus and continuing the journey.[14] Farmer hardly experienced fear alone. After endorsing the Ride, King refused to join Farmer and the Nashville contingent. The young people were furious with King and called him a coward.

After 360 riders had been arrested and jailed, Robert Kennedy again acted. He ordered the Interstate Commerce Commission [ICC] to ban segregation within interstate terminals. This mandate essentially ended discrimination in interstate travel. Although CORE initiated the "Freedom Rides," its role as a civil rights organization faced the prospect of being eclipsed by SNCC. The daring students forced the federal government into unequivocal support for the Civil Rights Movement, something that previous generations of black leaders failed to accomplish.

Energized by SNCC's successful forays into the South but fearful of a diminished role as leaders, the traditional "old guard" sprang into action. They initiated their grab for power by attacking the Kennedy Administration for being "cautious and defensive." Wilkins publicly announced his "disappointment with Mr. Kennedy's first year."[15] But if attacks against the Administration were designed to ingratiate African American leaders with the black electorate, the strategy failed miserably. Instead, the attack displayed an ever widening gulf between traditional black leaders and the masses. While the leadership expressed disappointment with Kennedy, the larger African American community showed continuous support for the Administration. As Kennedy's mystique grew within the black community, the prestige of black leaders steadily declined.

Despite public utterances ridiculing the Administration's support for civil rights, traditional black leaders had far more in common with strategists of the New Frontier than imagined. Both black leaders and the Administration approached resolutions to racial problems cautiously and concentrated on issues peripheral to the black majority. Neither fully understood the emotions and views of the black masses, addressed concerns over employment, nor gauged the extent of resentment building within the African American community.

In February 1963 Kennedy informed Congress about his desire to establish equality throughout the nation. Inequities in voting, housing, education, employment, and public accommodations, he avowed, must be addressed and corrected. Unfortunately, Kennedy's appeal fell on deaf ears in Congress—the legislative body refused to take action that would mitigate black grievances. With Kennedy's inability to deliver salvation to the African American majority—and with King, Randolph, and Wilkins perceived to have the President's ear—those who criticized traditional leaders seemed vindicated. The strategy of non-violence appeared anachronistic and ineffective. Professor Kenneth Clark of CCNY, the man responsible for explaining the psychological damage of segregation on black children useful in the Brown deliberation, articulated a sense of the growing enmity arising with the black masses. These people, Clark observed, rejected the gradualism embraced by the Administration and black leaders. Policy makers seemed unwilling or unable to devise a meaningful change in the status of African Americans.[16]

As black feelings hardened against non-violence, King conceived of a masterful stroke to recapture his philosophy of non-resistance as a viable strategy. He knew how to regain momentum for himself and SCLC by focusing on Birmingham, Alabama, the bastion of the segregated South. King also knew how to use an unwitting accomplice in the quest for renewed power in Eugene "Bull" Connor, the Birmingham police commissioner. On May 3, 1963 Connor used police dogs and water hoses against demonstrators and redirected leadership of the Civil Rights Movement in America back to Martin Luther King, Jr. King effectively used police violence to garner national attention as the intellectual and spiritual leader of the movement toward civil rights. [17]

Through a questionable but effective use of children as demonstrators, his physical presence and emboldened strength of character—and Connor's tactics that aroused public indignation—King forced Birmingham to surrender. Influenced by the national outcry against Connor's brutality and moral righteousness of the demonstrators' cause, the city's leading citizens agreed to desegregate most public facilities in downtown Birmingham. Those within the white power structure also placed and promoted blacks to positions previously denied African Americans, and established a biracial committee to resolve interracial problems.

The successful foray into Birmingham offered two unanticipated and contradictory responses. In a positive sense, President Kennedy presented a sweeping Civil Rights Bill to Congress designed to make discrimination unlawful throughout the nation. If enacted by Congress the Bill would eliminate the need for lengthy and protracted demonstrations to desegregate the recalcitrant South. On the other hand, the inhumanity displayed by Connor and the Birmingham police had been nationally televised, heightened black anger, and increased the African American community's resentment toward law enforcement agencies. Black leaders responded to Connor's brutality with rhetoric as an expression of frustration and worked aggressively to achieve passage of a civil rights bill to stem anger in the black community. However the black masses cared little about a congressional Civil Rights Bill and would present their antipathy for racial discrimination through violent protests in the streets.[18] Eventually the civil rights revolution would create a divisive wedge between leaders who spoke for justice and those among the black public intent on creating mayhem to satiate their anger.

Events in Birmingham caused members of the black establishment—Kenneth Clark, along with entertainers Harry Belafonte and Lena

Horne, writer James Baldwin, playwright Lorraine Hansberry and others—to meet with Robert Kennedy. For three hours the group excoriated the Attorney General for the Administration's callous disregard for the health and safety of civil rights activists. One representative even declared that being in the same room with Kennedy made him feel like vomiting.[19]

Unlike the elite who verbally attacked Robert Kennedy, scores of angry blacks expressed their frustration with discrimination through overt demonstrations. During the summer of 1963 an estimated 14,000 demonstrators who took to the streets in southern cities like Birmingham, Nashville, Raleigh, Greensboro, and Albany were arrested. African Americans also launched demonstrations in Sacramento, Detroit, Philadelphia, Chicago, Columbus, Ohio, Cambridge, Maryland, and New York City.[20] No black leader held sway with those engaging in the spontaneous eruptions. Frustration propelled inner city blacks into a frenzied response against racism and their impoverished status.

After being responsible for the initial civil rights successes of the 1950s but shunted aside by aggressive young men and women during the early 1960s, "old guard" leaders experienced a diminution of their power. A generation gap had evolved; young people lost respect for the venerable leadership. Randolph existed as a forgotten relic, King had been perceived as timid, and Farmer's behavior on the most recent Freedom Ride caused daring youths from SNCC to view him as being cowardly. NAACP director Roy Wilkins, by young people's reasoning headed a moribund organization that appeared far too conservative to be effective. Collectively, the established leadership realized that they could maintain power within their race only by devising a venture that would galvanize the masses and lead them in a directed, concentrated civil rights endeavor. The means by which power could be restored appeared in the guise of A. Philip Randolph and Bayard Rustin; the plan involved a massive March on Washington.

As the individual selected to help traditional leaders regain power by taking care of the logistics for the demonstration, Rustin endorsed the concept of a march solely for idealistic reasons. He sought to commemorate the centennial of the Emancipation Proclamation and to draw attention to economic injustices inflicted upon the poor. Rustin's sense of nobility and altruism evolved early in his life. Born out of wedlock in the small town of West Chester, Pennsylvania on March 17, 1912, Bayard Taylor Rustin was raised by a progressive matriarch activist grandmother, Julia Rustin. Grandmother Rustin also worked as a Quaker nurse and served as a board member of the local NAACP. Grandfather Janifer catered for the wealthy families in the town and brought additional funds into the Rustin household. Nevertheless, Julia Rustin served as the pillar of the family and the greatest influence on Rustin's life.[21] Through his grandmother Rustin acquired a profound commitment to achieving racial equality, a sense of justice, a desire for black economic opportunity, and an unwavering belief in pacifism. Athletic, handsome, brilliant, and gifted with an outstanding tenor voice, as a student at West Chester's Henderson High School, Rustin seemed destined for success. After acquiring a checkered education at Wilberforce University, Cheyney State Teachers College, and City College New York, Rustin would prove invaluable as a spiritual leader and strategist within the Civil Rights Movement.

Rustin's thinking corresponded with the ideas on race and class held by A. Philip Randolph. Rustin eventually met and befriended Randolph, and supported the initial MOWM concept in 1941. At the time Rustin held responsibility for busing young people to Washington and acquired knowledge of organizational logistics. Although the March never materialized, Rustin gained from the experience; he continued to engage in humanistic endeavors and honed skills designed to benefit his race. In 1956 Rustin served as King's secretary during the Montgomery Bus Boycott and acquired additional organizational skills. He designed car pools, engaged in fund raising, and handled press relations. Rustin's diversified background as an organizer and human rights activist made him the logical choice to be accorded a greater leadership role in the burgeoning movement for black civil rights.[22]

In the winter of 1962 Rustin visited Randolph, the man who acted as his surrogate father and mentor. During the course of their conversation Randolph suggested that an event be planned to commemorate the 100th anniversary of the Emancipation Proclamation; he decided to lead an Emancipation March on Washington. The seventy-three year old Randolph asked Rustin to prepare a blueprint for the March—a suitable task that Rustin gleefully accepted. Within weeks Randolph received the plan, cleared it with the Negro American Labor Council, and solicited support from key civil rights leaders. James Farmer of CORE and John Lewis of SNCC accepted immediately, for they supported the concept of a mass action to really impress white America, garner support from blacks, and pressure the executive and legislative branches of government to initiate action to free blacks from generations of racial oppression. Martin Luther King, Jr., however, demonstrated a reluctance to participate. King preferred to remain independent from Randolph and had an inclination to organize his own direct action movement on the nation's capital.[23]

Randolph realized that King's involvement would lend prestige to the March. After persuading King to join in the March and receiving his endorsement, Young and Wilkins decided to participate. Randolph then enticed SNCC leader John Lewis to attend with the dual purpose of attracting black youths to the gathering and co-opting radicals into refraining from militant acts of defiance. The "old guard" did not intend to be embarrassed. The strategy worked. Lewis delivered a temperate speech and the radicals remained in check.

March organizers also recognized that President Kennedy should be informed about their plans. Thirty leaders, including the "big six," Randolph, King, Wilkins, Whitney Young, James Farmer, and John Lewis met with Kennedy on June 22, 1963. The President initially spoke of the collective need to find the best means for ensuring passage of the Civil Rights Bill. Kennedy argued that the Bill's passage would be jeopardized if blacks alienated Congress and organized street demonstrations. The President sincerely believed that the rumored March on Washington would be foolhardy.

Black leaders certainly desired passage of the Civil Rights Bill but, they differed with the President regarding the March. The representatives held greater interest in retaining control of the Civil Rights Movement than mollifying Congress. As the most senior member of the black contingent and organizer of the original March on Washington, Randolph articulated the thinking of the collective leadership. In responding to Kennedy's misgivings about the looming March, Randolph said:

> The Negroes are already in the streets. It is very likely impossible to get them off. If they are bound to be in the streets in any case, is it not better that they be led by organizations dedicated to civil rights and disciplined by the struggle rather than to leave them to other leaders who care neither about civil rights nor about non-violence?[24]

Kennedy accepted Randolph's reasoning because he wanted traditional black leaders to gain control of the Civil Rights Movement and lesson the influence of "would be" radical extremists.

Other black leaders attending the meeting regarding the March concurred with Randolph. Farmer of CORE said: "We would be in a difficult if not untenable position if we called the street demonstrations off and were defeated in the legislative battle. The result would be that frustration would grow into violence and demand new leadership."[25] In support for the March, King said: "[The March] could serve as a means through which people with legitimate discontents could channel their grievances under disciplined, non-violent leadership." Responding to the timing of the March, King concluded: "I have never engaged in any direct action movement which did not seem ill-timed."[26] In deference to his elders, John Lewis did not speak. His views would be expressed later.

Historian Arthur Meier Schlesinger, Jr. attended the meeting and came away with the realization that black leadership—particularly King—was self-serving. Schlesinger recalled that: "King ... gave newspapermen after the meeting the impression that the President had asked the group to call off demonstrations and that he had boldly refused—a posture calculated to improve his standing among Negroes but only tenuously related to what happened."[27] To maintain their hegemony black leaders collectively agreed, with silent acquiescence from Lewis, the March on Washington would go forward.

In many respects the 1963 March simultaneously represented the apogee and nadir of black leadership. Through the March, Rustin, Randolph, and King revealed black leadership's skill in organizing. The entire nation became fixated on Washington D.C., and informed about the moral righteousness of the civil rights cause. Additionally, the March comprised thousands of people from different races, religions, and colors sympathetic to the black cause for freedom and constituted the most diverse demonstration for freedom in human history.[28] Unfortunately, by focusing on personalities, organization, and control, an important reason for initially holding the March had been forgotten. Lewis offered comments about "immoral compromises, black citizens, and the black masses ..." and declared he was distressed "... by the conservative concerns of the establishment faction, black and white, that were trying to steer the movement with their own interests in mind rather than the needs of the people."[29] Although the affair proved festive, dramatic, logistically and politically successful, stimulated by King's "I Have a Dream Speech," and embraced by President Kennedy, the March ignored issues pertaining to the poor. While Rustin solicited funding for jobless workers to participate in the Movement, no funds were forthcoming. "The sponsors were preoccupied," in Rustin's words, "with the problem of dignity."[30] He might have also specified that "dignity" represented the primary objective of the black middle class rather than the principal concern of the African American masses.

The March on Washington broadened the Civil Rights Movement by bringing blacks and whites together on a massive scale. Randolph, King, Wilkins, Rustin, Farmer, and Young achieved a primary goal long desired by their predecessors; they had gained legitimacy for the Civil Rights Movement by garnering respect from a representative contingent of progressive whites. This broad spectrum of the white community joined black leaders and proclaimed before the entire nation and world that racial discrimination must end.

Among certain blacks the positive symbolism achieved through the March held minimum significance. While the March enabled the black bourgeoisie to acquire understanding and support for its definition of civil rights, the needs of the working class and poor remained unaddressed. Randolph, Rustin, and Young recognized that economic stability was essential for the stability of black society.[31] Yet, as organizers of the March, they decided against making a public statement equating racism with inferior class status. This, coupled with the requirement that Lewis temper his remarks caused SNCC members to feel betrayed by traditional black organizations; some boycotted what they deemed the Washington "love fest."[32] But perhaps the most immediate divisive factor that stood to undermine the Civil Rights Movement appeared in the divergence between the northern and southern black masses. Indeed, northern blacks, largely an urban populace, existed as a sullen, restive underclass devoid of hope. These people lacked a sense of community, family, self-discipline, and respect for the church as an institution that provided direction and a mechanism for survival. Conversely, black southerners grounded in institutional religion and bolstered by moral righteousness and their faith in God exhibited a sense of optimism. Southerners also gained encouragement from the national focus on their region since virtually all-renowned civil rights organizations—SCLC, SNCC, CORE, and the NAACP—focused exclusively upon discrimination and racism practiced in the South. Although black protests originated and became sustained by blacks residing in the North, those in closest proximity to the historical centers of agitation—Boston, New York, and Philadelphia—were abandoned, establishing an ominous portent for the future. Only one organization addressed the anger fomenting within black urban youth of the North—the Nation of Islam [NOI]—a group more commonly known as the Black Muslims.

The subtle and covert nature of northern racism and the sense of an improving racial climate provided the black bourgeoisie with a feeling of smugness and contentment for living outside the confines of the vicious, recalcitrant "white South." With the "better" class of African Americans feeling secure in their environment and remaining aloof from the masses, thousands of blacks confined to northern ghettos found few to speak on behalf of those unable to compete or adjust to life in post-industrial America. The individual most responsible for articulating the Nation's message to the disaffected African American youth in a manner alien to traditional black leaders was a Black Muslim known as Malcolm X. Born on May 19, 1925 in Omaha, Nebraska, Malcolm entered the world as the seventh child of Earl and Louise Little. Young Malcolm seemed destined to be at odds with white society. His father, a Baptist minister, preached a religion of black pride and disseminated the philosophy of Marcus A. Garvey. His mother, a native of Grenada in the British West Indies who looked white, taught Malcolm to hate the white blood that coursed through his veins and directed him toward pursuing an adversarial relationship with white America.

Racial hatred impinged severely on Malcolm after the family moved from Omaha to Lansing, Michigan. In 1931 his father died at the hands of white vigilantes. Earl Little's death forced the family into penury. The Little children were placed in a foster home and accelerated Louise Little's mental deterioration. In response to the unfortunate family circumstances, Malcolm became rebellious, engaged in petty theft, and misbehaved in school. As a teenager Malcolm moved to Boston and lived with an elder sister. In his late teens he migrated to New York City. Attracted to the seamier side of life and thrilled by the excitement found there, Malcolm entered a life of crime and eventually landed in jail.

By the age of twenty, Malcolm Little became an expert in the nuances of the alienated, asocial, dispirited black lower class. A drug addict, thief, and prison inmate, Malcolm seemed headed toward a life of destitution until he developed a thirst for education and became acquainted with the Nation of Islam and the teachings of Elijah Muhammad. Malcolm's intelligence and understanding of the black underclass enabled him to rise from a recruit and disciple of the Black Muslims to attain fame as the religious order's most prominent and recognizable spokesman.

Of all the black organizations established to free African Americans from oppression, the Nation proved most inclined to reach out to lower class elements within the race. Founded in 1931 by an obscure man named

W.D. Fard, the concept that God's true name was Allah and that the true religion was Islam became major tenets of the newly created sect. The religion imbued followers with strict guidelines on demeanor, diet, gender roles and family structure for the purpose of providing blacks with a positive self-image. Yet an additional idea conceived by Fard, the dogmatic tenet that equated white people with the devil, may have been the catalyst that attracted scores of blacks to the NOI.

Among the handful of converts to his fledgling Order, Fard selected Elijah Muhammad [née Elijah Poole] as the supreme minister. As head of the organization [Fard mysteriously disappeared], Muhammad decided to free blacks from white oppression by establishing Universities of Islam throughout the United States. The schools instilled students with a positive self-image and introduced procedures to free them from white oppression. By the mid 1950s Muhammad recognized Malcolm's dedication to Islam and selected him to become the primary founder of new temples, minister of the New York City mosque, and eventually, the key spokesperson for the Nation of Islam.[33]

When Elijah Muhammad appointed Malcolm X as the voice for the NOI, he offered a platform to the most controversial black leader since Marcus Garvey. Malcolm's rhetoric alienated middle class blacks and whites, and established the Nation of Islam as the pariah organization of the Civil Rights Movement. Malcolm X's condemnation of whites produced a two edged sword. His fiery oratory about "white, blue-eyed devils" resulted in hundreds of downtrodden blacks joining temples and becoming Muslims. On the other hand, venomous tirades against whites proved equally reprehensible; racism appeared odious regardless of the perpetrator's pigmentation. Evidence of public disdain for the Nation appeared through a 1959 television documentary entitled, "The Hate That Hate Produced." When the black bourgeoisie endorsed the documentary's validity, Malcolm X derided the black establishment, saying: "They were stumbling over each other to get quoted and make various reassuring statements [to white people].[34]

By the early 1960s a profound schism appeared between the Nation and traditional black leaders. Malcolm X led the Nation's counterattack against the established leadership. Essentially, the fundamental difference between the black bourgeoisie and the Muslims rested on a simple issue—whether blacks should integrate or voluntarily separate from white society. Confrontation between the "old guard" and the Nation came to a head in 1963. Malcolm X lampooned the March on the national capital as the

"Farce on Washington." An indignant Malcolm declared: "Yes, I was there. I observed that circus. Who ever heard of angry revolutionists all harmonizing 'We Shall Overcome...' while tripping and swaying along arm-in-arm with the very people they were supposed to be angrily revolting against?"[35]

But probably, the event that had the most significant impact on Malcolm X, traditional black leadership and the African American community at large occurred with the assassination of President Kennedy on November 22, 1963. While Malcolm X's scornful utterances about hypocrisy angered black leaders, his comments about the Kennedy assassination (he used inappropriate words that attributed the death to "chickens coming home to roost") provided his rivals with suitable reasons for discrediting him and lessening the effectiveness of the Nation. For Malcolm, the "fall out" from Kennedy's death would prove devastating. Jealous of Malcolm's popularity and concerned about the NOI's increasing marginality, Elijah Muhammad used the "chickens" statement as an opportunity to suspend Malcolm. The rift with Elijah Muhammad eventually resulted in Malcolm X's assassination in 1965.[36]

Conceivably, the demise of Malcolm X would have a greater negative impact on the African American community than the death of President Kennedy. A pilgrimage to Mecca altered Malcolm's racist thoughts. After his return to the United States, Malcolm presented a more moderate approach to resolve racial differences in America. Moderation, combined with his natural charisma, might have enabled Malcolm to restrain extreme elements within the black community and direct the masses toward a more positive response to President Johnson's "Great Society." Malcolm might have also instilled the black bourgeoisie with greater sensitivity toward the plight of the black masses. One can only speculate about what might have occurred to ameliorate the quality of life for the African American majority had Malcolm X lived.

African American leaders had grave misgivings about Lyndon Baines Johnson, the successor to Kennedy as President of the United States.[37] Johnson was a Texan whose grandfather fought for the Confederacy. Blacks also knew that to get elected to political office in the South, a successful candidate had to condone racial discrimination. However, black leaders could not discern that Johnson had a vision toward the future; he realized that southerners who continued living in a racist past wasted time, energy, and pursued an immoral purpose. Assuaging fears about his intentions, Johnson declared that his Administration would maintain continuity with his predecessor. He not only retained Kennedy's White

House staff, but also pledged to present Congress with a Civil rights Bill to honor the fallen President.

President Johnson demonstrated commitment to passage of the Civil Rights Bill by relying upon support from prominent blacks and "twisting" the arms of Congressional leaders. Historian Theodore H. White revealed that:

> In a seven-day period from November 29th to December 5th, one by one, he called to the White House every major Negro leader of the country; first, Roy Wilkins of the NACCP on Friday following the assassination; Whitney Young of the Urban League the following Monday; Martin Luther King on Tuesday; James Farmer of CORE on Wednesday. Simultaneously he called in all the legislative leaders to discuss civil rights....[38]

Unfortunately those blacks conspicuously absent from the President's invitation list included A. Philip Randolph, Malcolm X, Adam Clayton Powell, Jr., John Lewis, or anyone who represented the African American working class or poor. President Johnson firmly committed himself to achieving racial equality within the United States. Once again, the exclusion of any African American leader from the left would have ominous consequences for the black masses, and ultimately, the nation.

During the first six months of 1964 black leaders adopted a "wait and see" strategy. They knew a Civil Rights Bill was pending in Congress and anticipated its passage. For privileged African Americans, the quiet wait for civil rights seemed justified. Passage of the Civil Rights Act of 1964 suggested that the prayers of advantaged, "deserving" African Americans had been answered. The legislation passed by Congress on July 2, 1964 banned racial segregation in public facilities throughout the nation, stopped federal funds to public or private programs that practiced discrimination, and outlawed racial and sexual discrimination in employment.[39] African Americans with ambition and means could look toward a propitious future.

Although middle class blacks and the leaders who represented their interests had reason to feel confident about passage of the 1964 Civil Rights Bill, those who belonged to the masses displayed hostility almost immediately after the legislation passed. On July 16, 1964, the death of a fifteen year-old boy in Harlem named James Powell ushered in the radical phase of the Civil Rights Movement. After hearing about Powell's death at the hands of the police, Harlem erupted and precipitated riots throughout the eastern seaboard.[40]

The impetus for black anger stemmed in part from African American leadership's failure to draw attention to the demographic shifts occurring within the black population. While King and the leaders of SNCC and CORE brought—and rightly so—attention to racial discrimination in the South and the NAACP lent its prestige to promote the southern strategy, the black urban North remained external to the interests of civil rights activists. By the mid-1960s the majority of African Americans lived outside the old Confederacy and seethed with hatred about their status in society. The Civil Rights Bill failed to correct overcrowded living conditions in sordid dwellings, enhance the quality of education, or find work for the unemployed. Federal, state, and municipal governments ignored this group and none of the traditional black leaders spoke on their behalf. These people were desultory and unhappy. With access to television, the black masses found it difficult to accept penury while they observed the larger American society enjoying prosperity and success.

The conservative nature of the black middle class, coupled with their failure to raise issues relevant or pertinent in eradicating social ills related to repression, urban blight, and poverty, contributed to a growing lack of respect for all "old guard" leaders and organizations. The anger building within northern ghettos not only continued unabated, but also became augmented by nameless orators who verbally attacked "the [white] man" and his system. Black leaders found themselves engaged in a new kind of internecine warfare—the traditional leader in opposition to the "street radical." During the first half of the decade, only the flamboyant Congressman Adam Clayton Powell, Jr., who became adroit at using fiery rhetoric and inflamed passion, wrested what little respect the masses held for traditional black leaders. Therefore, a new phase of the controversy between integrationists and separatists embracing nationalist or nihilistic views would again become enjoined. However, instead of racial disturbances occurring in the South, East, or Mid-West, this time conflict surfaced in an unexpected quarter—the West Coast—in the Watts area of Los Angeles, California.

Few single events captivated the nation and revealed the dissension within black leadership more pointedly than the Watts Rebellion of August 11-18, 1965. Watts contained a new array of African American leaders and organizations intent on representing the black underclass. The involved parties included the Nation of Islam, cultural nationalists known as the

United Slaves [US], and the Black Panther Party [BPP].[41] The Nation of Islam endeavored to court favor within the black community by emphasizing decorum, support for independent black businesses, strong family values, and by extricating itself from involvement in Malcolm X's death. Since these precepts would lead followers toward middle class respectability, the philosophy endorsed by the NOI varied little from that of the NAACP and the National Urban League. Yet the Nation also gained adherents from lower class blacks by hurling invectives at white people, a position anathema to the NAACP and NUL. Although the Nation did not plan or direct rioters, the organization's rhetoric gave license for angry young men to loot white owned establishments in the black community. Moreover, the mood reflected among black youths revealed a decidedly NOI inclination to attack traditional black leaders. One young man said: "cuss 'em and spit on 'em—and black leadership generally." Another referred to Dr. King as "a misguided or misinformed individual."[42]

Cultural nationalists also impacted black residents in Watts, the most notable spokesperson being Maulana Ron Karenga (née Ronald McKinley Everett) of the US organization. Karenga advised blacks to recover their African heritage. He also spoke of "self-determination," "black power"; used the "self-defense" appeal proclaimed by Malcolm X, and cited Franz Fanon's concept of violence as a "cleansing force."[43] Compared to other alienated people in the African American community, cultural nationalists who embraced the US doctrine seemed moderate. Accustomed more to the use of exhorting rhetoric than violence, cultural nationalists expressed themselves through plays, art, artifacts, and other norms that placed Americans of African ancestry in a positive state of mind. The activities of Ron Karenga corresponded somewhat to LeRoi Jones in New York City. Both men believed that cultural institutions had to be established in the inner city in order to implement a positive program.[44]

While the Black Muslims used rhetoric to recruit members and the United Slaves appealed for support by advocating the importance of racial pride, the Black Panthers advocated the use of violence by wielding guns to achieve desired results. The Panthers evolved from the old left and established a reputation for carrying weapons as evidenced in the self-defense program founded by Bobby Seale and Huey Newton in Oakland, California. This, coupled with the origins of the "Black Power" movement that coincided with the Black Panther symbol that originated in Lowndes County, Alabama, gave rise to rhetoric that bordered on nihilism. One rioter rationalized his actions by declaring: "We haven't got anything, our parents didn't have anything, we are not looking to get anything, and we just don't give a damn." [45] White Los Angelenos had cause for concern.

Although intense rivalry prohibited the three organizations from working jointly to enhance the black community, they reached a unified consensus about the ineffectiveness of the customary leaders in Los Angeles. "Finger pointing" became raised to a new art form. Progressive white outsiders like Saul Alinsky could justifiably say: "The civil rights leaders are out of touch with the masses and the gut issues." Liberal members of the black elite engaged in similar recrimination. To deflect responsibility from the inadequacies in his role as NAACP branch director, Norman Houston blamed the black bourgeoisie and declared that the "'so-called' middle [class] Negro ... has not given support to the total problem [and] has caused great resentment." [46] Even Martin Luther King voiced displeasure with black leadership in Los Angeles. Visiting the city during the aftermath of the rebellion he noted: "What we find is a blind intransigence and ignorance of the tremendous social forces which are at work here." But in actuality, King himself failed to comprehend the depth of black resentment for those identified as being leaders. Before he left Los Angeles King finally admitted: "We as Negro leaders—and I include myself—have failed to take the civil rights movement to the masses of people." [47]

The violent protests of 1964-1965 that culminated in the Watts rebellion could be attributed to several factors that heightened expectations but contributed to unfulfilled results. Initiatives taken by Presidents Kennedy and Johnson failed to provide the immediate improvements promised in the New Frontier and Great Society. Tragically, blacks rioted after Congress passed the Manpower and Development and Training Act and the Vocational Educational Act in 1963 and after President Johnson announced his War on Poverty program in July 1964. Equally ironic, in August 1964, riots in Harlem, Brooklyn, Chicago, Philadelphia, Jersey City, and Patterson, New Jersey coincided with legislation designed to help black Americans improve prospects for economic success. Black leaders displayed their inability to act as power brokers and revealed a communication void existed within the African American community. Either the traditional leadership never learned how to access consistently decision makers in the Executive branch of government, or if aware of Executive and Legislative objectives for eradicating poverty, failed to communicate the federal government's plans to the masses. Civil rights leaders denounced the riots and called for a moratorium on demonstrations, but were unable to find an alternative to stem the anger and frustration of the black urban North.

Causes for the riots were complex, multifaceted, and seemed beyond the comprehension of contemporary black leaders or organizations. First, economic problems within the black community required resolution. Therefore, black representatives should have found ways to help publicize and implement the federal job training opportunities for the inner-city populace. Second, black leaders also seemed remiss in assessing the attitudes of African American youth, the element primarily responsible for the rioting. By focusing primarily on issues of interest to the black bourgeoisie, sable leadership neglected young people who operated outside the middle class value system. Thus, rioters exemplified the African American masses' disregard for traditional black leaders who achieved success through hard work, acceptance of mainstream folkways and mores, and cooperation with the white power structure. Finally, events in Southeast Asia—the escalation of United States involvement in Vietnam—gained ascendancy over poverty programs designed to help the black masses. Winning a war abroad eventually took precedence over finalizing black equity at home.

After President Johnson signed the Voting Rights Act in early August 1965, the federal government's primary interest in African Americans waned. Despite the Watts rebellion, the national focus shifted from civil rights to the war in Southeast Asia. Recognizing both alterations in the national mood toward civil rights and un-reconciled anger inculcated within the desperate black masses, key African American leaders sprang into action. Whitney Young revived the idea of developing a domestic Marshall Plan and A. Philip Randolph presented a "Freedom Budget for All Americans," a decade long project designed to inject economic resources into the African American community. Their efforts, however, proved to be exercises in futility. The Johnson Administration committed an additional $1,700,000,000 to winning the war abroad. There would be no domestic Marshall Plan or "Freedom Budget" to provide prospects for mitigating the black urban rebellions at home.

Between 1966 and 1968 the war in Vietnam escalated while accordingly, white America's interest in civil rights declined. Nevertheless, Whitney Young and the National Urban League gallantly worked to mitigate black anger by seeking funds for domestic programs. In addition to continuing its manpower and training programs, the NUL developed a Skills Bank program to upgrade the black work force. However, it was

King's assassination in April 1968 and the resultant riots that propelled leaders like Young into taking more aggressive steps to quell heightening restiveness within the black community. To appease angry African Americans, Young conceived of a "New Thrust" policy that endorsed the concept of "Black Power" and offered hope for the alienated and dispossessed black underclass. Young called for $1,500,000 in foundation funds to meet the "New Thrust" effort. Given the billions required to effect positive changes in black ghettos, the money requested was paltry and tantamount to admitting defeat in the attempt to absorb the masses into the larger American society. Nevertheless, Young felt a noble gesture must be made to achieve a heightened sense of pride and dignity. Ever optimistic, Young envisioned: "the emerging black middle class ... aiding their brothers in the slums."[48] However, with the black middle class finally being incorporated into mainstream America, Young's request garnered little if any support from the black bourgeoisie. The "New Thrust" effort died; the masses would remain mired in poverty.

Of all the prominent black organizations, SNCC appeared most likely to incorporate ameliorative economic policies like Young's "New Thrust" effort with appeals to racial unity. Just as John Lewis and members of SNCC sustained civil rights movements in the South during the early 1960s, by the end of the decade new leaders within the organization could be looked upon to deliver urban blacks in the North from privation. The individual prepared to lead young African American activists toward economic justice was native born Trinidadian Stokely Carmichael.

Born in 1942, the future SNCC activist migrated with his family to New York in 1953. Extremely precocious and self-confident, Carmichael attended the prestigious Bronx High School of Science and then matriculated to Howard University. At Howard Carmichael became active in student activities, and upon graduation, converted college activism into fieldwork with SNCC. Carmichael's bravery as a field worker in Lowndes County, Alabama [where he founded the Black Panthers] and in Mississippi, and his gift of rhetoric enabled him to rise in SNCC ranks and eventually become the organization's director in May 1966. As the chair of SNCC, Carmichael popularized the term "Black Power," and gave rise to hope for the masses. Although many people may be credited with coining the term, for Carmichael, the concept of "Black Power" evolved as an extension of early twentieth century "Garveyism." During the intervening years since Garvey, and particularly during the post World War II era, blacks needed a messiah or a message that would deliver them from long standing discrimination that stifled black economic, political, and social development. While King and Malcolm X provided the range of leadership necessary for deliverance, "Black Power" offered the slogan that generated a sense of unity and pride. Consequently, African Americans felt free to interpret the "Black Power" concept expansively to satisfy a particular need or faction. Understanding the varying mood and expectations of African Americans, Carmichael referenced "Black Power" ambiguously and used the term adroitly to maximize his influence.

Through SNCC Carmichael gained a means for championing "Black Power." Carmichael's anti-white comments evoked criticism from established black leaders and created a huge schism between young activists who sought to appeal to the masses, and the traditionalists who believed hard won respect from whites should be protected and secured. Rather than envision the controversy over the meaning of "Black Power" solely as a clash involving divergent emotions or ideas, the issue could also be seen as a perennial intra-racial clash that divided the class interests of the bourgeoisie from the survival needs of the masses. The white media condemned the alleged racism presented by Carmichael in his varying definitions of "Black Power." Traditional black leaders joined the press in condemning the SNCC leader and refused to acknowledge that Carmichael spoke on behalf of an alienated black audience. In fact, the black bourgeoisie showed a greater alarmed response to Carmichael than to the white media that denigrated his remarks.

Roy Wilkins of the NAACP led the initial attack against SNCC, Carmichael, and the "Black Power" slogan. At the annual NAACP conference of July 1966, Wilkins presented the initial salvo against Carmichael and SNCC when he told the gathering that "black power' means anti-'white power,'" and equated the term with black separatism.[49] Others within the established black power structure held similar opinions about anyone who threatened their relationship with whites and their dependency upon white support. Bayard Rustin declared that the "Black Power" construct "lacked any real value for the civil rights movement" and deemed the concept "positively harmful, utopian, and reactionary."[50] An additional breach between the establishment and Carmichael and SNCC occurred when Wilkins, Young, King, and Randolph asked the young radicals to call off an anti-Vietnam War protest. The black establishment feared that given the declining white interest in civil rights, white people would perceive a demonstration against the war as action representative of and attributed to the Civil Rights Movement. A disagreement on domestic strategies for aiding their race led to what appeared as the final disillusion of the relationship between the Carmichael-led SNCC organization and the moderate/conservative black leadership. When SNCC refused to endorse President Johnson's pending civil rights legislation arguing instead that existing legislation should be enforced, an irrevocable schism between young activists and the "old guard" occurred.

In many respects the "Black Power" controversy represented a final divergence between the black political establishment and the masses. By the late 1960s middle class integrationists successfully undermined years of segregation, and through their success theoretically, if not pragmatically, made race inconsequential. By recoiling from a black ethos represented by "Black Power," traditional African American leaders reduced race as a factor of American life that had existed since the nation's inception. The black masses' experiences evidenced by poverty, despondency, and alienation, conversely, attributed racial prejudice as the primary reason for their inability to assimilate into mainstream America. Therefore to maintain a semblance of self-esteem, the black underclass embraced black ethnicity by evoking hairstyles, dress, and slang that differentiated the black masses from the black bourgeoisie and white culture.

Contrary to the hopes of the nationally prominent black leaders, the term "Black Power" increased in popularity. The black masses not only embraced the slogan but some among the black intelligentsia like *Ebony* editor Lerone Bennett, Jr. endorsed the concept as well. A Louis Harris poll conducted during the mid-summer of 1966 found that more than half of the "Negro community leaders" supported and accepted Carmichael's concept of black power. While many prominent black leaders remained adamantly opposed to "Black Power," King, ever the cautious politician, sensed a need to mitigate his previous statements against the slogan by citing the need to develop a greater sense of racial pride within the black community.[51]

Eventually, Adam Clayton Powell, Jr. and Whitney Young broke ranks and became outspoken supporters for "Black Power." Powell's endorsement of the "Black Power" concept, however, caused Carmichael to have doubts about the "good" Reverend's sincerity. The publicity-seeking Powell claimed the term originated with him, creating concern among SNCC leaders that Powell would usurp the term for personal gain. SNCC had justifiable cause for suspicion. Powell announced plans for a Labor Day conference on "Black Power," a move designed to make him the pre-eminent spokesperson for the controversial term. Whitney Young, however, had a less ego gratifying idea in mind. Like members in the CORE hierarchy who recognized a dependency between their organization's success and a supportive black public, Young knew that the opinions of black residents of the urban North must be respected. Therefore, Young, as one enthusiastic supporter proclaimed, "came home." He openly supported "Black Power" and announced that "Ghetto Power in Action" would be the theme of the NUL's 59th National Conference in July 1969. True to his word, "Urban Power" served as the Conference theme.[52]

Despite Powell and Young's acceptance of "Black Power" as a rallying cry for angry, impoverished urban blacks, the issue sounded the death knell for militant and traditional leaders working collectively to resolve problems affecting African Americans. Traditional leaders, to the eventual disadvantage of the black masses, would gradually refrain from using race and racial inequity as the cornerstone for black amelioration. These same leaders also became disenchanted by Carmichael after he endorsed the concept of black retribution for past white misdeeds. Nevertheless, to Carmichael's credit, he ably represented a myriad of concerns that blacks had with racism and its relationship to political oppression and economic discrimination that frustrated African Americans for generations. He also spoke accurately of the distrust low-income blacks had in respecting black leaders who never fully understood or articulated the problems confronting the average black man, woman, or child. Unfortunately, when Carmichael stepped down as the SNCC chair, he further weakened the organization internally and made it more susceptive to external assaults. With perhaps tacit acquiescence from moderate and conservative black leaders, the federal government devoted considerable attention toward combating Carmichael and what was perceived as SNCC radicalism.[53]

Black leadership's attack on Carmichael seemed invalid except for one essential factor—the attackers envisioned themselves protecting enormous gains derived from the most successful decade of struggle in the history of civil rights. They reasoned that newly won middle class rights and freedoms could not be jeopardized by rhetoric designed to appease the surly masses. Black leaders also knew that white America's sense of guilt had reached a level of diminishing returns. In justifying their retreat from militancy and abandonment of the masses, traditionalists soon gained justification for their caution and public disagreement with SNCC. The promise of SNCC forged by previous idealistic leadership reached its demise when the organization selected Hubert [H. Rap] Brown as Carmichael's successor. Unfortunately for SNCC, Brown lacked the vision and discipline required to lead the organization beyond Carmichael's leadership; forge a new direction for the organization, and achieve pragmatic results.[54]

Internal changes within SNCC and societal pressures beyond SNCC's control would present any civil rights leader with a difficult task. With the election of Richard M. Nixon as President of the United States on a "law and order" platform, black militants could no longer speak or act with impunity. Any discussion designed to arouse the masses—ranging from active endorsement of "Black Power" to demands that solutions to racial problems outlined in the Kerner Commission *Report of the National Advisory Commission on Civil Disorders* be addressed—became passé and irrelevant. With these eventualities black leaders recognized the advantages in sacrificing the needs of the masses to protect the dignity of African American society's higher classes. Successes derived since Brown v. the Board of Education provided justification for the caution of traditional leaders.

The decade of the 1960s proved unique in the annals of African American leadership. Never before had so many black representatives embracing a myriad of perspectives to improve the lot of black people gained the ear of the American public. The majesty of King, steady demeanor exemplified by Wilkins, energy of Whitney Young, daring exhibited by John Lewis and Diane Nash, criticism evoked by Malcolm X, and the persistence displayed by Randolph left an indelible impact upon every conscious American regardless of race, region, creed, color or political ideology. The aforementioned leaders possessed middle class values and had a vested interest in making America a true democracy for all citizens. Even those like Stokely Carmichael and H. Rap Brown, late 1960s militants who received the scorn of traditional black leaders, should be commended for placing their lives in jeopardy to promote the cause of black freedom and human dignity.

In the final analysis traditional black leaders made a significant contribution to the United States. They forced the nation to redress wrongs inflicted upon African Americans specifically, but also brought the nation closer to realizing its democratic ideals and disseminating those ideals throughout the world. However, within the black community an interesting dynamic occurred. Aside from human rights accorded African Americans in the South, the true beneficiaries of the Civil Rights Movement belonged to those who comprised the black middle class. Life for black professionals improved immensely. Big business, the federal government, educational institutions, and welfare agencies recruited scores of middle class blacks and placed them in comfortable positions in an attempt to bridge the racial gulf. Prospects for the black bourgeoisie to acquire acceptance from white counterparts approached finality. For the black bourgeoisie the good fight ended and the struggle had been virtually won.

Ironically, gains African American leaders achieved for the black bourgeoisie occurred at a disadvantage to low-income blacks. Mainstream black leaders ignored the masses and eventually despised them for participating in urban rebellions. Without a clear direction toward amelioration forged by African American leadership, the black underclass would remain impoverished. By the end of the decade previously support-ive white liberals tired of civil rights and seemed most receptive to Daniel Patrick Moynihan's explanations that blamed blacks for the inability of Presidents Kennedy and Johnson to make greater headway in resolving the civil rights crisis.[55] Conservative whites displayed hostility toward African Americans by focusing on black civil unrest and placing the "law and order" candidate, Richard Nixon, in the White House. Furthermore, intra-racial schisms determined by class represented a widening gap between the black bourgeoisie and the masses. This divide would create enormous problems for African American leaders determined to extend the Civil Rights Movement into the 1970s, but prove advantageous for those who would thwart black progress.[56] While the intra-racial breach put civil rights activities in disarray as traditional black leadership elected to place racial differences and "blackness" on the social and political "backburner" to pursue the integrationist ideal, the white opposition would find an opportunity to emasculate the Civil Rights Movement. The conservative white opposition seized upon an invidious strategy to circumvent their black opponents. Eventually, the white conservative right would adopt the adage "if you can't beat them join them," usurp the concept of racial irrelevance from conservative/ traditionalists within the Civil Rights Movement, and use the irrelevance of race to the detriment of all African Americans.[57]

PART III

CONSCIOUSNESS OF SELF

9

THE NIXON YEARS AND THE
RETRENCHMENT OF CIVIL RIGHTS

During the 1970s African American leadership at once appeared triumphant and moribund. Leaders of the previous decade exacted concessions from white America that exceeded expectations held by the most sanguine black activists of previous generations. Civil rights leaders acquired support from the legislative, judicial, and executive branches of the federal government. Consequently, laws were passed that guaranteed blacks access to white schools, the right to vote, and the ability to frequent any restaurant, rest room, and sit unrestricted in public conveyances. An eager black middle class emerged from the pall of segregation to claim rights formerly denied African Americans. And yet progressive black leaders knew that their work remained incomplete; most African Americans remained mired in poverty. The abysmal living conditions experienced by the black masses required black leadership's undivided attention. Nevertheless, directors of traditional civil rights organizations faced a unique dilemma. Their sense of humanism demanded that action be taken to redress limitations attributed to racism that still affected low income African Americans. However, pragmatic strategists recognized that the application of former tactics—marches, boycotts, and harsh rhetoric—could alienate liberal whites and the black bourgeoisie, invaluable allies and the foundation of long-standing civil rights organizations. These conflicting issues placed black leaders in an awkward position that caused them to appear ineffective in the post-civil rights era.

Given the turbulent 1960s, black leaders of the 1970s had reason to pause and reflect. Just as historian Eric F. Goldman interpreted the Eisenhower years as an era when the nation required time to catch its breath in response to upheavals created by World War II, African American leaders needed to assess and consolidate their achievements and chart future directions for their race. The results of their efforts would prove consistent with trends established during the four previous decades—the black bourgeoisie's fortunes continued improving while, correspondingly, the quality of life experienced by the masses continued to erode.[1]

On the eve of the 1970s black leadership received a sense of directed purpose and an understanding of the arduous task ahead through examples established by Dr. Martin Luther King, Jr. Dr. King realized that the Civil Rights Movement needed to shift its emphasis from demanding racial equality to providing economic opportunities for the poor. His support for striking Memphis garbage workers provided the impetus for a new direction—a movement for human rights. King knew that accessing a desegregated restaurant was irrelevant if African Americans failed to earn a decent wage. When King was assassinated during a trash collectors strike in Memphis, Tennessee, his death symbolized both the importance of elevating the income and quality of life for the poor and the enormous obstacles awaiting anyone seeking economic justice for low income African Americans. Because the general public perceived the federal government preferred helping African Americans rather than whites, black leaders would find the quest for class elevation more arduous than eliminating racial barriers.[2]

Reverend Ralph David Abernathy succeeded King as the head of SCLC and endeavored to continue the fallen leader's work by dramatizing the plight of the poor. In May, 1968, Abernathy led a contingent of blacks, Native Americans, whites, and Mexican-Americans on a poor people's campaign to Washington, D. C. The SCLC sponsored activity led to the creation of Resurrection City, a symbolic campsite designed to publicize the woeful conditions experienced by disadvantaged Americans. Unfortunately for Abernathy and SCLC, the effort was poorly organized and in less than two months, disbanded without achieving any noticeable objective. Because Abernathy lacked the charisma, leadership skills, or political acuity of his predecessor, the failure of Resurrection City permanently damaged Abernathy's role as a leader and diminished SCLC's role as a viable civil rights organization.

Abernathy and SCLC hardly proved the sole exemplars of the declining influence of black leaders and organizations during the post civil rights era. CORE, the organization that gave birth to "Freedom Rides" and enlisted scores of SNCC members into its ranks, also lapsed into oblivion. With "Freedom Rides" rendered irrelevant after federal law declared segregation invalid, CORE had little reason to exist. Given the preservation and renewed dignity afforded the black middle class, those like James Farmer could stop making headlines and smugly congratulate themselves for a "job well done." The National Urban League and NAACP loomed as the only black organizations that survived the Civil Rights Movement relatively unscathed.

In Whitney Young the Urban League had a leader most in tune with the nuances of change and associated problems in the post civil rights era. Young recognized the sense of alienation harbored by the African American masses and acted as the impoverished black majority's most articulate spokesperson. Born in Lincoln Ridge, Kentucky on July 31, 1921, Young seemed destined to devote his life toward ameliorative activities. His father taught at and eventually served as principal of the Lincoln Institute, a high school based on the Washingtonian concept of industrial education. Laura Ray Young, Whitney's mother, served as the campus matriarch of the Institute. These loving parents made certain their son enjoyed a middle class lifestyle sheltered somewhat from the vicissitudes of the "Jim Crow" South.[3] Young matriculated to Kentucky State University intent on becoming a physician. After earning his undergraduate degree at Kentucky State, Young became one of the thousands of young men drafted to serve in World War II. As a sergeant in the army Young found his calling; he demonstrated a talent for mediation and decided upon a career to promote positive race relations. In 1946 he enrolled at the University of Minnesota and acquired a Masters degree in social work.

Between 1947 and 1953 Young worked for the Urban League in St. Paul, Minnesota and Omaha, Nebraska. Before becoming the Executive Director of the National Urban League in 1961, Young taught at the University of Nebraska and served as Dean of the Atlanta University School of Social Work. After establishing a reputation as a progressive leader of the NUL and demonstrating prominence in the civil rights movement as an aggressive moderate, Young vied with Dr. King for leadership within the black community. *Time* magazine described Young as the "most effective man in the nation when it comes to drumming up jobs for Negroes." Others considered Young the "most creative civil rights leader" in the nation. Therefore, Young's familiarity with the civil rights movement, understanding of the nuances of the black economic condition, recognition of the need for equal job opportunities, and application of creative strategies to keep the civil rights movement alive made him the logical successor to Dr. King. Thus with the theme "Ghetto Power in Action," Young presided over the League's 59th Annual Convention held in Washington D.C. in 1969 and prepared the NUL to meet the economic challenges facing the black community in the forthcoming decade. With Convention topics like "police-community relations," "the youth rebellion," "community control of education," "housing," "job discrimination and upgrading," and "health problems," the NUL's comprehensive agenda established Young as the foremost black visionary in African American society. Using the Convention as his forum, Young delivered a keynote address that anticipated the primary concerns of blacks during the 1970s. Young spoke about the League's economic security programs to end poverty and secure equality.[4] He also condemned the tactics of the Nixon Administration. In contrast to the League's historically conservative stance, Young threatened to use "more confrontation tactics" to redress African American grievances.[5]

Young focused on finding the means to limit black unemployment and marshaled forces within the Urban League to enhance the economic standing of the entire African American community. He produced a syndicated newspaper column that informed American society about racial, economic, and urban problems.[6] Under his guidance the NUL hired the African American professor Charles Hamilton of Columbia to articulate the new paradigm—employment—the key toward improving the debased condition of the larger black community. In an article entitled "Full Employment as a Viable Issue," Hamilton presented an agenda that transcended race and spoke to the correlation between unemployment and social problems. Hamilton contended that the focus on "full employment" would move beyond the 1960s protest style and end the national divisiveness caused by inter-racial conflicts. Equally important, Hamilton and the Urban League believed that "full employment" would ease racial tensions and create empathy for all marginalized people handicapped by joblessness and poverty.[7] By articulating the needs of the black community and then soliciting the assistance of corporations, foundations, and government agencies, Young continued in the tradition of previous Executive Directors and maintained the NUL tradition of job placement and training.[8] Young also continued speaking in a constructively militant vein until his untimely death in 1971. In many respects, the premature demise of King and Young in relation to the Civil Rights Movement held corollaries with the death of Abraham Lincoln after the Civil War. In each instance, gaining victories through the brutality of war would prove far easier than solidifying gains during a period of reconstruction.

Vernon Jordan succeeded Young as Executive Director of the Urban League. Born on August 15, 1935 in Fulton County, Georgia, Jordan would have a promising future. Influenced profoundly by an enterprising, ambitious mother named Mary Belle Jordan, Vernon E. Jordon Jr. realized early in life that he had unlimited potential. With a mother who served as the PTA president of every primary and secondary school Jordan attended, young Jordan received the best teachers schools had to offer. Fascinated by the classy demeanor attorneys displayed at the monthly Lawyers Club meetings that his mother catered, Jordan decided to pursue law as a career. During his senior year at the David T. Howard High School in Atlanta, Jordan established himself as an orator, a talent that contributed to success in his professional career.

Raised to think and act independently, Jordan broke away from friends and teachers who encouraged him to attend an historical black college and decided to attend DePauw University, a small predominantly white Liberal Arts school in Greencastle, Indiana. During his college years at DePauw, Jordan learned how to interact effectively with white people, gain confidence in his intellectual ability, and gain worldly experience working as a bus driver in Chicago.[9] After graduating from DePauw Jordan matriculated to the Howard University School of Law, joined Omega Psi Phi fraternity, met his future wife, Shirley Yarbrough, and completed his legal studies in 1960. Immediately after graduation, Jordan gained experience working as an attorney in Atlanta for Donald Hollowell, one of the very few African American barristers in the state of Georgia.

In 1961 Jordan made another important crossroads decision in his life when he decided to leave Hollowell and work under the direction of Ms. Ruby Hurley as the Georgia Field Director of the NAACP. As the Field Director Jordan bolstered the membership of local chapters, helped the chapters organize events, investigated allegations of racial discrimination, and decided when to summon the NAACP to address the problems at hand.[10] While the work placed him at the cutting edge of the Civil Rights Movement, he put his life in jeopardy, a fact realized when his counterpart in Mississippi, Medgar Evers, was ambushed and killed by a virulent racist. Throughout the 1960s Jordan continued building his resume as a civil rights activist while simultaneously becoming touted as one of the young African Americans most likely to succeed in corporate America. He left the NAACP to become the executive assistant to the director of the Southern Regional Council [SRC], an inter-racial organization that promoted racial tolerance and enhanced living conditions for southern blacks. During his tenure with the SRC Jordan became a Fellow at Harvard's Kennedy School. Training at Harvard enabled him to serve as an attorney for the Office of Economic Opportunity and eventually return to CRC to become director of the organization's Voter Education Project. As the Voter Education director Jordan acquired name recognition throughout the South, and eventually was named to head the National Negro College Fund. Jordan's training, organizational skill, and visibility made him the logical successor to Whitney Young as director of the National Urban League.

Immediately after taking the helm, Jordan provided the NUL with stellar leadership. The League prepared for the new decade in its annual convention with the theme, "Action for the 70's," focusing on topics that included economic development, education, voter registration, health, justice, housing, and social welfare. He also anticipated a need for African American unity in his keynote address, "A Call to Black Leadership." Jordan asked for dialogue among the many diverse factions within the black community so that a broad consensus could be attained to negotiate a resolution to America's continuing "race problem."[11] Jordan had his "Call for Black Leadership" realized, but the result of Jordan's "Call," bore fruit far different from what the NUL director envisioned.

In 1972 the first National Black Political Convention convened in Gary, Indiana, a convention that appeared to heed Jordan's "Call" for unity. Like its predecessor, the moribund National Negro Congress, "so-called radicals" provided the initiative to organize. This time cultural nationalists from the Black Power Movement and youthful activists representing SNCC provided the impetus for convening. Three factors enticed traditional black leaders to join their more aggressive counterparts: the popularity of the sweeping appeal of black power that encompassed both the African American elite and the masses; the rise of blacks as a strong national political force; and the void in leadership left by the death of Martin Luther King, Jr.[12]

Black delegates entered the Convention with great anticipation. Prospects for deciding an heir apparent to King seemed ripe. Young men and women had a rare opportunity to select a leader capable of providing direction for future civil rights endeavors. Equally important, virtually every prominent black leader attended. Included among the traditional-integrationists were Jesse Jackson, Mayors Carl Stokes of Cleveland and Richard Hatcher of Gary, Congressman John Conyers of Detroit, Manhattan Borough President Percy Sutton, Georgia State Representative Julian Bond of Atlanta, and Roy Wilkins of the NAACP. Others who participated in planning the conference included Congressman Charles Diggs, Coretta Scott King, California State legislators Willie Brown and Mervyn Dymally, Texas State Senator Barbara Jordan, California Congressman Augustus Hawkins, Roy Innis of CORE, Clarence Mitchell of the Washington Bureau NAACP, and of course, Vernon Jordan of the Urban League. African American leadership seemed poised to reach a consensus on how best to champion the cause of freedom and create greater opportunities for black people.[13]

The time also seemed propitious to introduce new ideologies that could be fashioned to meet the challenges of the post-civil rights era. However trouble brewed even before the conference began when black Congress-woman Shirley Chisholm of New York announced her candidacy for President of the United States. Chisholm made this decision without consulting with black leaders. She incurred additional enmity from black leaders when she campaigned more as a feminist than as a representative of black America.

Chisholm, however, represented only one of several problems facing the Conference where poor planning decisions and ego vested conferees placed personal ambition before the welfare of the race.[14] In order to establish a sense of unity by appeasing the diverse factions scheduled to attend the Gary conference, the organizers selected a triumvirate—Diggs and Hatcher who represented the traditional establishment, and poet and playwright Imamu Amiri Baraka (LeRoi Jones), the outspoken advocate for the nationalist position—to lead the convention. Obvious difficulties inherent in rule by troika occurred. The single-minded Baraka decided to seize the chairmanship and push his nationalist agenda. Recognizing weakness in the organizational conception of the Convention, in the opening session Baraka's New York delegation took the chairmanship from Diggs, brushed Hatcher aside, and named Baraka president of the gathered assembly.

Further divisiveness ensued when Baraka's platform committee presented radical proposals to the conferees that opposed busing (a traditionalist mainstay), supported the Arab position in the Middle East, and declared that 95 percent of the white people in America were racists. In frustration and disgust, Mayor Coleman Young and his Detroit delegation walked out of the Convention. A unified strategy never emerged.

The Convention debacle would have far reaching consequences for black leadership. A *Chicago Defender* editorial encapsulated the sad affair when it declared:

> ...out of the maelstrom of flamboyant, militant rhetoric ... no clear leadership has emerged. The convention was a babel of ideologies, half-baked dilettantism and infantile assumptions. It did not live up to its roseate promise. It had a chance to be a force in the consortium of American politics, it has muffed it.[15]

The negative impact of the National Black Political Convention of 1972 extended from Gary and permeated the entire black leadership cadre. Continuing personality and factional differences demonstrated that black leadership could be ignored by white power brokers because no collective sense within the African American community existed. The enormous ideological and institutional differences, coupled with personality conflicts, rendered the liberal contingent of black leaders impotent and the radical fringe inconsequential. Although radicals endeavored to initiate a new black political movement, their only measurable success appeared through the creation of the National Black Independent Party [NBIP], a Party that virtually expired before birth.[16] As the most significant legacy of the Convention Movement, the NBIP in essence, signaled the end of twentieth century black-nationalism.

The failed Convention Movement demonstrated unequivocally that a void in black leadership existed in the post-civil rights era. The enthusiastic but intemperate neo-radical contingent evidenced by Stokely Carmichael, H. Rap Brown, and eventually Amiri Baraka lacked the maturity, clairvoyance, and organizational skill necessary to complete the quest for absolute racial equality. By placing more emphasis on theoretical ideology than learning from history, and stressing absolutism rather than consensus, the youthful idealism of intrepid freedom riders gave way to proponents of bombast.

Since non-traditionalists like Baraka failed to provide viable direction, a new innovative organization never evolved to stimulate a broader concern for African American rights. Traditional leaders and institutions again had the opportunity to reassert their authority. The people primarily capable of holding the mantle of leadership hailed from established black organizations. Seniority dictated that Roy Wilkins and the NAACP rather than Vernon Jordan's National Urban League should fashion the direction taken by civil rights leaders and organizations during the 1970s.

Born the grandson of a slave, Roy Wilkins experienced privation at an early age. Wilkins' parents migrated from Mississippi to escape discrimination and settled in St. Louis, Missouri, the city where young Roy was born in 1901. The elder Wilkins, a proud man, earned little money as a laborer at a brick kiln. Meanwhile Roy's mother, a former school teacher, remained in poor health after her son's birth and died of tuberculosis early in the young boy's life. Fortuitously, after his mother's death, Wilkins' father sent Roy to St. Paul, Minnesota to be raised in relative comfort by an aunt and uncle. Wilkins held fond memories of his Uncle Sam Williams and the integrated community in which the family lived.[17] A precocious youth who enjoyed writing, Wilkins studied hard and matriculated to the University of Minnesota where he majored in sociology, joined Omega Phi Psi Fraternity, and edited *The St. Paul Appeal*, a local African American newspaper. Although the Twin Cities proved liberating for black Americans when compared to Mississippi or St. Louis, racial violence in America prompted Wilkins to join the local NAACP during his undergraduate years. A brutal lynching of three black men in Duluth, Minnesota in Wilkins' eighteenth year encouraged him to devote the remainder of his life fighting racial discrimination. After graduating from the University in 1923, Wilkins moved to Kansas City, Missouri, accepted a job as managing editor of a syndicated black newspaper, *The Kansas City Call*, and continued his work with the NAACP as the local branch's secretary.

The Call provided Wilkins with an excellent opportunity to combine journalism with civil rights. A series of editorials waged against the reelection of a segregationist Missouri senator displayed Wilkins' talent for writing and brought him to the attention of the NAACP's national office. In 1931 Wilkins left Kansas City for New York and became the assistant executive secretary to Walter White. The following year Wilkins went "under cover" and investigated the treatment of blacks employed on Mississippi flood-control projects. His report initiated a Senate investigation that resulted in the enhancement of working conditions for black laborers. In 1934 Wilkins succeeded Du Bois as editor of *The Crisis*, and served in that capacity until 1949 when he became the Acting Executive Secretary and eventually succeeded Walter White as head of the NAACP.

As a consultant for the American delegation to the United Nations and a strategist in the Brown v. Board of Education litigation, Wilkins earned his stripes as a fervent civil rights advocate.

The NAACP recorded its greatest successes during Wilkins' tenure as Executive Secretary. Between 1960 and 1970 the National Association attained its largest membership, most substantial income, and greatest influence in the long history of civil rights.[18] As the direct action approach of civil rights demonstrators garnered headlines, Wilkins aided protesters by ably directing the NAACP in using the legal system to probe for weaknesses in established laws, challenging courts to impose justice, and enforcing court mandated civil rights directives. Under his guidance traditional legal and political action programs used to end discrimination and segregation that plagued black Americans for centuries enjoyed their greatest success. With King deceased, and Abernathy, a well meaning but uninspiring head of SCLC, as the long-standing director of the NAACP Wilkins arguably became the most venerated civil rights leader in the nation.

President Richard Nixon provided Wilkins and the National Association with an abundance of opportunities to rally African Americans to the NAACP banner. Intent on slowing the movement toward integration, President Nixon forced Clifford Alexander, chair of the Equal Opportunity Commission to resign, and endorsed Daniel Patrick Moynihan's suggestion to practice "benign neglect" toward African Americans.[19] When Nixon nominated Judge Clement F. Haynesworth of Greenville, South Carolina to replace Associate Justice Abe Fortas as a member of the United States Supreme Court, he propelled the NAACP into action. Haynesworth had an unsavory civil rights record during his tenure as the chief judge of the Fourth Circuit Court. Therefore, Wilkins advised the President to withdraw the nomination.[20] Nixon ignored the admonition, and in response, Wilkins initiated a lobbying campaign against Haynesworth and forced the Senate to reject the nomination. Flush with victory after having engineered the Senate rejection of Haynesworth, Wilkins and the NAACP attacked Nixon for being a hindrance to civil rights.[21] The Association scourged the President for undermining the voting rights act, for refusing to support the Equal Employment Opportunity Commission [EEOC], and for not enforcing school desegregation.[22]

Although Wilkins emerged victorious in the encounter with Nixon, he and the NAACP would be frustrated by attitudinal changes within the black community. While militant separatists would no longer compete with the

NAACP for attention, black leadership faced another intra-racial problem—the black bourgeoisie's heightened indifference toward the condition of the masses. After years of labor to acquire civil rights culminated during the 1960s, the black bourgeoisie sought to extricate itself from civil rights battles. Middle class blacks displayed little inclination to offer time, effort, and money for further agitation despite the realization that a significant segment of the black population failed to benefit from civil rights efforts. Wilkins realized that the NAACP'S work remained undone. He began the decade of the 1970s with broad objectives in mind. Wilkins directed the NAACP to attack and erode bastions of racial discrimination in the armed services, education, employment, housing, and in the administration of justice. Branches in Philadelphia and Detroit, for example, looked into the building trades to secure employment for skilled and unskilled African Americans.[23] The efforts in Philadelphia and Detroit, while laudatory, seemed unique. Most local branches focused primarily on issues germane to the black middle class. Knowing the NAACP remained available to redress racial discrimination, middle class blacks bombarded local chapters with complaints against public agencies and private industries that prevented blacks from being up-graded or promoted to higher paying positions.[24] Satisfying the employment concerns of the more privileged blacks consumed the time and energy of NAACP branches throughout the nation.

Unfortunately for Wilkins and the NAACP, the black rank and file also failed to match the hierarchy's fervor to sustain the Civil Rights Movement. Wilkins had become a leader with a diminishing number of followers. Annual memberships for the NAACP declined from 461,957 in 1969 to 361,807 in 1970, resulting in a 25% loss, a trend that continued throughout the Nixon presidency.[25]

There were several reasons for African American apathy. Among the established "Old Guard," exhaustion and a need to consolidate gains loomed as a primary reason for the dissolution of civil rights fervor. Although Wilkins appeared ready to continue the fight for racial equality, the prior decade of agitation could not be sustained. It also seemed evident that employment for low-income blacks and busing to achieve educational equity failed to capture the public imagination like voting rights and desegregating lunch counters. After breakthrough issues pertaining to human rights were achieved and the Brown case ended de jure segregation, Americans concentrated on resolving the war in Vietnam rather than contain the civil rights war at home. Finally, the gradual but continuous movement of middle class African Americans to suburbia made successful blacks more eager to show how well "respectable Negroes" could "fit-in" and less inclined to take issue with racial slights. The opportunity for blacks to compete fairly and openly appeared at hand. Given the opportunities middle class blacks finally enjoyed, the black bourgeoisie seemed less inclined to threaten the status quo by agitating aggressively on behalf of the black masses.

Despite the ominous winds of change, the NAACP continued the battle to achieve full equality for African Americans. Herbert Hill, director of the Labor Department for the NAACP believed that acquiring jobs for every qualified African American and assuring that fairness in promotions would garner greater support for the Association. He found useful evidence that could increase membership rolls while simultaneously acquiring information necessary for accurately articulating the problems faced by African Americans. As early as 1971 unemployment among the black urban population proved comparable to black unemployment during the Great Depression. Indeed, by 1973, a third of the minority population lived below the poverty line, 500,000 more than the numbers mired in poverty the previous year. In the final analysis, the dismal record of black unemployment, the NAACP believed, was attributed directly to racial discrimination.[26] When the Nixon Administration retreated from civil rights in order to garner support from white voters, the NAACP prepared to fight. Wilkins instructed Hill to expand the staff and hire a full time lawyer to pursue and redress complaints on labor discrimination. The department investigated charges registered by textile workers in Virginia; truck drivers in South Carolina; steelworkers in Birmingham, Alabama and Columbus, Ohio; aerospace workers in Georgia; automotive workers in Indiana; and construction workers in Buffalo, Seattle, Pittsburgh, Chicago, Boston, New York, and New Orleans.[27] Using its customary use of litigation to redress grievances, Wilkins and the NAACP engaged in numerous lawsuits against the federal government, public agencies, and private corporations. Despite the enormous effort generated to secure employment for underemployed African Americans, the black masses found themselves worse off than before the advent of the Civil Rights Movement.

While Wilkins made noble attempts to aid jobless blacks, the NAACP maintained its reputation as the preeminent civil rights organization by promoting equity in education as the cornerstone of Association policy. Determined to see that school integration proceed, the NAACP monitored newly desegregated schools in both North and South. The Association took interest in elevating the academic achievements of low income blacks and advocated policies designed to make schools accountable for students' academic progress. In order to counter white resistance to its ameliorative efforts, the NAACP monitored the suspensions and expulsions of black students, gathered facts for litigation, and filed complaints with federal and state agencies related to education. Wilkins and the Association also carefully watched the Executive Department to counter anti-desegregation policies proposed by the Nixon Administration.[28]

Sensitive to the wretched living conditions experienced by urban blacks, the NAACP also worked assiduously to upgrade housing in low-income neighborhoods. The NAACP found that ghetto areas continued to grow larger, poorer and increasingly all-black while the surrounding suburban areas remained predominantly white.[29] To combat the housing problem, Wilkins authorized the Association to create a National Housing Development Corporation to find sponsors who could fund suburban housing for low and moderate income black families. The Association also lobbied key federal institutions like the U.S. Department of Housing and Urban Development [HUD], the Farmers Home Administration, the Federal Home Loan Bank Board, and Congress, encouraging the agencies to initiate programs that would alleviate black housing programs. The private sector received NAACP attention as well. Organizations ranging from the National Corporation of Housing Partnerships, the National Assistance Housing Council and the National Association of Home Builders to the American Bar Association and the Savings and Loan Industry were flooded with information to acquaint them about the plight of African American housing.

Keeping the entire race in mind, the NAACP introduced an ambitious housing sponsorship program to help poor and middle class blacks alike. Planners estimated that if contributing branches raised $27 million, 763 low-income black families would acquire proper housing. The black bourgeoisie would benefit from fund raising efforts as well. African American lawyers, architects, financiers, contractors, real estate managers and others would find gainful careers and business opportunities in the housing field.[30] Director Wilkins targeted HUD as the most viable agency prepared to hire "capable Negroes ... to fill top-level jobs" traditionally staffed by white professionals.[31] Since African American leaders perceived HUD support as crucial for acquiring better black housing, the NAACP took a profound interest in bolstering the agency within the Nixon Administration. HUD officials, in turn, welcomed Association assistance and incorporated NAACP ideas into the agency's federal housing programs.[32]

The Nixon Administration's pursuance of the "southern strategy"—playing the "race card"—forced Wilkins and the NAACP to deviate from non-partisanship and join the Democratic Party in attacking the President. Nixon became the object of black wrath when he played to anti-black forces of white society by undermining President Johnson's "Great Society" programs. NAACP Labor Director Herbert Hill spoke for many black leaders when he said: "Not since the early years of this century has an American President so openly and deliberately joined with enemies of black people. The Nixon Administration ... has made a calculated political sacrifice of principle and law that has dire implications for the future of American society." Wilkins added to the excoriation of Nixon by proclaiming: "President Richard Milhous Nixon ... continued to lead the fight against our hard-won gains.... The rallying call of [his] administration has been 'law and order' which means 'law and order' for Negro criminals."[33] Black leaders collectively resented Nixon's brand of "racist opportunism," enabling the NAACP to join demands for the impeachment of Richard M. Nixon, efforts that bore fruition in August 1974.

Wilkins' civil rights endeavors appeared sufficiently broad to satisfy every segment of the African American community. Although blamed for being overly cautious and endorsing gradualist policies at the height of the Civil Rights Movement, Wilkins maintained a relentless pursuit for black equality during the Nixon years. A firm believer in school busing to achieve racial equality, Wilkins used every means at his disposal to make education available to every black child in the nation. Wilkins fought against racial discrimination in labor unions, addressed problems associated with rural and urban poverty, and tried to enforce civil rights statutes promulgated during the Kennedy and Johnson Administrations. The Executive Director also supported the policy of affirmative action, investigated military justice cases, and, through local branches, made certain that the NAACP instituted new policies to help African Americans. These efforts ranged from the Community Development Block Grant Program to defend the rights of minorities in slum areas to the General Revenue Sharing Program, a policy designed to equalize civil service employment.

Ironically, the impeachment of Richard Nixon anticipated a similar problem experienced by Roy Wilkins. Less than two years after Nixon resigned from office, Wilkins found himself facing removal from office. Although Wilkins worked assiduously to remain current with the needs of

African Americans, his power within the NAACP board gradually waned. The initial sign of foreboding for Wilkins occurred in 1974 with the deaths of NAACP Board chair Bishop Stephen Gill Spottswood and Assistant Executive Director Dr. John A. Morsell. Both men worked closely with Wilkins and established a productive relationship with the Executive Secretary during the heyday of the Civil Rights Movement. However when St. Louis attorney Margaret Bush Wilson succeeded Spottswood as chair of the NAACP Board of Directors, change in the governance of the NAACP seemed imminent. This change would have negative ramifications for Wilkins and the National Association because Wilson never participated nationally in the civil rights struggles of the 1960s. Wilson held no particular loyalty to Wilkins, a venerable leader who survived decades of arduous civil rights work. Instead, she spearheaded a youth movement within the Association that required staff members to retire at sixty-five.[34]

In addition to personality clashes and "power grabs" that historically plagued the NAACP, several additional factors beyond the Association's control threatened Wilkins' leadership. With the declining economic fortunes of black workers between 1968 and 1974, the African American community faced destitution. Job losses and heightened unemployment among black youths undermined previous NAACP successes in procuring work for African Americans. Modest job achievements and successful litigation on behalf of workers in Birmingham, Alabama and Columbus, Ohio could hardly reverse the defeatism that began to pervade the Association. Correspondingly, housing conditions for black Americans worsened as white flight to suburbia continued, leaving the cities increasingly "black and poor."[35] Equally disconcerting, NAACP efforts to improve the quality of education for black children produced more pathos than success. African American parents and students complained about the disproportionate burden desegregation visited upon the black community through reassignment and busing. In the NAACP's own words, in the newly integrated schools: "Black ... youths who could not read, write, or add were graduated from high schools [and] gifted black students [in these predominantly white schools] were not being identified or encouraged to reach their full potential."[36] When the 67th NAACP Annual Convention convened in Memphis in the summer of 1976, conventioneers would be subjected to the frustrations of an angry Board eager to place blame for the race's receding status in American society.[37]

Executive Director Roy Wilkins became the Association's scapegoat for the decline in the status of African Americans. Prior to the National

Convention, the Board of Directors decided to "retire" Wilkins and replace him with Benjamin L. Hooks, a judge, minister, and member of the Federal Communications Commission. Wilkins seethed with anger, decided to strike back, and used the Convention to maintain his leadership role in the Association. In a carefully drafted statement, Wilkins presented his views on retirement before the plenary session by declaring:

> For the greater part of my adult life every moment of my time has been at the command of this organization. I believe that I have contributed in making the NAACP a respected and effective organization.
>
> It was with shock, then, that I learned that a campaign of vilification of me had been started after the death of Bishop Spottswood by certain members of the Board of Directors and continues until this day.
>
> I suppose I should laugh when one man says I am dishonest and a hundred honor me for my integrity. I suppose I should laugh when a woman [Wilson] who shows no knowledge of good administrative practices refers to my administration of the affairs of the NAACP as "horrendous." But how does one laugh when his heart is breaking?
>
> If God is willing I shall be at the St. Louis Convention as an active, directing member of the NAACP family.[38]

Chairperson Margaret Bush Wilson informed the gathering that the Board had been surprised by Wilkins' declaration, inferring he not only agreed to the conditions of his retirement, but also participated in the discussions and arrangements for selecting his successor.[39] And to emphasize the degree of Board sensitivity toward Wilkins, Wilson informed the conferees that Wilkins would be designated Executive Secretary Emeritus and received a pension complete with full medical coverage for the former director and his spouse.[40]

The treatment accorded Wilkins represented a sad episode in the annals of black leadership. Wilson and others failed to appreciate Wilkins' dedication and untiring work on behalf of his race. They also refused to recognize that he, along with A. Philip Randolph, represented the last bridge between the thoughtful race conscious activism of Du Bois and Walter White, and those with narrower, self-centered interests. Wilson and her contingent within the NAACP opposing Wilkins would prove to be exceptionally naïve and unmindful of Wilkins' experience and wisdom.

The Board envisioned that the flamboyance and vigorous oratory Hooks offered could appeal to a younger generation of African Americans. They perceived the ouster of Roy Wilkins as a triumph of the aggressive young militants over tottering, appeasing, civil rights Neanderthals. However by ousting Wilkins and appealing to youthful enthusiasts, the NAACP overlooked an increasingly common but unfortunate phenomenon evolving. Their efforts would provide a foundation for those who believed individual success would carry greater import than the sense of collective racial advancement. Events would prove that future leaders of the NAACP and other organizations appeared less inclined to act as visionaries who strategize to uplift the entire race than as power mongers eager for self aggrandizement. Benjamin L. Hooks succeeded Roy Wilkins as the NAACP director on August 1, 1977.

Hooks and the Board never anticipated the difficulties they would face in combating the subtle racism manifested among whites and the apathy among blacks who eschewed building upon civil rights gains of the 1960s. Indeed, the challenges awaiting Hooks could prove more arduous than the problems encountered by his predecessors. Hooks faced the impossible task of convincing progressive whites to sustain support for civil rights. For white contributors, the NAACP's past triumphs enabled foundations and major businesses to reduce financial support to the venerable organization; they assumed civil rights work had been completed.[41] Moreover, the white controlled media recognized that its public tired of the black struggle and therefore limited publicity about civil rights organizations and their activities. African Americans presented different problems for Hooks. The black bourgeoisie had become happily complacent; restrictions that prevented them from enjoying privileges comparable to whites had been removed. Hooks found himself in the unenviable position of convincing middle class blacks that the civil rights crusade must continue.

When the 69th Annual Convention convened in July, 1978, Hooks sensed an on-going concern about the dearth of media attention given to the plight of the black underclass. Recognizing the growing dichotomy between middle and low-income blacks, Hooks paraphrased the opening passage of the Dickens classic *Tale of Two Cities* and stated:

> It is the best of times because today we have more than one million Blacks enrolled in college; … yet hundreds of thousands of young people … are finishing school functionally illiterate.
>
> It is the best of times because today there are more than 100 million people at work in America, and … there are more than 10 million Blacks gainfully employed, yet … because more than six million people are jobless, the rate of unemployment among Black adults is double that of

whites, and among Black teenagers the unemployment rate is as high as 70 percent in some communities as hundreds of thousands of Black teenagers are unable to find a job.

It is the best of times because ... today more than 25 percent of Black families have achieved mythical 'middle-class income standards.' Yet ... 30 percent of Black families are below the officially-defined poverty level.

It is the best of times because we have started Black upward mobility. Blacks ... are cautiously admitted into the executive suites, a few more have joined the cabinets of presidents and become ministers of state and have entered other positions of influence and power. Yet ... the nation's commitment to affirmative action is being threatened on the altar of male supremacy, under the guise of combating reverse discrimination.[42]

Since white Americans preferred to see race relations in positive terms, Hooks' reference to the pejorative aspect of black America appeared anachronistic. Problems encountered by Wilkins and Hooks within the NAACP mirrored challenges faced by all post civil rights leaders. White denial, combined with middle class black complacency, suggested that little support existed for maintaining civil rights organizations and their programs.

Prospects for Hooks enlisting white support for the black masses appeared ominous given the scores of blacks who served as mayors of the nation's largest municipalities. Starting in 1967 with the elections of Carl Stokes (Cleveland), Dennis Hatcher (Gary, Indiana), and Walter E. Washington (appointed mayor of Washington, D.C.) as the first blacks to serve as mayors of major cities, African Americans were poised to make political gains by becoming chief executive officers in cities and towns throughout the nation. The decade of the 1970s proved particularly bountiful for African Americans becoming mayors. Kenneth A. Gibson became the mayor of Newark, New Jersey, in 1970, followed by James E. Williams, Sr., East St. Louis, 1971; Theodore M. Berry, Cincinnati, 1972 (selected by city council); Tom Bradley, Los Angeles, 1973; Coleman Young, Detroit, 1973; Maynard H. Jackson, Atlanta, 1973; Ernest Nathan Morial, New Orleans, 1977; Lionel J. Wilson, Oakland, 1977; Henry L. Marsh III, Richmond, Virginia., 1977; and Richard Arrington, Jr. gained office in Birmingham, Alabama in 1979. African American women also attained high elected office. When Lelia Smith Foley won the election to the mayoralty seat in Taft, Oklahoma in 1973, she became the first black female mayor in the nation. Even Mississippi placed a black woman in office when Unita Blackwell became the mayor of Meyersville in 1976.

While the scores of blacks elected or appointed to major offices suggested that African Americans had significant political clout and sable leaders gained respect from the black and white electorate, several significant realities went unnoticed. First, most of the cities headed by black mayors were financially strapped. White flight to suburbia significantly reduced the tax base, negatively impacting the quality of public schools and weakening the urban infrastructure dependent on services provided by the municipal government. Second, evidence that African Americans gained sufficient respect to acquire high political office suggested that social equality had been proffered and black middle class concerns addressed. Like middle class black peers who benefited from the Civil Rights Movement, despite being elected into office in part by black voters, black politicians remained insensitive to the needs of the masses. Third, election to high office in no way meant that African Americans had true power in the city, state, or nation. Rather, black mayors remained dependent upon largess offered by the very white corporate structure and institutions that maintained indifference or hostility toward blacks.[43] Moreover, the mayors realized they dare not alienate white society; prominent white people retained the reins of power in every major city, and on a whim, could undermine the mayors' authority.[44] And finally, no black mayor spoke publicly about possessing limited power. This kind of confession would prove black mayors functioned essentially as figureheads. For the high ranking black politician, the illusion of power seemed as important as power itself.

Perhaps the greatest manifestation of the new black politico who represented an amalgam of coalition builder, august figurehead, and the personification of the powerful mayor who "happened to be black" would be Tom Bradley of Los Angeles. Born in 1917 to a Texas sharecropper, Bradley moved with his family at age seven to Los Angeles. The family resided on Central Avenue and lived a harsh existence. Reserved, pensive, and academically inclined as a child, Bradley grew into a tall, sinewy young man who excelled in football and track and field at the Los Angeles Polytechnic High School. After graduating from High School Bradley matriculated to UCLA, married, became an officer in the Los Angeles Police Department, and obtained a degree from Southwestern Law School.

During the 1950s and 1960s Bradley became interested in politics and joined the liberal wing of the Democratic Party. Contacts Bradley made with the Jewish community and white labor leaders enabled him to form a bi-racial political base that propelled him on to a Los Angeles City Council seat. As a councilman, Bradley vaulted into national prominence through his outspoken criticism of Police Chief William Parker's handling of the Watts Riot. Bradley's candor enabled him to solidify his base among blacks, ingratiate himself among white liberals, establish the foundation for his initial run for mayor in 1969, and win the mayoral race in 1973. Bradley's victory demonstrated that a small but solid and well-organized black community, joined to a liberal white constituency, could elect an African American to the highest political urban office in America.[45]

Bradley's victory represented the best and worst of bi-racial politics. Although the African American community served as the base of his strength, as mayor, Bradley was indebted to a myriad of non-black groups. Therefore, Bradley's ability to help African Americans would be constrained by the need to spread largess among political allies that comprised liberal whites, Jews, and wealthy conservative entrepreneurs. In fairness to Bradley, he supported the election of blacks to councilmanic seats. However, in politically factionalized Los Angeles, racial commonalities held less relevance; while many blacks supported Bradley, his greatest detractors were also African American. Blacks who opposed the mayor did so because he placed the needs of the city before the expectations of the low-income black community. For Bradley, the choice seemed easy; he became a mayor who happened to be black rather than a black mayor. Indeed, Maxine Waters, chief deputy to a black city councilman, would emerge during Bradley's first term in office, as the strongest advocate for low-income blacks—far outstripping Bradley as a friend to the poor. Bradley simply failed to maintain support in poor black neighborhoods.[46] Tom Bradley's terms as mayor of Los Angeles clearly represented the divisiveness between middle and lower income blacks. The black bourgeoisie thought and acted like white peers and had a vested interest in supporting Bradley. But for the African American masses, Bradley appeared solely as a man devoid of racial consciousness. Indigent African Americans remained poor and black during Bradley's term in office.

Political scientists perceived black mayors, and particularly Bradley, as politicians incapable or unwilling to extend civil rights to impoverished and dispossessed African Americans. The harshest critics believed black mayors were subservient to dominating economic interests devoid of compassion for the black masses, but these critics should have recognized the limits of black mayors' power. At best, the mayors could merely raise minority concerns, sensitize police consciousness in its treatment of African Americans, and increase black presence in middle class jobs. Perhaps the most significant reality understood by black mayors who acquired office through a bi-racial mandate existed in their ability to convince the white electorate that control of the city and city policies would remain under white control. Between 1973 and 1977 Bradley revealed a profound understanding of coalition politics. Arguably, Bradley's terms as mayor made him the best black municipal chief executive in the history of the United States. Yet despite his success as mayor, the socioeconomic condition of the black underclass remained static and dismal.[47]

Given the limitations under which black municipal officials operated, concerns for the African American masses gained "lip-service" but little attention. During the administrations of most African American officials, cities became more segregated, impoverished, and black in composition. In fact, the decade replicated the 1960s when the Kerner report warned of a nation "rapidly moving toward two increasingly separate Americas" divided by race.[48] However instead of concluding that the nation was increasingly divided by color, additional caveats could be added. Divisiveness could be attributed to black and white "haves," and black and white "have nots." The admonitions of the Kerner Commission that most clearly stated what needed to be undertaken and accomplished to provide equal rights to African Americans received scant reference from black leadership. Finally, as the nation lacked the incentive to address problems of the black urban poor, African American officials lacked the nerve to challenge the status quo by drawing attention to the plight of downtrodden members of their race.

Black mayors could hardly envision themselves as being powerless and incapable of leadership. Election to high office—usually through the essential support of white constituents—suggested that these representatives of the "talented tenth" had become accepted as equal partners in America's political system. During the administrations of Nixon and Ford, an era of retrenchment for federal poverty programs, African American mayors refused to comment upon the increasing "ghettoization" of the inner city. The mayors' very presence suggested to the ever-complacent black middle class that racial progress continued. Moreover, those among the black intelligentsia who held reservations about the dearth of services provided to inner city residents muted their criticism. Few blacks seemed willing publicly to critique a "brother" in power. Mindful of their origins, black leaders increasingly represented the cautious, conservative views of the black bourgeoisie. Certainly, a candid revelation that attempts to acquire outside assistance for their municipality failed could reveal a lack of initiative as well as compassion for the poor. However, they said nothing. Again, those who should have expressed outrage about the decline in the quality of life within the inner city remained quiescent.[49]

With the election of James Earl "Jimmy" Carter to the White House in 1976, African American leaders believed they had an opportunity to aid their race. Blacks who participated in the election process had reason to feel elated by Carter's election largely because black voters overwhelmingly supported the Democratic Party. Members of the black establishment also had high expectations for the new administration. Appointments of Andrew Young (Ambassador to the United Nations), Patricia Harris (elevated to cabinet status as the director of HUD), and Eleanor Holmes Norton (as the chair of EEOC), were designed to reward the black electorate. Yet, these appointments failed to placate the black establishment. Roger Wilkins, Roy Wilkins' nephew, reflected the thinking of the black leadership cadre when he complained that Carter "ignored the largest pool of seasoned black governmental talent the country had ever developed."[50] Wilkins and other like-minded people believed the race's advancement could be measured primarily by placing scores of blacks in prominent positions rather than improving the condition of the African American majority.

By appointing Andrew Young as the United States Ambassador to the United Nations, Carter selected an African American with the greatest potential to ascend to the highest level of black leadership. Born on March 12, 1932 in New Orleans to Andrew, Sr. and Daisy Fuller Young, a dentist and school teacher respectively, Andrew, Jr. was raised in a comfortable middle environment with strong Congregational religious beliefs. Precocious, with a profound interest in reading, young Andrew skipped immediately from first to third grade. As the smallest boy in class attending a school full of bullies, Andy Young mastered the art of diplomacy to ensure his survival, and acquired training that enabled him to interact effectively with people from diverse nationalities, races, religions, and political persuasions.[51]

During his early years in New Orleans Young learned the credo espoused by Du Bois that "The Negro race, like all races, is going to be saved by its exceptional men." Therefore, Young appreciated the concept of serving his race—a race suffering grievously from America's racist past. After attending Dillard and Howard Universities for his Bachelor's degree, Young prepared for the ministry at Hartford Divinity School, performed volunteer work in post-War Austria, and ministered to a small black congregation in Thomasville, Georgia. While ministering in Thomasville Young decided to head a black voter registration drive and had his initial encounter with Martin Luther King, Jr., a man who had a significant impact on Young's life. In the late 1950s Young served as an executive for the National Council of Churches in New York City. There, he acquired familiarity with the white establishment in the North and learned to appreciate the role of powerful church organizations in national and international affairs. At this time in his life Young also decided that the Bible spoke to oppressed people everywhere. He applied Social Gospel principles reminiscent of the late nineteenth century to relieve social and economic oppression and restore human dignity.

The southern "Sit-in" Movement caused Young to apply his concept of religious activism. He wrote Dr. King and volunteered to join in the Civil Rights Movement, eventually becoming a member of the SCLC staff. As a committed civil rights activist Young displayed a calm, intrepid demeanor and served as one of King's most able lieutenants. After Dr. King's death Young became active in Democratic Party politics. He articulated support for Hubert Humphrey in the 1968 presidential election. Despite Humphrey's defeat, Young remained enamored with politics. He resigned from SCLC to represent Atlanta's Fifth Congressional District in the 1970 congressional elections. At this time he developed a rapport with and befriended Jimmy Carter, the successful Georgia gubernatorial candidate. Thus, when Young entered Congress in 1972, he acquired intimate knowledge of politics and was poised to campaign actively for Carter in twenty-seven states and fifty-one cities during the 1976 presidential election. When Young's help proved invaluable in helping Carter win the election, the president-elect decided upon a fitting reward. Since Young shared Carter's view on human rights and established himself as a liaison between the United States and the Third World, as Carter's supporter and friend, the humanitarian and internationalist Andy Young received the first prestigious appointment of its kind ever awarded an African American. Andrew Young became the first of his race to receive an appointment as the United States Ambassador to the United Nations.

As the UN Ambassador, Young acted as an idealist intent on placing America "on the right side of the moral issues of the world." He ignored political sensibilities and expressed himself candidly on international issues without regard to alienating countries allied with the United States. History professor Kenneth O'Reilly summarized Young's contentious tenure as America's ranking foreign diplomat by declaring:

Critics said he practiced 'Open Mouth Diplomacy.' Young called Cuba a more-or-less stabilizing influence in Angola; dismissed Britain, Sweden, and Russia as racist nations; labeled former Presidents Nixon and Ford racist to the bone; championed the cause of 'political prisoners' (poor blacks apparently) in this country; blamed the America bashing so common at the UN by reference to white racist attitudes and other Eurocentric sins; and had nice things to say about the Palestine Liberation Organization (PLO).[52]

Young's support for the Palestinian position eventually sealed his doom in the Carter Administration. By obfuscating in regard to an unauthorized conference with the PLO's chief representative, Carter demanded that Young tender his resignation as the UN Ambassador. Young took his "firing" stoically and remained loyal to the President. However, the repercussions accruing from Young's dismissal had dire portents for the African American community and comprised far more than what Carter dismissed as "a mountain made out of a molehill." Obviously, the Israeli lobby held far more power than the African American community, particularly when the titular head of black America could be dismissed from an enormously high administrative post with impunity.

Young's position became vulnerable, in part, because of the waning influence of black leaders. Beset by a series of misadventures like the National Black Political Convention fiasco, Wilkins' ouster as Executive Director of the NAACP, and recurring factionalism that undermined black organizations, African American leaders became unable to appeal to the moral consciousness of white America. However Young also unconsciously contributed to his demise as black America's most prominent leader. Influenced by religious tenets and moral righteousness derived from the Civil Rights Movement, Young ignored the retreat of liberal whites from civil rights causes. He also failed to notice that the "talented tenth" emulated their white counterparts and tired of issues for disadvantaged people—black, white, or Palestinian—at home or abroad. Therefore, Young functioned as a black leader devoid of any concrete base of support.

With Andrew Young's departure from the Cabinet, Vernon Jordan of the Urban League appeared as the only black leader with an organizational following capable of extending the successes of the Civil Rights Movement to the masses of black Americans. Jordan had emerged from Whitney Young's shadow and evolved as a formidable leader of the NUL in his own right. Beginning in 1975, Jordan had the Urban League prepare an exhaustive, analytical, report on the status of African Americans in a number of critical areas including economics, employment, education, social services, the black family, and housing.[53] However, as a political realist, Jordan elected to steer a neutral course and refrained from attacking the Carter Administration over the retreat from Affirmative Action, reduction in federal funds for social needs, and the sacrifice of job programs in favor of incentives for the business establishment.[54] While Jordan acknowledged that blacks lost momentum generated during the 1960s and that black family income had declined during the 1970s, he failed to reproach the Administration for the lamentable economic condition of black Americans. Rather, something he deemed "'new negativism' inflation and the generally unfavorable economic conditions throughout the decade as contributory factors" for black regression.[55] Jordan even defended Carter's decision to accept Ambassador Andrew Young's resignation, a position that resulted in a "sit-in" in the Urban League office in October, 1979 with the charge that Jordan was not representative of black America.[56] This charge, unfortunately, could hardly be leveled solely at Vernon Jordan. Events would prove Jordan to be unequivocally race conscious compared to others put forward to represent African Americans.

In a desperate effort to draw attention to the issues facing African Americans in the forthcoming decade, political science professor Ronald Walters of Howard University wrote an alarmist article for the *New York Times*. He echoed Jordan's admonition about the plight of African Americans. Walters faulted whites for being indifferent to the black condition. But he also criticized the black middle and upper income elite. While the ratio of prosperous blacks increased to comprise approximately 25 percent of all black families, their good fortune enabled pubic policy decision makers to abandon the African American masses. Walters held African American leaders responsible for abdicating their role as "race" representatives and concluded his commentary by declaring:

> ...worsening social conditions, unattended by social policy and action, are again separating blacks' local and national leaders from the legitimacy conferred by the black masses because of the leaders' inability to influence the conditions that satisfy human needs by so-called normal politics. In such a situation, the prospect of a return to destruction is possible.[57]

Although venerable civil rights organizations like the NAACP and National Urban League had difficulty addressing the needs of disadvantaged blacks, one organization—the National Council of Negro Women [NCNW] increased in prestige and political influence. As an organization that evolved from Mary McLeod Bethune's leadership of the National Association of Colored Women, the NCNW was founded in 1935 as a black women's movement for constructive action. The organization came to prominence during the turbulent 1960s and extended its influence nationally and internationally throughout the 1970s.

Under the able leadership of Dorothy Irene Height the NCNW grew exponentially. Height possessed the qualities of a vigorous leader. Born in Richmond, Virginia on March 24, 1912, she was raised in Rankin, Pennsylvania and educated in New York City, earning Bachelor's and Master's degrees at New York University, and pursuing additional study at Columbia and the New York School of Social Work. She initially gained recognition as a leader in the Harlem YWCA, a position that propelled her into a national leadership role as a NCNW volunteer and eventually President of Delta Sigma Theta Sorority. After becoming the NCNW president in 1957, Height acquired stature as an organizational leader comparable to King of SCLC and Wilkins of the NAACP. During her fifteen year tenure (1965 to 1980) the NCNW sponsored forty national projects related to women, youth, employment, education, the African Diaspora, and extended their work to encompass internationalism and women's issues.[58]

An obvious void in African American leadership became evident during the 1970s. No African American leader presented a viable philosophy or strategy that offered hope to the black masses or encouraged white Americans to sustain the Civil Rights Movement. In fairness to black leaders, executive directors within the NAACP and National Urban League sought to maintain the hard won gains achieved during the 1960s. They were particularly vocal in bringing forward issues dealing with African American poverty. Unfortunately, few members among the African American "rank and file" or black bourgeoisie demonstrated any interest in sustaining the quest for civil rights. While the black bourgeoisie retained its position in society and even flourished, confusion and disillusionment became infused among the African American masses in a manner representative of the degradation preceding the Civil Rights Movement. Contending forces involving class, race, and personal ambition would determine the role and direction taken by African American leaders in the ensuing decade.

10

THE WANING OF BLACK LEADERSHIP

On December 13 and 14, 1980, an obscure but enormously significant meeting took place at the Fairmont Hotel in San Francisco. Thomas Sowell, Sr., conservative black economist and Fellow at the Hoover Institute, convened an alternative conference designed to discuss new policy directions for African Americans. Sowell intended to move blacks away from the "old civil rights movement" toward a more enlightened policy that would ameliorate the African American condition. The unique conference purportedly contained African Americans from diverse ideologies and political persuasions, but when reviewing the eighteen blacks and five whites attending the two-day meeting, an overwhelming number comprised conservatives far to the right of mainstream African American society. By design, none of the attendees hailed from a civil rights organization. The only semblance of objectivity appeared in the presence of Bernard E. Anderson, Director of the Social Sciences Division of the Rockefeller Foundation; T.V. talk show host Tony Brown; Chuck Stone, Senior Editor of the Philadelphia *Daily News*, and professor Charles V. Hamilton of Columbia University. The remainder comprised conservative businessmen, social theorists, and politicians aligned with the Republican Party.

Henry Lucas, Jr., former executive committee member of the Republican National Committee, clarified the reason for the gathering when he said:

This forum is to make known to this administration ... that here are black people ... who are competent, who are talented, who think differently, who want to examine the past; people who ... are willing to say that some approaches have not worked and that we do need a change.... Hopefully, this administration ... will begin to solicit the advice of those of us who are participative (sic), in these types of forum.[1]

Of course a sincere interest in aiding black Americans remained a paramount possibility, but the rationales for adopting strategies different from liberal black leadership suggested those presenting new ideas had ulterior motives. Black conservatives placed themselves in the good graces of the new administration to show why Reagan and his advisors could solicit their expertise as black problem solvers.

Sowell opened the convention by declaring the meeting served as a gathering of like-minded people who purposely intended to ensure that conservative policies would gain credence and eventual success within African American society. He cited the debased economic condition and limited financial progress made by blacks during the preceding decade. Instead of attributing the worsening social problems—disintegrating families, skyrocketing unemployment, and heightened incidence of crime inherent in black society to poverty, Sowell blamed the problem on excessive government bureaucracy. Although Sowell's assessment would appear too naïve and simplistic for this Harvard trained economist to declare or believe, his comments evoked a sense of unanimity among those in attendance. Dan Smith, Commissioner of California State for Economic Development, agreed with Sowell and proposed that new African American leaders be created to help blacks create their own wealth without federal assistance. Similar pronouncements came from Wendell Wilkie Gunn of Pepsico; economics professor Walter E. Williams of George Mason University; Maria Lucia Johnson, an attorney for the Lambert, Griffin, and McGovern Law Firm; and Clarence M. Pendleton, Jr., President of the San Diego Urban League.

Those attending the meeting also held different opinions from traditional black leaders concerning the best means for resolving educational problems within black America. Sowell, Williams, and Clarence Thomas (serving at that time as an aide to Senator John C. Danforth of Missouri) debunked liberal theories contending that class status, black role models, integration, and decent facilities enhanced a child's ability to learn. Instead, attendees proposed that a laissez-faire approach be adopted.

Thomas, though born poor, attended parochial schools that provided financial assistance from the white run diocese, declared: "...we need to look more to ourselves for solutions...definitely putting the primary responsibility for the solution to these problems, on ourselves."[2] At face value the Thomas declaration appeared sincere. Black self-reliance served as a fundamental objective since the days of Booker T. Washington. Yet for one dependent upon white largess throughout his entire life, Thomas' appeal to self-reliance would eventually prove self-serving and disingenuous.

With Edwin Meese III, the confidant of President-elect Ronald Reagan in attendance to give the summary address, faithful black Republicans took heart; they had ingratiated themselves with a powerful ally. Meese's comments stipulated that color would have no impact on decision making for the new administration, and that Reagan and staff intended to relate to blacks with similar ideas and values. Thus, the Fairmont Convention had far more to do with assembling conservative African Americans who would be supportive of the Reagan Administration's agenda than promoting black interests. The conferees espoused a doctrine of righteousness that called for developing black self-reliance rather than encouraging strategies designed to solicit federal assistance for an African American agenda. In a sinister vein, Reagan conservatives convinced Sowell and other black conferees that states rights rather than civil rights, and individualism instead of federal subsidies best served the interests of African Americans.

Meese deemed the conference "a significant beginning," an event that would serve as a prelude to black thinking for the next decade. Knowing his audience and how to play to their vanity, he declared: "There are going to be black people on the White House staff, but they are not going to be there simply as ambassadors to other black people. They are going to be there because they have a substantive role to fulfill...."[3] Meese's statement about a different thinking cadre of black leaders for the next decade proved prophetic. During the Reagan and Bush administrations blacks who gained prominence in public life, with few exceptions, would be conservative and identified largely with the American rather than the African American establishment.

Edwin Meese represented most white conservative ideologues who opposed federal support for African American advancement. Perceiving liberal enactments of the 1960s—busing, affirmative action, and job programs—inimical to the interests of white people, Meese and other Reagonites decided, as Omi and Winant related: "to rearticulate ... the meaning of race and the fundamental issues arising from racial inequality."[4] Meese and influential members of the Reagan Administration would come to represent a unique amalgam of the "Old" and "New Right"—combining the anti-federal government stance and black antipathy to create the Reagan Revolution. These "revolutionaries," neo-conservatives comprised primarily of white men, sought to reverse civil rights gains made during previous administrations by marginalizing blacks under the guise of "states rights."[5]

Even before Reagan's victory in the 1980 presidential election, civil rights organizations like the NAACP and National Urban League lost their penchant for carefully reviewing the candidates.[6] While they held deep resentment toward President Carter for his apparent indifference toward their race, leaders from each of the civil rights agencies merely held reservations about a Reagan presidency. When Reagan neglected to address the NAACP's national convention and elected instead to appear in the "deep South" to extol the virtues of "states rights," civil rights leaders had cause for being wary. Nevertheless, the Urban League retained an open mind toward Reagan.[7] When Reagan addressed the League's 70th annual convention, the attendees seemed thrilled by his presence and interrupted his speech fifteen times with applause. Atlanta delegate Lyndon Wade observed: "I was awed by his plea for black support and the substantive treatment he gave the issues...." Earl Caldwell, a black columnist for the *New York Daily News* noted that "The reception that Ronald Reagan, the conservative, got rivaled the one that had been given ...to Ted Kennedy, a politician whose name has always been magic in gatherings of blacks." And an official from the District of Columbia said: "I don't think that a Reagan presidency would be the disaster some blacks are saying it would be."[8]

Perhaps the most significant indicator revealing the conservative mood of the Urban League could be observed in the conclusions of the NUL report, "Black Progression-Black Regression." Maudine Cooper, who supervised the research, noted that "traditional liberal programs such as affirmative action, subsidies, and some special training programs 'result in dependence, rather than independence....'"[9] Cooper's conclusion comported with the conservative Reagan ideology, but seemed ironic given the general decline in the standing of living among significant numbers of low-income African Americans. Although the black press held severe reservations about Reagan, and the NAACP had been insulted by what appeared to be calculated indifference toward the organization's existence, the Urban League's apparent endorsement of a conservative position on federal largess suggested that black leaders of the post-civil rights era had reached a comfort zone. Unlike previous Urban League officials, current members appeared uninterested in the amount of assistance presidential candidates from either party would offer the black community. With unwarranted bravado Vernon Jordan declared: "The black strategy should be to hang loose and make the candidates come to us. No one can win without the black vote."[10]

Leaders within the National Urban League, more than any other civil rights organization, had to recognize the increasingly blighted conditions evident in ghettos throughout the United States. Wretched housing conditions, unemployment, and other conditions that exemplified poverty served as grounds for the NUL's creation and continued existence. During the 1970s Vernon Jordan spoke candidly about the woeful economic problems in the black community and directed his concerns to the nation's power elite. An unfortunate event, however, would sap the NUL of its vitality. An assassination attempt in 1979 severely wounded Jordan and incapacitated him for more than a year. Jordan's misfortune placed the NUL in a directionless holding pattern, rendering the League unprepared for the challenges resulting from the 1980 presidential election.

While the Urban League appeared significantly out of touch with the needs and thoughts of the masses during Jordan's convalescence, the NAACP faced different problems. Association executives became mired in internal fights that detracted from the organization's effectiveness. Directors became particularly concerned about their inability to attract sufficient numbers of people to join the Association, a failure that ultimately led to the forced resignation of Executive Director Roy Wilkins. Problems hardly abated with the removal of Wilkins. After Wilkins' departure a clash occurred between NAACP Board President Margaret Bush Wilson and Benjamin Hooks, the new Executive Director. Rather than serve as a unifying force within the black community, Wilson seemed more inclined to emulate Representative Shirley Chisholm. By demonstrating a propensity for independence and divisiveness and promoting opposition from black men, Wilson diverted attention away from a new civil rights agenda toward inter-personal vindictiveness.

Wilson's background suggested she would have a promising career as an NAACP executive. A native of St. Louis, Missouri, Bush's entire family played active roles in the local NAACP branch. After graduating from Talladega College and the Lincoln University School of Law, Wilson soon proved to be an aggressive opponent of racial discrimination, rising to a leadership position on the local executive board to eventually become president of both the St. Louis and Missouri State Associations. While working as a volunteer within the NAACP, Wilson acquired experience with federal agencies. Eventually she became a U.S. Attorney at the Department of Agriculture, gained an appointment to the Anti-Poverty and Civil Rights task force, and rose to become the Deputy Director of the St. Louis Model Cities Agency. Wilson's outstanding work in Missouri eventually garnered her national acclaim and election as president of the Association's National Board in 1975. Strong willed and uncompromising—Wilson orchestrated Wilkins' ouster as Executive Director—she held antipathy for anyone likely to challenge her authority. Although largely responsible for selecting Benjamin Hooks as Wilkins' replacement, her dictatorial style angered Hooks and created dissension within the entire Association.

Wilson's high-handed approach to leadership soon grated on organizations beyond her control. Mindful of her personal success in working with federal agencies and eager to bolster Association funds, Wilson decided to support President Carter's plan to encourage gas and oil deregulation. She fervently believed in a partnership between "big government, the big minority (blacks), and big oil." This decision placed the Association at odds with the National Urban League, the Congressional Black Caucus, as well as members of the NAACP Board. Scores of indigent blacks became subjected to the capriciousness and rising prices encouraged by oil magnates.[11] Despite warnings that her support of President Carter would cause ill feelings between the Association and other black organizations, Wilson used her position as NAACP president to coerce the Association into following her lead in support of deregulation. Therefore, prior to the presidential election of 1980, Wilson engaged in actions that alienated the NAACP from its base—upwardly striving people who sacrificed their meager finances to support the Association.

Wilson's mistakes and miscalculations enabled the NUL's Vernon Jordan to be perceived as the most prominent black leader in the United States. Given the internal problems within the NUL and NAACP, Reaganites recognized the time was propitious for developing a coalition of black conservatives who could dissuade African Americans from endorsing liberal Democratic Party causes. Soon after Ronald Reagan became president, Vernon Jordan sensed problems for blacks and placed blame for the weakening status of the black masses squarely on the shoulders of the President. Though "disappointed" by Reagan's reluctance to support the 1965 Voting Rights Act and school integration, and by the appointment of insensitive Negrophobes like William Bradford Reynolds and Edwin Meese to influential positions as (ironically) Assistant Attorney General for Civil Rights and Attorney General respectively, Jordan remained optimistic. "Dialogue between black leaders and the Administration," he contended, "will continue and will produce positive results in spite of our differences."[12] The Urban League director adroitly promoted an open public relationship between black leaders and Reagan. Jordan also declared that Reagan is a good man who is frank and forthright in presenting his position.

Jordan's resurrection as the African American community's most prominent leader proved short lived. The Administration encouraged Congress to authorize cuts in social programs. However, neither Jordan nor any other black leader offered rejoinders to mitigate the negative consequences of federal cutbacks. This silent response raised even greater concern about the effectiveness of traditional civil rights leaders. "In past months," Sheila Rule of the *New York Times* reported, "community activists and others have characterized their national leaders as being out of touch with the masses of blacks and afraid to wage a real fight against injustices for fear of alienating white businesses that provide financial support."[13] Her critique went uncontested.

John E. Jacob, the successor to Vernon Jordan as Urban League director, constantly demanded training and jobs for the poor. He approached corporate America—big business and industry—to sustain hope and find fresh opportunities for disadvantaged blacks, but, like Jordan, his efforts achieved little to ameliorate conditions in inner city black communities. Without external pressures being mounted by African American lobbying organizations, neither the private sector nor the federal government had reason to assist needy black Americans.

Unfortunately for the NUL, the NAACP—the organization that traditionally pressured the federal government and the white establishment into aiding blacks—imploded and faced total disintegration. While the conflict between Margaret Bush Wilson and Benjamin Hooks continued to simmer, a new problem surfaced that added to the comical, yet tragic image being created by leaders within the NAACP. Now, serious questions would be raised about the viability and relevance of the organization and the sanity of its leadership. In May 1982, the NAACP sued the NAACP Legal Defense Fund [LDF] for using the NAACP name. Given the Reagan Administration's retrenchment toward enforcing civil rights mandates and plight of low-income blacks, a suit over the use of the NAACP name appeared ludicrous. However, from the perspective of the NAACP Board of Directors, the suit had validity because the LDF took credit for NAACP successes. Although the two organizations severed ties in 1957, the parent organization believed that the LDF siphoned recognition and philanthropic donations away from the parent body. Rather than settle the dispute amicably out of court, rancor between the two groups became public, causing columnist William Raspberry to liken the squabble reminiscent of "Amos 'n Andy's" battle between Calhoun and the Kingfish.[15]

The rift between the NAACP and the LDF enabled "naysayers" like black Harvard professor Martin Kilson to ask whether the National Association should remain in existence. Kenneth Clark, the black social scientist who provided the intellectual framework for strategies leading to the favorable Brown Decision of 1954, provided an even more damning voice opposing the continued existence of the NAACP. Others declared the National Association irrelevant because of a decline in membership. Some people criticized the organization for downsizing that scaled back its voter registration drive and black employment campaign. Others became disenchanted with the NAACP because the Association failed to attract top executives to participate in leading the organization.[16]

Pressures generated by the NAACP/LDF debacle caused dissension between Board President Wilson and Executive Secretary Hooks to reach a breaking point. Animus between the two leaders came to a head in May 1983 when Wilson placed Hooks on an eight day suspension. In response, Hooks lobbied the Board to remove Wilson. Internal bickering within the NAACP eased somewhat when the Board removed Mrs. Wilson and replaced her with Kelly Miller Alexander. When Wilson vindictively proclaimed that the National Office had no idea about the number of members within the organization, charged that the accounting procedures were highly irregular, and accused Hooks of bilking the NAACP by lining his pockets with Association funds, personal differences between two people cast aspersions upon the entire organization.[17]

Troubles within the NAACP stemmed from several unfortunate realities. First, the Hicks-Wilson dispute represented the frustration of powerlessness—a factor that became evident when the two leaders found themselves unable to alter the nation's indifference toward the welfare of African Americans. Rather than fight an unconquerable foe—the staid conservatives who launched a conservative backlash toward black Americans—the combatants sought victory at each other's expense.

Second, black leadership appeared tired, elderly, and mired in the past. After providing a foundation for civil rights successes for the next generation, the "old guard" failed to share power and train potential leaders for future civil rights struggles. They also proved incapable of stimulating young people to exceed their accomplishments in race conscious endeavors. Third, younger people refused to see civil rights work as being challenging, rewarding, or relevant. Without experiencing completely the degradation of "Jim Crow," young middle class adults demonstrated complaisance and satisfaction with their status in society. And finally, black leaders in the NAACP faced a daunting task. They had to convince the nation that the quest for civil rights must continue regarding issues pertaining to social policy and economic equality.[18]

Perhaps the most chilling indictment of the NAACP existed in its failure to generate support from the primary beneficiaries of its efforts—the black middle class. With greater opportunities available for black professional and skilled workers during the post civil rights era, aspiring African Americans focused primarily on personal career objectives. Unlike predecessors who condemned racism and pricked the conscience of an ashamed America, this group focused on their current financial situation. The black bourgeoisie acted selfishly with some justification. The economic recession of the 1970s, in which middle class black families declined from 12 to 9 percent, encouraged the black bourgeoisie to feel less charitable toward disadvantaged members of their race and more inclined to devote time and energy toward self-preservation. Mindful of its long existence on the periphery of white middle class society, current economic problems discouraged the black bourgeoisie from shouldering responsibilities for the masses. Without strong endorsements from the black bourgeoisie, therefore, leaders of civil rights organizations experienced a diminution of support from their most reliable ally.

While the NAACP and NUL collectively spoke of problems encountered by scores of African Americans—segregated and inferior education, chronic unemployment, family instability, welfare dependency, inadequate health and social services, deteriorating housing, crime and inequities in the criminal justice system—the black bourgeoisie and their white peers hardly cared. Most middle class blacks and whites, focused on personal and career development, family, and pursued hedonistic endeavors. Therefore, it became difficult for those in the hierarchy of the NAACP to lead if those upon whom they depended for moral and financial support elected not to follow.[19] Indeed, declining support for the National Association led to a public debate about the relevance of the NAACP with Dr. Kenneth Clark presenting a critical assessment while Tony Brown of *Tony Brown's Journal* and Dr. Alvin F. Poussaint of Harvard University defended the Association. Though the debate never threatened black people's survival directly or immediately, internal dissension allowed for a far more insidious development. An increasing contingent of blacks perceived the NAACP as being weak, believed civil rights activity to be in remission, and sought wealth, power, and personal aggrandizement by siding with conservative Reaganites.[20] In order to retain its role as a champion of the race, justify its existence, and retain black support, the NAACP contemplated political action. Although divided by factionalism and in a weakened organizational state, the NAACP prepared to battle Ronald Reagan.

Reagan's indifference and hostility toward African Americans stood to rejuvenate the black bourgeoisie's interest in the NAACP. Aside from addressing the Urban League's national convention in August 1980, Reagan virtually ignored African American problems and refused to meet with NAACP leadership. By 1983 Reagan no longer received "benefits of the doubt" from African American leaders. With just cause, disgruntled blacks hurled a bevy of criticisms against Reagan and his Administration. Reagan's point man on civil rights insulted the very concept the term "civil rights" conveyed. Yale and Vanderbilt educated "blue blood" William Bradford Reynolds dedicated himself to ending racial quotas, undermining affirmative action, terminating "forced" busing, and questioning remedial programs designed to help blacks gain equality in America.[21] Unfortunately, African American leaders failed to find appropriate measures to forestall Reynolds' purposefully destructive policies.

Reagan provided additional insult to injury by supporting tax exemptions for schools like Bob Jones University that discriminated by race. He also attempted to abolish the Legal Services Commission and pack the Civil Rights Commission with individuals who shared his conservative philosophy. Reagan's insensitivity toward blacks emboldened the apolitical NAACP and changed the Association from a politically contemplative entity into an organization that engaged in direct political involvement. In breaking with the precedent of political neutrality adopted by previous Executive Directors, Benjamin Hooks decided that he and the NAACP would work strenuously to defeat Reagan and the G.O.P. at the polls.[22]

Decades of political neutrality left the NAACP bereft of an action plan to battle the Reaganites. Thus, when the politically naive NAACP decided to confront seasoned political veterans of the Reagan camp, an uneven fight commenced. Convinced that their use of the race card would pay dividends but mindful of the sensibilities of politics, Reagan advisors decided upon a novel strategy. After the failed attempt to alter the political composition of the Civil Rights Commission by removing liberal commissioners like the prominent African American scholar Mary Frances Berry, Reaganites decided to promote a "color blind" policy that eliminated race from consideration for jobs. However, Reaganites decided upon a shrewd political maneuver; they decided to place blacks sympathetic to their cause in key positions. Reagan advisors merely had to find the right kind of blacks with elitist class leanings, blind ambition, and sufficient self-loathing to attack affirmative action and federal social and economic programs beneficial to African Americans. These so called champions of conservative values would serve as a black phalanx promoting the anti-black sentiments inherent in Reagan Republicanism. Hooks and the NAACP would be out maneuvered; they had no answers for combating this opportunistic black conservative vanguard.

As one of the few conservative black Republicans, a staunch supporter of Reagan in the 1980 presidential election, and a long time associate of Reagan aide Ed Meese, Clarence Pendleton, Jr. possessed the ideal qualities Reaganites coveted in a black man deemed proper for a White House appointment. Born in Kentucky in 1930 and educated at Howard University, Pendleton moved to San Diego, California where he became chair of the San Diego Transit Corporation. Having distinguished himself in this position, Pendleton eventually served as director of the San Diego Urban League. In this capacity, Pendelton baited affirmative action advocates and national black leaders. With a warped perspective of what blacks needed to enjoy full American citizenship, Pendleton attacked black leaders and declared:

> I say to America's black leadership open the plantation gates and let us out. We refuse to be led into another political Jonestown as we were led during the presidential campaign. No more Kool-Aid, Jesse (Jackson), Vernon (Jordan), and Ben (Hooks)! We want to be free.[13]

The Reagan Administration immediately realized Pendleton possessed the proper mode of thinking for their kind of governmental appointee. When Pendleton enabled two white businessmen to use the San Diego Urban League as a front to qualify for special preference and thereby acquire government contracts, he became a man they could trust.[14]

Pendleton, therefore, became the Reagan Administration's appointee to head the Commission on Civil Rights [CCR], the first of a series of black public figures who actively and willingly helped undermine programs beneficial to African Americans.

Pendleton took the concept of "a color blind society" to lengths that even baffled the Reagan Administration. Using absurd reasoning and no respect for protocol, Pendleton chastised the President for holding a meeting with black federal officials in June, 1984 to discuss the Administration's civil rights record and said:

> Such meetings are contradictory to what...I believe about working toward a race and gender-neutral and color blind society....Meetings or briefings convened for groups by color, ethnicity or gender are divisive at best....You did not appoint people by color or gender. Why convene them for the same reason?[15]

In this case Reagan remained unaffected by Pendleton's chastening remarks. Although his detractors labeled him a fool, Pendleton played his role sufficiently well as a black opponent of civil rights to maintain his position as the CCR chair until Reagan retired from office.

While Pendleton appeared as the most "colorful" appointee used to dismantle civil rights policies, other blacks proceeded to carry out the Administration's "Negrophobe" mandate in a quiet but systematic manner. Included among other African Americans who became senior officials in the Reagan Administration were Housing and Urban Development [HUD] Secretary Samuel Riley Pierce, Jr.; Clarence Thomas, Chair of the Equal Employment Opportunity Commission [EEOC]; and National Security Advisor Colin Powell. While Powell's appointment may be attributed primarily to the high qualities he exhibited as a career army officer, the Pierce and Thomas appointments raised eyebrows. Each of these men demonstrated qualities useful to conservative Republicans but questionable in regard to the advancement of African Americans.

Samuel Pierce, perhaps more than any other black bureaucrat in the Administration, represented the ambiguous role of a "figurehead-dupe" and "race champion" that confounded traditional civil rights leaders. Born on September 6, 1922 in Glen Cove, Long Island, New York, Pierce enjoyed a comfortable middle class lifestyle and distinguished himself as a scholar-athlete in high school. Pierce matriculated to Cornell University where he played football and graduated Phi Beta Kappa. After serving in the Second

World War, Pierce returned to Cornell to pursue a law degree. After graduation Pierce became an assistant district attorney in New York City and came to the attention of Governor Nelson Rockefeller. Rockefeller respected his work in litigation and praised Pierce within Republican Party circles. In 1955 President Eisenhower enabled Pierce to become an assistant to the Under Secretary of Labor, and in 1970 President Nixon made him the first African American to serve as a general council to the Treasury Department.[16]

On December 22, 1980 President-elect Reagan selected Pierce to join his cabinet as the Secretary of Housing and Urban Development. As a cabinet member Pierce played a Janus-faced role. Representing blacks in a positive, pro-active sense, Pierce ardently attempted to protect HUD from massive budget cuts proposed by the White House budget office. Pierce also spoke out on behalf of civil rights issues and served as a moderating force opposed to the strident conservatives within the Administration. On virtually every issue sensitive to his race—the Voting Rights Act of 1982, maintenance of affirmative action, and the Bob Jones University tax exemption controversy—Pierce placed himself squarely in the African American camp. However, Pierce's pro-black stance became negated by one obvious reality; he presided over the dismantling of HUD programs that provided low and moderate-income homes desperately needed by the African American underclass. Adding insult to the injury inflicted by budget cuts, Pierce defended his actions before Congress, arguing that the cuts, though inimical to blacks, were economically necessary.[17] While Pierce should be credited for opposing Administrative policies harmful to the black community, he appeared more as a black figurehead than as someone beneficial to African American society. On more than one occasion the Reagan Administration advocated positions harmful to blacks that exceeded the views of the American public. Pierce had every opportunity to emulate William H. Hastie who, by protesting virulent racist Administration policies of the 1940s, gained more through resignation than remaining as a token sycophant. Given the insensitivity of the Reagan Administration toward blacks after the enormous sacrifices made to acquire dignity during the Civil Rights Movement, how could less be asked of Samuel Pierce, Jr.?

The role Pierce played as an administration insider demonstrated that the responsibility of conservative African American leadership had changed. Although similarities existed between Pierce and Frederic Morrow—both served as confidents to Presidents—Pierce represented the high visibility of a ranking official with immediate access to the White House. While Morrow lurked in the shadows, Pierce held an exalted cabinet position. Scores of African Americans had cause to seek his influence and guidance. But unlike Morrow who relied upon subservience and connections to achieve personal success, Pierce, like many subsequent black conservative leaders of the post-civil rights era, subscribed to the notion that his appointment had been determined by personal qualities rather than by race. He seemed to presume that success had been acquired by industriousness and strict adherence to the Protestant Ethic rather than by a selective, insidious use of affirmative action. Indeed, Edwin Meese's declaration at the Fairmont Conference that black appointees "are not going to be ambassadors to black people"—implying that they are serving the public as true, bona fide, acceptable Americans—evidently had been endorsed unquestionably by Pierce. Secretary Pierce served as a living example of the new black conservative. He and other similar minded African Americans believed that a black man integrated into society had been judged "by the content of his character" rather than "by the color of his skin."

Clarence Thomas far exceeded Pierce as a black Reagonite responsible for reversing the progress African Americans made during previous administrations. The grandson of a sharecropper, Thomas exemplified the "rags to riches" story proudly cited by patriotic Americans. Born June 23, 1948 in the Pinpoint community near Savannah, Georgia, Thomas attracted the attention of a Catholic order that enabled him to escape the life of a backward rustic to attend St. Benedict's, a black elementary school in Savannah. Later, Thomas and another boy became the first blacks to attend the all-white Catholic boarding school, St. John Vianney Minor Seminary High School. After graduating from high school, Thomas attended Immaculate Conception Seminary in Missouri between 1967 and 1968. During his tenure at Seminary he impressed his instructors and gained financial support to attend the College of the Holy Cross, a small liberal arts school in Worchester, Massachusetts. At Holy Cross Thomas experienced a momentary epiphany, posing as a radical occasionally attired in army fatigues and combat boots in keeping with college protests in vogue during the late 1960s and early 1970s. After graduating from college with honors, Thomas enrolled through an affirmative action program at the Yale University Law School. After graduating in 1974 Thomas moved to Missouri and served as the Assistant State Attorney.

Through his work as a state attorney Thomas came to the attention of Missouri Senator John Danforth who hired Thomas as his legislative assistant. With Danforth's tutelage and recommendation, Thomas became the Assistant Secretary for Human Rights in the U.S. Department of Education and served from 1981 to 1982. Almost immediately after assuming office, Thomas came to the attention of President Reagan. Thomas attracted attention because, in the words of William Bradford Reynolds, he represented "the epitome of the right kind of affirmative action." [18] Thomas' "correctness in thought" landed him an appointment as chair of the Equal Employment Opportunity Commission. During his tenure as head of EEOC, Thomas consistently demonstrated that the Reagonites selected the right man to carry out the conservative agenda. He spoke out against affirmative action, opposed quotas, disregarded class action suits with racial overtones, and eclipsed the enforcement power of the Commission. Furthermore, on several occasions, Thomas had been brought into court because he refused to investigate discrimination complaints registered by women and minorities. For obvious pragmatic but insidious reasons, the Reagan Administration placed Pendleton [CCR], Pierce [HUD], and Thomas [EEOC] in key administrative positions to reverse legislative programs created during the civil rights era. These clever maneuvers—using blacks as promoters of Administration policies—eased the conscience of fair-minded whites and undermined the credibility of progressive blacks who accused Reagan and his advisors as being racists. As black agents doing the Administration's bidding, Reagan's anti-civil rights agenda continued unabated.

Queries must be raised to ascertain black conservatives' motivation for participating in the retrenchment of civil rights. At best, extreme naiveté could explain the Pendleton, Pierce, and Thomas perspective on power and race in Reagan's post-civil rights America. As the "Great Communicator," Reagan possessed a unique ability to make Americans feel included, comforted, and important. Therefore, conservative African Americans, like their white counterparts, found comfort in and identified with Reagan's sense of a "color-blind" society. On the other hand, the aforementioned black conservatives may be deemed delusional, sincerely believing they gained accesses to the most powerful positions of government because of talent and perseverance. Since the triumvirate apparently accepted racism stoically during their formative years with the assumption that trust in white people and the denial of racism could eventually prove advantageous, their current positions seemed warranted and therefore confirmed their belief in

America. Speculation notwithstanding, the black representatives had been carefully selected by the Reaganites for utilitarian purposes—providing assistance in dismantling policies advantageous to African Americans. By holding key positions within the Administration and perceiving themselves as invaluable policy makers serving the larger American society, Pendleton, Pierce, and Thomas represented an evolving trend in black leadership. People of African ancestry would be available to engage in activities designed to limit black access to rights and privileges available to white Americans.

Progressive African American leaders had cause for believing that blacks in the Reagan Administration acted as traitors to their race. Among people victimized by oppression, individuals with deficiencies of character could easily succumb to overtures made by those in dominant positions. Thus, blacks suffering severely from the indignities of a slave heritage and subsequent racial discrimination could unwittingly engage in self-hatred, identify with white oppressors, and betray their race. However, the role played by neo-conservative African Americans confounded progressive black leaders. These black conservatives gained powerful positions because of their race yet maintained views at significant variance with both traditional African American leaders and the black masses. Usually blacks occupying exalted positions served as prideful men and women who instilled a sense of pride throughout the entire African American public. They functioned as genuine leaders who promoted black causes and used their prestige to enhance the reputation of and create opportunities for their race. Therefore, traditional black leaders had difficulty demanding the recall of unresponsive black bureaucrats overtly opposed to views common among the majority of African Americans. Progressive-minded blacks seemed stunned. At most, they grumbled about "race traitors" in private.

Leaders within the NAACP and Urban League never generated calls for demonstrations or rallies demanding the removal of Pendleton, Pierce, and Thomas. Without the application of outside pressure to hold the Administration and its black representatives accountable for nefarious actions against African Americans, Reagan Negrophobes like Reynolds and Meese carried out policies designed to dismantle civil rights gains with impunity. Established black leaders and organizations regrettably dispensed far more energy fighting internal wars than working aggressively to have destructive black public officials removed from office.

Frustrated by their dwindling role in the conservative oriented America of Ronald Reagan, African American leaders embarked upon a desperate move to regain recognition and power; they decided to elect one of their own, Jesse Jackson for president. In a bizarre sense, Jackson shared some commonalities with the "Great Communicator" himself. Both Reagan and Jackson suffered the pangs of a dysfunctional family, had problematic relationships with their fathers, possessed enormous presence, and captivated people by their personality and oratory. The two men also exuded extreme confidence and eschewed book learning for instinctive creativity. Both captivated people by offering homilies and demonstrating charismatic qualities with whom the "so-called" common people could identify.[19] Reagan and Jackson also coveted public affirmation—both needed constant reinforcement to demonstrate their pronouncements and ideologies enjoyed a massive following.

Jesse Jackson evolved as an interesting representative of leadership during the post-civil rights era. Born on October 8, 1941 as the bastard son of Noah Robinson and Helen Burns in Greenville, South Carolina, the circumstances of his birth left Jackson with a profound sense of insecurity. He coveted love from a father figure, and in the absence of that love, learned instinctively to serve as a paternal role model for his people. Being black, poor, and illegitimate, Jackson decided to recreate himself dramatically and positively so people would take notice. Jackson, consequently, fashioned himself as a black messiah who would lead African Americans to the "Promised Land."

At an extremely early age Jackson's mother and grandmother recognized that young Jesse possessed a unique gift. As a child Jackson revealed an enormous vocabulary and an uncanny knack for learning. By fourteen Jackson sported a size 14 shoe and reached six feet four inches in height. Stimulated by a need to compensate for his lowly origins, Jackson demanded attention from authority figures and sought to prove that he "was somebody." Because of his obsession to be recognized and respected, Jackson worked extremely hard in school to enhance his natural abilities as a student, athlete, and leader. He impressed his stepfather, Charles Jackson, sufficiently to cause his mother's husband to adopt Jesse as his own son. Jackson's demonstrated prowess as a student-athlete and enormous personality in high school eventually won the respect and adulation of his natural father as well as the larger black community that shunned him during his early childhood.

Segregation in Greenville failed to stifle Jackson's talent and ambition. His exploits on the gridiron as a star quarterback earned him a football scholarship at the University of Illinois. However, Jackson's initial foray into the North proved disappointing. Unfamiliar with the nuances of northern racism and discrimination practiced at Illinois, at the end of his first year Jackson transferred to North Carolina Agricultural & Technical (A & T) College at Greensboro, one of the South's historically black colleges and universities. At A & T Jackson demonstrated a talent for leadership, became president of the student body, joined Omega Phi Psi Fraternity, and met his future wife, Jacqueline Lavinia Brown. He also attended A & T at a propitious time; fellow classmates organized "sit-ins" at the Woolworth lunch counter and initiated the activity that reenergized the Civil Rights Movement. Though perhaps the most famous and popular man on campus, Jackson refused initially to lead or participate in the protest movement. He preferred to remain on the sidelines and pursue his degree. But after being emboldened by a direct student plea for his leadership and support, and deriving personal security and political sophistication through his close relationship with Jacqueline Brown, Jackson led his first march in downtown Greensboro in 1962. Never again would Jackson refrain from demonstrating to redress legitimate grievances of the indigent, defenseless, and maligned of society.

During his undergraduate years Jackson fell under the able guidance of President Samuel Proctor. Dr. Proctor, an ordained Baptist minister, endorsed Jackson's career decision to enter the ministry and aided his matriculation to the Chicago Theological Seminary. The academic rigor at Seminary, however, failed to curtail Jackson's desire for leadership. In the spring of his first year, Jackson decided to become directly involved in civil rights activities. He led a contingent of fellow students (all of whom were white) to Selma, Alabama where he met Martin Luther King, Jr., the man most influential in launching Jackson's career as a civil rights activist and leader. From King, Jackson learned how to lead more effectively by enhancing his charismatic standing within the African American community. Eventually Jackson acquired a high position within the Southern Christian Leadership Conference and earned the opportunity to head SCLS's Operation Breadbasket in Chicago. Under Jackson's direction Breadbasket increased revenues entering the South Side of Chicago by $22 million.[30] These successes heralded the arrival of Jesse Jackson as a pre-eminent civil rights leader.

Soon after King's death a problematic relationship developed between Jackson and SCLC. Temperamentally incapable of blunting his desire to succeed King as head of the entire organization, Jackson's ambitions created a rift between himself and the SCLC leadership. He eventually resigned from the Conference, journeyed back to Chicago, and established his own organization. He adopted the term "Rainbow Coalition" as the rallying motto for a unique intra-racial political movement, and created People United to Save Humanity [PUSH] to make the nation's wealth available to the disadvantaged and poor. The "Coalition" and PUSH collectively enabled Jackson to extend his political appeal to low income blacks by incorporating them into the political system and establishing a profound sense of pride among the African American masses. By fostering a sense of hope that civil rights gains would benefit blacks on the periphery of American society, he enlisted a coterie of supportive whites and legitimized his role as a national leader.

By 1980 Jackson established himself as the living symbol of the post-civil rights era. While he recognized that no one could supplant King as the exemplar of the Civil Rights Movement, Jackson found the means for establishing himself as a celebrity. First, he adopted a catchy motto that enthralled people alienated from mainstream America. Mutual admiration became established between Jackson and his audience through his trade-mark refrain "I am...somebody."[31] In addition, Jackson courted the support of wealthy liberal whites like Hugh Hefner, the founder and editor of *Playboy Magazine*. By associating with stars, Jackson received the aura of stardom in his own right. Finally, Jackson acquired a Tudor style residence in an upper middle class area on Chicago's South Side and became an excellent negotiator and an un-elected politician with a national following. Thus with grit, mottos, PUSH, and extreme self-assuredness, Jesse Jackson became recognized, in a 1983 ABC poll, as the most prominent and influential African American leader in the nation.[32]

While every black leader recognized that the retrenchment of federal programs during the Reagan presidency severely impacted low-income blacks, only Jackson developed a strategy designed to provide the African American community with encouragement. In the summer of 1983 he launched a major voter registration campaign to garner sufficient numbers of black voters to defeat Reagan in the 1984 presidential election. His rhetoric made the registration drive plausible to people who traditionally refrained from voting. Attracting an audience and effectively using histrionics in a patented speech he declared:

> Our time has come! From the slave ship to the championship, from charity to parity, from the outhouse to the courthouse to the statehouse to the White House-from disgrace to amazing grace-our time has come! In 1980,

Reagan won by the margin of our nonparticipation. Won eight southern states by 182,000 votes, while three million blacks there were unregistered. All those rocks, little David, just layin' around. There's a freedom train a-comin'. Only you got to register to ride. Hands that once picked cotton can now pick presidents. Our time has come![33]

The thrill Jackson derived from exhorting his followers to register and vote elicited the response "Run, Jesse, Run," an idea that gave Jackson cause to reflect about the possibilities for his own election to the presidency. Jackson realized that every black he encouraged to participate in the political process existed as a potential vote for his own candidacy and made prospects propitious for a run to the White House.

Black frustration with the Reagan Administration encouraged African American leaders throughout the nation to hold a series of private conferences to develop plans that could unseat Reagan in the forthcoming election. Throughout the summer leaders proposed a series of strategies that could defeat Reagan. Some advocated an "integrationist" position and decided to work with influential white politicians. They discussed the qualities of white candidates, and debated which, among white contenders, blacks should support. Others endorsed a black empowerment position and advanced the selection of an African American candidate for president. However, the prevailing question that transcended the black versus white candidate issue was the candidacy of Jesse Jackson. A candidate like Jackson who appealed to the masses did not necessarily garner the endorsement of the black elite. Andrew Young rather than Jackson appeared as the better candidate.

Established black leaders recoiled at the thought of Jesse Jackson running for president. Included among the Jackson detractors were mayors Coleman Young of Detroit, Richard Arrington of Birmingham, Tom Bradley of Los Angeles, Benjamin Hooks of the NAACP, Coretta Scott King, and naturally, Andrew Young. Young spoke for many Jackson detractors when he deemed the Jackson candidacy "extremely dangerous" because important votes would be siphoned away from Walter Mondale, the Democratic Party's standard-bearer.[34] Additionally, the black establishment perceived Jackson as being ego driven, domineering, self-serving, and an uncontrolled maverick. However, circumstances dictated that black leaders would be unable to check the Jackson advance. As the only black leader willing and prepared to make an attempt to become the United States

President, Jackson had the opportunity to enhance his reputation as the foremost black spokesperson in America.

Jackson's critics failed to recognize that he served as a precursor to the expanded role expected of the post-civil rights leader. Now that African Americans had been embraced (generally) by the larger society, black leaders could be expected to establish interests in questions pertaining to class, environmental, international, and broad social issues. A Civil Rights Movement for black people had become passé, a phenomenon Jackson clearly understood. His call for a suspension of nuclear arms development in the United States, a decrease in defense spending, increased allocations for education and public works projects, job retraining, recognition of Cuba, ending South African apartheid, and the creation of a Palestinian state revealed an enormous departure from African American liberation movements of previous decades. With Jackson raising global issues and appearing nationally as an American leader "who happened to be black," respect for African Americans as United States citizens evolved from theory to reality. With Jackson's successes African Americans presumably assumed a sense of racial pride and contentment in knowing Jackson had become a leader willing to represent every citizen of the United States. Those presumptions would prove misleading and erroneous. Jackson remained on the periphery of the black and white establishment.

Through fund raising efforts Jackson became the first national black leader to enjoy a bountiful lifestyle. For generations black ministers engaged in the customary practice of exhorting parishioners to gratify the Lord by placing money in the collection plate. Jackson, however, raised alms giving to a new level when he solicited funds for his presidential campaign. By the mid 1980s Jackson's income reached $200,000 annually, and by the decade's end he acquired more than $1,000,000 in assets. Few would question his need to raise money to support his family, but the upper class life style, in contrast to the life of penury experienced by his aides who went weeks without pay, certainly raised questions about Jackson's priorities. Few prominent African Americans perceived Jackson as the moral successor to Dr. Martin Luther King, Jr.[35] And perhaps fewer still agreed to accept Jackson as the sole spokesperson for the African American community.

Walter Mondale rather than Jackson would win the democratic primary races and launch an unsuccessful run for president in 1984. Nevertheless, by running for President of the United States, Jackson made a statement on behalf of African Americans. Jackson delivered a stirring address before the Democratic Convention and established a national reputation for himself and his race as power brokers in national elections. To demonstrate the newly acquired sense of inclusion, Jackson campaigned extensively on Mondale's behalf and encouraged more African Americans to cast votes in a presidential election than in any previous election in the nation's history. Moreover, the enormous black turnout resulted in scores of black mayors being elected throughout the nation and enabled the Democratic Party to retain its majority in the United States Senate. John Conyers of Michigan described Jackson as the John F. Kennedy of black America. Even Coretta Scott King and Andrew Young embraced him and rescinded previous misgivings about his style and character; Jackson must have believed that he inherited the mantle of leadership from Martin Luther King.[36]

The presidential election of 1988 represented a pleasant watershed for Jackson and African Americans. Jackson evolved as the most popular and influential black leader of the decade. He held an enormous mandate of support from the black community and gained a following among a cross section of white Americans. After spending years establishing his credibility as a legitimate presidential candidate, Jackson reached the apex of his popularity when he finished first or second in forty-six primary elections and caucuses. He entered the Democratic national convention only eight hundred votes short of the majority required for nomination. Just as Reagan found the means of appealing to an alienated white constituency and conservative blacks, Jackson connected with the idealistic and/or disadvantaged from either race. Although he lost his bid for the Democratic nomination to Michael Dukakis (who lost in the general election to George Herbert Walker Bush), Jackson emerged as the first true black presidential candidate in the history of the United States.

Ironically, Jackson's rise to prominence occurred concomitantly with a general diminution in the influence of black leadership. Neither the NAACP nor the National Urban League made a concerted effort to advance the Jackson candidacy for president. Instead, each organization focused on mending differences with President Reagan. Benjamin Hooks of the NAACP asked Reagan to meet with black leaders, something the President refused to do early in his second term. John E. Jacob, Executive Secretary of the Urban League also implored Reagan to heal the breach with blacks and respond to the needs of the poor.[37] Because of previous presidential snubs, NAACP and Urban League officials were far more dedicated to reestablishing the long-standing relationship between the White House than supporting Jesse Jackson.

Despite entreaties from penitent black leaders, Reagan, as historian Kenneth O' Reilly observed, had no time for the civil rights establishment. By ignoring leaders of the NAACP and NUL, Reagan demonstrated that the importance of civil rights organizations in the United States had been severely diminished. Emboldened by Reagan's coolness toward African Americans, opportunistic black conservatives attacked both the civil rights agencies and blacks dependent upon their support. Conservative black Harvard economist Glenn C. Loury blamed blacks for the crime and poverty rampant in the African American community, a position, if true, negated the need for the National Urban League. Economist Walter Williams of George Mason University proved equally contemptible of his race. Williams faulted organizations like the NAACP for being outmoded, and for defending black murderers who deserved to die. The death penalty, he argued, "is not a civil rights struggle....Those people are in jail because they murdered people."[38] Loury and Williams acted as Reagan lieutenants—black bulldogs that barked for the President and enabled "the Great Communicator" to remain mute on questions pertaining to black civil rights.

The nadir of the Civil Rights Movement could be observed in the extreme financial distress evident in the NAACP. A contented black middle class enjoying the benefit of civil rights success no longer had cause to bankroll the NAACP. Unable to retain a significant number of dues paying members, the organization found itself unable to meet rent payments for its national office in Manhattan. After moving briefly to Brooklyn, the Board decided to relocate the national headquarters to Baltimore, Maryland. Hooks and members of the Board placed a positive spin on the move, declaring that the Association would be able to purchase a National Office building, and insisted that relocating the office to Baltimore would allow the organization to be closer to power brokers in Washington, D.C.[39] Though trying to remain optimistic, the Association found itself at a decided disadvantage when trying to demonstrate any major success (other than defeating the nomination of Robert Bork to the Supreme Court and encouraging Congress to override Reagan's veto of the Civil Rights Restoration Act) achieved during the Reagan Administration.

Although leaders in civil rights organizations saw their influence wane as the conscience of America, individuals who participated in and served as leaders in politics remained as a force to champion the black agenda. With the exception of Jesse Jackson, only Kweisi Mfume, a Congressman from Maryland, and Willie Brown, the Speaker of the House in the

California State Assembly, appeared as the most logical leaders capable of speaking on behalf of the African American community. Both men experienced deprivation as children and possessed uncanny political acumen and survival skills. They also held common views about the best way African Americans could help their race, believing that black representatives should operate within the system.

Of all late twentieth century black leaders, Kweisi Mfume probably encountered and transcended the greatest obstacles. Born Frizzell Gray in Turners Station, Maryland, PeeWee—as affectionately known by family and close friends—was the first of Mrs. Mary Elizabeth Gray's four children. Though a loving, caring, religious woman, Mary Gray could not stave off the brutality visited upon the family by Clifton, her mean-spirited husband. The physically abusive Clifton Gray constantly demeaned his son. In 1959 the elder Gray deserted the family, leaving his wife and children destitute. The following year Elizabeth Gray moved her family to Baltimore. There, young Frizzell ran with a group of young toughs, and when his mother died, he became both inconsolable and irresponsible. Although Frizzell quit school to work and support his sisters, he also exhibited the asocial behavior of a ghetto gang member. Surly, insensitive, vicious, and promiscuous—he sired five children with four different women—Frizzell "PeeWee" Gray seemed destined for jail or an early grave.

In the summer of 1972, Gray experienced a religious epiphany.[40] Using the moral values instilled by his mother and Dr. Martin Luther King, Frizzell changed his name to Kweisi Mfume [Conquering Son of Kings] and completed his formal education at the Community College of Baltimore, Morgan State University, and Johns Hopkins. He also found employment as a disc jockey, married, won a seat on City Council, and in 1986, had the honor to represent Maryland's Seventh Congressional District in Congress. As a fledgling Congressman Mfume proved to be extremely intelligent, articulate, studious, and concerned about elevating the quality of life for his constituents.

Deeply committed to helping the black underclass with whom he easily identified, Mfume appeared as the black leader least likely to place personal gain before his race. A credo to which Mfume subscribed—"The worst thing you can do as a leader is to surrender to your ... ego"[41]—set him apart from Jesse Jackson and other prominent contemporaries. In 1987 he attached a rider to Housing Bill H. R. 4 to ensure that HUD would carry out the mandate for spending $30 billion on public assistance, rural housing, and community development.[42] Mfume would continue efforts to pass legislation advantageous to the disadvantaged and poor during the administration of President George H.W. Bush. Nevertheless, when competing against entrenched political conservatives of the late 1980s, most of the legislation Mfume initiated failed to receive congressional endorsement and become law.

Prospects for leading blacks toward a more propitious future existed in a man located far from the center of political power in Washington, D.C. Willie Lewis Brown, Jr. resided in San Francisco, California and represented the Golden State as Speaker of the State Assembly. Brown appeared as a man with the political savvy capable of rescuing blacks from continuous degradation. Born into poverty on March 20, 1934 in Mineola, Texas, Willie Brown would spend his entire adult life responding, in some manner, to his origins as an impoverished black male from the South. Brown's mother, Minnie Collins Boyd, produced five children, with Willie being the second youngest sibling. Although small in stature, young Willie Jr.'s domineering personality and extraordinarily high intelligence enabled him to become the primary focus of the entire family. Growing up on the Collins family homestead, Brown learned how to become resourceful, cunning, self-indulgent, and opportunistic—qualities that would augur well for one destined to spend his entire adult life in politics.

After graduating from Mineola Colored High School in 1951, Brown moved to San Francisco and lived with a maternal uncle. Brown enrolled at San Francisco State where, after stumbling initially because of inadequate preparation, he quickly adjusted to meet the academic rigor of college life. During his undergraduate years he joined the Alpha Phi Alpha Fraternity, became active in the San Francisco branch of the NAACP, ran hurdles on the track team, and developed an interest in politics. After graduating from college in 1955, Brown enrolled at the Hastings College of Law and displayed a talent for leadership. His classmates voted him class president, and from that election forward, Brown flirted on the edges of political decorum, pushing the envelope as far as possible to satisfy his personal ambitions.

Brown graduated from Hastings in 1957 and opened a law practice with Terry Francois, a friend and fellow within the militant faction of the NAACP. As an attorney, Brown made his living defending pimps and prostitutes and other sordid elements within San Francisco society. Brown recalled: "I made cash money every day representing whores. I became the whores' lawyer.... [43] At this time Brown also became active with the Young Democrats and maintained his affiliation with the NAACP branch in San Francisco. As chair of the legislative committee, Brown demonstrated a facility for organization and achieving success. During his tenure as legislative chair, the local chapter made considerable strides toward eliminating racial discrimination in the Bay Area. Through the efforts of Brown, along with law partner Francois, African Americans obtained jobs at the airport, dairy companies, and hotels. As a defense lawyer and leader within the San Francisco Chapter of the NAACP, Brown established a reputation as an energetic, intelligent young man dedicated to protecting and assisting black people.

Brown came to the attention of influential San Franciscans by attacking a "Jim Crow" covenant that prohibited blacks from purchasing homes in an upscale development known as Forest Knolls. When Brown went through the motions of trying to purchase a home in the development and met with refusal, he became a cause celebre within the liberal establishment. Brown adroitly organized a protest movement that launched his political career. Jazz pianist Oscar Peterson and Dianne Berman [the future Senator Dianne Feinstein] joined Brown on the picket line and enabled him to gain sufficient recognition to run for and eventually win a seat in the State Assembly.

As a member of the Assembly, Brown exhibited skills displaying both a keen understanding of politics and personal style destined to be successful in his political career. He traded votes, bent the rules, maintained his central beliefs, and worked hard at his profession. Like others among the new black politicos, Brown was subjected to questions about his sincere interest in promoting black amelioration. Like every black politician who had formed a racial coalition to gain an elected seat, Brown's racial loyalty was questioned by militant African Americans who believed him to be "a tool of white liberals and black reactionaries."[44] Few among the extreme factions appreciated Brown for what he was—a great African American exemplar of a political chameleon who knew how to take risks and win.

During his early years as an Assemblyman, Brown gradually used events to gain personal recognition within the state and eventually, the nation. The volatility of the 1960s taught Brown that holding office without power rendered black people powerless and rendered a black leader's role as politician inane. Therefore, he voluntarily expressed his opinions on a myriad of topics. He initially gained acclaim by supporting the movement against the Vietnam War and discovered his call for peace proved personally beneficial. In 1965 the Sacramento Capital Press corps named Brown the Outstanding Freshman legislator. Later that year Brown further enhanced his reputation by publicly analyzing causes for the Watts Riot and meeting black dignitaries like Julian Bond, Malcolm X, Jesse Jackson, and Martin Luther King, Jr. Brown had become the most visible black member of the Legislature, and for justifiable reasons. More than any other politician or leader, Brown understood the concept of power. He willingly used any legal method to acquire and maintain authority, control people, and assure his continuation in office. Indeed, power became his obsession. During the formative stages of his career, Brown decided that the best way to obtain and hold power existed from the vantage of an insider rather than as a strident external voice playing to the crowd but lacking influence.

Brown came into prominence as a national power broker in 1968. Given the significance of California's electoral vote and the need for a Democratic presidential nominee to carry the state, black votes became crucial for a candidate hoping to win the presidential election. Therefore, when Robert Kennedy courted Brown's support in his presidential bid, the role of Willie Brown as a prominent black leader became firmly established. Uncommonly smart and shrewd, the original "Slick Willie," (according to President Bill Clinton) came into fruition. Brown concurred with the sobriquet, because for a black politician like himself, he said: "The only ray of sunshine comes from outsmarting the system."[45] The year 1971 marked Brown's acceptance among skeptical blacks as a powerful force among the highest assemblage of African American leaders. Brown's stature as an eminent leader became finalized at the Northlake meeting that took place outside Chicago where he and others decided whom to support in the 1972 presidential election.

Brown's prowess as a politician and national power broker emerged at the 1972 Democratic National Convention held in Miami, Florida. A battle on the convention floor raged over getting the California delegation seated, a contest between the forces of George McGovern and those contesting his nomination. Brown supported McGovern, seized the opportunity to speak before the entire convention before a nationally televised audience, and delivered a three-minute electrifying address. "For one time in our lives," he thundered, "this convention should hear from grassroots working Democrats." "Seat my delegation.... I desire no less! Give me back my delegation."[46] The convention hall erupted, McGovern won the presidential nomination, and Brown gained recognition as the most powerful black politician in the United States.

Ironically, Brown's success may be deemed the crowning point and nadir of the Civil Rights Movement. Through Brown African Americans held sufficient power to select a presidential candidate. However, with McGovern's overwhelming defeat to Richard Nixon, an African American being instrumental as a presidential power broker no longer seemed viable. Recognizing this change, subsequent black leaders often appeared more inclined to engage primarily in self-aggrandizing activities rather than work exclusively on behalf of their race.

The great Frederick Douglass and Martin Luther King Jr. maintained reverence for their people and became champions of their race.[47] Willie Brown and his post-civil rights movement contemporaries, on the other hand, could not approach the adulation of Frederick Douglass or Martin Luther King Jr. Anticipating this drift toward individualism that would be displayed by "high profile" African Americans, Brown pioneered the movement of black leaders who used race pragmatically to acquire personal wealth and status.

Race loyalty failed to deter the pragmatic Willie Brown as evidenced by his split with the NAACP. In 1974 Brown advised the NAACP to avoid polarizing issues and adopt policies designed to garner power for the organization. Brown publicly opposed busing and school integration and encouraged the Association to focus on acquiring power through wealth, a position the NAACP ignored to its eventual detriment. Although the NAACP's National Office ignored Brown's suggestions, Willie Brown heeded his own advice. He invested in oil and gas drilling ventures, an Oakland radio station, a pharmaceutical company, real estate partnerships, and became the first black public leader to generate personal wealth without depending on white largess.[48]

Throughout the 1970s Brown solidified himself as a power broker in California and the entire nation. As the chair of the California Assembly Ways and Means Committee, Brown honed his administrative skills, displayed his superior intellect, and gained respect from his Republican adversaries. He constantly demonstrated his skill as a political power broker and effectively used people to achieve personal goals. Although Brown overtly blasted opponents, he quietly cooperated with political foes in caucus rooms away from the public eye. As his public stature grew, Brown exhibited a corresponding interest in clothes, cars, and women. Brown's hedonistic lifestyle occurred without damaging his standing with constituents. Clearly, Brown assessed his strength and realized he could act with impunity regarding his personal life.[49]

By 1980 Brown seemed poised to grab the brass ring—Speaker of the House in the California Assembly. Having secretly befriended the

Republicans in the Assembly by offering them responsible committee appointments and finessing members of his own party, Brown became Speaker on December 2, 1980—a position he held for the next fourteen years. But as Speaker, Brown faced a quandary. He had to decide whether to spend more time focusing on black issues, or rather, alienate the black middle class further by overtly courting the favor of whites. For Brown the choice was easy—he had already disavowed school integration and precipitated a break with the NAACP and traditional black leadership. Brown's centrist views alienated him from the extremes within the black political spectrum. The radical contingent already labeled him a "sell-out" and the dupe of white liberals, while those from the African American establishment perceived him as being non-supportive and indifferent to his race.

Having planned successfully to acquire the position of Speaker, Willie Brown charted an independent course. As perhaps the shrewdest black leader since Booker T. Washington, Brown combined ego, pragmatism, and politics to remain in power and achieve goals that he believed improved the black condition. He used the Black American Political Association of California to promote black political leaders and prevent black districts from being gerrymandered. Brown also became instrumental in raising money for Democratic Assembly candidates. These efforts enabled Brown to become the most powerful Democrat in California and one of the most influential Americans in the nation.

Brown unfortunately exhibited a fault that plagued African American leaders throughout the century. Like Washington, Du Bois, Walter White, and Jesse Jackson, Willie Brown was exceedingly egocentric. Former Assembly Speaker Jess Unruh observed: "He likes to share in the credit, and to the extent that he can get all the credit.... He's not ideologically driven. He is result driven, and he likes to be in the play. He likes to be the key player.[50] The insatiable desire to be "top dog" explained, in part, Brown's tepid support for Tom Bradley, the African American mayor of Los Angeles favored to win the 1982 California gubernatorial election. Bradley narrowly lost the election to Republican candidate George Deukmejian primarily because black constituents failed to support Bradley. Some political pundits held Brown responsible for Bradley's defeat. Rather than actively campaign for Bradley, Brown decided to focus primarily on protecting the Democratic majority in the Assembly to maintain his position as Speaker. No single individual or issue, including the election of

Tom Bradley as California's first black governor, was allowed to eclipse the importance of the consummate politician, Willie Brown, Jr.

As an ostentatious public figure, Brown had no equal. In July, 1984 Brown hosted his "Oh What A Night" party during the Democratic National Convention. For an estimated 10,000 people, the party cost $250,000 to stage and surpassed the hoopla surrounding the nomination of Walter Mondale for President. To remain in the political limelight Brown accepted donations from a broad spectrum of interest groups. He received more money from the tobacco industry—over $660,000—than any public official in the nation. School teachers, trash haulers, trial lawyers, bankers, trade organizations, and unions also showered Brown with money. Consequently, Brown could enjoy a lavish lifestyle and dispense political favors with care and calculation. He befriended the rich and famous and appeared on the cover of *GQ Magazine*. Francis Ford Coppola encouraged Brown to play a cameo role in The Godfather, Part III. Willie Brown could hardly be classified solely as a politician or celebrity; Willie Brown had become an institution.

Although Brown possessed a temper and would speak publicly about individuals with whom he differed, he always remained the calculating politician. Unlike most black leaders, Brown refrained from spending considerable time vociferously attacking President Reagan. He recognized Reagan's popularity, and in turn, Reagan—though he differed politically with Brown—respected Brown's influence.[51] Brown also acted with political acumen in regard to legislation. While disagreeing personally with the politically popular "three strikes" law, a law that incarcerated black men to a greater extent than any other group, Brown avoided risking his stature by opposing the referendum. From Brown's pragmatic, self-centered perspective, low income and disadvantaged blacks would simply be allowed to "strike out."

Despite Willie Brown's considerable skills, he, like leaders in the NAACP and National Urban League, became stymied during the conservative administrations of Reagan and Bush. The Brown legacy established during his tenure as Speaker must be measured by his ability to protect disadvantaged blacks from suffering more grievously at the hands of conservative Republicans. Brown dissuaded the Assembly from imposing severe budget cuts that reduced welfare spending for the indigent. He served as an ardent defender of affirmative action, and worked incessantly to improve the quality of education for students and enhance salaries and working conditions for teachers. Given his steady climb to the pinnacle of

political success, Brown believed that education offered the most efficacious means for blacks to become part of mainstream America.

During the Reagan dominated decade of the 1980s, black leadership
faced a quandary. They found themselves incapable of coping effectively
with conservative and reactionary forces intent upon fiscal conservatism
that proved deleterious to African Americans. The leading civil rights
organizations pledged to find jobs for unemployed youths, lesson crime and
teenage pregnancy, enlist the support of active young adults, gain economic
parity for blacks, strengthen the black family, stimulate urban revitalization,
and improve the quality of education in inner city public schools.[52] With
conservatives in control of the White House who would not be influenced
by liberally inclined civil rights groups, black leadership's attainments fell
far short of outlined goals. The median black income was approximately 57
percent of white income. Moreover, though African Americans comprised
only 12 percent of the population, 48 percent of the homicides, 46 percent
of the rapes, and 62 percent of those arrested for robbery involved blacks.[53]

With the reduction of federal funds needed to sustain civil rights
organizations and the black bourgeoisie enjoying its wealth derived from
opportunities acquired during the civil rights era, black leadership's base
of support evaporated. Accordingly, the Executive Branch's indifference
toward African Americans occurred at a most inopportune time. With white
sensitivity toward African Americans in remission and black pride and
initiative reflected solely in the nostalgia of the 1960s, black progress not
only stopped, but more importantly, showed evidence of decline. Individual
successes of leaders like Jesse Jackson, Kweisi Mfume, and Willie Brown
had limitations. PUSH existed as a fledgling organization whose success
could be attributed solely to Jackson's magnetism. Mfume played an active
role in the Congressional Black Caucus. But like the NAACP and NUL, the
members of the Caucus found themselves rendered innocuous. They served
primarily as a "rubber stamp" for the Democratic Party.[54] And Brown,
arguably the brightest and most astute black politician of the twentieth
century wielded little influence nationally with conservative Republicans.
The G.O.P. would be more inclined to listen to Thomas Sowell than Willie
Brown. With Jackson's defeat in the 1988 Democratic Primary and Vice
President George Bush's ascendancy to the White House, prospects for
black amelioration appeared bleak. Black liberalism became passé. The
primary voices exercising influence would be confined to black conservatives who followed the lead of the conservative white power structure.

11

GATEKEEPERS AT THE DOOR

Like the 1890s, an era requiring new leadership to prepare black people for eventualities of the twentieth century, a similar need occurred at the dawn of the new millenium. Problems unique to the twenty-first century demanded attention. Because of difficulties associated with leading a maligned race, representatives from the two eras encountered different obstacles. Leaders on the eve of the twentieth century faced the dilemma of second class citizenship inherent in segregation. Every black leader recognized problems associated with the "color line" equally affected every African American. A century later—the 1990s—another similar dilemma regarding equality appeared. This time black leadership would be expected to assess whether opportunities derived from integration applied equally to all segments of African American society. Black conservatives believed the Civil Rights Movement had achieved the necessary objectives. They argued that a "color blind" society existed where those with talent and an industrious nature acquired rights and enjoyed privileges their abilities warranted. Conversely, a more liberal contingent of black leaders hardened by decades of civil rights struggles contended that a disproportionate number of African Americans remained segregated and functioned outside mainstream America. This group would continue to serve as the conscience of America and insist that every black man, woman, and child have the opportunity to succeed. Since no consensus existed among black leaders regarding the universality and efficacy of integration as the panacea for achieving racial equality, an ideological stalemate regarding the black condition existed. An amalgam in thought between the differing camps would be essential if black leaders were to lead their race successfully into the twenty-first century.

Optimistic, industrious, and ambitious blacks who acquired high profile positions refrained from commenting on the inequities of "the color line." Invariably, their reticence resulted in promotion to a more prestigious, visible position. However, those dissatisfied with the marginalized condition of the black population encountered opposition from a bevy of influential, conservative whites who believed that African Americans had received greater opportunities than other American citizens. Given the burgeoning number of black professionals, politicians, athletes, and other African Americans recognized as successes, white liberals [and certainly black and white conservatives] believed the needs of disadvantaged African Americans could be ignored. Therefore, those black leaders intent on marshalling forces to extend civil rights programs to lowly African Americans faced an uphill battle. Three high profile blacks unwittingly made the task of progressive leaders more arduous and contributed to the plight of the masses. By the 1990s all would demonstrate to white Americans that democracy worked, the inequities of racism passed, that Americans are forgiving people, and that African Americans became fully embraced by the larger society.

The achievements of Barbara Jordan, Muhammad Ali, and Ron Dellums enabled whites to expiate their guilt and withdraw support for programs that could enhance the lives of the African American underclass. Among this triad of storied blacks, Barbara Jordan became the first to represent herself as an integrationist—a patriotic American who happened to be black.[1] Born on February 21, 1936, Barbara came into the world as the third daughter of Benjamin and Arlyne Jordan. Jordan's early life would be directed by her ebony complexion and gender, handicaps that caused her father and grandfather to demand that she cultivate her mind, work, and achieve.[2] As a teen, Jordan developed a sense of personal pride and confidence. Imposing in size and height (5'8" and 175 pounds) and voice, she appeared dignified, cultivated, self-assured, and prepared to attain personal goals by practicing law. In 1952 Jordan enrolled at Texas Southern University where she came under the tutelage of Dr. Tom Freeman, a man who became her debate coach and mentor. As a key to the Texas Southern debate team, Jordan gained the opportunity to leave the confines of the segregated South—through debate competitions in northern cities—to vie successfully against students from prestigious universities (Jordan and teammate Otis King debated and tied competitors from Harvard).

At this juncture in her life Jordan experienced the initial throes of race consciousness. With an unfailing interest in studying law, Jordan enjoined concerns about her future career with the limitations placed upon blacks in the segregated South. Therefore, she decided to leave Texas and enroll at the Boston University School of Law. As a fledgling law student, Jordan discovered that her segregated background had been debilitating and rendered her unprepared for the rigors of legal studies. Nevertheless, with sleepless nights and perseverance, Jordan graduated from law school, returned to Houston, Texas, and began her political career as a volunteer for the Harris County Democrats.

By 1960 Jordan had successfully canvassed blacks, whites, unionists, political activists, liberals, and won their collective support. She joined the NAACP and the Harris County Council of Organizations, the dominant black political organization in the area, and realized her future existed as a public figure in politics. After running for and winning a seat as the first black female state senator in Texas history, Jordan developed her reputation as a charming, cunning, and an effective legislator, and learned who had power within the "old boys" network.

While serving her second term in the Texas Senate, Jordan demonstrated the skill of a consummate political pragmatist. She developed close alliances with members of the conservative white establishment by endorsing their pet projects. In return she gained support and favors for her constituents and acquired power and influence for herself. Jordan soon became recognized as one of the most formidable power brokers in Texas politics. When Jordan won election to the House of Representatives in 1972, she appeared ready to extend her influence to the halls of the United States Congress.

Within weeks of the Congressional swearing in ceremony, Jordan received an appointment to the House Judiciary Committee, an appointment that would garner her national acclaim. Jordan came to the nation's attention on July 25, 1974. That evening she delivered an eleven-minute television address before millions of Americans and explained why President Richard Nixon should be impeached. During the impeachment hearings no other member of the committee approached Jordan's style, elocution, or erudition, or raised questions that guaranteed Nixon's resignation from office. From that day forward Jordan established a place for herself as a formidable figure in the annals of United States history, a reputation that became embellished during the administration of President Gerald Ford.

Throughout her many terms in Congress Jordan distinguished herself as an influential national leader. By using peers within the Texas delegation as a powerful base, Jordan operated independently from the dictates of liberal Democrats and the conformity of the Congressional Black Caucus [CBC]. Jordan willingly accepted resentment from peers within the CBC to achieve what she believed to be a higher purpose. Jordan's strategic thinking and uncanny instinct for political bargaining came to fruition when she encouraged the white majority in Congress to pass the Voting Rights Act of 1975.[3] Jordan's efforts made her a celebrity. By January, 1976, she ranked fourth among the twenty women most admired by the American people behind "First Lady" Betty Ford, Rose Kennedy, and Shirley Temple Black (Jackie Kennedy Onassis ranked tenth and Queen Elizabeth twentieth). Jordan again came to public attention when she delivered a riveting keynote address at the Democratic National Convention in 1976 and contributed immensely to Jimmy Carter's successful run for president. Jordan's personality, intelligence, presence, and political acumen easily separated her from other members of the contemporary black leadership cadre.

Jordan enjoyed an accomplished career despite, as a southern born black woman, being a political anomaly. Jordan's successes as a black congresswoman appear even more daunting because independence and popularity disturbed members of the Congressional Black Caucus. Although jealous of her popularity, survival instincts forced those within the CBC to register complaints about Jordan's imperious style privately for fear that public critiques would alienate their black constituent base. Jordan also acquired great wealth during her celebrity—becoming the first African American woman to serve on a major bank board in the nation—and still maintained a direct link to the humblest members of her race. Jordan's public life presented other contradictions that would mar the career of less talented people. She mastered the art of compromise, but exhibited an acid tongue in criticizing perceived enemies of her people, like President Ronald Reagan.[4] Though she appeared unprincipled, given her penchant for finding ways to ingratiate herself with white conservatives, Jordan became known as an uncompromising moralist and unreconstructed optimist. She represented blacks specifically but worked in the interest of the entire American public. She also brought new meaning to the idea of a centrist, an African American leader universally loved and admired by blacks and whites, wealthy and poor, friends and opponents alike. No black spokesperson since King held the esteem of Barbara Jordan. Her death in January 1996 marked a watershed in the annals of black leadership.

While Jordan functioned as a centrist who championed the cause of her people by reminding the larger society that all was not well, Cassius Marcellus Clay, Jr. emerged and evoked within white America a sense of smugness and belief that American egalitarianism truly existed. Clay (later known as Muhammad Ali) inadvertently became used as an example of the African American who transcended black racial chauvinism, gained favor among a forgiving white public, and gave license to the popular belief that the United States contained a "color-blind" society.

Born to Cassius M. and Odessa Clay in Louisville, Kentucky on January 17, 1942, the younger Clay descended from proud antecedents. Sheltered from the overtly hostile racism in the "deep South," the mild segregation of Louisville enabled Cassius and younger brother Rudolph to lead a relatively comfortable lifestyle in a stable, Christian household. A chance encounter with Joe Morgan, a white police officer and boxing enthusiast who consoled young Clay who lost his bike to a thief, led to Clay's pugilistic career. Under the tutelage of Morgan and a black man named Fred Stoner, Clay made the 1960 Olympic boxing team and won a gold medal in the light heavyweight division. Clay turned professional after his Olympic triumph and eventually became heavyweight champion of the world when he defeated Sonny Liston on February 25, 1964. Extraordinarily handsome and possessed with an enormous talent for boxing and a colorful personal style, Clay gained enormous popularity; but soon after defeating Liston, Clay became a member of the Nation of Islam and changed his name to Muhammad Ali. Ali's identification with the Muslims made him an immediate pariah to white Americans generally and to the conservative black middle class in particular.

As a Black Muslim, Ali served as the most recognizable member of the organization. A disciple of Elijah Muhammad, by default Ali endorsed the harsh, anti-white rhetoric of "Messenger" Muhammad and his brand of separatism that countered the integrationist ideology of the black bourgeoisie.[5] Ali compounded his public relations debacle by refusing to be inducted into the armed services. Former heavyweight icon Joe Louis excoriated Ali's decision, believing that as a world champion, Ali should represent all the people rather than a religious sect. Compared to other offended people, Louis' criticism seemed mild. Arthur Daley of the *New*

York Times summarized the national disdain for Ali when he said: "Clay could have been the most popular of all champions. But he attached himself to a hate organization, and antagonized everyone with his boasting and his disdain for the decency of even a low-grade patriotism."[6] The hatred America directed toward Ali resulted in a three year suspension from boxing and the loss of his title as world heavyweight champion.

Ordinarily, the decisions Ali made—joining the Black Muslims and refusing to serve in the military—would have terminated his career as a professional boxer and celebrity. Fortunately for Ali, the timing proved propitious for anyone who decided to be a conscientious objector during the 1960s. As public disgust for the Vietnam War intensified, Ali's stand on the draft enabled him to regain popularity. Ali's fortunes continued to brighten after Elijah Muhammad died in 1975. The vitriolic statements Muhammad, and indirectly, Ali made about white people would be forgotten when Ali found the opportunity to declare he held no enmity toward white Americans.[7] President Ford even invited Ali to the White House in an effort to foster reconciliation between the races. After his retirement in 1979, rapprochement between Ali and mainstream America intensified. As Americans recounted his fabled fights with Joe Frazier and George Foreman, and developed sentimentality toward Ali because of slurred speech and involuntary twitching cause by Parkinsonism, virtually all animosity concerning Muhammad Ali disappeared. Andrew Young observed: "Muhammad was probably the first black man in America to successfully break with the white establishment and survive."[8]

Ironically, Ali's restoration may be perceived as both a blessing and a curse. While most people would agree that Ali gained redemption with the white public, the price for his redemption conceivably had a deleterious effect on disgruntled, frustrated blacks who continued suffering from racism. For if the white establishment reasoned that Ali's "transgressions" could be tolerated, the concept of equality, fairness, and decency—sentiments that served as foundations for American democracy—remained extant. Consciously or unconsciously, America's horrific treatment of blacks became expiated, in part, by embracing Ali as a heroic, returning, prodigal son.

The career of Ron Dellums furthered the perception that equanimity existed between blacks and whites during the 1990s. Although perceived by detractors as being brash, arrogant, unpatriotic and aligned with a white-hating black sect, Ali's impact on American society would only be symbolic and therefore inconsequential. By contrast, Dellums raised the ire of the white establishment because of his intelligence, candor, leftist principles, and uncompromising position on issues that could have financial repercussions and create security problems for the entire nation. In some circles, Dellums posed a threat to the United States of America. The role he played as a black leader inspired debate about his nationalism and race consciousness.

Born in 1935 to Verney and Willa Dellums in a middle class household in West Oakland, young Ron was raised in a dignified, intellectual environment that fostered upward mobility for African Americans. An uncle, C. L. Dellums, served as a protégé of A. Philip Randolph and succeeded Randolph as head of the Brotherhood of Sleeping Car Porters. Dellums' father, a well read, learned man, integrated the Oakland docks, and with brother C. L.'s initial assistance, enjoyed a successful career as a longshoreman. Willa Dellums became a pioneer as well. She became the African American community's first professional beautician, the first black to work downtown at the J.C. Penney Store, and the first African American to clerk in the Oakland government offices.[9]

Dellums' parents provided him with educational training that prepared him for success. After attending St. Patrick's Catholic School, Westlake Jr. High, and Oakland Technical High School, Dellums contemplated attending the University of California, Berkeley. Although precocious, Dellums proved a desultory student and enlisted in the Marine Corps rather than attend college. Discharged in 1955, Dellums enrolled at San Francisco State to complete his undergraduate education. Upon receiving his baccalaureate and a Masters in social work from the University of California, Dellums delved into his profession in the greater Oakland community and became a high-ranking administrator. Ambitious and intent on advancement, Dellums prepared to take leave from his administrative duties and acquire a Ph.D. from Brandeis University. However, the "new-left" movement that evolved in northern California's East Bay caught Dellums' attention and lured him into politics. When the Berkeley Democratic Club endorsed his successful run for a seat on City Council, Dellums became enthralled with politics. By 1969 Dellums became part of a coalition comprising blacks, whites, Latinos, Asians, socialists, and gay rights people. Collectively, the coalition formed a political majority in the Seventh Congressional District, a District that eventually elected him to the United States House of Representatives in 1970. Dellums' victory marked the first time in history that an African American represented an over-whelmingly white (72 percent white vs. 17 percent black) constituency. As an African American representing a white, "left-wing" district, Dellums' effectiveness as a legislator would be severely tested.

Although a proud black man, Dellums became recognized in Congress more for his leftist ideology than for promoting the cause of his race. A founding member of the Congressional Black Caucus, Dellums' foray into politics pertained primarily to alleged war crimes committed by the United States in Vietnam rather than to the direct domestic concerns of black people.[10] The second major contribution Dellums made as a congressman occurred when he investigated complaints made by homeless and welfare dependent white females in Bangor, Maine. These activities hardly endeared Dellums with African Americans dedicated to ameliorating conditions blacks faced in inner-city neighborhoods.

Dellums represented the diversified interests of black congressional representatives of the post-civil rights era. Hardly unmindful of the plight of blacks, Dellums worked with prisoners' rights groups and anti-death penalty advocates who espoused civil rights for inmates. He proved instrumental in establishing policies and proposing legislation that would lead to divestment of American companies in South Africa, efforts that contributed to the end of Apartheid, black self-determination, and the eventual liberation of black South Africans. Nevertheless, most of Dellums' thoughts and deeds pertained to matters that were leftist, often self-aggrandizing, and irrelevant to downtrodden African Americans. In his autobiography Dellums proudly recalled his refusal to be searched by the California Department of Corrections guards during an excursion to San Quentin. He also mentioned serving as the United States representative attending groups like the World Peace Council and Socialist International where he served as Vice President of the Democratic Socialists of America.

Dellums seemed to derive more pleasure converting peers to his ideas and being respected as a congressman of equal stature than for achieving objectives specifically designed to benefit his race. He relished being praised by colleagues who respected his vote to curtail arms shipments to Israel and for his opposition to funding the development of the MX missile.[11] When a member of Congress congratulated Dellums for his principles and tenacity, he fondly remembered: "I was pleased. Finally someone from the conservative wing of the party had chosen to take time to hear me."[12] Inexplicably, Dellums never referenced recognition he received for contributions he made to the black community.

Further evidence of Dellums' focus on his need for acceptance by conservative factions appeared through his role as a member of the House

Armed Services Committee [HASC]. Dellums constantly proposed military budget cuts and enjoyed being known as a radical political gadfly who happened to be black. He fondly reminisced about the compliment paid him by Newt Gingrich for elevating the level of debate on nuclear disarmament. Once again Dellums rejoiced in knowing that he "had earned the respect of ... [his] colleagues ... and that he "had finally arrived in Congress."[13] For Dellums, final appreciation of his talents and acceptance by the power elite occurred on January 27, 1993 when Congress selected him to chair HASC with the full support of Gingrich.

For his efforts Dellums deserved praise rather than derision. During his tenure in Congress, Dellums supported a broad range of issues that affected people from California to South Africa. Dellums, as with other members of the CBC, responded to the changing political milieu by shying away from exclusively black concerns and adopting more comprehensive roles as public officials. According to Dellums, members of the CBC functioned as legislators rather than black politicians when he declared:

> Our task force concluded that for the Black Caucus to be effective we had to acknowledge that we were legislators ... and were not in a position to be all things to all people.... The NAACP, CORE, SNCC, the Black Social Workers Association, the National Bar Association, the National Medical Association, other civil rights groups ... all existed to further the interests of their members and our communities. If we were to try to do the job of all these organizations ... we would fail our constituents at the most fundamental level.[14]

With the reasoning of Dellums and the CBC, the most essential reason for the prior existence of African American leaders elected to high political offices—advocating for and protecting the welfare of black people—became less relevant. Thus, the reserved role of congressional black leaders during the post civil rights era can be more clearly understood. Equally important, the reluctance of the CBC to safeguard African American interests by publicly addressing the aggressive actions of black conservatives must also be understood in this novel context. CBC reticence, however, emboldened black reactionaries and provided them with the incentive to push the white conservative agenda forward with relative impunity.

If the changing political climate dictated that civil rights organizations rather than the CBC had primary responsibility for looking after African

American interests, the caretaker task fell primarily under the auspices of leaders within the NAACP. In 1989 Executive Director Benjamin Hooks addressed the 80th anniversary of the Association and defined the issues facing blacks during the 1990s. He saw the widening income gap between blacks and whites resulting from black unemployment and underemployment as a primary concern. Next, limited educational opportunities encountered by inner city youths and the dearth of qualified teachers represented a second problem requiring resolution. Hooks also spoke of asocial behavior—drug abuse, teenage girls having babies, and crime—as additional factors undermining the African American community.[15] Evidently, Hooks' charges to the membership were ignored. After his retirement the NAACP would spend an inordinate amount of time addressing leadership problems involving the new Executive Director, Benjamin Chavis, Jr.

As the new NAACP director, Chavis sought to attract a younger, more vibrant, aggressive element of blacks into the Association. Unfortunately, Chavis made a series of disastrous mistakes soon after succeeding Hooks in 1993. When Chavis aligned the NAACP with Louis Farrakhan and the Nation of Islam and the controversial anti-Semitic professor, Leonard Jeffries, NAACP members became angry and contemptuous of the Executive Director. Chavis, unfortunately, compounded his mistakes by spending $300,000 in organization money to settle a sexual discrimination and harassment lawsuit, charging more than $32,000 to the NAACP for clothing, children's toys, and airplane trips for relatives, and presenting the Association with an approximate debt of $3.8 million. Although Chavis' expenditures seemed comparable to Board Chairman William F. Gibson (who allegedly spent more than $100,000 of the Association's funds for personal matters), the sordid financial situation caused the NAACP considerable embarrassment.[16]

Chavis proved extremely naïve politically and completely inept as an administrator. Chavis' anticipated dismissal occurred on August 20, 1994.[17] With the ouster of Chavis, and subsequently Gibson, the Association found itself without a leader for the first time in eighty-five years. In order to rectify its leadership problems, the NAACP Board thought carefully before filling the vacated positions. Myrlie Evers-Williams eventually replaced Gibson to chair the NAACP Board of Directors, and Kweisi Mfume, former head of the CBC succeeded Chavis as Executive Director. Mfume's selection injected a sense of optimism into the beleaguered Association. His congressional experience suggested he possessed the acumen to mend fences, and his "street smarts" provided him with the ability to understand and reach out to disadvantaged, low income African Americans.

Black *Washington Post* columnist William Raspberry had queries about the selection of Kweisi Mfume as the Executive Director of the NAACP. Raspberry wondered whether Mfume would continue in the time honored tradition of previous civil rights leaders and focus on external forces—racist whites—as being the primary cause of African American problems. Or rather, as Raspberry hoped, would Mfume look internally and lead blacks toward self-criticism and direct reform from within.[18] Raspberry's comments regarding the direction he suggested Mfume take as the Executive Director of the NAACP reflected the tenor of the time. By ignoring entirely the residual effects of racism, the better classes of Americans took their good fortune for granted and self-righteously attributed their high socioeconomic status to industry and intelligence. Black and white conservatives had few qualms about on whom to place the blame for the unfortunate condition of destitute African Americans— they placed the responsibility entirely at the feet of blacks who comprised the "unwashed masses." Thoughts that Raspberry presented to readers of the *Post* comported with the ulterior motives of conservatives who wished to redirect the nation from federalism and social altruism toward individualism and states rights.

Even before the appearance of Raspberry's column, conservative Republicans had already effectively used aforementioned blacks to dismantle federal programs. The coterie of so called leaders functioned as people with "black skin and white masks."[19] Selected for their conservative views, these individuals appealed to members of the white establishment who intended to implement policies designed to return the nation to an earlier America unencumbered by federal mandates. Collectively, conservative whites endeavored to lessen the power of the federal government, place individualism before larger societal interests (with the exception of the abortion issue), eradicate affirmative action, and terminate welfare. By engineering the ouster of the Democrat Jim Wright as Speaker of the House and on the heels of the 1994 Republican victory in Congress, the new Speaker, Newt Gingrich felt empowered to implement his "Contract for America." This gave license for "moss back conservatives" to augment efforts designed to limit federalism by using "selectively safe" blacks to do their bidding.

In an attempt to continue the "Reagan Revolution" through the "Contract for America," Gingrich Republicans continued to dismantle civil rights gains of the 1960s. They found more "suitable," pliant blacks to place in governmental agencies, appoint to court benches, select for elected legislative offices, hire for broadcasting positions, and designate for other positions that influenced public opinion. Blacks, rather than whites therefore, led the charge against legislative and judicial decisions that had favored African Americans. Thus as blacks continued serving as the primary attack force against civil rights, the conservative agenda toward African Americans retained legitimacy within the larger American society. As Walters and Smith correctly asserted in *African American Leadership*, "their role [was] not to lead black people but to lead white opinion about black people."

Joining opportunistic blacks willing to assist in terminating civil rights gains during the previous Reagan and current Bush Administrations were professors like Thomas Sewall, Walter Williams, Martin Kilson, and Shelby Steele. Collectively they gave additional voice to the self-help and "tough love" panaceas evoked by the conservative white establishment. Also joining the black conservative coalition were black Republican Congressmen Gary Franks and J.C. Watts from Connecticut and Oklahoma, respectively, and talk show hosts Larry Elder and Allen Keyes—political pundits who endorsed the conservative agenda by broadcasting their aversion to programs designed to improve conditions for African Americans.[20] The decade of the 1990s also became witness to two of the most visible men of what Derrick Bell dubbed "super standing." One, the previously mentioned arch-conservative Clarence Thomas who acquired a seat on the United States Supreme Court, and the other, California businessman Wardell [Ward] Connerly, a man dedicated to creating a "color blind" society. Clarence Thomas and Ward Connerly stood out as the individuals most responsible for trying to help the conservative white establishment promote their agenda of retarding black progress. Each man seemed to relish their role as a single handed "Negro wrecking crew" responsible for undermining opportunities that blacks fought and died for during the Civil Rights Movement.

With wily cynicism, President George Herbert Walker Bush selected Thomas to succeed Justice Thurgood Marshall in 1991 as the black representative on the United States Supreme Court. Angry and apparently chided during his formative years by African American children for being poor, dark complexioned, simian featured, non-athletic, a possibly crude pursuer of women, but intelligent, Thomas exhibited animus toward his race, a quality deemed useful for the Bush Administration. President Bush recognized the advantages of placing a mediocre black conservative like Thomas to the bench rather than selecting a more talented African American, Native American, Latino, Asian or white. Nevertheless, the most surprising aspect of the Thomas nomination appeared through the tepid response of black leadership to the conservative nominee. Thomas' prior decisions suggested that he would undo the work of the first black justice—the race conscious Thurgood Marshall. After Thomas proclaimed himself a legal proponent of "original intent," a position [referred to the "Founding Fathers" original Constitution without amendments], that if interpreted absolutely, would return all African Americans to chattel slavery, Thomas should have been pilloried in the black press and excoriated by African American leaders.[21] Instead, Thomas survived public scrutiny of his legal opinions and entered the conformation hearings relatively unscathed.

While the Congressional Black Caucus and many civil rights organizations opposed the Thomas nomination, polls revealed that most blacks supported Thomas' candidacy.[22] The only certainty involving the Thomas nomination would be the demonstrated inability of black leaders to exercise sufficient influence to keep Thomas off the bench. Anita Hill, an African American woman who accused Thomas of making unwanted sexual advances, loomed as the greatest threat to the nomination. However, black leaders never rallied to Hill's defense. Instead, black, like white Americans, appeared more interested in the sensationalism of the Thomas-Hill controversy than acquiring information on whether Thomas would become a fair and objective jurist. Consequently, the Hill-Thomas controversy garnered opposition primarily from a feminist rather than an African American perspective. Without a well organized black opposition, liberal members of the Senate Judiciary Committee likely to oppose the Thomas nomination received little incentive to risk their political future by supporting an unresponsive African American electorate. Questionable black leadership, in part, enabled conservative members of the Judiciary Committee to confirm the Thomas nomination.

The Black leadership's muted response to Ward Connerly, the most rabid opponent of affirmative action, also raised interesting questions about elite members of the race who allegedly labored on behalf of African American rights. Born June 15, 1939 in Leesville, Louisiana to Roy and Grace Connerly, "Billy Boy," as his father nicknamed him, became traumatized by his father's flight from the family and mother's early death.[23] His formative years were spent living with an Aunt Bert and Uncle

James Louis, and with his domineering grandmother "Mom" Mary Soniea in Del Paso Heights, a suburb of Sacramento, California. Their collective tutelage taught Connerly the value of hard work and instilled in him the unshakable belief that every black person born in America could become a success. According to other relatives, Connerly's grandmother also imbued him with a sense of racial self-hatred, a feeling that would have a significant impact upon educational opportunities and contracts for African Americans.

After attending American River Junior College and Sacramento State College where he became the only black in a white fraternity and the first black student body president, Connerly graduated and took a job with the State Department of Housing and Human Development. His work attracted the attention of a young assemblyman named Pete Wilson. In 1969 Wilson invited Connerly to join the newly created assembly Committee on Urban Affairs and Housing which drafted housing legislation for federal antipoverty programs. From this initial encounter, Connerly gained wealth and the friendship of an extremely ambitious California politician.

By the early 1970s Connerly joined the Republican Party. Impressed with the individualism and business focus of the G.O.P. [and on the advice of Wilson], he founded Connerly and Associates, a consulting firm involved with public housing. When Wilson won the California gubernatorial election in 1990, Connerly became the "go-to-guy" who ran interference for Wilson, a role that resulted in his appointment to the Board of Regents of the University of California. As a Regent, Connerly climbed on to the national stage; he displayed a unique black perspective on racial diversity through his opposition to affirmative action. Connerly eagerly spearheaded the move to end affirmative action at the University of California by encouraging the Regents to terminate gender and race from admissions, hiring, and contracting at the University's nine campuses.

Connerly's effectiveness in removing affirmative action from the University of California won plaudits from white conservatives. When Tom Wood and Glynn Custred, two white academics responsible for creating the California Civil Rights Initiative [CCRI], had problems garnering sufficient support to have the referendum known as Proposition 209 placed on the 1996 state ballot, they sought Connerly's assistance. Connerly agreed to serve as co-chair of the initiative and used his time, energy, and race to fight what he deemed racial and gender quotas that were inimical to whites. With Wilson's assistance, Connerly gathered 700,000 signatures in three months to have Proposition 209 placed on the ballot. A grateful Tom Wood declared: "Without Ward and Pete Wilson, CCRI wouldn't have made it on the ballot."[24]

Connerly took pride in being steeped in controversy and for being known as a liberal black's worst nightmare. As a black male, Connerly had few positive relationships with African American boys or men. He had no respect for a father who allegedly deserted him, or for black boys who probably bullied him during his adolescence. Connerly only held his Uncle James, Booker T. Washington, and Martin Luther King, Jr. in high esteem. Even worse, he held blacks in disrepute and saw no advantage in having racial diversity, but rather, defined true diversity as amorphous qualities inherent in "the individual's heart and soul."[25]

The dissension Connerly created extended to his family. Connerly claimed he was raised in poverty, "ate nothing but sweet potatoes morning, noon, and night," and sold eggs to make ends meet. Connerly declared his was a story of rags to riches—rising from the ghetto to having access to the State Capital as a confidant to the Governor. However, Connerly's relatives dispute his recollection of being raised in poverty. As one relative recalled: "It (his upbringing) was very middle class. There was no poverty. There was none of this dirt-poor business. There were no chickens. Nobody sold eggs." Another relative simply declared: "Wardell hates being black," a notion supported by Connerly's closing statement in his autobiography where he asked "librarians and bookstore owners not to put *Creating Equal* in the African American section."[26]

Connerly's motives for supporting Proposition 209 also remained questionable. Connerly declared that the initiative was designed solely to eliminate discrimination. However others feel that loyalty to Wilson—who endeavored to use the anti-affirmative action stance as a means for reaching the White House—served as the underlying reason for Connerly's actions.[27] Connerly, and the Proposition 209 proponents, also used the terms "civil rights" as an obfuscating euphonium that confused voters into thinking an affirmative vote corresponded directly with Martin L. King, Jr.'s concept of equality.

Although CCRI threatened the existence of affirmative action in California, few prominent state or national African American leaders spoke out vigorously against CCRI or Ward Connerly. With the exception of Jesse Jackson, Constance Rice, a legal defense attorney employed by the NAACP, California State Senator Diane Watson, and Representative Maxine Waters, no nationally prominent African American leader vigorously campaigned against Proposition 209 or devised a successful strategy to lessen Connerly's effectiveness. Additionally, no significant protest could be heard from any civil rights entity or organization including—the Congressional Black Caucus, the National Urban League, NAACP headquarters, the African Methodist Episcopal Church, or the Southern Christian Leadership Conference.

Connerly declared that nothing could deter him from his honorable purpose to help create a color-blind society in America. This self-proclaimed, "highly principled" man believed he must continue on his chosen path despite students marching in protest against him, bullets riddling his office windows, or critics branding him with a series of epithets like "strange fruit," "angry 'oreo,'" "Uncle Tom," "sellout of his people," and "lawn jockey for the ruling class."[28] Despite his claims to the contrary, Connerly's efforts to achieve fairness, a "color-blind" society, appear at best disingenuous. Connerly could never convince any rational person that white people no longer consider race as a factor in American society or that white people achieve promotions and elected office solely on merit. Equally astonishing, Connerly's demand for entrance into the University of California based on criteria perceived more stringent than Ivy League Universities defies comprehension. Without a degree from any of the University of California campuses, an Ivy League institution, or a graduate or professional school, one must ask how Connerly could be considered credible or knowledgeable about the standards for admission into highly competitive college or university. Given Connerly's denial of American racism and ignorance of the academic selection process [allegedly he never took the Scholastic Aptitude Test because he transferred from American River Junior College directly into the California State University, Sacramento], the pejorative sobriquets about him from the perspective of objective critics deserve some merit.

Flush with victory after the passage of Proposition 209, Connerly founded the American Civil Rights Institute, carried his brand of equal rights to the states of Washington and Florida, and intended to propagate his ideas throughout the entire nation. In addition to removing privileges derived by gender and race, Connerly even spoke of establishing an absolute meritocracy regardless of race, gender, or socioeconomic class. In addition to eliminating racial and gender preferences, Connerly's pronouncement meant that he intended to prevent those of privilege with money and influence from using personal clout to gain admission or provide opportunities for friends, associates, and family members. This idea "died aborning." Evidently people of high standing and influence informed Connerly that he made a faux pas. Since then, Connerly remained silent about meritocracy being applied to members of the establishment.

Since white people have been perfectly capable of protecting their interests in regard to blacks for hundreds of years, a logical question must be raised about Ward Connerly. Why would a black man voluntarily act as the leading proponent against affirmative action? Aside from racial self-hatred engrained in him by an allegedly bigoted grandmother and his personal demons concerning his race that haunt him, Connerly sincerely believed in the righteousness of his cause. Nevertheless, a sense of ambition, national visibility, and a desire for power can not be omitted as primary reasons for Connerly's actions.[29] In many respects, Connerly resembled the infamous World War II collaborationist Vidkun Quisling, the Norwegian leader who supported the Nazis at the expense of his country. While Connerly should not be equated with the Nazis, he easily qualifies as a collaborationist, an opportunistic person who identified more with powerful interests than with people who share his racial ancestry.

In the twentieth century blacks who served in the United States Congress traditionally served as representatives of their people ranging from Congressmen George Henry White of North Carolina (1897-1901) and Oscar DePriest (1929-1935) and to Massachusetts Senators Edward K. Brooke (1966-1978) and Carol Moseley-Braun of Illinois (1993-1999) regardless of party affiliation. Gary Franks of Connecticut (1990-1996) and later Julius Caesar [J.C.] Watts of Oklahoma [1994-2002] became the first African American to break from what the Thernstroms declared to be the "monolithically liberal stance of African Americans in Congress." While Franks initially joined the Congressional Black Caucus and remained until barred from attending, Watts never joined the CBC. Watts' decision made sense considering the overwhelming white constituency he represented. Watt's role as a conservative black politician would also raise interesting questions about the future direction of African American leadership.

J.C. Watts added luster to the conservative movement in the United States. A native of Eufaula, Oklahoma and former football star at the University of Oklahoma, Watts became the first black Republican elected to Congress from the "deep South" since Reconstruction. An ordained minister, Watts' straight-forward approach and sincerity appealed to the predominately white constituency in his Congressional District. As a black Republican, Watts believed that less government is best for Americans generally and African Americans in particular. Strong family values, the eradication of welfare, and a balanced budget, he contended, would ensure meant a better future for subsequent generations. Moreover, he suggested, all Americans would benefit from the self-sufficiency encouraged by the Republican Party.[30]

Fortunately for Watts, his personality, athletic ability, and overall talent enabled him to rise from poverty to gain acclaim in the halls of Congress. While he proudly referred to his parents as those who instilled positive values among the Watts siblings, he failed to recognize the reality of many contemporary black households headed by a single female parent unable to provide the virtues of deferred gratification to her progeny. Watts embodied positive qualities of Americans—the vibrancy, opportunity, competitiveness, and energy that made the nation great. Obviously Watts and others like him deserved praise for their achievements; But platitudes, self-satisfaction, and contentment projected by Watts never resolved the enormous problems evident in black America. Watts extolled the virtues of America without addressing the duplicity inherent in a society with a pronounced racist foundation that relegates a disproportionate number of blacks to a permanent underclass.

As a member of the black conservative vanguard, Watts helped the Republican Party undermine civil rights gains with relative impunity. Surprisingly, few black spokespersons seemed to criticize Watts or care about the diminution of opportunities for struggling African Americans needing housing, jobs, and better education for their children. Indeed, Watts became the most noteworthy black member of Congress to break intentionally from the tradition of black leaders who made efforts to protect the interests of their race by being a decided outsider, declaring: "I did not come to Congress to become a black leader or a white leader, but a leader."[31] Watts' declaration represented America's move toward conservatism during the 1980s and 1990s. The political climate caused black politicians to gravitate toward a conservative agenda or remain silent, often to the disadvantage of the larger African American society. Calculating white politicians correctly gauged the African American elite's contentment and relative silence of black politicians.[32] Indeed, the expansion of the numbers of middle class and elite blacks created the illusion that "all is well" among African Americans. Unfortunately few black leaders, including J. C. Watts, spoke for the speechless masses.

While other blacks in the United States Congress worked far more than Watts as advocates for African Americans, at the very best, members of the Congressional Black Caucus engaged in a holding action against entrenched forces determined to sacrifice disadvantaged blacks for other priorities like increased defense spending and a balanced budget. The CBC represented the most vigorous and successful voice that challenged the conservative ideologies of Presidents Reagan and Bush. But its successes failed to counteract or render inoperative the cadre of "created" black leaders, the "new conservatives" who did the bidding of influential white conservative Americans.[33] Although Congressmen William Clay of Missouri declared "that inner city blacks need the same kinds of dollar infusion that built suburbia," and Julian Dixon of California added: "on the floor of the Congress, in committee hearings, before the press and across America, we have spoken out against policies which undermine the enforcement of civil rights and civil liberties ... "[34] information about CBC activities had not been disseminated among the black electorate. The black underclass remained helpless, devoid of hope, and uninformed.

The reputation of the Congressional Black Caucus as an entity that championed the rights of African Americans became further sullied by the unfortunate circumstances involving Lani Guinier. Guinier came to national attention as President William Jefferson Clinton's nominee for Assistant Attorney General for Civil Rights within the United States Justice Department. A former NAACP attorney and tenured professor at the University of Pennsylvania Law School, Guinier acquired a reputation as an able scholar possessing expertise on the 1965 Voting Rights Act. Guinier also attracted attention because of her outspoken commitment to civil rights in opposition to the twelve years of Reagan-Bush Republicanism and the offensive actions of William Bradford Reynolds who headed the Justice Department's Civil Rights Division.[35]

Guinier used a public ceremony as Justice Department nominee to present her vision. She proclaimed that the Justice Department should act on behalf of "the constituency of the Civil Rights Division—the disabled, the discriminated against, the marginalized Americans."[36] Guinier's views were distorted by Clint Bolick and other members of the reactionary "right-wing" that disparagingly referred to her as a "Quota Queen" who favored blacks. Pressure exerted by the conservative right caused Clinton to blink, back away, and withdraw White House support for his nominee. Guinier's demonization not only made Clinton look timorous, but equally significant, had a sobering impact on high profile black leaders. Although Guinier voiced dismay about the erosion of support from Hillary and Bill Clinton and law school classmates—a not unexpected lesson of betrayal taught by her father—she became particularly distressed by the retreat demonstrated by the black bourgeoisie generally and the CBC in particular.

Guinier expected someone, an individual or organization, to come forward from the black community to defend her against those who sullied her reputation, demonstrate the importance of her nomination as Assistant Attorney General, and force Congress to conduct hearings on her confirmation. Although Guinier might have appeared petulant when she charged the civil rights establishment with deserting her to maintain close ties with the White House, no black leader or African American organization staunchly defended her candidacy, including members of the CBC. The Guinier episode proved the civil rights establishment to be impotent, timid, and focused primarily on maintaining the semblance of self-importance. Guinier learned that black leadership intended to manage rather than resolve civil rights problems and President Clinton discovered anew that traditional black leadership—those who carried the mantle of civil rights responsibilities—could be charmed and then forgotten.[37]

Prospects for the reinvigoration of civil rights as a viable issue improved with high profile positions acquired by Andrew Young and General Colin Powell. Young's renewed claim to fame may be related directly to his role as co-chair of the Atlanta Committee for the Centennial Olympic Games of 1996. While his prominence extended back to the 1960s Civil Rights Movement, the Andrew Young of the 1990s perceived himself more as a business promoter than a civil rights advocate. As one who risked his life during the Civil Rights Movement of the previous generation, Young could hardly be expected to continue marching and singing "We Shall Overcome." Young's perspective had broadened. Since voting rights and social integration had been largely achieved, Young concentrated on economic development as the panacea that would enable African Americans to realize their potential as viable contributors to the larger American society. He also felt that a black and white partnership based on mutual economic interests would enable the entire African American community to prosper. According to Young, the successes of the Centennial Olympic Games of 1996 exemplified this very point.

With advice from Young, black leaders in Atlanta pressured the white establishment into making economic opportunities available for their community. Beginning with black leaders' involvement with the Metropolitan Atlanta Rapid Transit Authority—which guaranteed African American business and laborers work, to building the new Atlanta airport and successfully acquiring the 1996 Olympic Games—the entire black community became partners in the city's urban development. Drawing upon their civil rights heritage, Young and other southern black leaders found effective means toward obtaining opportunities for their race.

Like many progressive minded individuals, Young has been the object of criticism. Some contended, and with some justification, that the Atlanta games encountered far more difficulties than previous Olympiads. Transportation proved abysmal, many African American venders lost money because the local Games Committee skirted the black community, and southern arrogance allegedly precluded the Atlanta Olympic Committee from seeking advice from cities like Los Angeles which held an enormously successful Olympiad in 1984. If Young's premise rested upon the notion that common economic interests produce inter-racial accord and resultant success, a "naysayer" would contend that the idea spoke more to his religious faith in people than to the reality of individual greed. Black cynics perceived Young as a defender of the establishment like other African American leaders of the 1990s. However, Young can hardly be labeled a self-serving black conservative. Gracious and deeply committed to finding ways to ameliorate conditions for his race, Young represented a unique kind of black leader—a respected leader with power and influence within black and white society.

Ever mindful of the debased condition experienced by many African Americans, Andrew Young replicated Whitney Young and recommended that a domestic Marshall Plan be implemented on behalf of the black community. Unfortunately, neither of the Youngs had been able to impart his views to other African American leaders to the extent that black representatives could influence the larger white society. Andrew Young contended, for example, that a national free trade agreement with black America would be mutually beneficial for all Americans.[38] Nothing happened! Although easy to comprehend why Young's altruism toward blacks would have little impact on conservative white politicians, queries must be raised about his ineffectiveness among blacks. Why did the African American majority ignore this charismatic and daring figure to support Louis Farrakhan and Jesse Jackson? Why have black leaders overlooked his wisdom and experience? While Young believed that a domestic Marshall Plan was needed to salvage black America, why have insufficient efforts been made to support him and the demands he makes upon the federal government? Perhaps Andrew Young had been too self-effacing. Perhaps his moral principles prevented him from compromising his values and engaging in self-aggrandizing activities in order to remain in the national limelight. Black and white American leaders—as well as Young himself—should answer these questions.

General Colin Powell, like Young, possessed enormous talent and charisma. Born to Jamaican immigrants in Harlem in 1937 and raised in the South Bronx, Powell's leadership qualities became molded by family, formative years spent in a multi-racial environment, and the United States Army. Unlike many prominent African Americans whose personal history comprised a "rags to riches" saga—and who purposely forget their origins—Powell acted differently. Army training camps located in the "deep South" enabled Powell to recognize the depth of racism in the United States.[39] Furthermore, Powell extolled the virtues of black troops by supporting a monument honoring the Buffalo Soldiers, endorsed the concept of affirmative action, and served on the boards of the United Negro College Fund and Howard University.[40]

As a keenly perceptive and intelligent man, Powell appreciated the fundamental differences between African Americans whose heritage was rooted in the United States and blacks of West Indian origin. African Americans lacked the independent spirit of West Indians. Thus Powell realized that the self-assuredness, pride, and industriousness of his immigrant parents propelled him toward success. In addition, Powell's military experience allowed him to believe that merit, rather than color, predominated—a factor that encouraged him to join the Republican Party. Powell summarized his political philosophy by declaring he was a fiscal conservative with a social conscience. Nevertheless, his endorsement of the G.O.P. placed him outside the political norms embraced by the overwhelming majority of African Americans.

In many respects, Powell existed as an anomaly among black Americans. He identified with the poor and dispossessed. He understood how racism limited African American potential, and his support of affirmative action separated him from most black conservatives. But Powell also retained an unwavering confidence in the American system. As a beneficiary of the white power structure, Powell accepted his good fortune with grace and humility. His confident demeanor, penchant for efficiency, commanding presence, and fair complexion made him the first black of prominence that made race appear irrelevant. With a profound sense of loyalty to his parents' adopted nation and as a proud military man, Powell extolled the virtues of the United States, the nation that enabled him to become one of the most recognized black men in the world. White people embraced Powell because he represented the American success story—the popular notion that ability supercedes poverty and race. Although inspiring and competent, Powell never became recognized as a leader of African Americans. Once again he epitomized a man of prominence who happened to be black rather than a black leader.

Given the significant gains African Americans achieved during the last quarter century, the advent of a strong black conservative movement seemed plausible. Indeed, the ambivalence of black leadership toward affirmative action may be observed through their muted response to the innovative program's vocal opponents. Since the gains African Americans made politically, economically, and socially appeared greater than even the most optimistic human rights advocate of the 1960s could have imagined, contented blacks endeavored to bolster their status among white peers. To achieve this end, some contended that equal opportunity existed and declared racism and "Jim Crow" had met their proper demise. Some like Ward Connerly argued vociferously against the unconstitutionality of any kind of preference based on race or gender. Still others felt that any kind of preference for African Americans "rained on their parade." Collectively, these conservative proponents protected their self-interests—their perception of reality—and in turn displayed overt hostility toward those dedicated to assisting the black underclass.

While the affirmative action issue produced a muted response from black leadership, the Oakland School Board's decision to institute "Ebonics"[41] in its public schools created a maelstrom. Nearly every outspoken prominent black leader castigated the Board's decision. Oakland contained a large African American population with an abysmally low performance record in the public schools. Therefore the Board endeavored to elevate academic performance by validating language usage in the home and community. Responding to distortions presented through the media about the novelty of Ebonics (the use of black English as a learning device had been instituted previously in other school districts) and fearing that the public would assume that blacks were incapable of learning proper English, black leaders nationwide launched a furious and angry attack. In contrast to the muted response to Ward Connerly and Proposition 209, African American leaders unanimously castigated the Oakland School Board's decision to endorse Ebonics as a distinct black language. No African American leader or organization came to the Board's defense. Although scores of inner city public schools nationwide failed to address satisfactorily the academic needs of black youths, the Board stood alone in advocating its revolutionary proposal designed to enhance learning for disadvantaged African American children. Public denunciation of the Board even exceeded opposition voiced against Booker T. Washington who espoused "industrial education" i.e. manual arts training as the only curriculum to be offered southern blacks during the early twentieth century.

Here, a tragedy of the first order may be observed through the reluctance of black leadership to give voice to the welfare of disadvantaged black children. Educators knew that self-esteem exists as a factor essential for achieving high academic performance. Black leaders, however, jumped to negative conclusions about Ebonics, castigated the Board for its "folly," and equated—in no uncertain terms—Ebonics with heresy. The Ebonics issue closed without any alternative proposals offered by national black leaders to enhance the educational progress of children in the Oakland School District or other school districts with a preponderance of African American children.

By the 1990s every major city within the United States had an African American mayor; therefore, conservative black and white leaders received additional reinforcement that all was well. Further evidence of the passing of the infamous "color line" had been demonstrated by blacks elected to the United States Senate and House of Representatives, and an appointment to the United States Supreme Court. African Americans could even brag about a black governor of Virginia, a Fortune Five Hundred C.E.O., and a Chairman of the Joint Chiefs of Staff. Years of struggle to gain white acceptance as humans, as Americans, as equals, and eventually as prominent members of the establishment neared completion. Complaisance among black leadership could be understood in the context of the nation's racist past. If not for the desperate status of the black underclass, African American representatives could be forgiven for celebrating and adopting the French cliché "Laissez le bon temps rouler"—"Let the good times roll" in regard to the positive developments in American race relations.

Although President Clinton contributed to the comfortable ambiance and complaisance that pervaded black leadership, his initial opportunism exceeded his interest in allying himself with African Americans. During the 1992 presidential campaign Clinton excoriated Sister Souljah (Lisa Williamson) for her negative comments about white people in the aftermath of the Los Angeles riots that stemmed from police officers being exonerated after beating Rodney King. Clinton followed this attack by demeaning Jesse Jackson, declaring publicly in Jackson's presence that Jackson would not be his Vice Presidential running mate. Even after his victory Clinton responded favorably to conservative whites. He not only dropped the aforementioned Guinier, but also removed an excellent black candidate, President Johnnetta Betsch Cole of Spelman College in Atlanta, from the short list of candidates being considered for Secretary of Education.[42] Blacks remained pawns in America's political chess games and black leaders seemed powerless to stem the continuous use of race by opportunistic white politicians.

Despite initial problems with Clinton, blacks embraced the President and became counted among his most consistent devotees. His endorsement of policies favorable to blacks in education, labor, support for affirmative action, and role in trying to end the political upheaval in Haiti allowed the initial ill will to be forgotten. Clinton also gained support because Republicans who viciously attacked the President were also perceived to harbor views inimical to blacks. By default, Clinton's accusers helped the President bond with the African American community. By the end of his second term blacks became so enamored with Clinton that some jokingly referred to William Jefferson Clinton as the first African American President.

Clinton's popularity in the black community paradoxically contributed to the ever-waning influence of traditional black leaders. The Reverend Al Sharpton acted to fill the void. Sharpton, a short, stocky man with a unique coiffure of pressed, flowing hair started his career in Brooklyn, New York as a loud mouth rabble-rouser. He referred to white people as "faggots," denounced blacks that opposed him as "yellow niggers," or "cocktail-sip Negroes," and preached class conflict.[43] Sharpton first came to national attention in 1987 over the Tawana Brawley affair. Brawley, a girl of 15, accused three white men in upstate New York, including Steven Pagones, a former prosecutor and son of a white judge, with rape. When authorities doubted her story Sharpton aggressively came to Brawley's defense by appearing in TV talk shows and organizing news conferences to attack the alleged perpetrators. In the subsequent trial, the jury decided Brawley perjured herself, exonerated the officers, and allowed Pagones to sue Sharpton and eventually win a $60,000 judgement for defamation of character. The ten-year-long case, along with his role in protesting the death of a black man in the Bensonhurst section of New York, kept Sharpton before the national media. Throughout the 1990s he would become perceived as a "poor man's" Jesse Jackson—a gadfly who traveled from his New York City base throughout the East Coast to address real or imagined racial slights and garnered recognition for himself.

Al Sharpton operated as a 1990s combination of Marcus Garvey and Adam Clayton Powell, Jr. He attracted attention from whites, appealed to an alienated segment of the black population, and acquired recognition as an African American spokesperson. Here the association between Sharpton and his predecessors ends. Garvey was a visionary and Powell, though extremely egotistical, proved capable of using wit and charm to benefit his race. Sharpton, conversely, presented his people with more style than substance or success. Although influential New York politicians met with Sharpton and offered him "lip-service," hardly any of the white leaders seemed inclined to take Sharpton seriously or consider him a forceful change agent likely to threaten their hegemony. Moreover, while black traditionalists approved some of the issues Sharpton supported that encompassed the unwarranted treatment of African Americans, they would undoubtedly disapprove of him as the race's messenger. Sharpton adroitly understood contemporary culture required sensationalism (he engaged in a fist fight with Roy Innis of CORE fame on the Morton Downey, Jr. show) in order to grab attention, and respected sensationalistic orators like Jesse Jackson and Louis Farrakhan as "attention grabbers." When Sharpton's voice and presence in the 1990s became comparable to or exceeded presidents Julian Bond of the NAACP, John E. Jacob of the National Urban League, or Joseph Lowery of SCLC, progressive, respected black leadership reminiscent of previous years became a forgotten legacy.

Despite Sharpton's attempt to gain recognition as the most preeminent black in the nation, throughout the 1990s Jesse Jackson and Louis Farrakhan appeared as the African Americans most likely to be heralded by the masses as leaders. Since the death of Dr. Martin Luther King, Jackson perceived himself as the person most qualified to represent and speak on behalf of African Americans. Internationally, Jackson rescued hostages from the clutches of Saddam Hussein and negotiated the release of American servicemen from Slobadan Milosevic of Serbia. Jackson also remained extremely active at home. In the 1990s he used his Rainbow Coalition cohorts to energize the black electorate and strengthen the Democratic Party. Through the Coalition Jackson increased black voting strength, placed more black candidates in political office, and prepared to exact concessions from the Democratic Party.[44] Jackson also seized the opportunity to make his presence known at every site that could enhance his celebrity. Issues ranging from controversial personalities like Rodney King, Mike Tyson, and O.J. Simpson to the high school fistfights at Decatur, Illinois attracted Jackson like a moth to a light bulb.

Momentarily, Minister Louis Farrakhan eclipsed Jackson as the most prominent African American of the 1990s through his leadership of the

Million Man March. Born in 1934 in the Bronx to a West Indian woman named Mae Clark, and given the birth name Louis Eugene Walcott, young Louis intimately learned about urban poverty. He became angry and militant. After attending two years of college in North Carolina, Louis had become a fine violinist, earned a living as a calypso singer known as "The Charmer," married, and converted to Islam after meeting Malcolm X. After changing his name to Louis X (and eventually Louis Farrakhan), by the early 1960s Farrakhan headed a new mosque in Boston. After Malcolm X fell out of favor with Elijah Muhammad, Farrakhan became positioned to head the Nation of Islam after Minister Muhammad's death.

The dramatic, imposing Farrakhan had long appealed directly to the alienated, disaffected blacks who comprised the lower middle class and poor. An excellent orator, Farrakhan presented his audience with a profound and logical message on black self-help. Charismatic and with a brilliant mind, Farrakhan also possessed outstanding organizational skills as attested by the successful March that occurred in Washington in October 16, 1995. Thousands flocked to the nation's capital not only to vent their frustration, anger, and personal grievances, but also to raise self-esteem among black men. Equally important, the March emphasized the need for positive behavior in the black community—extolling the importance of the family, the expectation of husbands to respect their wives and support their children, and highlighting the problems associated with premarital sex and illicit drugs.

While Jackson and Farrakhan arguably attracted more attention than any other black leaders of the decade, the results of their efforts seemed negligible. Jackson succumbed to his own narcissism. He became larger than the organizations he directed. Unfortunately, his desperate need for publicity that resulted in quick headlines, colorful "sound-bites," and timely "photo-ops" lessened his effectiveness as a leader because of over-commitment and the absence of follow-through. Farrakhan also possessed severe limitations. For reasons only Minister Farrakhan can explain, the deserved accolades he received for planning the Million Man March became overshadowed by his deliberate and relentless bating of Jews. Farrakhan's rhetoric offended Jews, Gentiles, blacks, and whites. By having allegedly referred to Jews as "bloodsuckers," deeming Judaism "a gutter religion," identifying Israel as "an outlaw state," and proclaiming Hitler "a great man," Farrakhan had questions raised about the underlying motives of the March (other than symbolism) before the first marcher arrived in the District of Columbia.[45] He also alienated white Americans and the State Department with his flirtatious relationship with Muslim leaders like Muammar Muhammad al-Qadhafi of Libya. While Farrakhan's support for co-religionists caused him to support the Palestinians, it would seem that the Arab-Israeli conflict—its causes and effects—had little bearing upon impoverished African Americans.

The decade of the 1990s witnessed the near invisibility of liberalism or liberal black leadership and the unmistakable rise to prominence of African American conservatives. Unfortunately, black conservative thought seemed one-dimensional and self-delusional. While the "right-wing" declared affirmative action was reverse discrimination and detrimental to whites, conservative blacks ignored the unspoken reality that many successful whites enjoyed privileges derived from being white and well connected. Conservative blacks also ignored the years of African American repression that excluded blacks from opportunities afforded whites. Instead, many among the high profile "right-wing" black contingent befit the categorization described by Frantz Fanon in *Black Skin White Masks*, Paulo Freire's *The Pedigogy of the Oppressed*, and Stanley Elkins' *Slavery*.[46] Black conservatives of the 1990s served as classic examples of the oppressed identifying with the oppressor. Their sense of inferiority never escaped them regardless of attainment because subliminally, they never exorcized the demon of racial inferiority from their minds. These prominent blacks believed, with justification, that aggressive attacks against affirmative action and other policies beneficial to minorities would ingratiate them with influential whites.

Regrettably, Jackson and Farrakhan remain the only black leaders of prominence reaching out to the African American masses. Each man has presented creative ideas designed to promote better living conditions in African American society. In the broadest sense, however, their accomplishments appeared meager for several reasons. First, neither seemed willing to share the spotlight with others. Second, each man appeared more gifted in offering rhetoric than in sustaining ideas with "follow-up" activities. A third factor which undermined Jackson and Farrakhan's efforts evolved from the long-standing problem black leaders displayed for generations—the inability to establish and maintain positive intra-racial bonds. Collectively, these factors prevented African American leaders who have expressed concerns about the welfare of the black majority at the close of the millenium from effecting positive changes in the larger black society. The reticence and impotence of traditional black leaders and organizations enabled black conservatives to be perceived by both the white establishment and the black masses as protectors of the status quo rather than representatives of their race.

Unlike black leaders of the previous century who devoted themselves to ending racial discrimination and creating opportunities for African Americans, high-profile blacks on the eve of the twenty-first century acted to help the white establishment maintain hegemony in the judicial, executive, and legislative affairs of the nation. By operating on the premise that the United States has fulfilled its constitutional obligations pertaining to "life, liberty, and pursuit of happiness," African American leaders at the dawn of the new century became—at the expense of the black masses—"gatekeepers at the door."

Epilogue

Tragically, African American leaders represent a declining influence as the conscience of the United States, a reality manifested in the 2000 presidential election. In Florida, the pivotal state that determined who would be the nation's new chief executive, scores of African Americans were disenfranchised by devious and questionable acts undertaken by supporters of George W. Bush. The national media and strategists for the Democratic and Republican Parties, however, haggled about accepting dangling, pregnant, or "dimpled chads" rather than addressing grievances of thousands of blacks prevented from having their voting preferences recorded. Black leadership's response to the sordid political affair in Florida seemed virtually non-existent. Only Jesse Jackson garnered temporary attention from the national media. NAACP Executive Director Kweisi Mfume, though outraged and actively seeking to garner support for the black Floridians, proved impotent and ineffective in his leadership role. Leaders from the National Urban League, SCLC, and other black organizations expected to rally to the defense of the African American electorate became conspicuously absent. Without the inclination or ability of black leaders to protect their race by using moral suasion or agitation to influence the white public to respect the black voter, African American influence in the social, economic, and political life in the United States remains marginalized.

The tepid national response to black disenfranchisement in Florida presents a pathetic legacy to the civil rights efforts of previous African American leaders. Throughout the twentieth century outspoken black representatives had cajoled, admonished, shamed, and eventually forced white people into rescinding discriminatory practices that prevented African Americans from enjoying all privileges guaranteed to citizens of the United States. Intrepid leaders used legal and extra-legal methods to effect changes that not only liberated a significant number of African

Americans from omnipresent racial discrimination, but more importantly, forced American society to recognize that every citizen—regardless of race, gender, creed, color, sexual orientation, or physical challenge—deserved the right to "life, liberty, and the pursuit of happiness." Since a measurable number of blacks gained prominence and wealth, the white public believed the nation's obligation to provide civil rights to blacks and others could be terminated despite egalitarianism espoused in the Constitution remaining unfulfilled.

Talented blacks like Colin Powell [Secretary of State], Rod Paige [Secretary of Education], Condoleezza Rice [National Security Advisor] and other high-profile minorities in the Bush administration lend credence to the myth that racial discrimination is defunct in the United States. Although competent and well meaning, none (with the exception of Powell) make any pretense of supporting an agenda of specific importance to the African American community that encompasses the elimination of poverty, stabilizing family life, improving housing conditions, and acquiring gainful employment for young adults. Furthermore, no George W. Bush appointee seems likely to ridicule a G.O.P. program inimical to blacks that advocates diminished federal expenditures on social services, the elimination of affirmative action, and judicial decisions that reverse advances made during the Civil Rights Movement. To the "conservative establishment," the primary purpose of their sable auxiliaries appeared to be "window dressing" rather than competency or charting a new direction to enhance the quality of life for African Americans.

Additional reasons for whites being less "guilt laden" may be attributed to other icons who happened to be black. Basketball star Michael Jordan, talk show host Oprah Winfrey, American Express CEO Kenneth I. Chenault, and the "poster boy" of golf Eldrick "Tiger" Woods gained national and international celebrity with race being deemed irrelevant because the public persona of these talented people exhibited little reference to "blackness." Former basketball great Ervin "Magic" Johnson, tennis sisters Venus and Serena Williams, and comedian Eddie Murphy remain among the few renowned blacks, through diction, appearance, and commentary, that exhibit a black cultural presence. Yet regardless of the presence or absence of a black visible consciousness of high-profile African Americans, disadvantaged blacks require far more than symbolic "firsts" in high profile positions to ease the conflicts, tensions, poverty, and pressures of inner city life.

Since prominent blacks enabled white Americans to rid themselves of guilt and embrace the assumption that blacks enjoy the same privileges as whites, imperfections within American democracy continue. White conservatives, specifically members of the Republican Party, believe the federal government should ignore inequities and terminate social programs deemed essential for black progress. Stephan and Abigail Thernstrom add to the mystique that black Americans make gains commensurate to their industry and talent. In their quantitatively convincing study *America in Black and White*, the Thernstroms convey an impression that African American leaders have served their race and nation well. Furthermore, they argue that the successes enjoyed by the black bourgeoisie have been under reported, while the converse, the belief that most black Americans are impoverished ghetto dwellers, remains an exaggerated, erroneous stereotype. Although the Thernstroms' treatise suggests racism had been virtually eliminated, the "playing field" is level, and that all is well in black and white America, no effective rejoinder has been offered by black leadership to quell the misrepresentations presented by conservative politicians and scholars.

Unfortunately, black leadership failed to counter these arguments and convince white America that civil rights efforts should be sustained as long as the masses remained under served, under educated, and under employed. In part, national indifference to the African American plight may be attributed to the black bourgeoisie's inability to demonstrate that the nation's best interests are served if the lowly condition of the black underclass is addressed. In a special edition of *Time Magazine* published in 1995, the editors posed two unanswered questions that addressed the future prospects of the nation in the twenty-first century. One question pertained to the quality of public education in our nation's primary and secondary schools, and the other raised questions about the quality of life enjoyed by the disadvantaged minority population in the United States. Since most blacks and an increasing number of Latinos reside in the low income inner-city and attend substandard schools, the *Time* queries raise serious questions about the ability of the United States to remain a dominant world power. History dictates that world empires decay from within rather than falling prey to hostile, outside forces intent on destroying the predominant civilization.

Those who would speak for the black community, however, find themselves at a disadvantage. Because integration allowed the black bourgeoisie to leave black enclaves, those who previously agitated for the rights of African Americans lost touch with the black underclass—its value system, perceptions, lifestyle, and problems endemic among low income people. Between 1930 and 2000 the fortunes of middle class blacks improved while the gap between the African American establishment and the black masses increased exponentially with each passing decade. Therefore, without understanding the people they were expected to represent, it became difficult, if not impossible, for the "talented tenth" to recommend, implement, or endorse ameliorative strategies designed to benefit disadvantaged blacks.

Black leaders also failed to deal effectively with the insidious aspects of racism that severely affected the black masses. Vestiges of slavery, "Jim Crow," and other nefarious aspects of America's racist past have a continuing effect upon large segments of the African American community. Union discrimination prevented black men from acquiring work and confined African Americans to low income neighborhoods. An inferior educational system limited black upward mobility. Unfair applications of the law evidenced by racial profiling by law enforcement agencies rendered blacks defensive and insecure. These realities retarded the development of scores of African Americans and kept the race mired in poverty. Since a disproportionate number of African Americans remain poorly educated, jobless, incarcerated, prone to premature violent deaths, suffer from unwed motherhood, survive on welfare, and face lower life expectancy rates than whites, blacks as a race have yet to enjoy the full comforts of citizenship. When the desultory condition of the African American masses becomes the topic of conversation, blame is usually attributed to the long-standing victims of racism instead of those who eschew responsibility for or contribute to the servile condition of disadvantaged blacks.

Some among the black elite elect to forget the past and appear disinclined to recognize they profited from programs and laws that evolved from the Civil Rights Movement. They extol the virtues of industry and individualism and ignore benefits derived from auspicious personal circumstances attributed to birth, class and certain God-given gifts that enabled them to take advantage of the social upheavals of the 1960s. Equally disturbing is the assumption among increasing numbers of the black bourgeoisie who believe that the United States has become a "color-blind" society. These comfortable blacks insist that like whites, successes they enjoy occurred exclusively from personal attributes—hard work, sacrifice, tenacity, intelligence, an engaging personality, and other factors that enable the gifted to succeed.

Further evidence of black leadership's waning concern about the plight of the black proletariat occurred through their application of Moynihan's concept of "benign neglect." Few would begrudge ambitious, achievement oriented civil rights activists like Andrew Young and Vernon Jordan from serving on corporate boards, participating with the white elite as national power brokers, or sharing personal success stories on the lecture circuit. However, these dedicated leaders neglected to recruit or train successors equally committed to achieving race conscious goals. Moreover, their absorption into the white, elite oligarchy gave credence to the perception that America currently exists as a nation devoid of all manifestations of discrimination directed toward blacks.

W.E.B. Du Bois anticipated that the post civil rights generation of black leadership would become complacent. When the "talented tenth" failed to come to his defense during the hysteria of the McCarthy Era, Du Bois made a prescient observation. In *Battle for Peace*, the brilliant scholar and leader perceived that class divisions among African Americans would grow as racial discrimination decreased. By the close of the twentieth century Robert C. Smith's *We Have No Leaders* and Earl Ofari Hutchinson's *The Disappearance of Black Leadership* confirmed Du Bois' premonition. These intellectuals argue that the race conscious support and protection black leaders previously offered no longer seemed viable at the dawn of the new millenium. Du Bois' declining faith in black leaders as protectors of the defenseless, dependent, and despondent African Americans proved justified as the nation and world entered the twenty-first century.

Complaisance perhaps remains the greatest impediment to improving the condition of the black majority. The prospects for witnessing the evolution of effective, race-conscious leaders appear remote and commitment to clearly articulated goals non-existent. Middle class blacks enjoy the comforts warranted by their status and seem disinclined to alienate the white power structure that embraces fiscal conservatism and displays an overt disinclination to aid the poor. Given the enormous problems currently facing the black community, the void in leadership is most unfortunate. No forums have been convened, think tanks created, investigations undertaken, or plans established to reverse the desolation inherent among destitute blacks. These oversights become particularly distressing since the life expectancy of impoverished blacks declined during the 1990s and the conditions of life in certain inner city slums is more deplorable than cities located in third world countries.

Given the enormous gains black leaders achieved for their race, criticism directed toward black leadership might seem inappropriate. In the face of enormous obstacles, African American leaders endeavored to serve blacks to the best of their ability. Black leadership worked assiduously to make race less of a factor in limiting black progress. Black leaders effectively eroded the throes of discrimination, enlisted the assistance of the masses and progressive white people, and put "Jim Crow" to rest. Although exorcizing racism from white Americans proved a daunting task, black leadership still should have done more to convince white people that helping the black masses could prove beneficial for the entire nation. Regrettably, African American leaders allowed white people off the proverbial hook before equality had been achieved. Initial accomplishments gave way to indifference and complaisance, an ominous portent for the future of African Americans and the entire nation.

Traditional African American leaders representing the comfortable black bourgeoisie like the Congressional Black Caucus and NAACP posture instead of lead. They suggest that a strong black presence exists to stand guard against reactionary forces that would threaten the black community. White power brokers know, however, that black leadership collectively is vested in the system, possesses little revolutionary fervor, and demonstrates no inclination to assist the black underclass by demanding that business and governmental institutions aid their less fortunate brethren. What happened to the domestic Marshall Plan? Why has the "talented tenth" found it impossible to bring the African American masses into the political, economic, and social mainstream of American society? Since blacks historically have been instrumental in moving the country closer to the ideals espoused in the Declaration of Independence and the Constitution, why have contemporary leaders failed to rouse the nation from inertia to help America realize its potential for establishing an egalitarian society? Without a national or international crisis to transform the American attitude from indifference to beneficence toward the black underclass, it seems highly unlikely that white or black leaders will insist that considerable economic resources be invested to ameliorate conditions experienced by the black masses. At the commencement of the twenty-first century, the black proletariat reverted to the non-entity status described in Ralph Ellison's *The Invisible Man*, a concept readily embraced alike by black and white American leadership. Unless significant strides are taken to bolster the socioeconomic condition of the African American masses, the black majority may be treated like Native Americans—ignored and forgotten.

Black leaders should employ three distinct plans to enhance the quality of life for the African American underclass. First, black leaders must critique, mentor, and develop mutual respect and pride so sorely lacking in the black community by promoting and instilling the concept of race consciousness among the defeated, downtrodden masses. Black leadership rather than white benefactors is responsible for devising and applying strategies needed to end the violence, irresponsibility, and indolence prevalent in urban ghettos of our nation. Social service agencies like the National Urban League should enlist support from an array of middle class blacks to canvass the African American community and eliminate the defeatism and despair evident within the black proletariat. Second, a process must be established to neutralize the "Negro Quislings," toadies selected by the powerful white elite to undermine civil rights gains. "Self-hating" people like Supreme Court Justice Clarence Thomas and Ward Connerly should not be allowed to render opinions and promote policies inimical to the interests of the overwhelming majority of the black populace. Finally, black leadership must resume its role as the conscience of America. Sable leaders should develop multiple strategies to influence white public opinion about the pragmatic advantages in eliminating racism, a persistent plague that keeps our nation divided.

Given the queries raised in *Time Magazine*, one may assume that the key to the success of the United States depends largely on black leaders, those who have represented the largest racial minority population that suffered continuously from racial discrimination. Black leadership must develop a new sense of purpose and forge a binding relationship with the white power elite and other minority populations to lead the nation and world into the new millenium. It is imperative that the "talented tenth" continuously prick the conscience of white America so that all—black and white, rich and poor, male and female—have an equal opportunity to enjoy the American dream.

Notes to Chapter 1

1. Kenneth O'Reilly, *Nixon's Piano: Presidents and Racial Politics from Washington to Clinton*, (New York: The Free Press, 1995), pp. 13-61.
2. See Michael Omi and Howard Winant, *Racial Formation in the United States From the 1960s to 1990s*, (New York: Routledge, 1994), pp. 14-15.
3. Benjamin Quarles, *Frederick Douglass*, (New York: Atheneum, 1968), pp. 66-67.
4. Quarles, *Douglass, op. cit.*, pp. 96-98.
5. Joanne Grant, *Black Protest: History, Documents, and Analysis 1619 to the Present*, (New York: A Fawcett Premier, 1968), pp. 161-162. For an extensive discussion on the role of African American leaders in the national limelight during the era of Reconstruction see Howard N. Rabinowitz, ed., *Southern Black Leaders of the Reconstruction Era*, (Urbana: University of Illinois Press, 1982), Part I.
6. Hollis R. Lynch, *Edward Wilmot Blyden: Pan-Negro Patriot 1832-1912*, (New York: Oxford University Press, 1967), pp. 3-9.
7. Lynch, *Blyden, op. cit.*, pp. 67-77.
8. Howard Brotz, (ed.), *Negro Social and Political Thought, 1850-1920*, quoted from Frederick Douglass, "The Civil Rights Case," October 22, 1883, (New York: Basic Books, Inc., 1966), pp. 298-301.
9. Brotz, *Negro Social and Political Thought, op. cit.*, quoted from Garnet, "The Past and the Present Condition, and the Destiny of the Colored Race," 1848, pp.199-200.
10. Earl Ofari Hutchinson, *"Let Your Motto be Resistance:" The Life and Thought of Henry Highland Garnet*, (Boston: Beacon Press, 1972), p. 199.
11. Willard B. Gatewood, *Aristocrats of Color: The Black Elite, 1880-1920*, (Bloomington: Indiana University Press, 1993), pp. 4, 19, 98, and 347.
12. Gatewood, *Aristocrats of Color, op. cit., Passim.*
13. August Meier, *Negro Thought in America, 1880-1915:Racial Ideologies in the Age of Booker T. Washington*, (Ann Arbor: The University of Michigan Press, 1968), p. 66, fn. 15.

14. Victor Ullman, *Martin R. Delany: The Beginnings of Black Nationalism*, (Boston: Beacon Press, 1971), pp. 20-34.

15. Ullman, *Martin R. Delany, op. cit.*, pp. 58-60. Also see Jessie Carney Smith, (ed.), *Black Firsts: 2000 Years of Extraordinary Achievement*, (Detroit: Visible Ink Press, 1994), p.219.

16. Ullman, *Delany, op. cit.*, pp. 115-21.

17. Ullman, *Delany, op. cit.*, pp. 436-37, 469, 500, and 507-19.

18. Meier, *Negro in America, op. cit.*, p. 42 and Rayford W. Logan, *The Betrayal of the Negro:From Rutherford B. Hayes to Woodrow Wilson*, (Toronto, Canada: The Macmillan Company, 1969), p. 322.

19. Wilson Jeremiah Moses, *The Golden Age of Black Nationalism, 1850-1925*, (Hamden, Connecticut: Archon Books, 1978), pp. 72-73.

20. See Louis R. Harlan, *Booker T. Washington: The Making of a Black Leader, 1856-1901*, (New York: Oxford University Press, 1972), p.24.

21. W.E.B. Du Bois, *The Souls of Black Folk, Three Negro Classics*, (New York: Avon Books, 1965), p. 215.

22. Harlan, *Washington, Black Leaders, op. cit.*, p. 161.

23. Harlan, *Washington, Black Leaders, op. cit.*, pp. 157-8.

24. Harlan, *Washington, Black Leaders, op, cit.*, pp 168-69 and 299.

25. The only possible exception would be the erratic T. Thomas Fortune, a native Floridian who became a journalist and eventual editor of the *New York Age*. See Emma Lou Thornbrough, *T. Thomas Fortune: Militant Journalist*, (Chicago: University of Chicago Press, 1972), pp. 217-218, 320-321, and 350. Also see Harlan, *Washington, Black Leaders, op. cit.*, p. 192.

26. Harlan, *Washington, op. cit.*, pp. 279-80.

27. Booker T. Washington, *Up From Slavery*, (New York: Gramercy Books, 1993), p. 162.

28. I. A. Newby, (ed.), *The Development of Segregationist Thought*, quoted from John T. Morgan, "The Race Question in the United States," (Homewood, Illinois: The Dorsey Press, 1968), pp. 22-23.

29. C. Vann Woodward, *A History of the South: Origins of the New South, 1877-1913*, (Baton Rouge: Louisiana State University Press and the Littlefield Fund for Southern History of the University of Texas, 1951), p. 330.

30. See C. Vann Woodward, *The Strange Career of Jim Crow*, (New York: Oxford University Press, 1974), p. 82.

31. David Levering Lewis, *W.E.B. Du Bois: Biography of a Race, 1868-1919*, (New York: Henry Holt and Company, 1993), p. 11.

32. Elliott M. Rudwick, *W.E.B. Du Bois: Propagandist of the Negro Protest*, (New York: Atheneum, 1968), pp. 15-16. This information is derived from *Darkwater*, p. 9, an autobiography Du Bois penned in his later years after experiencing considerable disillusionment with the United States and leaders from a predominately English background.

33. Lewis, Du Bois, *Biography of a Race, op. cit.*, p. 31.

34. By the advent of the Civil War, approximately one third of the students attending Oberlin were black. See Jessie Carney Smith, *Black Firsts: op. cit.*, p. 98.

35. Quoted from *Autobiography*, p. 12 found in Lewis, Du Bois, *Biography of a Race, op. cit.*, p. 66. Also see Adolph L. Reed, Jr., *W.E.B. Du Bois and American Political Thought: Fabianism and the Color Line*, (New York: Oxford University Press, 1997), pp. 53-56.

36. Lewis, Du Bois, *Biography of a Race, op. cit.*, p. 77.

37. See Lewis, Du Bois, *Biography of a Race, op. cit.*, p. 107; Meier, *Negro Thought, op. cit.*, pp. 80-82 and, Du Bois, *The Souls of Black Folk, Three Negro Classics op. cit.*, p.245.

38. Lewis, Du Bois, *Biography of a Race, op. cit.*, p. 111.

39. Lewis, Du Bois, *Biography of a Race, op. cit.*, pp. 122-23.

40. See Michael B. Katz, *Class, Bureaucracy, and Schools: The Illusion of Educational Change in America*, (New York: Praeger Publishers, 1972), pp. 43 and 106-113. Also see Henry Allen Bullock, *A History of Negro Education in the South: From 1619 to the Present*, (New York: Praeger Publishers, 1970), pp. 85-107.

41. Lewis, Du Bois, *Biography of a Race, op. cit.*, p. 149. Quoted from *Autobiography*, p. 182.

42. Lewis, Du Bois, *Biography of a Race, op. cit.*, pp. 161-164.

43. Lewis, Du Bois, *Biography of a Race, op. cit.*, p. 169.

44. Lewis, Du Bois, *Biography of a Race, op. cit.*, p. 170 quoted in Harlan, (ed.), B.T. Washington papers, IV, p. 321.

45. See Robert Green McCloskey, *American Conservatism in the Age of Enterprise 1865-1910*, New York: Harper and Row, 1951), pp. 42-71. Also see Henry Steele Commager, *The American Mind: An Interpretation of American Thought and Character Since the 1880s*, (New Haven: Yale University Press, 1970), pp. 202-215.

46. Samuel P. Hays, *The Response to Industrialism, 1885-1914*, (Chicago: University of Chicago Press, 1966), pp. 76-78.

47. W.E.B. Du Bois, *The Philadelphia Negro*, (New York: Schocken Books, 1967), pp. 388-392.

48. John D. Hicks, *The Populist Revolt: A History of the Farmers' Alliance and the People's Party*, (Lincoln: The University of Nebraska Press, 1961), pp. 55, 61-84.

49. C. Vann Woodward, *Tom Watson: Agrarian Rebel*, (New York: Oxford University Press, 1972), p. 220.

50. Woodward, *Tom Watson, op. cit.*, p. 221. Also see Morton Keller, *Affairs of State Public Life in Late Nineteenth Century America*, (Cambridge: The Belknap Press of the Harvard University Press, 1977), pp. 573-74.

51. Beverly Washington Jones, *Quest for Equality: The Life and Writings of Mary Eliza Church Terrell, 1863-1954,* (Brooklyn, New York: Carlson Publishing, Inc., 1990), pp. 11-12.
52. Jones, *Quest for Equality, op. cit.,* pp. 22-23.
53. Darlene Clark Hine, Elsa Barkley Brown, and Rosalyn Terborg-Penn (eds.), *Black Women in America: An Historical Encyclopedia,* Vol. I, (Bloomington: Indiana University Press, 1993), pp. 275-278.
54. Logan, *Betrayal of the Negro, op. cit.,* pp. 242-43.
55. Woodward, *Strange Career of Jim Crow, op. cit.,* pp. 17-18. See particularly the discussion of the treatment accorded blacks who attended the Noyes Academy in Canaan, New Hampshire in 1835. Also see Hutchinson, "*Let Your Motto Be Resistance, op. cit.,* pp. 5-6.
56. Woodward, *Strange Career of Jim Crow, op. cit.,* p. 69.
57. Woodward, *Strange Career of Jim Crow, op. cit.,* pp. 70-72.

Notes to Chapter 2

1. Peter Bergman, *The Chronological History of the Negro In America,* (New York: Harper and Row, 1969), p. 327.
2. William Stanton, *The Leopard's Spots: Scientific Attitudes Toward Race in America 1815-1859,* (Chicago: University of Chicago Press), 1960, p. 3.
3. Stanton, *Leopard's Spots, op. cit.,* p. 15.
4. Stanton, *Leopard's Spots, op. cit.,* pp. 16-17.
5. Stanton, *Leopard's Spots, op. cit.,* pp. 33-53.
6. Stanton, *Leopard's Spots, op. cit., pp.* 66-71.
7. See Mary Taylor Blauvelt, "The Race Problem," *The American Journal of Sociology,* [hereafter AJS] (Chicago: University of Chicago Press, 1900-1901), IV, 662.
8. See Sarah E. Simons, "Social Assimilation, Part I, AJS, 1900-1901, VI, 790-815; "Social Assimilation, Part II," AJS, 1902, VII, 543; Richard Wright, review of W.H. Thomas's *The American Negro,* AJS, VII, 850; Paul S. Reinsch, "The Negro Race and European Civilization," AJS, (1905-1906), XI, 154-166; and Charles A. Ellwood's review of George Merriam's *The Negro and the Nation,* AJS, 1906-1907, XII, 275.
9. Mildred I. Thompson, *Ida B. Wells-Barnett: An Exploratory Study of an American Black Woman, 1893-1930,* (Brooklyn, New York: Carlson Publishing Co., 1990), pp. 11-12.
10. Thompson, *Barnett, op. cit.,* p. 23.
11. Thompson, *Barnett, op. cit.,* p. 27. Quoted from Ewing, "The Heart of the Race Problem," *Atlantic Monthly,* January-June, 1909, p. 389.
12. Linda O. McMurry. *To Keep the Waters Troubled: The Life of Ida B. Wells,* (New York: Oxford University Press, 1998), p. 260.

13. Thompson, *Barnett, op. cit.*, pp. 34-36.
14. McMurry, *Keep the Waters Troubled, op. cit.*, p. 263.
15. Ray Stannard Baker, *Following the Color Line: American Negro Citizenship During the Progressive Era,* (New York: Harper and Row, 1964), pp. 109-121.
16. August Meier, *Negro Thought in America 1880-1915,* (Ann Arbor: The University of Michigan Press, 1968), pp. 172-73. Also see Thompson, *Barnett, op. cit.*, p. 74. Although Washington gave the impression of indifference or opposition to black suffrage, he subtly encouraged whites to refrain from disenfranchising blacks. See "Open Letter to the Louisiana Constitutional Convention," February 19, 1898, Cary D. Wintz (ed.) *African-American Political Thought 1890-1930: Washington, Du Bois, Garvey, and Randolph,* (Armonk, New York: M.E. Sharpe, 1996), p. 3.
17. Meier, *Negro Thought in America, op. cit.*, p. 112. Also see Louis Harlan, *Booker T. Washington: The Making of a Black Leader, 1856-1901,* (New York: Oxford University Press, 1972), p. 320. Also see John Hope Franklin and August Meier (eds.), *Black Leaders of the Twentieth Century,* Louis R. Harlan, "Booker T. Washington and the Politics of Accommodation," Urbana: University of Illinois Press, 1982), p. 3.
18. See Meier, *op. cit., Negro Thought in America,* p. 111. Also see Stephen Mansfield, *Then Darkness Fled: The Liberating Wisdom of Booker T. Washington,* (Nashville, Tennessee: Highland Books, 1999), p. 120 and Lewis R. Harlan, *Booker T. Washington, The Wizard of Tuskegee, 1901-1915,* (New York: Oxford University Press, 1983), pp. 417-428.
19. Manning Marable, *Black Leadership,* (New York: Columbia University Press, 1998), pp. 26-29.
20. Marable, *Black Leadership, op. cit.*, p. 33.
21. David Levering Lewis, *W.E.B. Du Bois: Biography of a Race, 1868-1919,* (New York: Henry Holt and Company, 1993), pp. 238-239.
22. Harlan, *Washington, The Making of a Black Leader, op. cit.*, pp. 321-322.
23. *Ibid*, p. 145.
24. Lewis, *Du Bois, Biography of a Race, op. cit.*, pp. 241-242. Also see Washington to Du Bois, October 26, 1899, Wintz, *American Political Thought, op. cit.*, pp. 33-34.
25. Harlan, *Washington, Making of A Black Leader, op. cit.*, pp. 262-266. Lewis, *Du Bois, op. cit.*, p. 230 and Thompson, *Wells-Barnett, op. cit.*, pp.78-79.
26. Harlan, *Washington, Wizard of Tuskegee, op. cit.*, pp. 39-40. Also see Emma Lou Thornbrough, *T. Thomas Fortune: Militant Journalist,* (Chicago: The University of Chicago Press, 1972), p. 204 and 226-227.
27. Harlan, *Washington, Making of a Black Leader, op. cit.*, pp. 268-271.
28. Lewis, *Du Bois, Biography of A Race, op. cit.*, pp. 274-275.
29. See Meier, *Negro Thought in America, op. cit.*, p. 115.

30. Harlan, *Washington, Wizard of Tuskegee*, p. 17.
31. Lewis, *Du Bois, Biography of A Race, op. cit.*, pp. 253-256.
32. See Leon Litwak, *Trouble in Mind: Black Southerners in the Age of Jim Crow,* (New York: Alfred A. Knopf, 1998), pp. 144-149.
33. Lewis, *Du Bois, Biography of a Race, op. cit.*, pp. 243-245.
34. W.E.B. Du Bois, *The Souls of Black Folk, Three Negro Classics,* (New York: Avon Books, 1965), pp. 241 and 246.
35. Du Bois, *Souls of Black Folk, op. cit.*, pp. 146-249.
36. Lewis, *Du Bois, Biography of a Race, op. cit.*, p. 264.
37. Du Bois, *Souls of Black Folk, op. cit.*, p. 215.
38. Lewis, *Du Bois, Biography of A Race, op cit.*, p. 311.
39. Harlan, *Washington, Wizard of Tuskegee, op. cit.*, p. 51. Also see Adolph L. Reed, Jr. *W.E.B. Du Bois and American Political Thought: Fabianism and the Color Line,* (New York: Oxford University Press, 1997), pp. 60-61.
40. See Stephen R. Fox, *The Guardian of Boston: William Monroe Trotter,* (New York: Atheneum, 1970), pp. 5-6, and 9-19.
41. Lewis, *Du Bois, Biography of a Race, op. cit.*, p. 304.
42. Lewis, *Du Bois, Biography of a Race, op. cit.*, p. 276.
43. Kenneth O'Reilly, *Nixon's Piano: Presidents and Racial Politics from Washington to Clinton,* (New York: The Free Press, 1995), p. 73.
44. See John D. Weaver, *The Brownsville Raid,* (New York: W.W. Norton and Company, 1970), pp. 97-98, 188, 199, and 273-274. Also see O'Reilly, *Nixon's Piano, op. cit.*, p. 73.
45. Dickson D. Bruce, Jr., *Archibald Grimké: Portrait of a Black Independent,* (Baton Rouge: Louisiana State University Press, 1993), pp. 154-159.
46. Ray Stannard Baker, *Following the Color Line: American Negro Citizenship in the Progressive Era,* (New York: Harper and Row, 1964), pp. 3-11, 15.
47. Lewis, *Du Bois, Biography of a Race, op. cit.*, p. 334.
48. Program, The Seventy-Fifth Anniversary of Sigma Pi Phi, "Sigma Pi Phi and Regional Organizations, p. 4, Sadie T. M. Alexander Papers, Box 71, File 6, Archives, University of Pennsylvania [hereafter UPA].
49. See "Sigma Pi Phi Fraternity; A Brief History," Sadie T. M. Alexander Papers, Box 71, File 7, UPA.
50. Willard B. Gatewood, *Aristocrats of Color: The Black Elite, 1880-1920,* (Bloomington: Indiana University Press, 1993), pp. 234-236.
51. Charles H. Wesley, *The History of Alpha Phi Alpha: A Development in College Life,* (Washington, D.C. The Foundation Publishers, 1937), p. 41. Also see Lawrence C. Ross, Jr., *The Divine Nine: The History of African American Fraternities and Sororities,* (New York: Kensington Publishing Corp, 2000), pp. 5-7.

52. Majorie H. Parker, *Alpha Kappa Alpha Through the Years: 1908-1988*, (Chicago: The Mobium Press, 1990), p. 10. Also see Ross, *Divine Nine, op. cit.*, pp. 165-166.
53. Darlene Clark Hine, Elsa Barkley Brown, and Rosalyn Terborg-Penn (eds), *Black Women in America: An Historical Encyclopedia*, I, (Bloomington: Indiana University Press, 1993), pp. 23-24.
54. Harlan, *Washington, Wizard of Tuskegee, op. cit.*, pp. 86-87.
55. Lewis, *Du Bois, Biography of A Race, op. cit.*, pp. 308-309.

Notes to Chapter 3

1. Charles Flint Kellogg, NAACP: A History of the National Association for the Advancement of Colored People, 1909-1920, Vol. I, (Baltimore: The Johns Hopkins Press, 1967, p. 9. Also see David Levering Lewis, W.E.B. Du Bois, Biography of a Race, 1968-1919, (New York: Henry Holt and Company, 1993), pp. 387-388.
2. Ovington fondly remembered the organization's founders by declaring: "One was the descendant of an old-time abolitionist, the second a Jew, and the third a southerner." Quoted from Lewis, Du Bois, Biography of a Race, op. cit., p. 389. Also see Kellogg, NAACP, op. cit., p. 12.
3. Lewis, *Du Bois, Biography of a Race, op. cit.*, p. 391.
4. Ibid. Kellogg, *NAACP*, I, *op cit.*, pp. 20-22.
5. See Kellogg, *NAACP*, I, *op. cit.*, pp. 23-24, and Lewis, *Du Bois, Biography of a Race, op. cit.*, p. 391.
6. William Toll, *The Resurgence of Race: Black Social Theory from Reconstruction to the Pan-African Conferences*, (Philadelphia: Temple University Press, 1979), p. 110.
7. Quoted from Washington in Lewis Harlan, *Booker T. Washington, The Wizard of Tuskegee*, (New York: Oxford University Press, 1983), p. 359.
8. Harlan, *Washington, Wizard of Tuskegee, op. cit.*, p. 364.
9. See Kellogg, *NAACP*, I, *op. cit.*, pp. 70-72. Also see Harlan, *Washington, Wizard of Tuskegee, op. cit.*, p. 376-378.
10. August Meier, *Negro Thought in America 1880-1915*, (Ann Arbor: The University of Michigan Press, 1968), pp. 208-209.
11. Lewis, *Du Bois, Biography of a Race, op. cit.*, p. 400.
12. Kellogg, *NAACP, op. cit.*, p. 83, fn. 65.
13. Lewis, *Du Bois, Biography of a Race, op. cit.*, p. 394.
14. Lewis, *Du Bois, Biography of a Race, op. cit.*, p. 395.
15. The Committee was divided almost evenly by race. Black members included Reverend William Henry Brooks, Charles E. Russell, and Bishop Alexander Walters of New York City; Dr. Owen M. Waller of Brooklyn, New York; Professor William L. Bulkley of Ridgefield Park, New Jersey; Archibald

Grimké of Boston; W. S. Scarborough of Wilberforce, Ohio; Ida Wells-Barnett, and Dr. Charles E. Bentley of Chicago; Dr. William Sinclair and R.R. Wright, Jr. of Philadelphia; Lafayette M. Hershaw, Mary Church Terrell, and Reverend J. Milton Waldron of Washington, D.C.; Du Bois of Atlanta; and Leslie Pinckney Hill of Manassas, Virginia. Kellogg, *NAACP*, I, *op. cit.*, pp. 29-30 and pp. 300-301.

16. William Loren Katz, *Eyewitness: A Living Documentary of the African American Contribution to American History*, (New York: A Touchstone Book, 1995), p. 326. Also see Dickson D. Bruce, Jr. *Archibald Grimké: Portrait of a Black Independent*, (Baton Rouge: Louisiana State University Press, 1993), pp. 174-175.

17. See Lewis, *Du Bois, Biography of a Race, op. cit.*, pp. 218-226.

18. Henry Lewis Suggs, *P.B. Young Newspaperman: Race, Politics, and Journalism in the New South 1910-62*, (Charlottesville: University Press of Virginia, 1988), pp. 15-16. Also see Kellogg, *NAACP*, I, *op. cit.*, p. 49.

19. Kellogg, *NAACP*, I, fn. 25, *op. cit.*, p. 51.

20. See Kellogg, *NAACP*, I, *op. cit.*, p. 53.

21. See Kellogg, *NAACP*, I, pp. *op. cit.*, 57-65.

22. Harlan, *Washington, Wizard of Tuskegee*, p. *op. cit.*, 404.

23. Harlan, *Washington, Wizard of Tuskegee*, *op. cit.*, pp. 341-342.

24. See Kellogg, *NAACP*, I, *op. cit.*, p. 157.

25. Harlan, *Washington, Wizard of Tuskegee*, *op. cit.*, p. 355.

26. Harlan, *Washington, Wizard of Tuskegee*, *op. cit.*, p. 356.

27. Harlan, *Washington, Wizard of Tuskegee*, *op. cit.*, pp. 440-441 and 450-451.

28. See Harlan, *Washington, Wizard of Tuskegee*, *op. cit.*, p. 323.

29. Three important books discuss the multi-faceted reasons for black migration associated with World War I. For an eyewitness account see Emmett J. Scott, *Negro Migration During the War*, (New York: Arno Press and the *New York Times*, 1969), pp. 26-70. For a more recent discussion see Florette Henri, *Black Migration: Movement North, 1900-1920*, (New York: Anchor Books, 1975), pp. 175-207 and 269-305. And to understand the role and impact of African American soldiers in heightening black pride see Arthur E. Barbeau and Florette Henri, *The Unknown Soldiers: Black American Troops in World War I*, (Philadelphia: Temple University Press, 1974), *Passim*.

30. Kellogg, *NAACP*, I, *op. cit.*, pp. 125-126, 129-130, and 186.

31. Kellogg, *NAACP*, I, *op. cit.*, p. 131.

32. Kellogg, *NAACP*, I, *op. cit.*, fn. 17, p. 93.

33. Kellogg, *NAACP*, I, *op. cit.*, p. 87.

34. See Kellogg, *NAACP*, I, pp. 133-134. Also see Willard Gatewood, *Aristocrats of Color: The Black Elite 1880-1920*, (Bloomington: Indiana University Press, 1993), p. 65.

35. See Kellogg, *NAACP*, I, *op. cit.*, pp. 189-190 and 194-196.

36. The incipient black middle class displaced a strong need to create social organizations during the early twentieth century. All black collegiate fraternities and sororities, with the exception of Sigma Gamma Rho Sorority (1922) and Iota Phi Theta Fraternity (1963) were founded between 1906 and 1920. Jones and Sadie Alexander became charter members of their respective organizations while others like Du Bois, Addams, and Woodson entered the Black Greek System as honorary members or in graduate chapters. See Lawrence C. Ross, Jr., *The Divine Nine: the History of African American Fraternities and Sororities*, (New York: Kensington Publishing Corp., 2000), *Passim*.

37. A compromise was reached and the three African Americans were allowed to remain in the ABA. Since future applicants to the American Bar Association were required to self identify by race, subsequent black attorneys were prevented from joining the ABA. See Kellogg, *NAACP*, I, *op. cit.*, pp. 199-201.

38. Peter M. Bergman, *The Chronological History of the Negro in America*, (New York: Harper and Row, Publishers, 1969), p. 361.

39. See Kellogg, *NAACP*, I, *op. cit.*, pp. 214-215.

40. Kellogg, *NAACP*, I, *op. cit.*, pp. 220-221.

41. Du Bois held complex views toward the war, viewing the confrontation from both an American and African perspective. See Wilson Jeremiah Moses, *The Golden Age of Black Nationalism 1850-1925*, (Hamden, Connecticut: Archon Books, 1978), pp. 225-331; Editorial "Close Ranks," *The Crisis*, Vol. 16, No. 3, (July 1918), p. 111. Also see Lewis, *Du Bois, Biography of a Race, op. cit.*, pp. 555-557.

42. Hawkins's pamphlet was entitled "What Does the Negro Want? Fourteen Articles Setting Forth What the American Negro Expects as a Basis for Democracy at Home." See Rayford W. Logan and Michael R. Winston (eds.), Dictionary of American Negro Biography, (New York: W.W. Norton and Company, 1982), p. 295.

43. Nancy J. Weiss, *The National Urban League 1910-1940*, (New York: Oxford University Press, 1974), pp. 30-33.

44. Guilford Parris, *Blacks in the City: A History of the National Urban League*, (Boston: Little, Brown, and Co, 1971), pp. 76-77, and 80-83.

45. Kellogg, *NAACP*, I, *op. cit.*, p. 266. Quoted from *The Bee*, September 1, 1917. Also see Weiss, *Urban League, op. cit.*, pp. 59-60.

46. See Kellogg, *NAACP*, I, *op. cit.*, pp. 266-269. Also see Weiss, *Urban* League, *op. cit.*, pp. 133-134.

47. Judith Stein, *The World of Marcus Garvey: Race and Class in Modern Society*, (Baton Rouge: Louisiana State University Press, 1986), p. 35.

48. According to Judith Stein, these views originated with Garvey in Jamaica. See Stein, Garvey, *op. cit.*, pp. 33-34.

49. See Stein, Garvey, *op. cit.*, p.84. Also see Moses, *Black Nationalism, op. cit.*, pp. 211-215.
50. n.n., *The Crisis*, "The Massacre of East St. Louis," Vol., 14, No., 5 (September, 1917), p. 219. Also see Marcus Garvey and Amy Jacques-Garvey (eds.), *Philosophy and Opinions of Marcus Garvey*, Part II (New York: Atheneum, 1969), pp. 128-129.
51. Elliot M. Rudwick, *Race Riot at East St. Louis, July 2, 1917*, (Carbondale: Southern Illinois University Press, 1964), pp. 27-40 and 50-53. Also see Kellogg, *NAACP*, I, *op. cit.*, p. 221, see fn.48.
52. See *The Crisis*, Vol. 14, No. 5, (September, 1917), 216, and Rudwick, *Race Riot., op. cit.*, p.66. Quoted from the *California Eagle*, July 21, 1917.
53. Kellogg, *NAACP*, I, *op. cit.*, p. 225, fn. 488.
54. *Crisis*, "Massacre, "*op. cit.*, (September, 1919), 219.
55. William R. Tuttle, Jr., *Race Riot: Chicago in the Red Summer of 1919*, (New York: Atheneum, 1972), pp. 32-66. Also see Kellogg, *NAACP*, I, *op. cit.*, pp. 236-238.
56. Kellogg, *NAACP*, p. 238. Also see James Weldon Johnson, "The Riots," *The Crisis*, Vol. 18, No. 5 (September, 1919), 243; F.S. Kelley "The Outer Pocket," *The Crisis*, Vol. 18, No. 6, (October, 1919), 288; and Walter White, "Chicago and Its Eight Reasons," Vol., 18, No. 6, (October, 1919), p. 297.
57. W.E.B. Du Bois, "Opinion," *The Crisis*, Vol.; 18, No. 5, (September, 1919), 231.
58. See Kellogg, *NAACP*, I, *op. cit.*, p. 236.
59. Kellogg, *NAACP*, I, *op. cit.*, pp. 241-245. Also see Stern, *Garvey, op. cit.*, p. 55.
60. Kellogg, *NAACP*, I, *op. cit.*, p. 246.
61. See quote from Du Bois, *The Crisis*, Vol., 20, No.3 , (July, 1920), 117.
62. Kellogg, *NAACP*, I, *op. cit.*, p. 292.
63. See Stein, *Garvey, op. cit.*, p. 57.
64. Garvey, Randolph, and Powell formed a rump group, met in the home of black millionaire, Madam C. J. Walker, and formed the International League of Darker Peoples. See Stern, *Garvey, op. cit.*, pp. 49-50.

Notes to Chapter 4

1. David Levering Lewis, *W.E. B. Du Bois: The Fight for Equality And the American Century, 1919-1963*, (New York: Henry Holt and Company, 2000), pp. 1-4. Henry Lewis Suggs, *P.B. Young Newspaperman: Race, Politics, and Journalism in the New South 1910-1962*, (Charlottesville: University of Virginia Press, 1988), pp. 47-48.
2. Kenneth T. Jackson, *The Ku Klux Klan in the City: 1915-1930*, (New York: Oxford University Press, 1967), p. 15.

3. Scott Ellsworth, *Death in a Promised Land: The Tulsa Race Riot of 1921*, (Baton Rouge: Louisiana State University Press, 1982), p. 14.

4. Ellsworth, *Death in a Promised Land,"* *op. cit.*, pp. 15-16.

5. The exact number of people killed in the riot remains unknown, with estimates ranging from 26 to 200 blacks dead and more than 300 wounded. Ellsworth, *Death in a Promised Land, op. cit.*, p. 70. Also see *New York Times*, May 31, 1996.

6. Walter White, "The Eruption of Tulsa, *Nation*, CXII (June 29, 1921), 909-910.

7. *Ibid.*

8. See Ellsworth, *Death in a Promised Land, op. cit.*, p. 103.

9. The Rosewood incident first became apparent to the general public on the Maury Povich Show of January 18, 1993. Michael D'Orso, *Like Judgment Day: The Ruin and Redemption of a Town Called Rosewood*, (New York: G.P. Putnam's Sons, 1996), p. 152.

10. D'Orso, *Like Judgment Day, op. cit.*, pp. 1-10.

11. William Loren Katz, *Eyewitness: A Living Documentary of the African American Contribution to American History*, (New York: Simon and Schuster, 1995), pp. 379-380.

12. Evidently Walter White perceived Sweet as an arrogant ingrate. See O.H. Sweet, M.D. to Mr. William Pickens, December 20, 1930, "Sweet Case," NAACP Papers, Library of Congress, Washington, D.C. Also see John Hope Franklin, *From Slavery to Freedom: A History of Negro Americans*, (New York: Alfred A. Knopf, 1967), p. 484.

13. Willard B. Gatewood, *Aristocrats of Color: The Black Elite, 1880-1920*, (Bloomington: Indiana University Press, 1993), pp. 332-333.

14. Gatewood, *Aristocrats, op. cit.*, p. 336.

15. Faith Berry, *Before and Beyond Harlem: A Biography of Langston Hughes*, (New York: Wings Books, 1992), pp. 2-3. Also see Arnold Rampersad, *The Life of Langston Hughes: 1902-1941, "I Too, Sing America,"* I (New York: Oxford University Press, 1986), pp. 7-8.

16. Gatewood, *Aristocrats, op. cit.*, p. 338

17. Berry, *Before and Beyond Harlem, op. cit.*, pp. 84-85. Also see Rampersad, Life of Langston Hughes, I, op. cit., pp. 50-51, 56-57.

18. Raymond Pace Alexander, "Forward," May, 1931, Box 85, Folder 12. Also see "Our Local and National Bar Association: Their Aims and Purposes," circa 1929, Raymond Pace Alexander Papers, Box 95, Folder 18, Archives, University of Pennsylvania [hereafter RPA,UPA].

19. See "Politics and the Law," pp. 1-2, Box 95, Folder 19, RPA,UPA.

20. James Welden Johnson, *Along This Way,* (New York: The Viking Press, 1933), pp. 78-79.

21. Johnson, *Along This Way, op. cit,* pp. 365-366.

22. Johnson, *Along This Way, op. cit.*, p.367.

23. Johnson, *Along This Way, op. cit.*, p 373.
24. Raymond Pace Alexander, "The Struggle Against Racism in Philadelphia From 1923 to 1948," Box 71, Folder 10, Sadie Taylor Mosell Alexander Papers, Archives, UPA.
25. Parris and Brooks, *Blacks in the City, op. cit.*, p. 197.
26. Parris and Brooks, *Blacks in the City, op. cit.*, pp. 136-137. Also see Nancy J. Weiss, *The National Urban League 1910-1940*, (New York: Oxford University Press, 1974), pp. 207-208.
27. Guichard Parris and Lester Brooks, *Blacks in the City: A History of the National Urban League*, (New York: Alfred A. Knopf, 1971), pp. 156-158. Also see Weiss, *National Urban League, op. cit.*, pp. 43-46.
28. Parris and Brooks, *Blacks in the City. op. cit.*, p. 170.
29. Parris and Brooks, *Blacks in the City, op. cit.*, p.171. For an interesting discussion of the term "opportunity" in conjunction with "crisis," the title of the NAACP's magazine, see Weiss, *National Urban League, op. cit.*, p. 69.
30. Parris and Brooks, *Blacks in the City, op. cit.*, p. 171.
31. Parris and Brooks, *Blacks in the City, op. cit.*, p. 172.
32. Parris and Brooks, *Blacks in the City, op. cit.*, pp. 181-183; and Weiss, *The National Urban League, op. cit.*, pp. 181-187.
33. Paula F. Pfeffer, *A. Philip Randolph, Pioneer of the Civil Rights Movement*, (Baton Rouge: Louisiana University Press, 1991), p. 24. Also see Parris and Brooks, *Blacks in the City, op. cit.*, pp. 184-185.
34. Parris and Brooks, *Blacks in the City, op. cit.*, pp. 184-185, quoted from T. A. Hill, "The Dilemmas of Negro Workers," *Opportunity* (February 1926), 39.
35. Parris and Brooks, *Blacks in the City, op. cit.*, p. 184.
36. Parris and Brooks, *Blacks in the City, op. cit.*, p. 185.
37. Nancy Weiss speaks disparagingly of the Urban League's successes. Yet, without League efforts, she concedes that the urban black proletariat in northern cities would have fared worse. Weiss, *The National Urban League, op. cit.*, pp. 307-309. Also see Parris and Brooks, *Blacks in the City, op, cit.*, pp. 185-186.
38. See Lewis, *W.E.B. Du Bois: Fight for Equality, op. cit.*, pp. 57-58.
39. W. Burghardt Turner and Joyce Moore Turner, (eds.), *Richard B. Moore, Caribbean Militant in Harlem: Collected Writings 1920-1972*, (Bloomington: Indiana University Press, 1992), p. 35.
40. Turner and Turner, *Richard B. Moore, op. cit.*, p. 38.
41. Turner and Turner, *Richard B. Moore, op. cit.*, p. 49
42. As one of the first NLUCAN fellows, Owen's radicalism deeply embarrassed the League. See Parris and Brooks, *Blacks in the City, op. cit.*, pp. 152-154 and Weiss, *The National Urban League, op. cit.*, p. 79.
43. Parris and Brooks, *Blacks in the City, op. cit.*, p. 153.

44. Randolph and Owen later altered their view toward Grimké and used him effectively to fight Du Bois. See Dickson D. Bruce, Jr. *Archibald Grimké: Portrait of a Black Independent*, (Baton Rouge: Louisiana State University Press, 1993), pp. 237-238. Also see Parris and Brooks, *Blacks in the City, op. cit.*, p. 153.

45. Parris and Brooks, *Blacks in the City, op. cit.*, pp. 153-154, quoted from *The Messenger*, December, 1920.

46. Pfeffer, *Randolph, op. cit.*, p. 20. James Weldon Johnson, *Black Manhattan*, (New York:Atheneum, 1968), p. 246.

47. William H. Harris, *Keeping the Faith: A. Philip Randolph, Milton P. Webster, and the Brotherhood of Sleeping Car Porters, 1925-1937*, (Urbana: University of Illinois Press, 1991), p. 15.

48. See Harris, *Keeping the Faith, op. cit.*, pp. 2-3.

49. Pfeffer, *Randolph, op. cit.*, pp. 21-22.

50. See Pfeffer, *Randolph, op. cit.*, pp. 281-305. Also see Harris, *Keeping the Faith, op. cit.*, pp. 67-68 and 145.

51. Amy Jacques-Garvey (ed.), *Philosophy and Opinions of Marcus Garvey*, (New York: Atheneum, 1969), "The True Solution of the Negro Problem," I, pp. 52-53; "An Appeal to the Conscience of the Black Race to See Itself," II, pp. 22-26; and "Aims and Objects of Movement for solution of Negro Problem," II, pp. 37-43. Also see John Hope Franklin and August Meier, *Black Leaders of the Twentieth Century*, (Urbana: University of Illinois Press, 1982), Laurence W. Levine, "Marcus Garvey and the Politics of Revitalization," 117-119.

52. Rupert Lewis, *Marcus Garvey: Anti-Colonial Champion*, (Trenton, New Jersey: Africa World Press, Inc., 1988), pp. 61-62.

53. Philip S. Foner, (ed.) *W.E.B. Du Bois Speaks: Speeches and Addresses 1920-1963*, (New York: Pathfinder Press, 1970), pp. 11-20.

54. Pfeffer, *Randolph, op. cit.*, p. 15.

55. Pfeffer, *Randolph, op. cit.*, p. 16.

56. Lewis, *Du Bois: Fight for Equality, op. cit.*, p. 57-58 and 78. It is important to note that some members of the black elite also initially supported Garvey. Also see E. David Cronin, *Black Moses: The Story of Marcus Garvey*, (Madison: University of Wisconsin Press, 1968.), pp. 69-70.

57. *Ibid.*

58. See Cronin, *Black Moses, op. cit.*, pp. 103, and 188-191.

59. Quoted from *Amsterdam News*, November 30, 1927 in Cronon, *Black Moses: Marcus Garvey, op. cit.*, p.143.

60. See Elinor Des Verney Sinnette, *Arthur Alfonso Schomburg: Black Bibliophile and Collector*, (Detroit: Wayne State University Press, 1989), pp. 134-148.

Notes to Chapter 5

1. Guichard Parris and Lester Brooks, *Blacks in the City: A History of the National Urban League*, (Boston: Little, Brown, and Company, 1971), p. 204.
2. Parris and Brooks, *Blacks in the City, op. cit.*, pp. 218-219. For an extensive discussion about the problems faced by Executive Director, Eugene Kinkle Jones who headed the Urban League, see Nancy J. Weiss, *The National Urban League: 1910-1940*, (New York: Oxford University Press, 1974), Chapters 15 through 17.
3. Parris and Brooks, *Blacks in the City, op. cit.*, p. 265.
4. Parris and Brooks, *Blacks in the City, op. cit.*, p. 212.
5. Weiss, *National Urban League, op. cit.*, p. 163-164. Also see B. Joyce Ross, *J.E. Spingarn and the Rise of the NAACP, 1911-1939*, (New York: Atheneum, 1972), pp. 19-20.
6. See Parris and Brooks, *Blacks in the City, op. cit.*, pp. 229 and 231-233.
7. Parris and Brooks, *Blacks in the City, op. cit.*, p.235. Weiss, *The National Urban League*, op. cit., p. 269.
8. Parris and Brooks, *Blacks in the City, op. cit.*, pp. 240-243.
9. Although William J. Wilson's *The Declining Significance of Race* and Michael Omi and Howard Winant's *Racial Formation of the United States* argue that profound divisions occurred during the 1960s, origins of this phenomenon took place during the New Deal. Ross, *Spingarn, op. cit.*, pp. 130-131. Also see Parris and Brooks, *Blacks in the City, op. cit.*, p. 214.
10. Quoted from T. A. Hill, "The National Urban League," *Southern Workman* (May, 1936) 138. See Parris and Brooks, *Blacks in the City, op. cit.*, p. 247.
11. NUL audited statement for 1935 and 1936. National Urban League Headquarters Office, New York, *Ibid.*
12. Parris and Brooks, *Blacks in the City, op. cit.*, p. 274.
13. Quoted from L. B. Granger's "Reminiscences," Parris and Brooks, *Blacks in the City, op. cit.*, p. 254.
14. Parris and Brooks, *Blacks in the City, op. cit.*, pp. 258-259.
15. See Eric Hobsbawm, *The Age of Extremes: A History of the World, 1914-1991*, (New York: Vintage Books, 1994), pp. 54-84.
16. Philip S. Foner and Herbert Shapiro (eds.), *American Communism and Black Americans: A Documentary History, 1930-1934*, (Philadelphia: Temple University Press, 1991), p. x. For the most definitive discussion of blacks and the CPUSA see Wilson Record, *The Negro and the Communist Party*, (New York: Atheneum, 1971), pp. 120-183.
17. See William A. Nolan, *Communism Versus the Negro*, (Chicago: Henry Regney Company, 1951), pp. 25-31.

18. W. Burghardt Turner and Joyce More Turner, (eds)., *Richard B. Moore, Caribbean Militant in Harlem: Collected Writings 1920-1972*, (Bloomington: Indiana University Press, 1992), pp. 46-48.

19. Foner and Shapiro, *American Communism and Black Americans, op. cit.*, pp. xi-xii.

20. Foner and Shapiro, *American Communism and Black Americans, op., cit.*, pp. xv-xvi.

21. Foner and Shiparo, *American Communism and Black Americans, op. cit.*, p. xvii.

22. See John P. Davis, "Let Us Build a National Negro Congress," National Sponsoring Committee, National Negro Congress, October, 1936, *Passim*.

23. See flyer, Call for National Negro Congress; Davis, "Let Us Build a National Negro Congress," *op. cit.*, p.30; and Peter M. Bergman, *The Chronological History of the Negro in America*, (New York: Harper and Row, 1969), pp. 472-473. Also see Supplementary Memorandum to the Report on the National Negro Congress from Mr. Wilkins, March 10, 1936, *Passim*, Box C-383, NAACP Papers, Library of Congress (hereafter NAACP, LC).

24. "Call for National Negro Congress," flyer, *op. cit.*

25. Wilkins, Memorandum on the NNC, *op cit.*, pp. 5-7.

26. See Program, Second National Negro Congress, Urban Archives, Temple University.

27. Bergman, *The Chronological History of the Negro in America, op. cit.*, p. 479.

28. Excerpt from letter from Charles H. Houston written at Toledo, Ohio, January 21, 1936, Box C-383, NAACP, LC.

29. Walter White to A. Philip Randolph, February 3, 1936, and Randolph to White, February 4, 1936, Box C-383, NAACP, LC.

30. This held true for black churches and other organizations as well. White to Arthur Fauset, April 4, 1938, Box C-383, NAACP, LC. Also see Paula Pfeffer, *A. Philip Randolph: Pioneer of the Civil Rights Movement*, (Baton Rouge: Louisiana State University Press, 1991).

31. Interview with Arthur Huff Fauset, September 21, 1974. While Fauset suggests that Randolph's naiveté allowed the CPUSA to undermine the NNC, as early as 1925 Randolph held strong reservations about the communists. See William H. Harris, *Keeping the Faith: A. Philip Randolph, Milton P. Webster, and the Brotherhood of Sleeping Car Porters, 1925-1937*, (Urbana: University of Illinois Press, 1991), p. 115.

32. Record, *Negro and the Communist Party, op, cit.*, pp. 197-198.

33. Pfeffer, *A. Philip Randolph, op. cit.*, p.38.

34. Quoted from Randolph, "Why I Would Not Stand for Re-election in the National Negro Congress," *American Federalists* (July, 1940), 24-25 found in Pfeffer, *A. Philip Randolph, op. cit.*, p. 40.

35. Raymond Wolters, *Negroes and the Great Depression: The Problem of Economic Recovery*, (Westport, Connecticut: Greenwood Publishing Corporation, 1970), pp. 7-34.

36. See Darlene Clark Hine, Elsa Barkley Brown, and Rosalyn Terborg-Penn (eds.), *Black Women in America: An Historical Encyclopedia*, Vol. I, (Bloomington: University of Indiana Press, 1993), pp. 113-127.

37. Evidence of primary concern for the black middle class as opposed to the interests of the masses can be seen throughout NAACP correspondence. Two specific items illustrate this point. First, NAACP success in defeating Bill H.R. 5733—an industrial commission to investigate and resolve economic problems among African Americans may be observed through the following: Walter White to Franklin D. Roosevelt, August 16, 1935, Official File 93, Franklin Delano Roosevelt Library, Hyde Park, New York [hereafter FDR Library]. For a second example see Report of the Secretary of the District Branch NAACP, p. 2, June 20, 1939, I, Box G-38, NAACP, LC.

38. See *Philadelphia Tribune*, February 20 and December 4, 1930, July 8, 1937, and May 4, 1939. And see for *Philadelphia Independent*, September 23, November 22, and November 29, 1936.

39. Parris and Brooks, *Blacks in the City, op. cit.*, pp. 238-239.

40. Parris and Brooks, *Blacks in the City, op. cit.*, pp. 220-224 and 227-239.

41. Wolters, *Negroes and the Great Depression, op. cit.*, pp. 238-241.

42. See Wolters, *Negroes and the Great Depression, op. cit.*, p. 246.

43. W.E.B. Du Bois, *Dusk of Dawn*, (New York: Shocken Books, 1968), p. 297.

44. David Levering Lewis, *W.E.B. Du Bois: The Fight for Equality and the American Century*, (New York: Henry Holt and Company, 2000), pp. 334-348.

45. See Circular letter from Campbell C. Johnson, Esq., March 27, 1936, Box 2; Dr. M.O. Bousfield to FDR, April 21, 1936; and Reginald Barrows to FDR, April 2, 1935, Official File 93, Box 2, FDR Library.

46. B.M. Pettit, a white man who served as the New Deal's Assistant Director of the Division of Housing cited the opinion of Roscoe Conkling Bruce, a black elitist from New York who advocated housing solely for the African American upper crust. See Notes on Advisory Committee Meeting, October 24, 1935, Philadelphia Housing Association Papers.

47. See *Chicago Defender*, June 6 and June 13, 1936.

48. See "Has the Roosevelt New Deal Helped the Colored Citizen?," Official File 93, FDR Library.

49. *Chicago Defender*, May 11, 1935; Frank Young to Roosevelt, September 8, 1936, Presidents Personal File, 30 Colored Matters, FDR Library; and *Amsterdam News*, November 18, 1939.

50. See *Chicago Defender*, March 4 and April 22, 1933, May 5 and June 23, 1934. See Gertrude A. Ayers to White, Copy, Trade School Situation, November 1931, I G-142; and Dr. H. Claude Hudson to William Pickens, October 28,

1933, I G-17, NAACP Branch Files, L.C. Also see "The Progression of the Teaching Profession," p. 11, March 16, 1939, Pennsylvania State Archives; Mr. Connie Jones to Frost, May 3, 1937 and Memorandum to Mr. Marshall and Wilkins from CHH, May 10, 1937, I G-144 NAACP Files, L.C.

51. Presumably, few among the masses knew graduate schools existed. Roger Goldman with David Gallen, *Thurgood Marshall: Justice For All*, (New York: Carroll and Graff Publishers, Inc., 1992), p. 30.

52. Goldman and Gallen, *Thurgood Marshall, op. cit*, p. 30. Also see Alton Hornsby, Jr., *African American History: Significant Events and People from 1619 to the Present*, (Detroit: Gale Research Inc,.1991), pp. 83-84 and Bergman, *Chronological History of The Negro in America, op. cit.*, pp. 481 and 484-485.

53. Thurgood Marshall, Procedure to Equalize Educational Opportunities, June, 1935, Box 85, Folder 30, RPA, UP.

54. Ironically, the greatest debates concerning public schools outside the segregated South pertained to maintaining segregation to protect black teachers. For information about integration see Rev. Sheldon Hale Bishop of New York to Walter White, January 10, 1933, I G-143, and H. Claude Hudson of Los Angeles to William Pickens, October 28, 1933, I C-17, NAACP Files, LC; Floyd Logan to Walter Biddle Saul, December 7, 1934, Series I, Box 2, Logan Papers, Temple Urban Archives; *Amsterdam News*, February 18, 1939; *Chicago Defender*, March 4, April 22, and May 5, 1933; and letter from Herbert E. Turner, President Chicago NAACP to mayoral candidates, January 28, 1931, I G-49, NAACP Files, LC. And for the debate between black segregationists vs. integrationists see Gunnar Myrdal, *An American Dilemma*, II, (New York: McGraw-Hill Book Company, 1964), pp. 901-902; Interview with Dr. Ruth Hayre, former Superintendent of Schools, Philadelphia, July 18, 1992; and Memorandum to Walter White for Roy Wilkins, January 14, 1935, I C-290; Katheryn M. Johnson to Walter White, March 3, 1930, I G-49 NAACP Files, LC.

Notes to Chapter 6

1. See Arthur R. Ashe, Jr., *A Hard Road to Glory: A History of the African-American Athlete 1919-1945*, Vol. II., (New York: Amistad Press, 1988), p. 83.

2. Gunnar Myrdal, *An American Dilemma*, Vol. II, (New York: McGraw Hill Book Company, 1964), p. 1009. Quoted from the *New York Times*, July 20, 1942.

3. James MacGregor Burns, *Roosevelt: The Soldier of Freedom*, (New York: Harcourt Brace Jovanovich, Inc., 1970), p. 54. Also see Paula F. Pfeffer, *A.*

Philip Randolph: Pioneer of the Civil Rights Movement, (Baton Rouge: Louisiana State University Press, 1991), p. 46.

4. Herbert Garfinkel, *When Negroes March: The March on Washington Movement in the Organizational Politics for FEPC*, (New York: Atheneum, 1969), pp. 19-21.

5. Garfinkel, *When Negroes March, op. cit.*, p. 33.

6. *Ibid.* Quoted from Walter White, "Negroes," the New International Yearbook for 1940," p. 537.

7. Garfinkel, *When Negroes March, op. cit.*, p. 38.

8. Rayford Logan, (ed.), *What the Negro Wants*, (New York: Agathon Press, Inc,. 1969), p. 130.

9. Garfinkel, *When Negroes March, op. cit.*, p. 39. Quoted from "The President, the Negro, and Defense," *Opportunity* XIX, (July, 1941), 204.

10. See Garfinkel, *When Negroes March, op. cit.*, p. 41.

11. Garfinkel, *When Negroes March, op. cit.*, p. 41.

12. See Andrew Buni, *Robert L. Vann of the Pittsburgh Courier: Politics and Black Journalism*, (Pittsburgh: The University of Pittsburgh Press, 1974), pp. 3-6.

13. Buni, *Vann, op. cit.*, p. 300.

14. Buni, *Vann, op. cit.*, pp. 302-306.

15. Garfinkel, *When Negroes March, op. cit.*, p. 77. Quoted from *Daily Worker*, June 26 and 27, 1941.

16. Garfinkel, *When Negroes March, op. cit.*, p. 94.

17. Garfinkel, *When Negroes March, op. cit.*, p. 109.

18. See Peter M. Bergman, *The Chronological History of the Negro in America*, (New York: Harper and Row, 1969), p. 499. Also see Henry Lewis Suggs, *P.B. Young Newspaperman: Race, Politics, and Journalism in the New South 1910-62*, (Charlottesville: University of Virginia Press, 1988), pp. 120-121.

19. Walter White, *A Man Called White: The Autobiography of Walter White*, (Bloomington: Indiana University Press, 1948), p. 225.

20. See Guichard Parris and Lester Brooks, *Blacks in the City: A History of the National Urban League*, (Boston: Little Brown, and Company, 1971), pp. 304-305; John Hope Franklin, *From Slavery to Freedom: A History of Negro Americans*, (New York: Alfred A. Knopf, 1967), p. 599; and Suggs, *P.B. Young, op. cit.*, pp. 133-134.

21. White, *A Man Called White, op. cit.*, pp. 207-208.

22. White, *A Man Called White, op. cit.*, pp. 220-223 and 242-252.

23. See Logan, *What the Negro Wants, op. cit.*, pp. 110-111.

24 Henry L. Stimson, the Secretary of War, believed in the inferiority of blacks, and General George C. Marshall, Chair of the Joint Chiefs of Staff, sincerely believed that desegregation would destroy the morale within the Armed

Services. See John Morton Blum, *V Was For Victory*, (New York: Harcourt Brace Jovanovich, 1976), pp. 184-185.

25. Charles E. Francis, *The Tuskegee Airmen: The Men Who Changed A Nation*, (Boston: Branden Publishing Company, 1993), pp. 245-248.

26. For extensive discussion of General Benjamin O. Davis Jr.'s role in World War II, see Benjamin O. Davis, Jr., *An Autobiography: Benjamin O. Davis, Jr.: American*, (Washington: Smithsonian Institution Press, 1991), Chapters 4 through 6.

27. See. Francis, *Tuskegee Airmen, op. cit.*, pp. 193, 197-199, and 205-207.

28. See Francis, *Tuskegee Airmen, op. cit.*, pp. 230-236.

29. Frances, *Tuskegee Airmen, op. cit.*, p. 195.

30. *Ibid.*

31. For an extensive discussion on the integration of the United States Air Force, see Davis, *op cit*, pp. 153-165. Also see Francis, *Tuskegee Airmen, op. cit.*, p. 195.

32. See Jervis Anderson, *Bayard Rustin: Troubles I've Seen*, (Berkeley: University of California Press, 1998), p. 127.

33. Francis, *Tuskegee Airmen, op. cit.*, p. 255. Also see Parris and Brooks, *Blacks in the City, op. cit.*, p. 340.

34. Parris and Brooks, *Blacks in the City, op. cit.*, pp. 313-314.

35. Parris and Brooks, *Blacks in the City, op. cit.*, p. 339. Quoted from NUL Annual Reports from 1950.

36. *Ibid.*

37. Robert C. Weaver, *The Negro Ghetto*, (New York: Harcourt, Brace and Company, 1948), p. 125.

38. Weaver. *The Negro Ghetto, op. cit.*, pp. 130-132.

39. Robert Frederick Burk, *The Eisenhower Administration and Black Civil Rights*, (Knoxville: University of Tennessee Press, 1984), pp. 6-8.

40. Weaver, *The Negro Ghetto, op. cit.*, 136-138.

41. Weaver, *The Negro Ghetto, op. cit.*, pp. 298-299.

42. See Blum, *V Was For Victory, op, cit*, pp. 215-216 and Alton Hornsby, Jr., *Chronology of African-American History*, (Detroit: Gale Research Inc., 1991), pp. 91 and 94. See Weaver, *The Negro Ghetto, op. cit.*, pp. 298-299.

43. Nina Mjagkij, *Light in the Darkness: African Americans and the YMCA, 1852-1946*, (Lexington: The University Press of Kentucky, 1994), pp. 8, 18, and 85.

44. Mjagkij, *Light in the Darkness, op. cit.*, p. 110.

45. Mjagkij, *Light in the Darkness, op. cit.*, pp. 125-132.

46. Darlene Clark Hine, Elsa Barkley Brown, and Rosalyn Terborg-Penn (eds.), *Black Women in America: An Historical Encyclopedia*, I, (Bloomington: University of Indiana Press, 1993), pp. 152-153.

47. Hine, et. al., *Black Women in America*, II, *op. cit.*, p. 1302.

48. Weaver, *The Negro Ghetto, op. cit.*, p. 367.

49. *Ibid.* Quoted in The Church and Race Relations, Federal Council of the Churches of Christ in America, 1946, pp. 2-3.
50. Weaver, *The Negro Ghetto, op. cit.*, p. 368. Quoted in Seminar on Negro Problems in the Field of Social Action, National Catholic Welfare Conference, 1946, pp. 17 and 33.
51. See Arnold Rambersad, *Jackie Robinson, A Biography*, (New York: Alfred A. Knopf, 1997), pp. 36-82.
52. Myrdal, *An American Dilemma, op. cit.*, p. 1013.
53. Burns, *Roosevelt, op. cit.*, p. 355.

Notes to Chapter 7

1. David Levering Lewis, *Du Bois: Fight for Equality and the American Century, 1919-1963*, (New York: Henry Holt and Company, 2000), pp. 520-550.
2. Martin Duberman: *Paul Robeson: A Biography*, (New York: The New Press, 1989), p.18.
3. Duberman, *Robeson, op. cit.*, p. 149.
4. See Duberman, *Robeson, op. cit.*, pp. 186-187.
5. See Eric Hobsbawm, *The Age of Extremes: A History of the World, 1914-1991*, (New York: Vintage Books, 1996), pp. 58 and 124-125.
6. For a brief but comprehensive discussion of the American Communist Party's attempt to incorporate blacks into the movement see Philip S. Foner and Herbert Shapiro (eds.), *American Communism and Black Americans: A Documentary History 1939-1934*, (Philadelphia: Temple University Press, 1991), pp. xi-xxix.
7. See John Button, *The Radicalism Handbook: Radical Activists, Groups and Movements of the Twentieth Century*, (Santa Barbara, California: ABC-CLIO, Inc. 1995), pp. 282-283.
8. Duberman, *Robeson, op. cit.*, pp. 342-343.
9. Duberman, *Robeson, op. cit.*, P. 347, quoted from *Crisis*, May, 1949, p. 137.
10. Duberman, *Robeson, op. cit.*, p. 357.
11. Duberman, *Robeson, op. cit.*, p. 414.
12. Brian Urquhart, *Ralph Bunche: An American Odyssey*, (New York: W.W. Norton and Company, 1998), p. 45, quoted from Peggy Mann, *Ralph Bunche: UN Peace Maker*, (New York, 1975), p. 87.
13. Urquhart, *Bunche; op. cit.*, p. 53.
14. Urquhart, *Bunche, op. cit.*, p. 84.
15. Urquhart, *Bunche, op. cit.*, p. 92, quoted from "The Programs of Organizations Devoted to the Improvement of the Status of the American Negro," *Journal of Negro Education*, July, 1939.
16. Urquhart, *Bunche, op. cit.*, p. 198.
17. Urquhart, *Bunche, op. cit.*, p. 233.

18. Urquhart, *Bunche, op. cit.*, pp. 250-256.

19. See Robert Frederick Burk, *The Eisenhower Administration and Black Civil Rights*, (Knoxville: The University of Tennessee Press, 1984), p. 69.

20. See E. Frederic Morrow, *Forty Years as a Guinea Pig*, (New York: The Pilgrim Press, 1980), p. 17.

21. See Morrow to Walter White, November 22, 1939, NAACP Files, I G-54, L.C.

22. Morrow, *Forty Years, op. cit.*, p 61.

23, Morrow, *Forty Years, op. cit.*, pp. 100-104 and 152.

24. E. Frederic Morrow, *Black Man in the White House: A Diary of the Eisenhower Years By the Administrative Office for Special Projects, The White House, 1955-1961*, (New York: Coward McCann, Inc., 1963), pp. 245-264.

25. Morrow, *Diary, op. cit.*, p 266.

26. Morrow, *Forty Years, op. cit.*, p. 161.

27. See David Halberstam, *The Fifties*, (New York: Villard Books, 1993), pp. 131-143.

28. Burk, *Eisenhower, op.cit.*, pp. 120-121.

29. Burk, *Eisenhower, op. cit.*, p. 122.

30. See Lawrence Otis Graham, *Our Kind of People: Inside America's Black Upper Class*, (New York: Harper Collins Publishers, 1999), *Passim.*

31. See John Hope Franklin, *From Slavery to Freedom: A History of Negro Americans*, (New York: Alfred A. Knopf, 1967), p. 620; Peter M. Bergman, *The Chronological History of the Negro in America*, (New York: Harper and Row Publishers, 1969), p. 565.

32. See Will Haygood, *King of the Cats: The Life and Times of Adam Clayton Powell, Jr.*, (Boston: Houghton Mifflin Company, 1993), p. 25.

33. Haygood, *Powell, op cit.*, p. 172.

34. Haygood, *Powell, op. cit.*, p. 189.

35. *Haygood, Powell, op. cit.*, p. 193.

36. Haygood, *Powell, op. cit.*, p. 219.

37. See Morrow, *Diary, op. cit.*, pp. 34-37.

38. Marshall sent an outline of NAACP strategy to Raymond Pace Alexander of Philadelphia for review long before scholars like Roger Goldman and David Gallen suggest in *Thurgood Marshall: Justice for All*. See Procedure to Equalize Educational Opportunities by Thurgood Marshall, June, 1939, Box 85, Folder 30, Archives, RPA, UP.

39. Goldman and Gallen, *Marshall, op. cit.*, p. 84.

40. Goldman and Gallen, *Marshall, op. cit.*, p. 86.

41. Burk, *Eisenhower Administration, op. cit.*, p. 109.

42. Halberstam, *The Fifties, op. cit.*, pp. 539-544 and 546-563.

43. Burk, *Eisenhower, op.cit.*, pp. 207-208.

44. Morrow, *Forty Years, op. cit.*, pp. 173-177.

45. Morrow, *Forty Years, op. cit.*, pp. 176-177.

46. *Ibid.*
47. Morrow, *Forty Years, op. cit.*, p. 171.
48. Morrow, *Forty Years*, *op. cit.*, p. 191-192

Notes to Chapter 8

1. Milton Viorst, *Fire in the Streets:America in the 1960s*, (New York: Simon and Schuster, 1979), p. 95.
2. Viorst, *Fire in the Streets, op. cit.*, p. 94.
3. Viorst, *Fire in the Streets, op. cit.*, p. 95
4. John Lewis (with Michael D'Orio), *Walking With the Wind: A Memoir of the Movement*, (New York: Simon and Schuster, 1998), pp. 52-53.
5. Lewis, *Walking With the Wind, op. cit.*, pp. 56-59.
6. Viorst, *Fire in the Streets, op. cit.*, pp. 115-117 and Lewis, *Walking With the Wind, op. cit.*, pp. 102-117.
7. Lewis, *Walking With the Wind, op. cit.*, pp. 90 and 114.
8. *Ibid.*
9. Viorst, *Fire in the Streets, op. cit.*, pp., 119-122.
10. Viorst, *Fire in the Streets, op. cit.*, p. 123.
11. See E. Frederic Morrow, *Forty Years a Guinea Pig, (*New York: The Pilgrim Press, 1980), pp. 185-187 and 199-205.
12. Viorst, *Fire in the Streets, op. cit.*, p. 149.
13. Viorst, *Fire in the Streets, op. cit.*, pp. 137-138. Also see Lewis, *Walking With the Wind, op. cit.*, p. 113.
14. Viorst, *Fire in the Streets, op. cit.*, p. 156.
15. Arthur M. Schlesinger, Jr. *A Thousand Days: John F. Kennedy in the White House*, (Boston: Houghton Mifflin Company, 1956), p. 939.
16. Schlesinger, *A Thousand Days, op. cit.*, p. 958. Also see William M. Banks, *Black Intellectuals: Race and Responsibility in American Life*, (New York: W.W. Norton and Company, 1996), p. 146.
17. King also reestablished his role as the pre-eminent civil rights leader by writing the classic tome, "Letter from a Birmingham Jail." See Andrew Young, *An Easy Burden: The Civil Rights Movement and the Transformation of America*, (New York: HarperCollins, 1996), pp. 224-226. Also see Theodore H. White, *The Making of the President 1964*, (New York: Atheneum Publishers, 1965), pp. 167-171.
18. Benjamin Muse, The American Negro Revolution: From Nonviolence to Black Power 1963-1967, (Bloomington: Indiana University Press, 1968), pp. 63, 78-81, and 88-89.
19. Schlesinger, *A Thousand Days, op., cit.*, pp. 962-963.

20. See Schlesinger, *A Thousand Days, op. cit.*, pp. 964 and 974; Viorst, *Fire in the Streets, op. cit.*, pp. 221-222; and White, *The Making of the President, op. cit.*, pp. 170-171.
21. Jervis Anderson, *Bayard Rustin, Troubles I've Seen,* (Berkeley: University of California Press, 1998), pp. 7 and 24.
22. Viorst, *Fire in the Streets, op. cit.*, p. 211.
23. Anderson, *Rustin, op. cit.*, pp. 239-240.
24. Schlesinger, *A Thousand Days, op. cit.*, p. 969.
25. Schlesinger, *A Thousand Days, op. cit.*, p. 970.
26. *Ibid.*
27. Schlesinger, *A Thousand Days, op., cit.*, p. 971.
28. Viorst, *Fire in the Streets, pp. op. cit.*, pp. 199, 215-216.
29. Lewis, *Walking With the Wind, op. cit.*, p. 224.
30. Viorst, *Fire in the Streets, op. cit.*, pp. 230-231.
31. Viorst, *Fire in the Streets, op. cit.*, p. 231.
32. Clayborne Carson, *In Struggle: SNCC and the Black Awakening of the 1960s,* (Cambridge: Harvard University Press, 1981), p. 94.
33. See Alex Haley, *The Autobiography of Malcolm X,* (New York: Grove Press, Inc., 1965), pp. 206-217.
34. Haley, *Autobiography, op. cit.*, pp. 242-243.
35. Haley, *Autobiography, op. cit.*, p. 284.
36. See Gerald Horne, *Fire This Time: The Watts Uprising and the 1960s,* (Charlottesville: University of Virginia Press, 1995), p. 19. Also see Lewis, *Walking With the Wind, op. cit.,,* p. 317.
37. Viorst, *Fire in the Streets, op. cit.*, p. 173.
38. White, *Making of a President, op. cit.*, p. 44.
39. Bernard J. Firestone and Robert C. Vogt, (eds.), *Lyndon Baines Johnson and the Uses of Power,* (New York: Greenwood Press, 1988), p. 105.
40. White, *Making of the President, op. cit.*, pp. 221-223.
41. Horne, *Fire This Time, op. cit.*, p. 5.
42. Horne, *Fire This Time, op. cit.*, pp. 100-102 and 122-124.
43. Horne, *Fire This Time, op. cit.*, pp. 200-201.
44. See Harold Cruse, *The Crisis of the Negro Intellectual: From Its Origins to the Present,* (New York: William Monroe and Company, Inc., 1967), pp. 367-368. Also see Michael Omi and Howard Winant, *Racial Formations in the United States From the 1960s to the 1990s,* (New York: Routledge, 1994), pp. 40-41.
45. Horne, *Fire This Time, op. cit.*, p. 100.
46. Horne, *Fire This Time, op. cit.*, pp. 172-178.
47. Horne, *Fire This Time, op. cit.*, p. 183. Quoted from the *Los Angeles Times*, August 18, 1965.
48. Parris and Brooks, *Blacks in the City, op. cit.*, p. 464.
49. Carson, *In Struggle, op cit.*, p. 219.

50. Carson, *In Struggle, op. cit.*, p. 220.
51. Carson, *In Struggle, op. cit.*, pp. 222-223.
52. See News Release, July 1, 1969, National Urban League papers and *Washington Post*, July 29, 1969, Schomburg Library, New York.
53. See Carson, *In Struggle, op. cit.*, pp. 244-264.
54. The black establishment could never take Brown seriously. In a letter dated February 21, 1968 from the Parish Prison in New Orleans, Brown encouraged blacks to engage whites in a fight to the death. See "A Letter From Prison From H. Rap Brown," SNCC papers, 1959-1972, Reel 3, Schomburg Library, New York.
55. Daniel Patrick Moynihan, "The President and the Negro: The Moment Lost, *Commentary* Vol. 43 (February, 1967), 31-45.
56. Omi and Winant, *Racial Formation in the United States, op. cit.*, pp. 90-91.
57. Omi and Winant, *Racial Formation in the United States*, op. cit., pp. 53-76 and 96.

Notes to Chapter 9

1. See H. Viscount Nelson, "Philadelphia's Thirtieth Ward, 1940-1960," *Pennsylvania Heritage*, Vol. V., No. 2, (Spring 1979), 14-18.
2. Michael Omi and Howard Winant, *Racial Formation in the United States From the 1960s to the 1990s,* (New York: Routledge, 1994), pp. 114-118.
3. Dennis C. Dickerson, *Whitney M. Young Jr. Militant Mediator*, (Lexington: The University Press of Kentucky, 1998), pp. 24-27.
4. "Press Release," National Urban League, July 28, 1969; Schomburg Library, New York, New York, hereafter SL
5. *Evening Star*, July 28, 1969, SL.
6. See "Press Release," National Urban League, July 28, 1969, SL.
7. See Robert C. Smith, *We Have No Leaders: African Americans in the st-Civil Rights Era*, (Albany: State University of New York Press, 1996), pp. 25-26.
8. William M. Banks, *Black Intellectuals: Race and Responsibility in American Life*, (New York: W.W. Norton and Company, 1996), pp. 150-151.
9. Vernon E. Jordan, Jr. (with Annette Gordon-Reed), *Vernon Can Read: A Memoir*, (New York: PublicAffairs, 2001), pp. 88-107.
10. Jordan, *Vernon Can Read, op. cit.*, p. 152.
11. Press Release, National Urban League, 1970; Keynote Address, Sixtieth Anniversary, National Urban League, July 19, 1970, SL.
12. Smith, *We Have No Leaders, op., cit.*, pp. 33-34.
13. *Ibid.*
14. Smith, *We Have No Leaders, op. cit.*, pp. 39-41.
15. Smith, *We Have No Leaders, op. cit.*, p. 53.
16. Smith, *We Have No Leaders, op. cit.*, pp. 64-75.

17. Roy Wilkins, *Standing Fast: The Autobiography of Roy Wilkins*, (New York: The Viking Press, 1982), pp. 26-32.
18. *NAACP Annual Report*, 1969, p. 5.
19. Wilkins, *Standing Fast, op. cit.*, pp. 333-334.
20. *NAACP Annual Report*, 1969, *op. cit.*, p. 6. Also see NAACP Annual Report, 1970, p. 5.
21. For an extensive discussion of Nixon's strategic use of race for political gain, see Kenneth O'Reilly, *Nixon's Piano: Presidents and Racial Politics from Washington to Clinton*, (New York: The Free Press, 1995), pp. 279-329.
22. *Amsterdam News*, January 1, 1970.
23. *Annual Report*, 1970, *op. cit.*, pp. 29-41.
24. *Annual Report*, 1970, p. 29.
25. *Annual Reports*, 1970-1973, *op. cit.*, p. 6.
26. Annual Reports, 1970-1973, *op. cit.*, p. 83.
27. See *Annual Reports*, 1971, p. 46; 1972, p. 60; 1973, p. 51; 1974, pp. 45-50.
28. Annual Report, 1971, pp. 50-51; 1972, pp. 65-68; and 1973, pp. 54-56.
29. Annual Report, 1970, *op. cit.*, p. 90.
30. *Annual Report*, 1971, *op. cit.*, p. 52.
31. *Annual Report*, 1971, p. 54; *Annual Report*, 1972, *op. cit.*, p. 72.
32. *Annual Report*, 1972, *op cit.*, p. 72.
33. See *Annual Reports*, 1972, *op. cit.*, p. 79, and 1973, *op. cit.*, pp. 5 and 67.
34. While Wilkins and other sitting senior staff members were exempted from the ruling and the insertion of mitigating language enabled the Board to wave the retirement provision, Wilkins's position became more tenuous. See *Annual Report*, 1974, p. 6.
35. *Annual Report*, 1976, pp. 38-42.
36. Annual Report, 1976, p. 45.
37. As early as July 1975 rumors floated concerning Wilkins's retirement, a charge Wilkins denied. See *Amsterdam News*, July 9, 1975.
38. *Annual Report*, 1976, pp. 54-55. Also see *New York Times*, July 2 and 3, 1976.
39. *Annual Report*, 1976, pp. 55-56.
40. *Ibid.*
41. *New York News World*, July 4, 1977.
42. *New York Daily World*, July, 1978, quoted from speech given at 69th Annual Convention, July 4, 1978.
43. See Otto Kerner, Chair, *Report of the National Advisory Commission on Civil Disorders*, (New York: A Bantam Book: 1968), p. 2.
44. *See Report of the National Advisory Commission, op. cit.*, pp. 389-402.
45. Raphael J. Sonenshein, *Politics in Black and White: Race and Power in Los Angeles*, (Princeton: Princeton University Press, 1993), pp. 76-83.
46. Sonenshein, *Politics, op cit.*, pp. 125-129 and 134.

47. Between 1973 and 1980 the Bradley Administration acquired millions in anti-poverty medical grants, but a significant amount of the funding became absorbed by areas with less need. Particularly devastating for the masses was the paucity of federal funds directed toward providing low-income housing. See Sonenshein, *Politics, op. cit.*, pp. 164-169.

48. *Report of the National Advisory Commission, op. cit.*, p. 407.

49. For an extensive discussion on the limitations of critical black thinking see Harold Cruse, *The Crisis of the Negro Intellectual*, (New York: Quill Press, 1984), *Passim*.

50. O'Reilly, *Nixon's Piano, op. cit.*, pp. 341-342.

51. Andrew Young, *An Easy Burden: The Civil Rights Movement and the Transformation of America*, (New York: Harper Collins Publishers, 1996), pp. 18-20.

52. O'Reilly, *Nixon's Piano, op. cit.*, p. 348.

53. Press Release, National Urban League, January 24, 1980, NUL papers, SL.

54. *New York Daily World*, August 10, 1978.

55. Press Release, NUL, January 24, 1980, *op. cit.*

56. See *New York Times*, October 19-20, 1979.

57. Ronald W. Walters, "Black America's Needs," *New York Times*, March 13, 1979.

58. Darlene Clark Hine, Elsa Barkley Brown, and Rosalyn Terborg-Penn, *Black Women in America: An Historical Encyclopedia*, I and II, (Bloomington: Indiana University Press, 1993), pp. 552-554 and 861-862.

Notes to Chapter 10

1. The Fairmont Papers: Black Alternative Conference, San Francisco, December 12-13, 1980, p. 92, SL.

2. Fairmont Papers, *op. cit.*, p. 68, SL.

3. Fairmont Papers, *op. cit.*, p. 161, SL.

4. Michael Omi and Howard Winant, *Racial Formation in the United States From the 1960s to the 1990s*, (New York: Routledge, 1994), p. 120.

5. Omi and Winant, *Racial Formation in the United States, op. cit.*, pp. 118-136.

6. The complacence of civil rights leaders must be understood in the context of the times. They decided not to rock the proverbial boat, realizing that blacks comprising a majority of the electorate could vote black candidates into office. Moreover, they sensed that the white electorate appeared sufficiently open minded to support a national holiday for Martin Luther King and the extension of the 1965 Civil Rights Act. See Katherine Tate, *From Protest to Politics: The New Black Voters in American Elections*, (Cambridge: Harvard University Press, 1994), p. 2.

7. *New York Times*, August 7, 1980.

8. *Wall Street Journal,* August 8, 1980.
9. *Ibid.*
10. See Joseph Kraft, *Staten Island Advance,* August 7, 1980.
11. *Wall Street Journal,* April 10, 1978.
12. *Christian Science Monitor,* July 31, 1981.
13. *New York Times,* July 25, 1981.
14. See *New York World,* December 8 and 31, 1981.
15. See *Staten Island Advance,* May 28, 1982 and *New York Times,* May 30, 1982.
16. *Time Magazine,* July 12, 1982.
17. *New York Times,* June 21, 1983 and *New York Tribune,* June 23, 1983.
18. *New York Times,* July 18 and 21, 1983.
19. See Allan Brownfeld, *New York Tribune,* August 27, 1983.
20. See *New York Times,* Letter to the Editor from Alvin F. Poussaint, July 28, 1983 and *The Harlem Weekly,* November 17-23, 1983.
21. Kenneth O'Reilly, *Nixon's Piano, President, and Racial Politics from Washington to Clinton,* (New York: The Free Press, 1995), pp. 362-363. Also see William Loren Katz, *Eyewitness: A Living Documentary of the African American Contribution to American History,* (New York: A Touchstone Book, 1995), pp. 543-550.
22. See *Time Magazine,* July 25, 1983, p. 24.
23. O'Reilly, *Nixon's Piano, op. cit.,* p. 373.
24. *Ibid.*
25. *New York Times,* July 4, 1984.
26. See Alton Hornsby, Jr., *Chronology of African-American History: Significant Events and People from 1619 to the Present,* (Detroit: Gale Research, Inc.: 1991), pp. 307-308.
27. Smith, *We Have No Leaders, op. cit.,* pp. 154-156.
28. O'Reilly, *Nixon's Piano, op. cit.,* p. 395.
29. Marshall Frady, *Jesse: The Life and Pilgrimage of Jesse Jackson,* (New York: Random House, 1996), pp. 206-207.
30. Frady, *Jesse, op. cit.,* p.202.
31. See Frady, *Jesse, op. cit.,* p. 260.
32. Frady, *Jesse, op. cit.,* p. 296.
33. Frady, *Jesse, op. cit.,* p. 306.
34. Frady, *Jesse, op. cit.,* pp. 308-309.
35. Frady, *Jesse, op. cit.,* pp. 326-327.
36. Frady, *Jesse, op. cit.,* p. 371.
37. *New York Times,* February 17, 1985 and *Los Angles Times,* January 17, 1985.
38. *The Washington Post,* June 30,1985. Also see *New York Times,* July 21, 1985.
39. *New York Times,* February 13, 1986.
40. Kweisi Mfume, *No Free Ride,* (New York: Ballantine Books, 1996), pp. 168-178.

41. Mfume, *No Free Ride, op. cit.*, p. 291.
42. Mfume, *No Free Ride, op. cit.* P. 295.
43. James Richardson, *Willie Brown: A Biography*, (Berkeley, University of California Press, 1996), p. 68.
44. Richardson, *Willie Brown*, p. 102, quoted from J. W. Woodard, "Political Affairs, The Primary Examined," *The Mallet*, June 6, 1964.
45. Richardson, *Willie Brown, op. cit.*, p. 163.
46. Richardson, *Willie Brown, op. cit.*, pp. 209-210.
47. Benjamin Quarles, *Frederick Douglass*, (New York: Atheneum, 1968), pp. 348-350.
48. Richardson, *Brown, op. cit.*, pp. 242-243.
49. Richardson, *Brown, op. cit.*, pp. 190-191.
50. Richardson, *Brown, op. cit.*, p. 299.
51. Evidence of Brown's influence with Reagan appeared when Reagan gave a personal tribute at the funeral of Brown's mother. See Richardson, *Brown, op. cit.*, p. xii.
52. See *Long Island Newsday*, August 6, 1982, *Christian Science Monitor*, March 7, 1986 and July 17, 1987, and National Urban League Conference, July 30, 1987, SL.
53. *The Washington Post*, January 15, 1988.
54. See Mfume, *No Free Ride, op. cit.*, p. 320.

Notes to Chapter 11

1. Mary Beth Rogers, *Barbara Jordan: American Hero*, (New York: Bantam Books, 1998), p. xiii.
2. Rodgers, *Jordan, op. cit.*, pp. 4-6.
3. Rogers, *Jordan, op. cit.*, pp. 240-255.
4. Rogers, *Jordan, op. cit.*, p. 320.
5. See Thomas Hauser, *Muhammad Ali: His Life and Times*, (New York: A Touchstone Book, 1991), pp. 122-123 and 130-139.
6. Quoted from *New York Times*, March 29, 1966. See Hauser, *Ali, op. cit.*, p. 147.
7. See Hauser, *Ali, op. cit.*, pp. 294-295.
8. Hauser, *Ali, op. cit.*, p. 511.
9. Ronald V. Dellums, *Lying Down with the Lions: A Public Life from the Streets of Oakland to the Halls of Power*, (Boston: Beacon Press, 2000), pp. 9-12.
10. Dellums, *Lying Down, op. cit.*, pp. 58-59 and 64-65.
11. Dellums, *Lying Down, op. cit.*, pp. 67-68; 72-73; and 78-80.
12. Dellums, *Lying Down, op. cit.*, p. 89.
13. Dellums, *Lying Down, op. cit.*, p. 116.
14. Dellums, *Lying Down, op. cit.*, p. 104.

15. See Program Report, NAACP Special Contribution Fund Address, 1990, NAACP files, Folder 2, Schomburg Library and *Los Angeles Times*, July 8, 1990.

16. See *New York Times*, November 8, 1994 and *Los Angeles Times*, July 10, 1995, p. A 25

17. For a detailed discussion about NAACP difficulties during Chavis' tenure, see *The Washington Post*, December 18, 1994.

18. William Raspberry, "Big Choice for Kweisi Mfume—and the NAACP, *The Washington Post*, December 15, 1995.

19. See Frantz Fanon, *Black Skin, White Masks: The Experiences of a Black Man in a White World*, (New York: Grove Press, 1967), pp. 11-12.

20. Ronald W. Walters and Robert C. Smith, *African American Leadership*, (Albany: State University Press of New York, 1999), pp. 81-82.

21. The endorsement of "original intent" which advocates judicial interpretations to the eighteenth century—in the strictest sense—would return Americans of African ancestry to slavery.

22. Stephen Thernstrom and Abigal Thernstrom, *America in Black and White: One Nation Indivisible*, (New York: Simon and Schuster, 1997), pp. 291 and 301.

23. See Ward Connerly, *Creating Equal: My Fight Against Race Preferences*, (San Francisco: Encounter Books, 2000), pp. 27-33; Barry Bearak, "Questions of Race Run Deep for Foe of Preferences" *New York Times*, July 27, 1997.

24. See Rich Lowry "Rolling Back Quotas, National Review, (September, 1996), 2-3.

25. Connerly, *Creating Equal, op. cit.*, p. 117.

26. Quoted from "I am not African-American," San Francisco's *Focus Magazine*, May, 1997, p. 60. Evidence of the extended family's disenchantment with Connerly also appeared on the television show "Sixty Minutes," November 9, 1997. Also see Connerly, *Creating Equal, op. cit.*, p. 279.

27. Connerly vehemently denied this accusation. However UC Regent Roy Brophy believed the Connerly lobbied the Regents to help Wilson's presidential aspirations. And though Wilson's bid in 1996 failed, he was expected to seek the presidential office in 2000. See "I am not African-American," *op. cit.*, p. 126. Also see William Bradley, "Pay Attention When Wilson Picks Fights," *Los Angeles Times*, November 6, 1997, p. B11.

28. Leon Worden, "Ward Connerly: One Man's Passion for Fairness," January 31, 1996, Synopsis OnLine.

29. See Ethan Watters, "Ward Connerly Won the Battle Now He's Facing the War," *Mother Jones* (November/December, 1997), p. 71. Also see an interview of Connerly conducted by Wallace Terry, "Why I Oppose Affirmative Action," *San Francisco Sunday Examiner and Chronicle*, May 31, 1998.

30. See Rep. J.C. Watts' Response to the State of the Union Address, August, 1997; Clint Parker, "Watts Speaks at Taylor Dinner, *Oklahoma Congressman,*

Copyright, Mountain Sentinel, 1997; and Willie A. Richardson, "From the Publisher," *Headway Magazine*, April, 1997.

31. Thernstrom and Thernstrom, *America in Black and White, op. cit.*, p. 301. Also see *Los Angeles Times*, February 22, 1999. Unconfirmed reports claim that Watts decided against running for reelection in 2002 because of disrespect he received from fellow Republicans. For a suggested confirmation about this interpretation see Earl Ofari Hutchinson, "A Black Republican Wises Up and Opts Out," *Los Angeles Times*, July 8, 2002.

32. Evidence of black satisfaction appeared through black leadership's muted response to the injustices imposed on the black community throughout the Reagan-Bush Administrations. See Mary Frances Berry, *Black Resistance White Law: A History of Constitutional Racism in America*, (New York: Penguin Books, 1994), pp. 243-244.

33. William L. Clay, *Just Permanent Interests: Black Americans in Congress: 1870-1992*, (New York: Amistad Press, 1993), pp. 340-341.

34. Clay, *Just Permanent Interests, op. cit.*, pp. 347-348.

35. Lani Guinier, *Lift Every Voice: Turning A Civil Rights Setback Into A New Vision Of Social Justice*, (New York: Simon and Schuster, 1998), pp. 32-33.

36. Guinier, *Lift Every Voice, op. cit*, p. 35.

37. Guinier, *Lift Every Voice, op. cit.*, pp. 141 and 147. Kweisi Mfume stated that he argued with President Clinton on Guinier's behalf and contended the CBC supported her nomination and rebuffed Clinton for abandonment. See Kweisi Mfume, *No Free Lunch: From the Mean Streets to the Mainstream*, (New York: Ballantine Books, 1996), pp. 327-332.

38. Andrew Young, *An Easy Burden; the Civil Rights Movement and the Transformation of America*, (New York: Harper Collins Publishers, 1996), p. 527.

39. See Colin L. Powell, *My American Journey*, (New York: Ballantine Books, 1996), 33-34.

40. Powell, *My American Journey, op. cit.*, pp. 598-602.

41. Derived from the terms ebony and phonics, ebonics became a term which served as a euphemism for black English.

42. Kenneth O'Reilly, *Nixon's Piano: Presidents and Racial Politics from Washington to Clinton*, (New York: The Free Press, 1995), pp. 413-414.

43. Carl T. Rowan, *The Coming Race War in America: A Wake-Up Call*, (Boston: Little Brown and Company, 1996), p. 32.

44. Earl Ofari Hutchinson, *The Disappearance of Black Leadership*, (Los Angeles: Middle Passage Press, Inc., 2000), p. 79.

45. Rowan, *Coming Race War in America, op. cit.*, pp. 63, 71-72.

46. See Stanley Elkins, *Slavery: A Problem in Institutional and Intellectual Life*, (Chicago: University of Chicago Press, 1959), pp. 86-87; Frantz Fanon, *Black Skin White Masks: The Experiences of a Black Man in a White World*, (New

York: Grove Press, 1967), p. 100; and Paulo Freire, *Pedagogy of the Oppressed*, (New York: Continuum, 1989), pp. 30-32.

BIBLIOGRAPHY

A Note on Sources

Although many of the people now deceased mentioned in *Black Leadership* have manuscript collections available to scholars, this author elected to present readers with an overview of their life and contributions derived essentially from secondary sources. Monographs, biographies, and an occasional internet item provided information that placed the subjects into the historical context and presented a perspective on a particular subject's activities, and with quotes and paraphrases, thoughts. When available, autobiographies authored by subjects provided pertinent personal information about their origins, opinions, and rationalizations for strategies and decisions rendered that affected an organization, program, or event. Other primary sources included newspapers, magazines, various manuscript collections and interviews with the late Arthur Huff Fauset and Ruth Hayre.

Among the manuscript collections perused, the world-famous Schomburg Library is a must for anyone engaging in a comprehensive study of African American history and culture. Detailed information on the NAACP such as its Annual Reports, the National Urban League may be found there as well as information pertaining to the Student Non Violent Coordinating Committee. Newspaper clippings from the local press as well as columns and editorials about stories involving African Americans are contained there as well. A document containing minutes about the Fairmount Conference also proved most helpful. The Library of Congress is replete with information about the origins of the NAACP. This collection as well as documents from the Franklin D. Roosevelt Library, the Free Library of Philadelphia, and the Temple University Archives proved rich in information about blacks during the Great Depression. The University of Pennsylvania Archives contain the extensive papers of Raymond Pace and Sadie Taylor Mosell Alexander dating from the 1920s to the 1970s. These extensive papers contain correspondence ranging from people like W.E.B. Du Bois to Thurgood Marshall as well as some information about Sigma Pi Phi (The Boulé) and Delta Sigma Theta Sorority. Additional sources like the writings of Frederic Morrow are located in the Charles E. Young Library of UCLA.

Secondary Sources

Anderson, Jervis. *Bayard Rustin: Troubles I've Seen*. Berkeley: University of California Press, 1998.

Ashe, Jr. Arthur. *A Hard Road to Glory: A History of the African-American Athlete*. New York: Amistad Press, III Vols. 1988.

Baker, Ray Stannard. *Following the Color Line: American Negro Citizenship During the Progressive Era*. New York: Harper and Row, 1964.

Banks, William M. *Black Intellectuals: Race and Responsibility in American Life*. New York: W.W Norton and Company, 1996.

Barbeau, Arthur E. and Henri, Florette. *The Unknown Soldiers: Black American Troops in World War I*. Philadelphia: Temple University Press, 1974.

Bergman, Peter M. *The Chronological History of the Negro in America*. New York: Harper and Row, Publishsers, 1969.

Berry, Mary Frances. *Black Resistance White Law: A History of Constitutional Racism in America*. New York: Penguin Books, 1994.

Burk, Robert Frederick. *The Eisenhower Administration and Black Civil Rights*. Knoxville: University of Tennessee Press, 1984.

Button, John. *The Radicalism Handbook: Radical Activists, Groups, and Movements of the Twentieth Century*. Santa Barbara, California: ABC-CLIO, Inc., 1995.

Berry, Faith. *Before and Beyond Harlem: A Biography of Langston Hughes*. New York: Wings Books, 1992.

Blum, John Morton. *V Was For Victory*. New York: Haracourt Brace Jovanovich, 1976.

Brontz, Howard (ed). *Negro Social and Political Thought, 1850-1920*. New York: Basic Books, Inc., 1966.

Bruce, Jr. Dickson D. *Archibald Grimké: Portrait of a Black Independent*. Baton Rouge: Louisiana University Press, 1993.

Bullock, Henry Allen. *A History of Negro Education in the South: From 1619 to the Present*. New York: Praeger Publishers, 1970.

Buni, Andrew. *Robert L. Vann of the Pittsburgh Courier: Politics and Black Journalism*. Pittsburgh: University of Pittsburgh Press, 1974.

Burns, James MacGregor. *Roosevelt: The Soldier of Freedom.* New York: Haarcourt Brace Jovanovich, Inc., 1970.

Carson, Clayborne. *In Struggle: SNCC and the Black Awakening of the 1960s.* Cambridge: Harvard University Press, 1981.

Clay, William L. *Just Permanent Interests: Black Americans in Congress: 1870-1992.* New York: Amistad Press, 1993.

Commager, Henry Steele. *The American Mind: An Interpretation of American Thought and Character Since the 1880s.* New Haven, Connecticut: Yale University Press, 1970.

Connerly, Ward. *Creating Equal: My Fight Against Racial Preferences.* San Francisco: Encounter Books, 2000.

Cronin, E. David. *Black Moses: The Story of Marcus Garvey.* Madison: The University of Wisconsin Press, 1968.

Cruse, Harold. *The Crisis of the Negro Intellectual: From Its Origins to the Present.* New York: William Monroe and Company, Inc., 1967.

Davis Jr., Benjamin O. *An Autobiography: Benjamin O. Davis, Jr.: American.* Washington: Smithsonian Insstitution Press, 1991.

Dellums, Ronald V. *Lying Down with the Lions: A Public Life From the Streets of Oakland.* Boston: Beacon Press, 2000.

Dickerson, Dennis C. *Whitney M. Young, Jr.: Militant Mediator.* Lexington: The University Press of Kentucky, 1998.

D'Orso, Michael. *Like Judgement Day: The Ruin and Redemption of a Town Called Rosewood.* New York: G.P. Putnam's Sons, 1996.

Duberman, Martin. *Paul Robeson: A Biography.* New York: The New Press, 1989.

Du Bois, W.E.B. *Dusk of Dawn.* New York: Shocken Books, 1968.

_____. *The Philadelphia Negro.* New York: Schocken Books, 1967.

_____. *The Souls of Black Folk: Three Negro Classics.* New York: Avon Books, 1965.

Elkins, Stanley. *Slavery: A Problem in Institutional and Intellectual Life.* Chicago: University of Chicago Press, 1959.

Ellsworth, Scott. *Death in a Promised Land: The Tulsa Race Riots of 1921.* Baton Rouge: Louisiana State University Press, 1982.

Firestone, Bernard J. and Vogt, Robert C. (eds). *Lyndon Baines Johnson and the Uses of Power.* New York: Greenwood Press, 1988.

Fanon, Frantz. *Black Skin, White Masks: The Experiences of a Black Man in a White World.* New York: Grove Press, 1967.

Freire, Paulo. *Pedagogy of the Oppressed.* New York: Continuum, 1989.

Foner, Philip S. (ed). *W.E.B. Du Bois Speaks: Speeches and Addresses 1920-1963.* New York: Pathfinder Press, 1970.

Foner, Philip S. and Shapiro, Herbert (eds). *American Communism and Black Americans: A Documentary History, 1930-1934.* Philadelphia: Temple University Press, 1991.

Fox, Stephen R. *The Guardian of Boston: William Monroe Trotter*. New York: Atheneum, 1970.

Frady, Marshall. *Jesse: The Life and Pilgrimage of Jesse Jackson*. New York: Random House, 1996.

Francis, Charles E. *The Tuskegee Airmen: The Men Who Changed a Nation*. Boston: Branden Publishing Company, 1993.

Franklin, John Hope. *From Slavery to Freedom*. New York: Alfred A. Knopf, Inc., 1967.

Franklin, John Hope and Meier, August (eds). *Black Leaders of the Twentieth Century*. Urbana: University of Illinois Press, 1982.

Garfinkel, Herbert. *When Negroes March: The March on Washington Movement in the Organizational Politics for FEPC*. New York: Atheneum, 1969.

Garvey, Marcus and Garvey, Amy Jacques (eds). *Philosophy and Opinions of Marcus Garvey*. Part II. New York: Atheneum, 1969.

Gatewood, Willard B. *Aristocrats of Color: The Black Elite, 1880 -1920*. Bloomington: Indiana University Press, 1993.

Goldman, Roger with Gallen, David. *Thurgood Marshall: Justice For All*. New York: Carroll and Graff Publishers, Inc., 1992.

Graham, Lawrence Otis. *Our Kind of People: Inside America's Black Upper Class*. New York: Harper Collins Publishers, 1999.

Grant, Joanne. *Black Protest: History, Documents, and Analysis 1619 to the Present*. New York: A Fauset Premier, 1968.

Guinier, Lani. *Lift Every Voice: Turning a Civil Rights Setback Into a Civil Vision of Social Justice*. New York: Simon and Schuster, 1998.

Halberstam, David. *The Fifties*. New York: Villard Books, 1993.

Haley, Alex. *The Autobiography of Malcolm X*. New York: Grove Press, Inc., 1965.

Harlan, Louis. *Booker T. Washington: The Making of a Black Leader, 1856-1901*. New York: Oxford University Press, 1972.

_____. *Booker T. Washington: The Wizard of Tuskegee, 1901-1915*. New York: Oxford University Press, 1983.

Harris, William H. *Keeping the Faith: A. Philip Randolph, Milton P. Webster, and the Brotherhood of Sleeping Car Porters, 1925-1937*. Urbana: University of Illinois Press, 1991.

Hauser, Thomas. *Muhammad Ali: His Life and Times*. New York: A Touchstone Book, 1991.

Haygood, Will. *King of the Cats: The Life and Times of Adam Clayton Powell, Jr.*. Boston: Houghton Mifflin Company, 1993.

Hays, Samuel P. *The Response to Industrialism, 1885-1914*. Chicago: University of Chicago Press, 1966.

Henri, Florette. *Black Migration: Movement North, 1900-1920*. New York: Anchor Books, 1975.

Hicks, John D. *The Populist Revolt: A History of the Farmers Alliance and the People's Party.* Lincoln: University of Nebraska Press, 1961.

Hine, Darlene Clark, Brown, Eliza Barklay, and Terborg-Penn. *Black Women in America: An Historical Encyclopedia.* Vol. I and II. Bloomington, Indiana: Indiana University Press, 1993.

Hobsbawm, Eric. *The Age of Extremes: A History of the World, 1914-1991.* New York: Vintage Books, 1994.

Horne, Gerald. *Fire This Time: The Watts Uprising and the 1960s.* Charlottesville: Virginia University Press, 1995.

Hornsby, Jr. Alton. *Chronology of African American History: Significant Events and People from 1619 to the Present.* Detroit: Gale Research Inc., 1991.

Hutchinson, Earl Ofari. *"Let Your Motto Be Resistance:" The Life and Thought of Henry Highland Garnet.* Boston: Beacon Press, 1972.

_____. *The Disappearance of Black Leadership.* Los Angeles: Middle Passage Press, 2000.

Johnson, James Weldon. *Along This Way.* New York: The Viking Press, 1933.

Jackson, Kenneth T. *The Ku Klux Klan in the City: 1915-1930.* New York: Oxford University Press, 1967.

Jones, Beverly Washington. *Quest for Equality: The Life and Writings of Mary Eliza Church Terrell, 1863-1954.* Brooklyn: Carlson Publishing Inc., 1990.

Jordan, Vernon E. (with Gordon-Reed, Annette). *Vernon Can Read: A Memoir.* New York: PublicAffairs, 2001.

Katz, Michael B. *Class, Bureaucracy, and Schools: The Illusion of Educational Change in America.* New York: Praeger Publishers, 1972.

_____. *Eyewitness: A Living Democracy of the African American Contribution to American History.* New York: A Touchstone Book, 1995.

Kellogg, Charles Flint. *NAACP: A History of the National Association for the Advancement of Colored People, 1909-1920.* Vol. I. Baltimore: The Johns Hopkins Press, 1967.

Keller, Morton. *Affairs of State Public Life in Late Nineteenth Century America.* Cambridge: The Belknap Press, 1977.

Kennedy, David M. *Freedom From Fear: The American People in Depression and War, 19291945.* New York: Oxford University Press, 1999.

Kerner, Otto. *Report of the National Advisory Commission on Civil Disorders.* New York: A Barton Book, 1968.

Lewis, David Levering. *W.E.B. Du Bois: Biography of a race, 1868-1919.* New York: Henry Holt and Company, 1993.

_____. *W.E.B. Du Bois: The Fight for Equality and the American Century.* New York: Henry Holt and Company, 2000.

Lewis, John (with D'Orio). *Walking With the Wind: A Memoir of the Movement.* New York: Simon and Schuster, 1998.

Lewis, Rupert. *Marcus Garvey: Anti-Colonial Champion*. Trenton: Africa World Press, Inc., 1988.

Litwack, Leon. *Trouble in Mind: Black Southerners in the Age of Jim Crow*. New York: Alfred A. Knopf, 1998.

Logan, Rayford W. *The Betrayal of the Negro from Rutherford B. Hayes to Woodrow Wilson*. Toronto, Canada: The Macmillan Company, 1969.

_____. *What the Negro Wants*. New York: Agathon Press, Inc., 1969.

Logan, Rayford W. and Winston, Michael R. (eds.). *Dictionary of American Negro Biography*. New York: W.W. Norton and Company, 1982.

Lynch, Hollis R. *Edward Wilmot Blyden: Pan-Negro Patriot 1882-1912*. New York: Oxford University Press, 1967.

Marable, Manning. *Black Leadership*. New York: Columbia University Press, 1998.

Mansfield, Stephen. *Then Darkness Fled: The Liberating Wisdom of Booker T. Washington*. Nashville: Highland Books, 1999.

McCloskey, Robert Green. *American Conservatism in the Age of Enterprise 1865-1910*. New York: Harper and Row, 1951.

McMurry, Linda O. *To Keep the Waters Troubled: The Life of Ida B. Wells*. New York: Oxford University Presss, 1998.

Meier, August. *Negro Thought in America, 1880-1915: Racial Ideologies in the Age of Booker T. Washington*. Ann Arbor: University of Michigan Press, 1968.

Meier, August and Franklin, John Hope. *Black Leaders of the Twentieth Century*. Urbana: University of Illinois Press, 1982.

Mfume, Kweisi. *No Free Ride*. New York: Ballantine Books, 1996.

Mjagki, Nina. *Light in the Darkness: African Americans and the YMCA, 1852-1946*. Lexington: The University of Kentucky Press, 1994.

Morrow, E. Frederic. *Black Man in the White House: A Diary of the Eisenhower Years By the Administrative Office for Special Projects, The White House, 1955-1961*. New York: Coward McCann, Inc., 1963.

_____. *Forty Years as a Guinea Pig*. New York: The Pilgrim Press, 1980.

Moses, Wilson Jeremiah. *The Golden Age of Black Nationalism*. Hamden, Connecticut: Archon Books, 1978.

Muse, Benjamin. The American Negro Revolution: From Nonviolence to Black Power. Bloomington: Indiana University Press, 1968.

Myrdal, Gunnar. *An Ameican Dilemma*. II. New York: McGraw-Hill Book Company, 1964.

Newby, I. A. (ed.), *The Development of Segregationist Thought*. Homewood, Illinois: The Dorsey Press, 1968.

Nolan, William A. *Communism Versus the Negro*. Chicago: Henry Regney Company, 1951.

Omi, Michael and Winant, Howard. *Racial Formation in the United States.* New York: Routledge, 1994.

O'Reilly, Kenneth. *Nixon's Piano: Presidents and Racial Politics from Washington to Clinton.* New York: The Free Press, 1995.

Parker, Majorie H. *Alpha Kappa Alpha Through the Years: 1908-1988.* Chicago: The Mobium Press, 1990.

Parris, Guilford and Brooks, Lester. *Blacks in the City: A History of the National Urban League.* Boston: Little, Brown, and Company, 1971.

Pfeffer, Paula. *A. Philip Randolph: Pioneer in the Civil Rights Movement.* Baton Rouge: Louisiana State University Press, 1991.

Powell, Colin L. *My American Journey.* New York: Ballantine Books, 1996.

Quarles, Benjamin. *Frederick Douglass.* New York: Atheneum, 1968.

Rampersad, Arnold. *Jackie Robinson, A Biography.* New York: Alfred A. Knopf, 1997.

_____. *The Life of Langston Hughes: 1902-1941, "I Too Sing America."* Vol. I. New York: Oxford University Press, 1986.

Record, Wilson. *The Negro and the Communist Party. New York:* Atheneum, 1941.

Reed, Jr. Adolph L. *W.E.B. Du Bois and American Political Thought: Favianism and the Color Line.* New York: Oxford University Press, 1997.

Richardson, James. *Willie Brown: A Biography.* Berkeley: University of California Press, 1996.

Rogers, Mary Beth. *Barbara Jordan: American Hero.* New York: Bantam Books, 1998.

Ross, B. Joyce. *J.E. Spingarn and the Rise of the NAACP, 1911-1939.* New York: Atheneum, 1972.

Ross, Jr., Lawrence C. *The Divine Nine: The History of African American Fraternities and Sororities.* New York: Kensington Publishing Corp, 2000.

Rowan, Carl T. *The Coming Race War in America: A Wake-Up Call.* Boston: Little Brown and Company, 1996.

Rubinowitz, Howard (ed.) *Southern Black Leaders of the Reconstruction Era.* Urbana: University of Illinois Press, 1982.

Rudwick, Elliott M. *Race Riot at East St. Louis: July 2, 1917.* Carbondale: Southern Illinois University Press, 1964.

_____. *W.E.B. Du Bois: Propagandist of the Negro Protest.* New York: Atheneum, 1968.

Schlesinger, Jr., Arthur M. *A Thousand Days: John F. Kennedy in the White House.* Boston: Houghton Mifflin Company, 1965.

Scott, Emmett J. *Negro Migration During the war.* New York: Arno Press and the New York Times, 1969.

Sinnette, Elinor Des Verney. *Arthur Alfonso Schomburg: Black Bibliophile and Collector.* Detroit: Wayne State University Press, 1989.

Smith, Jessie Carney (ed.). *Black Firsts: 2000 Years of Extraordinary Achievement*. Detroit: Visible Ink Press, 1994.

Smith, Robert C. *We Have No Leaders: African Americans in the Post-Civil Rights Era*. Albany: State University of New York Press, 1996.

Stanton, William. *The Leopard's Spots: Scientific Attitudes Towards Race in America 1815-1859*. Chicago: University of Chicago Press, 1960.

Sonenshein, Raphael J. *Politics in Black and White: Race and Power in Los Angeles*. Princeton: Princeton University Press, 1993.

Stein, Judith. *The World of Marcus Garvey: Race and Class in Modern Society*. Baton Rouge: Louisiana State University Press, 1986.

Suggs, Henry Lewis. *P.B. Young Newspaperman: Race, Politics, and Journalism in the New South 1910-1962*. Charlottesville: University of Virginia Press, 1988.

Tate, Katherine. *From Protest to Politics: The New Black Voters in American Elections*. Cambridge: Harvard University Press, 1994.

Thompson, Mildred I. *Ida B. Wells-Barnett: An Exploratory Study of an American Black Woman, 1893-1930*. Brooklyn: Carlson Publishing Company, 1990.

Thernstrom, Stephan and Thernstrom, Abigail. *America in Black and White: One Nation, Indivisible—Race in Modern America*. New York: Simon and Schuster, 1997.

Thornbrough, Emma Lou. *T. Thomas Fortune: Militant Journalist*. Chicago: University of Chicago Press, 1972.

Toll, William. *The Resurgence of Race: Black Social Theory from Reconstruction to the Pan-American Conferences*. Philadelphia: Temple University Press, 1979.

Turner, W. Burghardt and Turner, Joyce More (eds.). *Richard B. Moore, Caribbean Militant in Harlem: Collected Writings 1920-1972*. Bloomington: Indiana University Press, 1992.

Tuttle, Jr., William R. *Race Riot: Chicago in the Red Summer of 1919*. New York: Atheneum, 1972.

Ullman, Victor. *Martin R. Delaney: The Beginnings of Black Nationalism*. Boston: Beacon Press, 1971.

Urquhart, Brian. *Ralph Bunche: An American Odyssey*. New York: W.W. Norton and Company, 1998.

Viorst, Milton. *Fire in the Streets: America in the 1960s*. New York: Simon and Schuster, 1979.

Walters, Ronald W. and Smith, Robert C. *African American Leadership*. Albany: State University Press of New York, 1999.

Washington, Booker T. *Up From Slavery*. New York: Gramercy Books, 1993.

Weaver, John D. *The Brownsville Raid*. New York: W.W. and Norton Company, 1970.

Weaver, Robert C. *The Negro Ghetto*. New York: Harcourt, Brace, and Company, 1948.

Weiss, Nancy J. *The National Urban League 1910-1940*. New York: Oxford University Press, 1974.

Wesley, Charles H. *The History of Alpha Phi Alpha: A Development in College Life*. Washington, D.C.: The Foundation Publishers, 1937.

White, Theodore H. *The Making of the President 1964*. New York: Atheneum Publishers, 1965.

White, Walter. *A Man Called White: The Autobiography of Walter White*. Bloomington, Indiana University Press, 1948.

Wilkins, Roy. *Standing Fast: The Autobiography of Roy Wilkins*. New York: The Viking Press, 1982.

Wilson, Sondra Kathryn. *In Search of Democracy: The NAACP Writings of James Weldon Johnson, Walter White, and Roy Wilkins (1920-1977)*. New York: Oxford University Press, 1999.

Wintz, Cary D. (ed.). *African-American Political Thought 1890-1930: Washington, Du Bois, Garvey, and Randolph*. Armork, New York: M.E. Sharpe, 1996.

Wolters, Raymond. *Negroes and the Great Depression: The Problem of Economic Recovery*. Westport, Connecticut: Greenwood Publishing Corporation, 1970.

Woodward, C. Vann. *A History of the South: Origins of the New South, 1877-1913*. Baton Rouge: Louisiana State University Press, 1951.

_____. *The Strange Career of Jim Crow*. New York: Oxford University Press, 1974.

_____. *Tom Watson: Agrarian Rebel*. New York: Oxford University Press, 1972.

Young, Andrew. *An Easy Burden: The Civil Rights Movement and the Transformation of America*. New York: Harper Collins Publishers, 1996.

Journals

Blauvelt, Mary Taylor. "The Race Problem." *The American Journal of Sociology*, IV, 662.

Du Bois, W.E.B. "Opinion," *The Crisis*, Vol. 18, No. 5, 231.

_____. Editorial. "Close Ranks," *The Crisis*, Vol. 16, No. 3, 111.

Ellwood, Charles A. Review of George Merriam's "The Negro and the Nation."*The American Journal of Sociology*, XII.

Johnson, James Weldon. "The Riots." *The Crisis*, Vol 18, No. 5, 243.

Kelly, F. S. "The Outer Pocket." *The Crisis*, Vol. 18;, No. 6, 288.

n.n. "The Massacre of East St. Louis." *The Crisis*. Vol. 14, No. 5, 216-219.

Reinsch, Paul S. "The Negro Raace and European Civilizations." *The American Journal of Sociology*, XI, 154-166.

Simons, Sarah E. "Social Assimilation, Part I." *The American Journal of Sociology*, VI, 790-815.

_____. "Social Assimilation, Part II." *The American Journal of Sociology*, VII, 543.

Wright, Richard. Review of W.H. Thomas' "The American Negro." *The American Journal of Sociology*, VII, 850.

White, Walter. "Chicago and Its Eight Reasons," *The Crisis*, Vol.. 18, No. 6, 297.

_____. "The Eruption of Tulsa." *The Nation*, CXII, 909-910.

INDEX

A

Abbott, Robert, 116
Abernathy, Rev. Ralph David, 226–27, 234
Abolitionist Movement, 40
Adams, Sherman, 180
Addams, Jane, 26, 65, 73
Affirmative Action, 249, 296, 305, 310
African American apathy, 235–36
African American Leadership, 294
African-American Leadership, Walters, Ronald W. and Robert C. Smith, ix
African Blood Brotherhood (ABB), 84, 101
African Exclusion Bill, 70
African Methodist Episcopal Church, 298
Alexander, Kelly Miller, 258
Alexander, Raymond Pace, 94
Alexander, Sadie T. M., 73
Alinksy, Saul quoted, 215
Allen, Richard, xii, 4
Amenia Conference (1916), 71
America in Black and White, Thernstrom, Stephan and Abigail, 315
American Bar Association (ABA), 73–74, 329n37
American Civil Rights Institute, 298
An American Dilemma, Myrdal, Gunnar, 145, 166–67, 176
American Federation of Labor (AF of L), 97, 118
American Journal of the Medical Sciences (1942), 36
American Negro Academy, 13, 29
American Negro Labor Congress (ANLC), 122
Amsterdam News, 101, 109
Anderson, Bernard E., 251
Anniston, Alabama, 201
Anti-Bookerite faction, 63
Antioch College, 28
Aristocracy (Black), 10–11
Armstrong, General Samuel Chapman, 14–15
Arrington, Richard, Jr., 242, 270
Atlanta Baptist College (Morehouse College), 44
Atlanta Constitution, 96
Atlanta Journal newspaper, 53
Atlanta riots (1906), 53, 61
Atlanta University, 45, 46, 50, 63, 65, 66
The Atlantic Monthly, 38
Atwood, Rufus, 125
Aycock, Charles B., 19

B

Baker, Ella, 198–99
Baker, Ray Stannard, 39, 40, 53, 65
Baldwin, James, 204
Baldwin, Jr., Mrs. William, 77
Ballou, General Charles C., 76
Baltimore Afro-American, 154